CINEASTE ON FILM CRITICISM, PROGRAMMING,
AND PRESERVATION IN THE NEW MILLENNIUM

CINEASTE

ON FILM CRITICISM, PROGRAMMING, AND PRESERVATION IN THE NEW MILLENNIUM

EDITED BY CYNTHIA LUCIA AND RAHUL HAMID

UNIVERSITY OF TEXAS PRESS
AUSTIN

Requests for permission to reproduce material
from this work should be sent to:
    Permissions
    University of Texas Press
    P.O. Box 7819
    Austin, TX 78713-7819
    utpress.utexas.edu/rp-form

The paper used in this book meets the minimum
requirements of ANSI/NISO Z39.48-1992 (R1997)
(Permanence of Paper). ∞

Library of Congress Cataloging-in-Publication Data

Names: Lucia, Cynthia A. Barto (Cynthia Anne Barto), editor. |
    Hamid, Rahul, (Editor), editor.
Title: Cineaste on film criticism, programming, and
    preservation in the new millennium / edited by
    Cynthia Lucia and Rahul Hamid.
Description: First edition. | Austin : University of Texas Press,
    2017. | Includes bibliographical references and index.
Identifiers: LCCN 2017010806| ISBN 978-1-4773-1340-4
    (cloth : alk. paper) | ISBN 978-1-4773-1341-1 (pbk. : alk.
    paper) | ISBN 978-1-4773-1342-8 (library e-book) |
    ISBN 978-1-4773-1343-5 (nonlibrary e-book)
Subjects: LCSH: Motion pictures—Periodicals. | Film
    criticism. | Motion pictures—Reviews. | Mass media—
    Technological innovations. | Mass media criticism.
Classification: LCC PN1995 .C48517 2017 | DDC
    791.43015—dc23
LC record available at https://lccn.loc.gov/2017010806

doi:10.7560/313404

Contents

Acknowledgments

Without the nearly one hundred contributors to the *Cineaste* symposia and interviews collected here—including film critics, programmers, curators, and preservationists—this volume would not have been possible. We thank them for generously investing and sharing their time, insight, and expertise.

Although our names appear as editors on this volume, it genuinely is a collaborative, collective effort involving the entire *Cineaste* editorial board, without whom the original symposia could not have been organized or published. Richard Porton was instrumental in conceiving and coordinating the four symposia on film criticism, with Robert Cashill playing a crucial role in "Film Criticism in the Age of the Internet." Jared Rapfogel was equally vital in shaping and organizing the symposia on film programming and film preservation. (In the introductions to the individual symposia, we acknowledge others beyond the editorial board members who helped bring these pieces to fruition.) The interviews collected here were conducted by *Cineaste* contributing editor Leonard Quart, editorial board members Richard Porton and Robert Cashill, as well as founder and editor-in-chief Gary Crowdus. It is through Gary's persistence, dedication, and intelligence, as well as his creative and collaborative vision, that *Cineaste* exists, has grown, and continues to thrive in the new millennium. Not only has Gary steered the magazine forward over the last fifty years, but also he is responsible for the magazine's layout and design, for its initial website construction, and for keeping it afloat through his administration of everything from grant applications, subscription renewals, and mailings to office space and so much more. Dan Georgakas, who until recently served as *Cineaste*'s chief financial officer, also has contributed invaluably through his writing and his often tedious, behind-the-scenes but crucial work. Without Gary and Dan, the magazine could not have survived and thrived. Barbara Saltz, our advertising representative, also has contributed significantly, as has contributing editor Roy Grundmann, who provided frequently sought advice. Many other past editorial board members, as well as present and former editorial associates and assistants, proofreaders, contributing writers, and interns, have helped make this volume possible through their dedicated efforts in support of the magazine.

We deeply thank Jim Burr, our terrifically supportive editor at the University of Texas Press, and our copyeditor, Abby Webber, along with the press's marketing and design staff. We also thank the press's two anonymous reviewers, both of whom read an early version of this volume and provided much-appreciated suggestions.

We express our gratitude to Rex Roberts, design and production editor at *Film Journal International* and friend, who generously volunteered his time to help prepare our illustrations.

We most importantly acknowledge our families, especially Raymond Lucia, Ragan Rhyne, and Oona and Olive Hamid, who patiently and uncomplainingly allowed for our distracted attention while we completed this project. We cannot thank them enough for their support and their love.

CINEASTE ON FILM CRITICISM, PROGRAMMING,
AND PRESERVATION IN THE NEW MILLENNIUM

Editors' Introduction

Cynthia Lucia and Rahul Hamid

Already in progress in the 1990s, the "digital revolution" both ushered in and dramatically defined the new millennium, radically altering so many fields, from communications, journalism, and travel to science and medicine. Whether considered revolution, evolution, devolution, or onslaught, the digital age has had a far-reaching impact, not only on the art and industry of film and television production, but also on the print media and the practice of film criticism.[1]

The seemingly limitless digital and Internet availability of films and the truly limitless availability of Internet publishing venues have notably narrowed *and* immensely broadened the field of film criticism. The profusion of blogs and news and entertainment sites has "democratized" the field, as is so often noted, providing access to intelligent, insightful writers—both amateurs and experts. At the same time, free access on the Internet has closed down more than a few print publications, including the mainstream movie magazine *Premiere*, which discontinued its print edition in 2010, while retaining an online presence. This trend, in turn, has decidedly diminished the number of salaried positions for professional critics. Several academic journals, like *Jump Cut*, likewise have transitioned from print to online editions. At the same time, the Internet has also given birth to well-regarded film sites, like IMDb, and online film journals, like *Senses of Cinema*, *Moving Image Source*, and *Rouge*.

Digital technology has even more fundamentally and profoundly altered filmmaking by allowing greater access to cheaper production platforms, not to mention special effects processes, while on the downside (as many preservationists believe) rendering celluloid all but obsolete. A virtual, numerical matrix, for better or worse—and likely for both better *and* worse—has largely supplanted the celluloid *material* of film art. Indexical, real-world tracings of once present people and places have vanished, with moments in time as easily fabricated as recorded. Such issues have prompted extensive theoretical deliberation, while also animating ongoing debates concerning film aesthetics, programming, and preservation. There is no denying that digitization has provided many more viewers access to myriad films previously available only by visiting far-flung archives. At the same time, the widespread theatrical exhibition of film on digital formats places pressures on repertory theaters devoted to screening films as originally intended to be shown. For preservationists, the unstable digital format likewise poses problems, even as digital technology measurably enhances the preservation process.

With such paradoxical complications and controversies in the air, *Cineaste* magazine has explored and continues to explore the opportunities and challenges of the digital age—and its impact on film criticism, programming, and preservation. Through a series of symposia devoted to those areas, *Cineaste* invited a range of prominent practitioners, drawing upon their professional expertise and experiences, to address a series of crucial questions.[2] Cineaste *on Film Criticism, Programming, and Preservation in the New Millennium* compiles these noteworthy symposia in a single volume, along with several relevant interviews. Originally published in *Cineaste*'s print edition from 2000 through 2013, the symposia included here have been widely requested for use as classroom resources and as essential research tools.

FILM CRITICISM IN THE NEW MILLENNIUM

Whether in print or on radio, TV, or the Internet—and mostly on the Internet—film reviews, criticism, and commentary have become more widely available than ever before. Yet much of it has seemed, to *Cineaste* and to serious readers, as instantly disposable—functioning as little more than a publicity conduit for major studio releases or as shallow "thumbs-up, thumbs-down" consumer guides for readers and potential viewers.

As a publication devoted to the art *and* politics of film, *Cineaste* encouraged critics, in its four symposia devoted to film criticism, to examine these issues, along with the pitfalls of sociological approaches to film criticism that often reduce films to social themes or "messages" at the expense of appreciating aesthetic aspects and artistic achievements. Another *Cineaste* concern is that film criticism be well written, with ideas—no matter how complex the level of argumentation or analysis—made accessible to readers who should find *pleasure* in reading. The strict dichotomy between journalistic and academic writing that has come to characterize the American film scene is, thankfully, largely absent in other national contexts. Why does this division persist in the United States? This question, among others, is addressed by several of our respondents.

Published in 2000, "Film Criticism in America Today" solicited the responses of top US film critics in addressing these concerns. Twenty-four critics—including Manohla Dargis, now of the *New York Times*; David Denby of the *New Yorker*; the late Stanley Kauffmann of the *New Republic*; the late Richard Schickel, then *Time* magazine critic; and the late Roger Ebert of the *Chicago Sun-Times*—define their professional roles, the qualities of superior film criticism, and the relationship between film critics and the film industry, as they have observed and experienced it.

Expanding the scope of this first symposium, in 2005 *Cineaste* published "International Film Criticism Today," posing to international film critics many of the same questions US critics had earlier addressed and additionally asking them to discuss the impact of globalization on film criticism and the film industry. Thanks to the Internet, the work of these prominent international film critics is now globally accessible. The twenty-two critics responding represent twenty nations and include Argentina's Quintín, *El amante cine*; France's Michel Ciment, *Positif*; Germany's Olaf Möller, independent critic; Hong Kong's Li Cheuk-to, *Economic Journal*; Italy's now deceased Tullio Kezich, *Corriere della sera*; Russia's Lev Karakhan, *Iskusstvo kino*; and Tunisia's Tahar Chikhaoui, *Cinécrits*.

Both symposia were inspired by the sense that serious attempts at film criticism—defined by in-depth argumentation and attention to a range of films, including international, independent, and auteur films (as opposed to generic or celebrity-driven studio movies)—were becoming more difficult to publish and that serious critical voices were becoming marginalized, if not silenced. Marketing and advertising pressures and the control of media outlets by fewer and fewer parent corporations, many of which also controlled film production and distribution companies, were increasingly influencing film criticism, whether overtly or indirectly—an unfortunate circumstance that continues to this day.

"Film Criticism in the Age of the Internet," published in 2008, and "Film Criticism: The Next Generation," published in 2013, not only are logical extensions of the first two symposia but also share inextricably related concerns centered on Internet venues, which, more often than not, appeal most strongly to younger generations of readers and critics. Among the twenty-three critics discussing the impact of the Internet are some who were earlier featured in "Film Criticism in America Today," along with a number of others, including Zach Campbell, *Elusive Lucidity*; J. Hoberman, then of the *Village Voice*; Robert Koehler, *Variety*; Amy Taubin, *Film Comment* and *Artforum*; and Stephanie Zacharek, then of *Salon*. When surveying critics aged thirty-five or younger about the role and qualities of effective film criticism, *Cineaste* received a plethora of responses—the majority of which were fittingly published on its website, www.cineaste.com—with the print edition featuring the responses included here, from Ben Kenigsberg, Gabe Klinger, Michael Koresky, Kiva Reardon, and Andrew Tracy.

The sheer number of Internet sites and blogs devoted to film has given rise to the common quip, "Everyone's a film critic"—whether uttered with conspicuous contempt or muttered in weary resignation. Has film criticism become the victim of a "dumbing-down" process promoted by the mainstream press and encouraged by sheer ubiquity? Or does the Internet provide intelligent, critically cogent voices otherwise overlooked? As already evident, the *Cineaste* symposia suggest that the Internet supports both sets of conditions. With that in mind, one modest goal of the 2008 symposium was to offer a guide for the perplexed Internet surfer who might as easily stumble upon a site seemingly written by a demented teenager as one written by an erudite expert. Although Internet blogs, in particular, rarely undergo rigorous editing, such sites are at the same time lauded as participatory spheres that help break down boundaries of age, geography, and social class. Neither mindless cheerleaders nor grumpy naysayers, the symposium participants express the hope that good criticism will predominate over bad, whether in print or on the Internet, and that increased bids for corporate and government control of cyberspace will not drown out or silence the many voices that constitute contemporary film criticism.

This hope also motivates the 2013 symposium, in which young critics admit that the digital era has its downside—particularly in the scarcity of archival 35 mm prints accessible in the age of DCP (Digital Cinema Package). These writers nevertheless insist that the Internet has engendered rich new opportunities for independent critical voices and for the cultivation of a collective cinephilia. Vadim Rizov, in his symposium contribution on the *Cineaste* website, points out that "the digital era's effect on cinephilia has been rather dazzling. . . . [T]he sheer amount of information has increased exponentially. . . . We may not have an indexical grasp of film history in all its aspects but we're much closer than before." Calum Marsh remarks, "I take it for granted that I can find any Jacques Rivette movie I want online, and I take it for granted that I can find fifty people online who'd like to toss opinions of *Out 1* (Rivette and Suzanne Schiffman, 1971) back and forth with me." Russian critic Boris Nelepo concludes that "new editions of DVDs continue to rewrite and complete the history of cinema before our very eyes."[3]

THE ART OF REPERTORY FILM EXHIBITION AND DIGITAL-AGE CHALLENGES

Another feature of film culture unfortunately taken for granted is repertory film exhibition. Although scholarly fields are devoted to in-depth study of film art and history, very little attention is paid to the practicalities of film exhibition, to the individuals and institutions presenting films past and present, or to the art of film programming. The most basic step in the reception of the art form—the environment and context in which films are, at least ideally, actually seen—is largely ignored. The consequences of this oversight are significant, given the rapidly changing nature of film projection and viewing in the digital age. As it becomes increasingly rare for viewers to watch films as originally intended, the lack of understanding of—or at least emphasis on—the mechanics of film exhibition becomes a fundamental concern. What, we must ask, is at stake in the transition from celluloid to digital, and in the experience of watching movies in isolation on DVD or on a computer instead of on the big screen with an audience?

Among the fourteen respondents tackling this question, while also defining their programming philosophies and discussing the basics of their work—from availability of quality prints to changing audience demographics, not to mention the future viability of repertory programming—are Bruce Goldstein, director of repertory programming at Film Forum in New York City; Haden Guest, director of the Harvard Film Archive; Richard Peña, former program director of the Film Society of Lincoln Center;

Marie Losier, filmmaker and former film programmer at the French Institute Alliance Française in New York City; and David Schwartz, chief curator at Museum of the Moving Image.

Digital formats, as noted, are rapidly consigning the celluloid film print to the status of an antiquated medium. In terms of contemporary film production, this means one thing: while many bemoan the fact that even the greatest filmmakers are increasingly turning to cheaper and more versatile video formats, most have also begun to come to terms with this inevitable shift, or at least to recognize that video has its own particular qualities and possibilities. When it comes to the exhibition of works from cinema's first century, however, the implications of the digital era are more alarming, as pressure mounts to present digital screenings of works created on film—tantamount to displaying a reproduction of a great painting in a museum and passing it off as the original. And the loss is immeasurable—not only of unmistakable qualities such as the sharpness, brightness, shading, and contrast of the image, but also of more intangible factors dancing at the edge of perception (the flicker embedded in the projection, or the materiality of the emulsion).

As unavoidable a part of film culture in the twenty-first century as DVD viewing may be, it remains vitally important for scholars, teachers, and cineastes to foster an awareness of the extent to which viewing contexts influence the way a film is perceived, as well as a sensitivity to how a particular film is affected by the circumstances in which it is viewed. There is no going back to the days in which theatrical exhibition was the only show in town, but just as the masterpieces of cinema's first century are inseparable from this mode of film viewing, new, rapidly proliferating modes are anything but neutral factors in how we experience cinema today, as symposia participants explain.

FILM PRESERVATION IN THE DIGITAL AGE

Film preservation and repertory film programming, of course, go hand in hand. Programmers are among the most influential of film preservation advocates, and some are themselves directly involved in film preservation. It should come as no surprise, then, that several of the same individuals are contributors to both the repertory and preservation symposia.

Although greater numbers of films become available every year thanks to digital technology, the misapprehension abides that most significant films of the past are accessible. While those seriously engaged in film culture are aware that vast numbers of films remain unavailable on home video, even they harbor the illusion that these films are simply waiting to be transferred to DVD or scanned for digital screening. The sad truth is that countless numbers of films have been irremediably lost—by some estimates as many as seventy to ninety percent of silent-era films no longer exist. As for noncommercial and nonnarrative films produced in the sound era (e.g., home movies, avant-garde cinema, and industrial, educational, scientific, and medical films), a similar number have vanished.

The increase in the number of films released on DVD has been an indisputably positive phenomenon, with movies appearing from throughout film history, from around the world, and even from previously neglected realms of film production (thanks to initiatives like Kino's Classic Educational Shorts DVDs and the National Film Preservation Foundation's ambitious series of Treasures from American Film Archives box sets). At the same time, the continual evolution of digital formats and their proven instability mean that even those works released on DVD are not entirely safe from the threat of loss.

A central theme, then, of *Cineaste*'s film preservation symposium is the digital revolution and its complicated and multidimensional impact on the field. Professionals discuss the changing landscape of film preservation, including funding challenges, factors determining the films to be preserved, those films and modes of filmmaking most threatened by extinction, and the potentially thorny issue of preservation versus access. Among the eleven preservationists and programmers sharing their knowledge are Margaret Bodde, executive director of the Film Foundation; Paolo Cherchi Usai, senior curator of film at George Eastman House (now the George Eastman Museum); Dennis Doros and Amy Heller, founders of Milestone Film & Video; John Ewing, director of the Cleveland Institute of Art Cinematheque; Annette Melville, director of the National Film Preservation Foundation; and James Quandt, senior programmer at the Toronto International Film Festival Cinematheque.

Although many film scholars, students, and viewers are accustomed to seeing films identified or marketed as "preserved" or "restored," few probably consider exactly what this means in terms of the processes by which films are brought back from a state of deterioration or from the brink of extinction. From its inception, the cinema has been haunted by the specter of decay and even of self-destruction. For decades, films were printed on nitrate stock—notorious for its extreme flammability. Prints exposed to excessive heat would simply burst into flame, sometimes during projection. Nitrate films also decomposed quickly when stored in less than ideal conditions. In the 1950s, a transition was effected from nitrate to acetate stocks, which were far more stable and safer than the earlier prints but also subject to their own forms of decay, including color fading, melting, and breakage.

Counterbalancing this potential for disintegration is the capacity to copy film prints many times over. Most Hollywood productions, for instance, saw hundreds and even thousands of prints produced for distribution throughout the world. But few of those prints were saved after a film's initial release had run its course. Outside of the commercial realm, the story is very different. Many home movies and avant-garde films were shot on 8 mm or 16 mm reversal stocks, which resulted not in a negative, but in a single, not easily reproducible print. These works are thus unique and closer to the status of paintings or sculptures than to that of photographs or film. And today, with the medium in the throes of transition from celluloid film prints to digital media, the cost of striking prints has risen so dramatically that the likelihood of films being reproduced photochemically (in their original celluloid format) remains more a theoretical possibility than a practical option.

While symposium contributors almost unanimously agree that digital media are not yet capable of replacing celluloid as a preservation format (since they cannot begin to compete with a film print's ability, under proper storage conditions, to resist deterioration for more than a century), they also concur that digital technologies have made possible previously unimaginable, albeit prohibitively expensive, methods of restoration. Perhaps the most significant role the digital revolution plays in film preservation is as an invaluable tool for providing access. After all, preservation is rendered virtually meaningless if films cannot be seen—by scholars at the very least and, ideally, by the public at large. As a tool for access, digital video is doubly beneficial—not only does it allow for far wider distribution than possible with film prints, but it also allows movies to be seen without risking damage to the original film materials.

Although most preservationists share (and to some extent are motivated by) a conviction that films should ideally be seen as originally intended, they are also deeply aware of the extent to which film history—just like other kinds of history—is determined by those particular films (or texts or artifacts) that survive to be experienced, studied, and integrated into contemporary culture. The mission to preserve films, in other words, is not a matter of safeguarding obsolete relics, but an activity that deepens our understanding of the past in order to enrich our present-day culture.

CINEASTE AND ITS PLACE IN FILM CULTURE

Much of the preceding information is culled from *Cineaste* editorials, and the symposia that follow are reprinted, with minor updating, from the pages of the magazine. It's possible, then, that those readers not already familiar with *Cineaste* will wonder about the nature, history, and mission of *Cineaste* as a film publication. The magazine celebrates its fiftieth anniversary in 2017—a remarkable achievement for an entirely independent, nonprofit film magazine that relies on an all-volunteer editorial staff and the talents of writers whose contributions earn only the most modest recompense. As the editorial in the fortieth-anniversary issue observes, "The roll call of American film periodicals that have ceased publication during *Cineaste*'s lifespan is a long one." With the exception of *Film Quarterly*, which first appeared in 1958 under University of California Press sponsorship, *Cineaste* is the oldest quarterly film publication in the United States.[4] The longevity and success of the magazine are due largely to its founder and editor in chief, Gary Crowdus, who remains at the helm and who nurtured the magazine from early mimeographed issues, when he was a film student at New York University, to the polished, full-color edition it is today. Surviving the dramatically changing landscape of print publication in the age of the Internet, the closing of large bookstore chains such as Borders—where *Cineaste* sold well—and the 2008 financial crisis that led many belt-tightening readers to deem magazine subscriptions a discretionary expense, *Cineaste* (rather miraculously) has continued to publish; the magazine remains present in bookstores, at institutional libraries, and on newsstands around the globe.

As both Crowdus's personal history of the magazine and the late film historian Robert Sklar's more formal history have detailed, the thirty-nine-page first issue—its masthead proclaiming it as "A Magazine for the Film Student"—was published in the summer of 1967, at a time when film production and film history/aesthetics were integrated programs of study (in contrast to the division typically found in most higher-education film programs today). *Cineaste*'s masthead has since evolved to adopt

"America's Leading Magazine on the Art and Politics of Cinema" as the publication's guiding principle. The magazine also has grown in length, spanning from sixty-five to eighty-eight pages, with some issues exceeding one hundred pages.[5] Reflecting its ongoing mission to provide in-depth coverage in accessible prose—eschewing the esoteric, jargon-laden language of 1970s French-influenced structuralist film theory, for instance— its title was changed from *Cinéaste* to *Cineaste* in 1978, with editors citing Marx and the best Marxist theoreticians as models who make "theoretical work accessible to large numbers of people."[6] In response to the social turbulence and the explosion of politically engaged cinema of the 1970s, the magazine declared its dedication to "cinema engaged in the movement for social change." Sklar points out that "the early 1970s appears as a period of extraordinary energy and hope for the magazine—combined with an ideological reticence that, to its editors' credit, reflected a refusal to embrace the propensity for sectarianism and dogmatism in the U.S. left."[7] With the dawn of the 1980s, according to Sklar, "*Cineaste* had articulated and begun consistently to demonstrate a standard of detailed, capacious, readable, and politically incisive film criticism," which "would stand the magazine in good stead as the Reagan Era dawned, and in the theoretical ideological controversies to come."[8]

Moving into the 1990s and the new millennium, as this volume's symposia demonstrate, the magazine has continued to pursue thoughtful coverage of the many aspects of film art, history, contexts, and trends as expressed through the varied perspectives of its contributors. Symposia such as those reprinted here, as well as special sections and supplements—devoted to such wide-ranging topics as, to name a few, film music; film editing; acting in the cinema; Shakespeare on film; Beur cinema; and the contemporary cinemas of Spain, Ireland, and Great Britain—have continued to appear in dedicated issues of the magazine. But it is *Cineaste*'s regular sections, appearing in every issue, that consistently reflect the magazine's mission: its feature articles on historical and contemporary film subjects; its comprehensive interviews; its in-depth film, DVD, and book reviews; and its "Short Takes" page dedicated to documentary films receiving only limited release. Sklar observes that "the magazine's interviews are likely to be of primary importance" when *Cineaste*'s history is ultimately assessed: they "set a standard for reaching out to politically minded filmmakers, writers, critics and other cinema workers and engaging them in probing give-and-take about their artistic and social values."[9]

Filmmakers Oliver Stone and John Sayles, echoing Sklar, have found the *Cineaste* interviews to be of special value, with Stone calling them "in-depth" and Sayles remarking that "*Cineaste* asks all the questions you wish the other interviewers asked."[10]

A mere handful of the hundreds of *Cineaste* interviews are reprinted in this volume, including those with the late, renowned *New Yorker* film critic Pauline Kael, cult film critic John Bloom (a.k.a. Joe Bob Briggs), the late film festival programmer/director Peter von Bagh, filmmaker/critic/festival director Mark Cousins, and Warner Bros. archivist George Feltenstein.

Like the interviews appearing regularly in the magazine, the contents of this volume serve as a primary research source—an archive for film scholars and cineastes who wish to gain access to and an understanding of a crucially transitional moment in film aesthetics, history, and technology through the expertise and insights of highly regarded film critics, programmers, and preservationists. More than a few of the contributors are also academic film scholars whose publications and teaching have been significantly influential.

It is a peculiar phenomenon, however—especially in the United States—that a strict division has often been drawn between film scholars/academics and film critics, with each group looking askance at the status and usefulness of the other. To be sure, some critics perceive the work of academics as pretentiously inscrutable, and some academics regard the work of critics as superficially lightweight. It has always been *Cineaste*'s unspoken mission to close this gap—a gap more perceived than real among those at the far end of either group. Like cinema itself, which began as an arcade amusement and rose to the status of an art form, film criticism began largely as a journalistic pursuit, with the finest journalists elevating discussion to serious, detailed consideration of film form and content. As film journalism led a transition to film scholarship, and as film studies grew as an academic discipline, a perceived need grew among film academics to assert the legitimacy of this emerging field in relationship to long-established humanities and arts fields like literature, philosophy, painting, and music—a tendency that gave rise to incisive, useful theoretical scholarship but also, in some instances, to arcane approaches and impenetrable prose. *Cineaste* has always included in its pages and on its editorial board members of both groups who are united by their commitment to making in-depth exploration of cinema subjects accessible. As this volume demonstrates, more than a few journalistic writers teach university film courses, and many academic film scholars publish engaging, readable works on film in a range of journalistic and scholarly sources.

As *Cineaste* editorial policy for five decades has successfully shown, the field of film studies must encompass the field of film criticism, as well as concerns about programming, preservation, and multiple other aspects of access. Thus, the most productive present and future ways of thinking about, understanding, and viewing films require collaborative inquiry and exchange among journalists, practitioners, and academics. In this spirit, we hope that the volume will be timely and useful to critics, scholars, historians, teachers, students, curators, distributors, programmers, and preservationists—not to mention those artists and technicians who create the cinema we enjoy and study in the first place.

While not an academic, peer-reviewed journal, *Cineaste* nevertheless operates as a publishing collective, with all decisions concerning its contents arising from careful deliberations among its editorial board members. Over *Cineaste's* half-century history, its editorial board has represented a mixture of academics, film distributors and programmers, journalists, and independent scholars—many of whom take on more than one of these professional roles. Their voluntary, collective work—including office duties centered on budgets and fundraising, promotional mailings, subscription processing, newsstand distribution, and website construction and updating—has been a genuine labor of love.

Among those in the film world and industry who recognize the quality of these efforts is former *Village Voice* film critic J. Hoberman, who has claimed that "*Cineaste* is a unique voice in U.S. film culture" in that it is "serious without seeming academic, political but not doctrinaire, always topical although seldom trendy." Yale University film professor and film theorist Dudley Andrew has pointed out that "*Cineaste* is tough and analytic, a vigilant magazine with a perspective. Yet there's an enthusiasm for films of every sort that makes it lively in a way no academic film journal ever is." Andrew's observation reflects *Cineaste's* central objective in attempting to reach an audience of educated, politically engaged film enthusiasts. Documentary filmmaker Ross McElwee has recognized this goal in observing, "So much of what is published in the United States about film and video is either superficial and glossy or pretentiously arcane and overly academic. *Cineaste* . . . manages to strike a balance between these two extremes, presenting readable but insightful analysis of films and filmmakers from around the world."[11]

Oliver Stone has pointed out that, among the many film publications he has read, "*Cineaste* ranks highly as a magazine with serious journalistic writing and true integrity. . . . [It] makes an important contribution to our filmmaking culture as it stands up for important causes and special films that would otherwise be lost in our mass consumption of pop culture."[12] The editors of this volume can only hope that the symposia collected here will confirm the impressions cited by others in terms of *Cineaste*'s scope, seriousness, and value to the varied groups that comprise American and global film culture in the new millennium.

NOTES

1. The section overviews in this introduction draw directly from *Cineaste* editorials devoted to the specific symposia topics. Introductions to each of the symposia and related interviews in the chapters to follow are slightly revised and updated versions of the material as originally published.

2. It must be noted that female film critics, as well as women in repertory programming and film preservation, are underrepresented here, a situation that reflects both the fields themselves and individual circumstances. Some of the women *Cineaste* approached declined to participate, citing professional and personal time constraints, just as several men did.

3. For these and other responses, see "Film Criticism: The Next Generation" at www.cineaste.com.

4. *Cineaste* 32, no. 4 (2007): 1.

5. See ibid., 34–37 and 38–42.

6. Ibid., 36.

7. Ibid., 35.

8. Ibid., 37.

9. Ibid., 34. Although the late Robert Sklar was a *Cineaste* board member, he was very much an independent voice as a film historian.

10. Quoted from the magazine's subscription flyer.

11. Ibid.

12. Ibid.

PART I

FILM CRITICISM IN
THE NEW MILLENNIUM

CHAPTER 1

Film Criticism in America Today
A CRITICAL SYMPOSIUM

Since its inception in the late 1960s, *Cineaste* has been dedicated to publishing and promoting serious film criticism, an effort to go beyond the mere consumer-guide function of most film reviewing and elucidate the broader artistic and social issues any film raises. In addition to critical essays on individual films, genres, and national cinemas, issues of *Cineaste* have contained articles on documentary criticism, film music criticism, and Marxist film criticism; articles on the work of a wide range of critics (including André Bazin, Pauline Kael, and Joe Bob Briggs); and interviews with prominent critics (including Vincent Canby, J. Hoberman, Pauline Kael, and Andrew Sarris).

In the years just before 2000, several film critics, especially those who came of age during the 1960s (a period that essayist Phillip Lopate has described as "The 'Heroic' Age of Moviegoing"), publicly voiced concerns about an overall decline of film culture in the United States, a noticeable dumbing down of both movies and moviegoing audiences, and their own waning influence as critics in such a degraded cultural environment. Many film critics, especially those writing for mainstream newspapers and magazines, feel increasingly embattled in their efforts to write serious criticism as they face off against commercial pressures from publishers, publicists, and film distributors, all of whom are principally interested in using critics as marketing aids. Indeed, many critics have been co-opted into the Hollywood movie-marketing machine, whether knowingly or otherwise. Whether or not

Originally published in *Cineaste* 26, no. 1 (Winter 2000); copyright © 2000 by Cineaste, Inc.

this state of affairs constitutes, as some believe, a "crisis," it has certainly left many film critics, as James Wolcott wrote in a recent *Esquire* magazine survey of the field, with "a group case of chronic depression and low self-esteem." Since 2000, when this symposium was first published, the situation has become grave indeed, with many major critics (some of whom participated here) losing their jobs and many important print publications either folding or transitioning to solely online formats.

This symposium provides a sense of the state of the vocation in late 2000 via the impressions of some of America's leading film critics at the time, whom *Cineaste* invited to sound off at a moment when print film journalism had entered a state of profound transition. *Cineaste* asked contributors to this critical symposium to focus their responses around the following questions, which led some to format their responses as essays and others to respond point by point in correlation with the questions. Next to each critic's name is his or her professional affiliation at the time of the symposium in 2000. Following each response is an expanded, updated biography of the contributor.

Cineaste, at the time, expressed the hope that the insightful and often impassioned comments of these highly regarded film critics would be of interest not only to fellow critics, aspiring critics, and scholars, but also to readers of criticism, moviegoers, and perhaps some members of the film industry.

1. What does being a film critic mean to you? (More specifically, why do you write film criticism? Whom do you hope to reach, and what do you hope to communicate to them?)
2. What qualities make for a memorable film critique? (Do you think such critiques tend to be positive or negative in tone? Is discussing a film's social or political aspects as important to you as its cinematic qualities and value as art or entertainment?)
3. How would you characterize the relationship between film critics and the film industry? Do you think film critics could be more influential in this relationship? How?
4. What are the greatest obstacles you face in writing the kind of film criticism you wish to write? (For example, does your publication require delivery of your copy on a short deadline after only one screening, limit the space available for your reviews, or dictate which films you should review? How difficult is it for you to keep up with all types of film releases?)

5. Do you have any pet peeves or personal frustrations that you'd like to address? Or would you like to share your critical credo or a favorite maxim about film criticism from a forerunner?

DAVID ANSEN, *NEWSWEEK*

The literary critic Harry Levin once said that in order to dissect something (he was talking about a play by Shakespeare), you have to kill it first. I don't agree. One of the challenges of writing movie reviews is keeping the patient alive while you perform your operation: you want to preserve the beating heart, the messy innards, of the thing itself. "A man watches a movie, and the critic must acknowledge that he is that man," Robert Warshow famously wrote. These are words that most good American critics live by. I may get paid to do my job, but I'll never lose the sense of myself as an amateur, and I don't want to. But there is more to it than mere subjectivity, one would hope. A movie critic is part mirror: a mirror that talks back to what it's reflecting, a mirror informed by all the images that have passed before it. Our readers and our editors may see us merely as consumer guides, but I still like to think that splitting the fine hairs of art takes us deeper into ourselves, can help us see the work—and by extension the world—with clearer eyes. Contrary to our enemies, critics (or at least the ones I care to read) are not frustrated artists picking apart art because we don't have the stuff to make it ourselves. We're more likely to be frustrated, wildly promiscuous lovers, in perpetual pursuit of the one we can lose our hearts to, one eye fixed on the object of our desire, panting to be seduced, the other coolly judging the quality and terms of the seduction.

Memorable reviews (I say this as a reader) are well-written reviews. I was infuriated by Pauline Kael's put-down of *Hiroshima, mon amour* when I read it as a fourteen-year-old, and I knew instantly she was someone whose views I was compelled to contend with. It's a review I've learned from, argued with, and never forgotten. A memorable review opens doors in your head, pulls the rug of received opinion out from under your feet, supplies a context to bounce your own ideas off of. It helps, of course (I say this as a critic), to have a memorable movie (good or bad) to write about; something you can sink your teeth into. By the time you get to contemplating shopworn summer sequels (whose audience couldn't care less what any critic thinks), your muse may feel a little punch-drunk. Still, hopefully, there will always be something going on inside or behind the movie you are writing about that bears scrutiny and can charge your mental batteries. The last part of your question (politics vs. entertainment) can be answered only on a case-by-case basis. There shouldn't be one answer to that question. The best critical minds are supple enough to juggle all these balls in the air at the same time, responding freshly to the matter at hand; the doctrinaire critic refuses to take a movie on its own terms, holding all up to the same predetermined notion of what Good Art (or Good Politics) is supposed to be. Little of interest can come of this.

Lopsided. That's the relationship today between film critics and the industry, now more than ever. Hollywood has all the power, much as they flatter you by misquoting your reviews in ads. It seems every year the big wannabe blockbusters, with their $40-million marketing campaigns, become more and more critic proof. It simply didn't matter what anybody had to say about *Mission: Impossible II*. Its success was eerily predetermined: Paramount succeeded in marketing a commodity the nation felt obliged to see, don't ask me why. The strange and scary thing was that the biggest hit of the summer was a movie nobody in the country was genuinely excited by: I've yet to encounter anyone who loved it. Say what you will about *The Phantom Menace* (I say it stinks), it at least evoked some honest enthusiasm. The critic's real power in Hollywood isn't about influencing grosses: it's about making reputations. As others have observed, it's really ego—not money—that runs the movie industry. One can never overestimate the easily bruised egos of filmmakers and studio executives, or how much they need us to feel good about themselves in the morning. There was nothing more revealing than the hissy fit James Cameron threw in the pages of the *Los Angeles Times* in retaliation for Ken Turan's attacks on *Titanic*. The entire world had fallen in love with his movie, he was drowning in money and Academy Awards, and the fact that Turan thought his movie was shit drove him mad: he literally called for the *Times* to serve up Turan's head on a platter. He wanted him fired.

Our relationship with foreign and independent films is another story. Lacking the millions for marketing, the smaller distributors need good reviews (and almost as important, good placement on page one of the Friday entertainment section) to sell their movies. A pan from the *New York Times* of a foreign art film can not only kill the movie in New York, it also may mean the movie never opens anywhere else in the country. (It took years for Leos Carax's *Les amants du Pont Neuf* to even open in New York after Vincent Canby savaged it at its New York Film Festival premiere.)

In a newsweekly, the biggest obstacle is space. Is there a magazine out-side of the *New Yorker* or *The Atlantic* that hasn't seen the pictures get larger, and the text smaller, in the past twenty years? There are wonderful movies I simply haven't been able to review because there was no room that week in the magazine. A last-minute breaking news story can rob your three columns in the back of the book. (It happened as I was writing this.) I was happy to get in a plug for *Human Resources*, but the review was literally two sentences long, accompanied by four stars: I had to be content to be a consumer guide, but I certainly wasn't being a critic. There are good journalistic reasons to choose to review the movies everyone will turn up to see, but was it more interesting to write a two-column review of *Gone in 60 Seconds* than it would have been to write about *Aimée and Jaguar*, a film that never quite made it into the magazine? Do I need to answer?

One of the great services that critics can provide is turning the audi-ence on to the best, freshest, most exciting new work in movies. Journal-ism used to be about that. But there's been a profound shift in the culture. Most editors today are more concerned with second-guessing their read-ers: what's the hot movie going to be? The media wants to be on the side of the winners. Magazines and newspapers think exactly like the studio execs: what sells tickets sells magazines. In the process, journalism has increasingly abdicated its power to set the agenda, to serve as a guide, to highlight what it considers to be the most worthwhile in favor of pander-ing to what it guesses will be the most popular. God forbid someone accuse you of elitism! In coverage of the arts, the monotone rules: everyone is lusting after the same stories, the same movies, the same stars to profile. Critics are by nature hierarchical. We have an innate belief in aesthetic priorities. And we are swimming against the tide. The harsh fact is that the culture doesn't have much use for real criticism these days. We're cheer-leaders or spoilsports, but we don't really matter the way we once did. But as Gilda Radner used to say, "Never mind." Pissing and moaning aside, it's a great gig. Sillier still, I believe in it.

In 2000 David Ansen was movie critic and senior editor for *Newsweek*, where he remained through 2008. He had been reviewing movies for the magazine since 1977 and continues to do so on a freelance basis. He was artistic director of the Los Angeles Film Festival from 2010 to 2014; served on the New York Film Festival Selection Committee from 1990 to 1998; and is a member of the New York Film Critics Circle, the National Society of Film Critics, and the Los Angeles Film Critics Association. He is a three-time winner of the Page One Award from the Newspaper Guild of New York. Beyond working as a film critic, Ansen has written television documentaries on Greta Garbo, Elizabeth Taylor, and Groucho Marx; he also wrote the narrative for *All about Bette*, a TNT documentary on Bette Davis that garnered the Ace Award. In addition, Ansen appears in the documentary *This Film Is Not Yet Rated*.

JAY CARR, *BOSTON GLOBE*

I write film criticism because it is by now as natural as eating and drinking and talking with my friends. In fact, it began years ago in New York, when not going to a new film and not talking about it for hours with your friends was unthinkable. You never know whom you're going to reach. Nor would you want to. One of the fringe benefits of writing, especially now that the Internet has been added to the mix, is that you never know who's going to read what you write. I like to be surprised by this, no less than I like being surprised by a film.

Your questions—please forgive me—seem naïve in a few respects. The relationship between critics and the film industry should always be mutually uneasy and best avoided, or minimized. Each is working a different side of the street. They're trying to sell their film. You're trying to evaluate it, or capture your response to it—phenomenological, political, sociological, wherever the ball lands. It's a mistake to go into a film with an agenda. Go in honestly, demandingly, with a sense of perspective and film history. Learn to ignore the hype and buzz. It only interferes with your job, which is to respond to a film.

Writing about films, especially for a daily newspaper, has never been an ideal situation, apart from the fact that you're paid to do it. Does my publication require delivery of my copy on a short deadline after only one screening? All the time. I write more than three hundred pieces a year. No point in whining about it. It just goes with the territory. You do the best you can. The stuff gets written, usually in the best way when you trust your perceptual and instinctual equipment and just let the film act on you. Once you do that, the review writes itself, taking its cue from the interaction between the film and your sensibility, wiring, intelligence, empathetic capacity, background, imagination, et cetera. Worst of all is to overlay the process with some agenda or filter. Just let it happen, and you'd be surprised how often the review emerges from whatever subterranean level it takes shape in. All you have to do is stand back and let it come, shaping the language a little bit.

Serious critical voices are used to being marginalized. They should be. They should stand off to one side of the mainstream, or at least stay out of bed with industry people adept at turning them into marketing adjuncts. The best critics usually are not celebrities. You can only be co-opted by the film industry if you allow yourself to be. So don't allow it. Just stand your ground, call your own shots, don't let people shove you around. There's no crisis in film criticism that hasn't always been part of the landscape, apart, that is, from finding a place that will pay you a decent salary and then leave you alone to do your job. There are fewer living-wage jobs for critics than there are for actors. That's the crisis. In the end, the stuff is out there with your name on it, finding its proper level. You put yourself on the line and let your writing do the talking—and the audience selection—for you.

After reviewing film, theater, and music for the *New York Post* and the *Detroit News*, Jay Carr joined the *Boston Globe* in 1983, where he was reviewing films at the time of this symposium. He left the *Globe* in 2002 and passed away in 2014 at the age of seventy-seven. Carr wrote prolifically for the arts pages of the *Globe* and appeared as a film critic for New England Cable News, where he hosted the Screening Room segment. He also wrote reviews for Turner Classic Movies and was the editor of *The A-List: The National Society of Film Critics' 100 Essential Films*. Carr received the George Jean Nathan Award for Dramatic Criticism, conferred by English department chairs from Cornell, Princeton, and Yale Universities.

GODFREY CHESHIRE, *NEW YORK PRESS*

I wrote my first film review in 1968, at the tender age of seventeen, for my prep-school newspaper. It was of *2001: A Space Odyssey*. Back then the year 2001 seemed inconceivably distant; now, of course, 1968 does. Lately I've had the occasion to think back on the kid who wrote that review and to wonder what he possibly could have been thinking.

I know he wasn't thinking of a career in film criticism. His plans were much grander, albeit entirely unformulated. Indeed, his self-created forum in the school paper was grander than any mere film-review slot. Very much under the sway of McLuhan, the kid was writing what he loftily described as a "media column." The first review he penned was of the phantasma-goric British TV series *The Prisoner*, which, like 2001, traded in deep-think symbolism. The kid took a certain type of esoteric exegesis to be a neces-sary and exciting part of the critic's duty, an opinion that would endure.

The kid was lucky starting out: he had a clear idea of his readership, and it was one he liked and felt intellectually engaged by. Later, he would decide that finding (or perhaps imagining) an intelligent audience was the cornerstone of any critic's effort to construct his own sense of mission. In the matter of readers, the kid's luck has endured, too.

What didn't endure, looking back, was a mental picture of the world as it relates to history and "media." Back then, and it wasn't entirely McLu-han's fault, the kid saw writing (which, truthfully, he didn't enjoy) as an unglamorous means to an end, and nearly outmoded. Audiovisual forms like film and TV, he thought, had come along to subsume, improve upon, and replace older arts like painting, novels, theater, and so on. Writing was on its way out; if one wrote about film, one did so to embrace and advance the cause of film, an exemplary winner in the evolutionary race of media.

Now, that picture looks almost exactly the opposite. Film not only is the medium that's clearly on its way out—in retrospect, it was only a brief technological adjunct to the five-thousand-year history of the larger, more essential medium. The name itself provides the metaphor. Film: a fleeting oil slick on the great ocean of writing.

That other, more encompassing term, *medium*, aptly suggests a "thing in-between," a space and means of transit for what really counts: *ideas*. That's what the kid was most interested in—and I still am. Ideas that reflect, direct, and, sometimes, correct the larger culture. Ideas counted as understandings that are not just profound but eminently practical—not only "life enhancing" but as necessary as a rudder and a steering mecha-nism are to a ship.

"Artists are the antennae of the race," said Ezra Pound, coining a meta-phor that also points toward the usefulness of critics, who at their best are artists of a sort. Pound also said, "What counts is the cultural level," giv-ing the critic marching orders that stress social responsibility as a guiding light and ultimate standard.

The critic's job in one word: discrimination. It follows that criticism is at its most vital when the most crucial distinctions are being made. In film, surely, that was the era when the form's trashy, populist roots and high-art potential were at their point of maximal tension/convergence, and artists

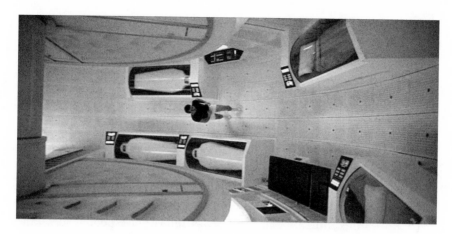

Figure 1.1. Stanley Kubrick's *2001: A Space Odyssey* (1968) inspired then teenage film critic Godfrey Cheshire to embrace criticism, in one form or another, as a career. © MGM, 1968.

and audiences were maximally invested in the drama and outcome of that catalytic interplay.

The mid-1950s to the mid-1970s, roughly. The great crest of the wave known as cinema (movies seen and practiced as a rigorous, refined art) is rightly identified with the era of cinematic modernism, when individual consciousness was exalted in terms that constantly referred to reading and writing: the auteur idea not only elevated the film director (excessively and insupportably, some said) but also the viewer-reader and the critic-exegete. This was the time when film critics, too, became stars, and when most currently prominent critics got their call.

Things have changed, but that's what things do. Cinema, as defined above, clearly has slipped from its position of cultural centrality, is no longer the idea that inspires passionate imaginations to, say, follow Godard toward Sartre, Velasquez, and Homer. But movies are still extraordinarily popular and, more important, are still capable of carrying ideas that unite emotion, intuition, soul, and logic, and thereby help distinguish the individual imagination from the increasingly ubiquitous mercantile-government infosphere.

Privileging the individual mind has been the essential task of art, criticism, and true education for at least a century. Today the task grows harder because of the difficulty of establishing formal parameters—and thus the conditions for discrimination—within the soup-like environs of electronic media and the culture they inevitably generate. Yet I have no beef with studio heads, publicists, media barons, or bottom-line-driven publishers. The only villains I see reside within the academy, where poisonous, antidemocratic ideas exercise a despotic sway and the responsibility of public dialogue and leadership long ago vanished. (For a generation now, academic film writing has been equated with disposable gibberish.)

Cinema, one of the Lumières famously said, is "an invention without a future." It's now clear that he was right, sort of. Yet rather than supposing that the future of film criticism is similarly foreclosed, I would prefer to note that the film criticism that has mattered most to me (and that I try to practice) is not exclusively or even primarily focused on film; rather, it uses film—a medium, after all—to discuss and connect people, ideas, the world.

Will film criticism outlive film itself? In a literal sense, that's virtually assured of being true. Yet I think it's true in a larger sense as well. Technological art forms are inherently short-lived. As one declines toward obsolescence, others arise—but the need for discussion and understanding goes on. At present, it seems to me, some of the key questions facing critics and thinkers of all stripes have to do with technology itself, and human limits.

Will humanity devise creations it finally can't control? Will it keep a rein on its twenty-first-century technology, or be overwhelmed or even replaced by it? Or is it possible that the next stage of evolution will involve a merging of man and machine? These are, in fact, the very same issues that, as magnificently expressed in *2001: A Space Odyssey*, long ago propelled one curious kid toward film criticism.

Godfrey Cheshire served as the film critic and executive editor of *Spectator* magazine of Raleigh, North Carolina, from 1978 to 1990. His criticism has appeared in the *New York Times, Variety*, the *Village Voice, Interview, Film Comment*, the *Oxford American*, and *Independent Weekly*; at RogerEbert.com; and in the *New York Press*, where he served as film editor at the time of this symposium. His interests include representations of the South, digital cinema, and Iranian film, a subject on which he contributed a feature to *Cineaste* (25, no. 4), focusing on the films of Abbas Kiarostami. Beyond working as a film critic, Cheshire wrote and directed the documentary *Moving Midway* (2007), which chronicles the complex historical and cultural factors at play when his cousin relocated the family's ancestral Southern home, Midway Plantation, to make way for a shopping center.

MIKE CLARK, *USA TODAY*

1. I've followed the movies aggressively each day of my life since age six (1953), and I always liked newspapers, so it was always a given in my own mind that I at least *might* end up reviewing. So on a purely personal "why" level, I figured that if seeing movies could be my job, it would leave me with more off-time hours for pursuit of other interests: reading, music, sports, and so on. To say nothing of raising a family in a very family-unfriendly profession (nighttime screenings and kids' homework don't mix).

Even at an early age, I was driven to earn this privilege, which I still think it is much of the time. I aggressively plotted a résumé that might make me look attractive to editors: college reviewing; working during my college years at one of the largest TV-station film libraries in the country; completion of all but the French requirement for an MA from NYU's cinema studies program; and working in the Library of Congress for two years helping compile the AFI's 1960s Catalog of Feature Films. The turning point came when I became the programmer—and later the director—of the AFI theater in Washington, DC, for eight years. Three of my 150 or so series were retrospectives on Cary Grant, James Stewart, and the favorite movies of François Truffaut—and all three made personal appearances.

Programming was an invaluable lead-in to reviewing because I frequently witnessed positive audience response to movies I'd always loved—and which, in many cases, the general public or critical establishment had undervalued. This gave me confidence in my personal taste, as did getting to see hundreds of vintage films in 35 mm (often nitrate) studio copies. The experience intensified a personal reaction to the perceived blather I sometimes saw in both popular and academic criticism, and I wanted to "set the record straight" from my own point of view. In the beginning, I wanted to bridge, for readers, older movies with contemporary movies—and as a programmer, I had often run double bills of, say, 1930s films and 1970s films with comparable subject matter. More recently, I've wanted to be a link from the old school (seeing movies in theaters) to the new (seeing them at home on DVD and with the right equipment).

2. I suppose few things are funnier than a cruel review of an inept or pathetically formulaic movie. From a work standpoint, these are always the ones that editors most prize and praise in so-called "best of the month" in-house citations. This is ironic, of course, because they are also the easiest to write.

Speaking purely as a reader and film enthusiast, my favorite reviews are the ones that rise to the occasion of "Event" movies—like David Denby's masterful 1988 defense of *The Last Temptation of Christ*. I also loved the reviews Vincent Canby used to write of edgy, auteurist works that a lot of the *New York Times* readership probably didn't embrace.

You can't live in a vacuum, and if the film itself has a political slant, you have to address it in some way. But the reality for me is that at *USA Today* I'm only going to get give-or-take five graphs for the whole package. And in this kind of "general interest" publication, readers will let your editors know in a blink that they don't want any movie critic's politics rammed down their throats, regardless of what they are. This is not necessarily a negative. I suspect that were we to go back and read the politically propelled film criticism of the 1960s and 1970s (from *Films in Review* on the Right to who-can-count-how-many? on the Left), they would read like quaint artifacts of an age.

3. The relationship between film critics and the industry is a mutually wary one, though I myself have never really had what I would categorize as a truly terrible experience. Every film critic at *USA Today* has duties in addition to reviewing first-run movies, and mine is the three-day-a-week process of putting together the Friday video column. When I began doing so in spring 1985, the massive weekly workload it takes effectively ended my career as an interviewer of actors and filmmakers or "interacting" with the industry; it's pretty tough to take "surround sound" on the road. For me, this has been a more than acceptable trade-off because my mail is, and has always been, about eight to one video over theatrical.

That's the purely personal answer. But speaking even objectively, I still feel queasy about the idea of palling around with filmmakers or studio personnel—though I certainly consider myself a social animal. Doing so just makes the job too difficult. I once spent a day with Sylvester Stallone and ended up really liking the guy. Yet I'd have almost rather not had the experience because I still have to deal with the fact that he's starred in a dozen or so of the worst movies ever made; I really wish I could say something nice about one of them, but I almost never can. Speaking just for myself, I think filmmakers and critics should stay on their separate sides of the street. Those who don't, always look a little to me like Pat Buchanan caught in the revolving door between TV commentating and running for president.

4. Space (or the lack of it) is the number one headache. It's been a built-in problem since the paper was launched in 1982—but when we

expanded the Friday Life section in March 1998, it was determined that all movie reviews would run on a Friday (rare Wednesday openings excepted). Until then, I had written occasional roundups of platformed independent films, and these packages ran during the week. Now everything runs on Friday—and the reviews compete for space with the major movie feature pieces, the paper's extensive TV coverage, my own video column, and much more. Space allocation is always tight—and it keeps shifting (usually shrinking) all the way up to the point when we're just a few hours away from shooting the copy up to the satellite. Maybe fifty percent of my reviews end up in print as I'd envisioned them.

The editors and I are in fairly harmonious agreement over what we'll review. It's a national paper, and most indies are not going to play ninety percent of the country—in theaters. But they'll be gettable on video—if not in stores, then certainly through online services. So we have to use common sense. Last year, I reviewed about 150 theatrical releases and about 480 videos or DVDs (about a 330 differential). I see about 220 films a year theatrically and at least that many on some home format. We have extremely early deadlines for a newspaper, and I have to write more reviews than I'd like to on a dime—but I usually get at least twenty-four hours to (literally) "sleep on it." Seeing a film for a second time before reviewing is virtually unheard of, and the time we're given to ruminate before writing is an obvious product of how soon the movie screens. As any critic will tell you: when it's in the studio's interest to screen a movie early, it will; when not, it won't.

5. I think too many critics are failing to address how movie watching has changed. Seeing a film at that Sony complex at New York's Sixty-Eighth and Broadway is one thing. Enduring the so-called moviegoing experience at more US theaters than not means crummy projection, shows not starting on time, coming attractions for seven bombs that do nothing but depress you, and concession-stand teens who put butter on your popcorn after you've asked them not to. Give me *Day of Wrath* on video over the years of wrath I've spent in multiplexes.

Seeing movies is a much more tactile experience than it used to be. I can now lie in bed with my Panasonic DVD Palm Player like I can with a book, listening to Peter Bogdanovich's commentary on *The Lady from Shanghai*. I can stop it and play it over as much as I want, then go downstairs to see the movie itself on a bigger screen. People all talk about the communal experiences of seeing movies in theaters, but for me, that usually means hearing two idiots in front of me talking. There always are going to be movies in theaters as long as teenagers want to get out of the house, but when even my son's baseball coach has a sixty-one-inch home screen, DVD, satellite dish, and monster surround sound, I think the idea of New York critics shunting in and out of small screening rooms is a little quaint.

Rude realities:

a. The film generation era of a quarter century ago is as dead as the rest of the 1960s and early 1970s. The college kids who spent time in rep theaters seeing *The Seventh Seal* and *Yojimbo* have been replaced by a generation that can annotate every episode of *The Brady Bunch* (and before that, *Mr. Ed*).

b. I have one son who's in a "gifted" school, another who's a rock 'n' roll jock, and about the only thing they agree on is that if a movie's in black and white, they'll probably refuse to watch it. I'm praying this will change, but I'm not taking bets.

c. The movie culture as my generation knew it was "over" once the studios started reporting the grosses (and sad to say, *USA Today* was the first to do so). Robert Altman and Martin Scorsese probably wouldn't have had careers had this industry-altering practice been in place in the early 1970s, because most of their movies would have been number fifteens on the week. *Nashville*, for instance, couldn't even do much business after making the cover of *Newsweek*.

d. For decades, more great Hollywood movies than not managed to link stars with provocative material. In other words, audiences wanted the emotional connection of seeing major actors with built-in emotional appeal starring in films with at least some socially relevant content. I still think they want them, but they rarely get them. Instead, it's either lightweight indie actors and indie budgets giving you the content without the production magic—or major stars so often appearing in formulaic junk for the one movie a year they choose to make. Is it any wonder that so many moviegoers regarded a Tom Hanks in a *Saving Private Ryan* as filling a huge void?

Mike Clark was senior film critic of *USA Today* at the time of this symposium and had previously been film critic for the *Detroit Free Press*. As director and program planner of the American Film Institute Theater of the John F. Kennedy Center for the Performing Arts, in Washington, DC, he created more than one hundred thematic film series. His writing appears in the Critical Mass section of *Entertainment Weekly* and in *Satellite Orbit* and *Satellite Direct* magazines. Clark has been a contributing editor to *Leonard Maltin's Movie and Video Guide* since 1974 and is a member of the National Society of Film Critics.

MANOHLA DARGIS, *LA WEEKLY*

1. It's a cool job. It means that I don't have to work behind a cash register and that I get to watch movies for a living, which, even after thirteen years, amazes me. It's an extraordinarily privileged way to make a living. As to whom I'm reaching and what I hope to communicate to the people who read me: the best I hope for is that I can turn someone on to a film or a filmmaker I love. If I can persuade someone to bypass the latest Jerry Bruckheimer blockbuster in favor of a local Leos Carax retrospective (or, even better, to check both out) then I'm happy.

2. Intellectual rigor, wit, a sense of film history, and a real engagement with both form and content can help make a film critique memorable. Good writing helps. It's easier for me to write a negative review than a positive one; explaining why I love something can be tough, which is why I work twice as hard on my more favorable reviews. As to whether or not the social and political aspects of film are as important as the aesthetic qualities, I find it impossible to separate these. The fact that form is content and content is form is always in my mind, even if I tend to skew toward one issue or another in my reviews. I would find it nearly impossible (not to say boring) to write reviews that are, essentially, checklists of preferred topics—I go where the film takes me.

3. The relationship between critics and the industry is, and probably always has been, overly cozy. There is the human factor, of course: nobody wants to live in a box, isolated from one's peers, and critics and industry types, filmmakers included, are essentially interested in the same things, movies. It is, in a word, fun, to talk to your peers about your shared obsession with movies. At the same time, too many critics, many of whom are unreconstructed geeks—this writer included—are too easily flattered by industry insiders. Critics love to be in the loop. We love to know what's going on, who's doing and saying what about and to whom. Industry types, most of whom live in an ostensibly more glamorous (certainly more

profitable) world than the rest of us, know how to play film critics. (We are the cheapest violins.) It's tough to give a bad review to a filmmaker who's told you that you are their favorite movie critic. Critics and filmmakers fraternize at their peril; certainly, we fraternize at the peril of our personal ethics. (Of course, I haven't even addressed the fact that, increasingly, film critics work for the same corporations that produce the entertainment they're meant to critique.)

4. I have the privilege of writing for a newspaper that essentially lets me write what I want. I'm the film editor at the *LA Weekly*, as well as a critic, which means that I also assign myself more or less the movies I want to review. (My colleague Ella Taylor and I have figured out a way to divvy up the movies to both our liking.) My primary frustration is that there are far too many films in release and rarely enough space in which to write about those films in great detail. I'm an overwriter, which means that I rarely seem to have enough space in which to get my ideas across. A feature review in the *Weekly* is about 1,200 to 1,300 words; I yearn for the luxury of more space. The other frustration comes from the industry itself, which tends to control access to films and filmmakers with a ferocity more suited to the Pentagon (which, in turn, could learn a few lessons in damage control from Pat Kingsley). Studios restrict access to the major releases such that I often don't see a movie until a day or two before my copy is due. This problem would be nonexistent if I didn't worry so much about running timely reviews. I used to think that one way to erode the industry's control over entertainment journalism would be to run reviews late; or, at least, past the day or week of the initial release. The problem now, however, is that many films (certainly "smaller" and foreign-language films) rarely stay in theaters for more than a few weeks. The opening weekend has become so crucial to a film's survival that if you don't run a review immediately, you can't help the film or serve your readers.

5. I don't have a personal credo or favorite maxim about film criticism from a forerunner to share; I would instead refer anyone interested in film criticism to the collected works of Manny Farber and Pauline Kael, my two irascible and deeply idiosyncratic film-critic heroes. I would also urge anyone interested in film criticism to check out the magazine *Film Culture*, which was founded by Jonas Mekas in 1955 and remains the essential American expression of true movie love. In the winter 1962/63 issue of the magazine, which features an image of filmmaker Robert Breer on the cover, the first three articles are Andrew Sarris's "Notes on the Auteur

Theory in 1962"; Manny Farber's classic essay, "White Elephant Art vs. Termite Art"; and Pauline Kael's review of *Shoot the Piano Player*. Everything you need to know about movie love, or pretty damn close to it, in sixteen passionate pages.

Manohla Dargis was film editor for the *LA Weekly* and film critic for *Harper's Bazaar* at the time of this symposium. She is currently chief film critic for the *New York Times* and was previously chief film critic for the *Los Angeles Times*. She has written film criticism for *Sight & Sound, Film Comment*, and the *Village Voice*, and her writing appears in several anthologies, including *Women and Film: A* Sight & Sound *Reader* and *American Movie Critics: An Anthology from the Silents until Now*. She is author of the British Film Institute monograph on Curtis Hanson's *L.A. Confidential*. Dargis served as both president and vice president of the Los Angeles Film Critics Association, and her work has been recognized through the Nelson A. Rockefeller Award conferred by Purchase College in 2012. She was a finalist for the Pulitzer Prize for Criticism in 2013, 2015, and 2016.

DAVID DENBY, *NEW YORKER*

Let's distinguish between self-pity and regret. The first is ridiculous and unworthy—we're all lucky enough to make a living by doing what we love. Initially, no one wanted or needed us, and we imposed ourselves, often in the face of disdain or indifference. So we've fought to become whatever it is we've become, and at this point, our survival is itself some sort of achievement, since, again, no one but a few enlightened editors and a minority of fervent readers really wants a serious movie critic around at this point. So self-pity should be easily extinguished by defiance. But regret is another story. To say that we live in a second-rate film culture that diminishes us all may be true or false, but the statement is not in itself a sign of weakness—it's a reflection on history. Nostalgia may be a muted form of grief.

Of course there are always good things coming out; there are always interesting things to write about. But as a culture, it's a shadow of what it was. Anyone who can't see that, admit that, live with that, is afraid that simple candor will propel him right out of a job. Yes, it would be nice if it were 1968 again and Godard were still riding high in the saddle, or 1972, with Coppola, De Palma, Scorsese, et al., breaking through, a time when critics were avidly read, argued over, played off against one another, even turned into minor household icons, et cetera. But we're a long way from those eras, and nothing like them is likely to appear in the immediate future. As I write this, it is the second week of October 2000, more than nine months into the year, and what has been released in the American cinema this year that one can unequivocally call first-rate? (That's a rhetorical question that may not need answering.) Or even inventive, bold, exciting? Nineteen ninety-nine, it turns out, was an anomaly: everyone in Hollywood was afraid of competing with *Phantom Menace,* and so a number of big, stupid projects were canceled or pulled back, and great things came out at the periphery of the studios, from the classics divisions or independents. In 2000, it's back to business as usual. I have no idea what the Internet and digital filmmaking will bring, but at the moment, despite all the ballyhoo about independent film and the democratization of production, producers are in control; no director, even if he or she has the talent, is likely to become an auteur in this system, and some of the best actors are fleeing to television. At the critical end, one result of the collapse has been the overpraise of mediocre movies—the feeble, repugnant *Chuck & Buck,* the soft and temporizing *Almost Famous.* These would not have been seen as good movies twenty-five years ago.

A severe downturn in quality hits an ambitious critic like an ax. He cannot fire up his work without being obsessed with his subject, yet in a bad period the movies do not always repay obsession. If he is very resourceful, and has the Devil's own wit, he can write his way out of trouble; or he can join the Righteous, disappearing into a film-festival and cultural-institute regimen of austere or merely high-minded films, praising "interesting" movies from Egypt—an arrogant form of denial. But if the dream of a great popular art form—the dream that animated Griffith, Chaplin, Keaton, Eisenstein, Gance, Renoir, Lubitsch, Ford, Welles, Truffaut, Kurosawa, Fellini, Scorsese—has died, then critics are dying too, for that dream also inspired Gilbert Seldes, James Agee, Robert Warshow, Andrew Sarris, and Pauline Kael. Formerly, a critic who got angry was in a good state of health—he was honestly expressing the betrayal of his hopes when something better was possible. But if the possibility of art is evaporating, if the system has no use for it, doesn't want to produce it, and wouldn't know what to do with it if anyone did produce it, then what is the point of a critic's putting down bad movies week after week or day after day? In such a case, rage threatens to go stale and collapse into ill humor—the prig's offended nostrils at the cotton-candy media carnival. At the moment, the movies are hardly good enough in general for a critic to say with love and hope in his heart that they are bad in particular. But we do it, of course. We do it, because we have to. But we face a relentless tide.

Like it or not, we are enmeshed in marketing, which has become not just a way of getting products to consumers but an ethos, a way of life, a law, a metaphysical imperative. To question its workings is to risk the charge of extreme naïveté. Yet the terrible thing about marketing is that most of it is indiscriminate, without special feeling for the product or the audience. There is a loud, agitated, relentless, and wearying quality now to the cycle of movie publicity, release, and withdrawal, a powerful disgust built into the operation of the huge machine itself. Whirlwinds of promotion often lead to a sudden collapse—all to be repeated the following week with a new movie, the instant monumental dissolved and reborn, dissolved and reborn. Critics want to stop the world and get off, but they can't. The marketing cycle controls most of them—us—as well. The studios have either marginalized us as cranks or reduced us to semi-irrelevance by surrounding us with hacks whom they create, nourish, and promote with junkets and blurbs. Most criticism has been pulled into the marketing system.

The situation may be particularly severe at daily newspapers. Newspapers are in desperate competition with other media merely to survive, and editors and writers at some papers may come under tremendous pressure to stupefy their movie coverage. A talented critic who is instinctively honest can get trapped as completely as a mediocrity. Editors, perhaps pressured by publishers (with marketing studies in hand), may ask critics to shorten and punch up their reviews, assign star or letter grades to the movies, omit qualifying paragraphs, lines of reasoning, evocation—everything that makes a review criticism and not thumbs-up-or-thumbs-down hackwork. The editor would be of much greater value to the critic and to the paper if he challenged him to become a provocative writer, thereby attracting new readers, but publishers may not see it that way, and all too often editors cut critics down to size any way they can. Frightened that readers will feel outclassed by a strongly worded opinion, they may tell the critic that he's "lost touch" with the audience; or they may publish opinions by ordinary folk or students to reveal the voice of "the people." What they really want—what they think readers need—are not reviews at all but endless feature coverage of movies and interviews with stars, so they require the critics to do double duty and join publicity junkets in New York or Los Angeles. The meaningless stories and fake interviews on local TV channels proliferate like kudzu.

Gently, ever so gently, with cunning and diplomacy, critics have to remind editors, and through them, if possible, publishers, that movies, however threadbare at the moment, can still be a great art form; that critics play a small but necessary role in the art of movies; and that newspapers and magazines have a responsibility to the audience—to defend the best possibilities of movies—that the audience isn't necessarily aware of. If editors won't trust the tastes of their critics, they could at least trust their own tastes, rather than follow the chimera of "what the public wants"—which is often just a meaningless rumble created by past hits, star power, and promotion. Critics handing out blurbs will stop playing the fool if only editors will ask them to stop. It is a strange profession. The critic is a creature of the city, dipping in and out of shadows, seeking enchantment through long moods of sardonic disaffection. He is devoted by necessity to craft, not (usually) to philosophy, and to steady work and small victories, not to triumph. For him, there is no triumph; instead there is service, a calling—though certainly not a humble calling—and the exacting toil of precision, fairness, and wit. A critic who can't write has little value as a judge.

Drama critics, by tradition, affect the debonair; they are men and women of the city, too—boulevardiers. But movie critics slouch and vegetate, cultivating endless memory and odd loyalties. They also cultivate hope. Obsessed with a performing art, critics need to feel that something is breaking out, that something good is opening. They may be outsiders, but the surge of excitement surrounding a new movie sweetens their moods as much as it does that of people working in show business. And like players everywhere, they hope to get lucky; they want to feel, exultantly, that they are riding the crest of a movement, or helping some new taste or sensibility make its way in the world, or perhaps marking the stages in a great director's or actress's career. In his own head (and even if the world will never agree), the critic likes to think he is playing some role in the way new movies are made and discussed. It's hard, at times, to think that now, but without thinking it, critics do not greet gently their moods at morning when they first sit down to write.

David Denby, along with Anthony Lane, worked as a film critic for the *New Yorker*, a position Denby took in 1998. In 2015 he left that post to become a staff writer for the magazine. He was previously film critic for the *Atlantic*, the *Boston Phoenix*, and *New York* magazine. His 1996 book on the undergraduate curriculum debates at Columbia University, his alma mater, *Great Books: My Adventures with Homer, Rousseau, Woolf, and other Indestructible Writers of the Western World*, has been published in thirteen international editions. His other books include *American Sucker* (2004), a memoir about the dot-com investment bubble; *Snark* (2009), an analysis of Internet sarcasm; *Do the Movies Have a Future?* (2012), a collection of his film writings; and *Lit Up: One Reporter. Three Schools. Twenty-Four Books That Can Change Lives.* (2016).

MORRIS DICKSTEIN, *PARTISAN REVIEW*

1. I write film criticism to communicate my excitement about movies, my thrill at the subtle craft and tremendous human insight that can go into them. The impact of movies is so visceral they can easily bypass the mind, turning us into passive spectators and shameless voyeurs. We all have our guilty pleasures. Writing about movies is a way of explaining them to ourselves, making sense of our own inchoate reactions in the guise of clarifying them for other people.

When I see a movie like Liv Ullmann's new *Faithless*, based on Bergman's autobiographical script, I'm blown away by the emotional intelligence of the author and actors. I hear echoes of a dozen other Bergman films, including *Persona* and *Scenes from a Marriage*, which once helped me understand how tortuously complicated people can be. I feel privileged to have lived during the decades when Bergman was working. When I read, say, André Bazin on Renoir's *The Rules of the Game* or on the ending of De Sica's *The Bicycle Thief*, where the boy, now grown up before his time, takes his defeated father's hand, I realize that film criticism, in its own way, can offer the same illumination as movies themselves, opening us up to the work as the work opens us up to the world around us.

2. A great film essay (like Bazin's on De Sica) is lit up by this quality of attention as well as the quality of its writing. This is hard to do on a tight deadline. Unfolding in real time, movies, unlike novels, fly by very quickly. We need to catch them on the wing, to grasp how they're put together. The best critics simply see and hear more than most people and describe it in ways that give us a deep shock of recognition. Their writing teaches us to see by helping us to think. Bad criticism offers pedestrian plot summary

laced with sweeping judgments—thumbs up or thumbs down. It's not grounded in any real film sense, or developed as coherent argument, or bolstered by any great feeling for context.

Politics is essential to how our world is organized, but criticism can be political in the bad sense, hanging on the well-meaning prejudices of the critic rather than the enacted politics of the work itself. Good critical writing brings to bear a universe of moviemaking on the current project: whatever the director, screenwriter, and actors have done before, the kind of material the movie emerges from and the genre it leans on or revises. Knowledgeable criticism connects the pressure points of the new to the complex history of art and technique.

It follows that honest writing about movies ranges from the deliriously enthusiastic to the cruelly but instructively negative. Being hard on what we hate gives validity to what we praise. It's vital to the health of a culture, to its critical standards, that shoddy workmanship, flawed talent, emotional dishonesty, and cynical expediency be pilloried for what they are—for degrading art. Bad art is a kind of mental pollution that has a suffocating effect on our common culture. This should make us angry. Good criticism at least ought to try to clear the air.

3. Unfortunately, movie critics have even less power than book critics or theater critics. The publicity machinery for commercial movies—the deceptive trailers, softball endorsements, talk-show interviews, and banal feature stories—is designed to create a buzz that makes criticism irrelevant. The movie review, conveniently timed to the actual release date, becomes one small blip in the promotional juggernaut. So the conscientious critic is reduced to mocking big-money movies, dismissing outright junk, and above all trying to get some attention for the small, honest movie that can barely afford to advertise. It's perhaps unfortunate that a strong drama critic can make or break a play, but this power can also be used to draw attention to unheralded work. A book reviewer can do more good for a first novel than damage to a presold bestseller. It goes without saying that movie critics should keep their distance from the industry: the more money at stake, the greater the likelihood of petty corruption and undue influence. If critics have no sense of vocation, no faith in the purpose and calling of criticism, they can be bought for very little, a junket here, a freebie there, without even knowing they've been had.

4. Rather than reviewing individual films, I tend to write longer pieces about batches of films. This means I'm usually taking stock of an interesting trend, such as the shifting currents of independent filmmaking, or a

Figure 1.2. In Vittorio De Sica's *The Bicycle Thief* (1948), the child offers a hand of forgiveness and support to his disgraced, defeated father.

whole genre, or a significant director's body of work. Writing for monthlies and quarterlies, at my own whim and on my own schedule, I treat new movies as an opportunity to take the long view, a privilege usually denied to working journalists. I've used new releases as ways of excavating what lay behind them, from horror films and Holocaust documentaries to classic boxing flicks, war movies, and films about returning veterans. Film history is integral to film reviewing; inevitably, this involves some social history as well.

5. The bane of film criticism today is the deadly work that passes for film scholarship, much of it intensely ideological, impenetrably theoretical, or both. Despite the valuable contributions of feminism to recent film criticism, academic film writing, like literary scholarship, has devolved into ideological critique, with a marked political accent, numb to both the complexity of art and the dynamic of human relationships, which is exactly where the classic directors are so strong.

The shift from auteurist film history, focused on talent and creative genius, to research on the workings of the film industry has changed the emphasis from the director to the producer, from individual artistry to collective enterprise, from the greatest, most memorable works to the most typical, most compromised, or most forgettable. (One influential film history focuses on a random selection of films.) We have traded insight for hindsight, intuition for information. With this academic turn, the role of the genuine film critic becomes more important, paradoxically, because it is now so rare. We have many eager reviewers, on- and off-line, but few critics with the mental equipment of Otis Ferguson in the 1930s; James Agee, André Bazin, Manny Farber, or Robert Warshow in the 1940s and 1950s; or Pauline Kael and Andrew Sarris in the 1960s and 1970s. These writers had passion, style, clarity, and freshness. Their laser-sharp writing gave them power within a burgeoning film culture; they were fortunate in when they were writing. The world of movies was opening up and they were acutely attentive to the movies as visual art, as popular culture, and as human drama. They enfolded movies not only in ideas but also in their own sensibilities, which were as distinctive and idiosyncratic as the directors they wrote about.

We are latecomers to an art now more than a century old, at a time when criticism itself may be losing its place. Our hope is that by knowing more we can see further, if only by standing on the shoulders of giants.

Morris Dickstein was film critic for the *Partisan Review*, as well as a member of its editorial board, from 1972 to 2003, when the magazine ceased publication. He teaches at Queens College and the CUNY Graduate Center, where he is a Distinguished Professor of English and Theatre and where he founded the Center for the Humanities in 1993. Dickstein is a member of the National Society of Film Critics; contributes regularly to the *New York Times Book Review* and the *Times Literary Supplement*; and has written for the *American Scholar*, *Bookforum*, and *The Nation*, among other publications. He is author of *Double Agent: The Critic and Society* (1992), *Leopards in the Temple: The Transformation of American Fiction, 1945–1970* (2002), *A Mirror in the Roadway: Literature and the Real World* (2005), and *Why Not Say What Happened: A Sentimental Education* (2015). His book *Gates of Eden: American Culture in the Sixties* (1978) was nominated for the National Book Critics Circle Award, and *Dancing in the Dark: A Cultural History of the Great Depression* (2009) was a finalist for that award and won the Ambassador Book Award for American studies.

ROGER EBERT, *CHICAGO SUN-TIMES*

1. I share my enthusiasm and disappointment. I try to encourage readers to look beyond the blockbuster publicity and seek out particular films they might find rewarding. I like to write about less obvious types of films: subtitled, documentary, independent, silent. I am interested in various projection formats, and have taken the side of celluloid against digital projection. I write for filmgoers, not filmmakers or distributors, and take as my guide Robert Warshow's comment, "A man goes to the movies. The critic must be honest enough to admit that he is that man." In other words, to borrow Warshow's phrase, I focus on "the immediate experience" and try not to let ideology or theory obscure what I feel emotionally.

2. A film review should be readable for itself, apart from its subject. It should be an essay using the occasion of a film to make comments not only about the film but also about the medium and, sometimes, life. Each film dictates the tone of its review. Sometimes a film wants to be discussed as art, sometimes as entertainment, sometimes as politics. My review of *The Patriot* tried to make clear that many moviegoers would find it an absorbing experience, while at the same time questioning its values and history.

3. The industry is uninterested in critics except as a tool of marketing. Many critics are more than happy to play along, trading quotes for junkets. Critics should not have a relationship with the industry, but with the art form. I frequently do not know the name of the studio releasing a given film, nor do I care. I do not follow or report on which studios are doing better or worse, and I try to avoid the media emphasis on box-office figures and "winning the weekend." Many writers on film are not critics but business journalists. A critic tries to view all films on more or less even ground, as experiences. Speculation on how well a film will perform should not be of much concern to a critic.

4. Of course my publication requires short deadlines and space limitations. Those are the conditions of journalism, and apply to most of us, whatever the specific deadlines and lengths may be. There is often only one opportunity to see a film before reviewing it, although I almost always go to a later screening of a film I have seen at a festival, to refresh my memory. My paper allows me up to one thousand words, sometimes even a little more, for each review, and I can write about any film that interests me. Small art-house releases get comparable play with big studio films. I review about 250 movies a year.

On television, we skew more toward wide-release pictures, because a show playing in two hundred markets must be aware of how many of those markets are ill-served by exhibitors. However, on every show we have one or two more specialized films, and will review films that are playing in only one or two cities if we feel they deserve attention.

5. I know that some of my newspaper colleagues have been told by editors that their reviews should reflect the tastes of the readers. This makes the public into a ventriloquist, and the critic into a dummy sitting on the public's knee. The critic should theoretically be better informed than the reader, and the reader should be grateful for that. There is too much catering to demographic groups. The first critic I read regularly was Dwight Macdonald, in *Esquire*. He was forty years older than me. I learned from him. When you find a critic who closely reflects your own tastes, knowledge, and experience, you can safely skip him, as you already know what he has to tell you. Better to seek a critic who is a good writer with provocative opinions, and forget about agreement.

At the time of this symposium, Roger Ebert was film critic for the *Chicago Sun-Times*, where he began in 1967. He was also cohosting *Ebert and Roeper*, a film criticism TV show that succeeded his TV series with fellow Chicago-based film critic Gene Siskel, who passed away in 1999. Ebert has the distinction of being the first film critic awarded a Pulitzer Prize for his reviews. His more than twenty books include the annual *Roger Ebert's Movie Yearbook*, *The Great Movies* (2003), and *Roger Ebert's Book of Film* (1996). In addition to working in print and television, Ebert founded the film criticism website RogerEbert.com and wrote the screenplays for Russ Meyer's *Beyond the Valley of the Dolls* and *Beneath the Valley of the Ultra-Vixens*. He was a lecturer in fine arts at the University of Chicago Extension and ran the Overlooked Film Festival, now known as Ebertfest, which takes place at the Virginia Theatre in Champaign, Illinois. Ebert lost his long battle with cancer in 2013, a struggle chronicled in the Steve James documentary *Life Itself*.

DAVID EDELSTEIN, *SLATE*

1. I began writing film and theater criticism because the real world was full of confusion and pain, and movies and plays were vital to my emotional well-being in ways that I didn't entirely understand. I turned to the work

of great critics (Pauline Kael, Kenneth Tynan, Manny Farber, James Agee, and many others) to help me account for my own responses. Later, when I began to write criticism, the goal became to explain my responses to myself—which isn't as easy as it sounds.

There's a joke about an art professor who says in his first lecture, "Right now, you don't know anything about art, but you know what you like. Well, at the end of this semester, you still won't know anything about art. But you'll know what I like." It's funny—except I think that knowing what a great teacher or critic likes, and why, is knowing a great deal. As a critic, the way that you react becomes the show: you teach by your own example. When you lead readers through your responses, the goal is not necessarily to change their minds (although convincing someone that the work of Roberto Benigni or Lars von Trier is less than meets the eye isn't a bad day's work). It's to bring to their attention some things they might have seen but didn't fully register, and to help them to think through all the implications. You can be a catalyst between a work and a reader, helping him or her digest it—extract the nourishment from a great film, and, of course, noisily excrete a bad one.

Anyone who dismisses critics or criticism in principle is implicitly saying that a work of art ends the moment it has been consumed—that it's not supposed to have any kind of afterlife. That's not just wrong: when you're dealing with a medium as powerfully manipulative as cinema, it's also dangerous.

2. My favorite critics manage to be evocative and analytical at the same time. They realize that the "meaning" of a film can be conveyed through artful description and even synopsis, and that you can capture what's most powerful about some movies just by focusing on the face or body of an actor. One of the reasons that Pauline Kael pissed off so many people is that she did a better job saying what a movie she hated looked like and what it was attempting to do than most of that movie's champions did—which made her maddeningly difficult to dismiss. You couldn't say to her, "You saw a different movie," because she saw more of it than you did.

I love critics who are entertainers, because that makes me want to read them. I don't even care if they sometimes lose control and appear foolish—in fact, I'm suspicious of anyone who doesn't lose control from time to time when talking about a movie they love or hate.

As for the question, "Is discussing a film's social or political aspects as important to you as its cinematic qualities and value as art or entertainment?" the answer is, "Of course!" But it's also important to say that a movie you agree with politically might be dreary and a movie you think is evil might work an audience over brilliantly. The important thing is for a critic to be true to his or her own responses, and to respect that those responses can be multitiered. Take that rabid vigilante remake of *Shaft*. I have to be able to admit that when the rich white racist beats the nice, unarmed black guy to death that I—along with everyone else in the crowd—want to see him die in agony. So on a primitive level, the movie works. And I can certainly understand the appeal to historically unem-powered African Americans to have a vigilante they can call their own. But then I have to be able to step back and say, "OK, it's a success on its own terms, but those terms stink." It is shocking to me how many critics let the vigilante messages of such films as *The Patriot* or the *Shaft* remake go unchallenged, simply because, as rabble-rousers, they "work."

3. The relationship between film critics and the film industry is an uneasy one, and I don't see how it could be otherwise. The industry would do without us if it could. Most studio executives, publicists, and filmmak-ers don't give a damn about a nuanced evaluation of their work. They want to sell tickets. Even the smart ones want to sell tickets. One reviewer whom I particularly detest, because almost every line he writes is suitable for blurbing, often is cited warmly by my filmmaker friends. They wouldn't dream of reading him for his critical (non)insights, but they appreciate his status among studio executives and publicists, and they're grateful for language that can so easily be plugged into ad copy and used to sell their work. I appreciate that a great popular critic can also be capable of stirring up excitement and getting butts into seats. But in the end, critical language and advertising copy are not the same, and to confuse the two is danger-ous. In general, there's too much tolerance within the critical profession for the buffoonish cheerleaders and blurb whores—although I'm not sure how we could be rid of them. Legally, anyway.

4. My publication lets me write about whatever films I want at virtually any length I want to write about them. That's the rare freedom of a serious Internet magazine whose editors trust its writers and don't hire and fire on the basis of "hits." I do feel some pressure to cover national releases more consistently than foreign "art" films, but that comes from my own desire to be read and not the dictates of my editors. Also, my magazine is a general-interest one with an emphasis on politics and culture; there's no mandate to cover every movie. I tend to write about smaller films only if I like them or if they're catching on with a sizable audience; I won't go out of my way to slam an art film just because it's there.

A problem that I share with most critics is getting to see the national, mainstream releases in a timely manner. Although my deadline is relatively flexible, I still resent it when I can't see a major release until the Tuesday or Wednesday before its Friday opening. (Isn't it funny how blurb whores get to see movies that the rest of us are told aren't finished? Or do they supply their blurbs without actually seeing the movies?)

On occasion, I have had to convince publicists that even though I write for an Internet magazine, I'm not going to dash home and post on the site that the movie's a dog ten days before its release. I think it's vital for critics to respect release dates. Those who violate them make it tougher for the rest of us.

5. The increasing inability of the general public to read and understand criticism is a source of frustration. There's this idea that the Internet will make it possible for different, less corporate voices to be heard, but, in some ways, because the medium is so interactive, there is more pressure for critics at big Web outlets to be mainstream friendly. No matter how highbrow your publication (and *Slate* is pretty pointy-headed), you're still confronted with anti-intellectualism at its most virulent. You get rage and ignorance—illiterate fulminations full of homophobia and racism and anti-Semitism, often from people who don't even seem to have understood what they've read.

A random example: the amount of hate mail for my irreverent but not even entirely unfavorable review of *Mission: Impossible II* was just staggering—hundreds of e-mails along the lines of these (original spelling and grammar intact):

It's only a movie, meant to provide a couple of hours of entertainment and escape from the routine of everyday life. Get a grip!

Movie critics are way over rated in the importance of their opinion and the need for them. Most people cruising for reviews aren't looking for dissertations. We are looking for a few object paragraphs.

I think you take yourself too seriously in this role and want to be a "literary critic" instead of a leisure movie reviewer. On both films I feel you delve a little to deep theses films r ment to entertain and to this extent they do a good job.

Give a straight forward review! You are trying to hard. In your first line of the review, give me the conclusion.

As with all critics, you talk too much!

Did you even watch the movie?!?!? It was awesome. Next time watch it instead of sticking your dick in your gay lover's ass. And don't publish something that isn't true.

Or that old standby, restated in scores of ways: "You're just jealous of Tom Cruise."

My response to that is: Sure I'm jealous of Tom Cruise, but I'm even more jealous of Daniel Day-Lewis and I usually give him good reviews.

David Edelstein was movie critic for the online magazine *Slate* at the time of this symposium and later became chief film critic for *New York* magazine. He is film critic for *Fresh Air* on National Public Radio and has appeared as commentator on *CBS Sunday Morning*. His film criticism has been published in the *New York Post*, the *Village Voice*, *Rolling Stone*, *Vanity Fair*, *Esquire*, *Variety*, and in both the *New York Times Magazine* and the newspaper's Arts and Leisure section. In addition to his film writing, Edelstein has written two plays, *Feed the Monkey* (1993) and *Blaming Mom* (1994), and, with Christine Vachon, coauthored the book *Shooting to Kill: How an Independent Producer Blasts through the Barriers to Make Movies That Matter* (1998). A member of the National Society of Film Critics, he has been credited with coining the term "torture porn" in his discussions of such films as *Saw* and *Hostel*.

GRAHAM FULLER, *INTERVIEW*

1. In the first place, I am wary of the definition "film critic." Does it refer exclusively to weekly and monthly film reviewers (including those magazine and newspaper journalists whose contributions to film culture are frequently negligible), or does it include scholars, historians, and film journalists who do not necessarily review films but whose work enhances the appreciation of a movie? Can professors who teach film studies be regarded as critics more or less than radio, TV, and tabloid "blurb whores"?

Is a regular *Time Out* reviewer, say, more of a critic than an author of academic monographs on film? These questions—partly rhetorical, I admit—are worth asking because film criticism, at its best, is a demanding discipline (if not an exact science) that has become increasingly trivialized in an oversaturated field.

Although I was the original film critic for the *New York Observer*, I have worked more as a "film editor" than as a reviewer in the last twenty years. For the past decade, however, I have written a serious monthly film column for the pop-culture magazine *Interview*, and I now also select and edit the film (and all arts-related) stories for the *New York Daily News* Sunday entertainment paper, *ShowTime*. I have also written on film for the *New York Times*, the British monthly *Sight & Sound*, *Film Comment*, and the *Village Voice*, and will shortly be completing a trilogy of interview-driven books on British TV/film auteurs (Potter, Loach, Leigh).

The film criticism I write is written out of a simple desire to share my interpretation of films with others and to contribute to the understanding of those films. Often I write about certain films or filmmakers because I must have my say on them (positive or negative), must contribute to the debate—examples this year include *The Virgin Suicides*, *L'humanité*, and *Dancer in the Dark*. Since I write for a number of very different readerships, I have no fixed idea of an audience.

"A man must have enthusiasms," said Al Capone (Robert De Niro) in *The Untouchables*, before bludgeoning an out-of-favor hood to death. I don't think I bludgeon, but I hope I share my enthusiasms with subtlety and taste.

2. Since the subject of this symposium is "serious" criticism, "a memorable film critique" is one that convincingly interprets a movie rather than one that focuses on its entertainment or commercial value or the critic's ability to entertain. Whether or not a critic likes or dislikes a film should emerge from a critique, though it is secondary to his/her ability to explain its meaning in historical, artistic, sociopolitical, and psychoanalytic terms. This can be done accessibly and with humor and style, but not if the reader comes away thinking about the critic's wit, erudition, verbal agility, ego, or thumbs.

Trade paper reviews are a thorny area. Always an invaluable source, *Variety* has had some excellent critics over the years, and yet the commercial imperative of its reviews, based as it is on speculation, is reductive, at least in the terms of the above criteria.

3. I do not know how *New Yorker* critic Anthony Lane responded when he learned that the film industry favors his reviews above those of other critics, per *Variety* (March 13–19, 2000), but hopefully it made him laugh. While Mr. Lane is not one of those writers likely to be impressed by such flattery, there are others who seem all too willing to write the reviews for which the industry hungers. The attacks leveled at critics by filmmakers in that *Variety* article are, meanwhile, a sign of rude health in the critical community, although what filmmakers generally think of critics and criticism is generally of no import.

I see no good reason why there should be any relationship between film critics and the film industry. Why should critics seek to influence the industry? There is no symbiosis and certainly no room for "synergy." I think as much aloofness as possible is healthy. How much a film costs and how it is marketed are interesting points but ultimately tangential to its meaning and value as a cultural artifact.

. 4. I have been lucky enough not to have been asked to write or review particular films against my wishes, but I know that there have been instances of critics on corporately owned publications having being pressured to review certain films and to review them favorably. There have, of course, been hundreds of films I have reviewed in one hundred words or less on which I could have expended one thousand words or more, but there are few quality publications around that allow such in-depth criticism: this journal aside, *Sight & Sound* and *Film Comment* remain preeminent. Since I arrived in New York in 1986, the *Village Voice* has, in my opinion, always offered the best-written and most authoritative criticism in a weekly format.

I try to see every film that is artistically or journalistically important, whether it is an *American Pie* or an *In the Mood for Love*. I will seek out on video those I miss in screenings. It's come to my notice that there is a broad middle ground of films that are made with no passion, purpose, or artistic ambition, and these I am trying to cut back on, but then you never know . . .

5. Criticism is a pursuit that is more passive than I am comfortable with, and it often brings to mind the saying, "Those who can do something, do it—those who can't, write about it." And yet there is an indescribable joy to be had in discovering a new filmmaker—a Hal Hartley or a Lynne Ramsay—and in calibrating and defining their work as essentially as you can.

Graham Fuller was film columnist for *Interview* magazine from 1991 to 2008, and he was editor for the *New York Daily News* Sunday entertainment section at the time of this symposium. From 1980 to 1983, Fuller was executive editor and essayist for *The Movie*, a comprehensive history of cinema published in weekly installments. His film criticism has appeared regularly in *Cineaste*, *Screen International*, *Sight & Sound*, *Film Comment*, and the *Arts Desk*, and his articles have appeared in the *New York Times*, the *Los Angeles Times*, the *Village Voice*, *The Guardian*, *Art Forum*, *Reverse Shot*, and *Vanity Fair*, among others. He is editor of the books *Potter on Potter* (1993), a collection of interviews with director Dennis Potter; and *Loach on Loach* (1999), interviews with filmmaker Ken Loach.

J. HOBERMAN, *VILLAGE VOICE*

1. I've been fascinated by films and filmmaking since I was a teenager thirty-odd years ago. I grew up in New York and I spent a good chunk of my adolescence educating myself at the Museum of Modern Art, the Bleecker Street Cinema, the New Yorker, and the Film-Makers' Cinematheque. I also read whatever I could find. My favorite films were Hollywood movies from the 1930s and 1940s, French New Wave, and what were then called underground movies—and to a degree that's still so, although my interests have broadened. I studied filmmaking in college and graduate school and made a few films. You could describe them as avant-garde and essayistic— they're still in distribution with the Film-Makers' Cooperative. Although I no longer make films, I write film reviews and film criticism (and film history and also teach and sometimes program) as a means of participating in and, hopefully, helping to build film culture. I'd like to convey that enthusiasm. For me, movies were the essential expression of the twentieth century, and nothing has displaced them yet. I've always thought that one of the great things about reviewing movies is that, given the breadth of the field, it ultimately allows you to write about just about anything.

2. I value good writing and lucid thinking. I also enjoy wit and I can appreciate nasty one-liners, but ultimately the ideas expressed are more important than the writer's personal opinion of the particular movie or director under discussion. I'm bored by too much subjectivity. I think it's self-indulgent. Perhaps it's too much to expect reviewers to be fully aware

of their own particular class biases or social prejudices (not to mention those of the publication for which they write), but it's up to the critic to explain why they like what they like. There's also a journalistic component to movie reviewing. I believe that it's a reviewer's job to place a movie in context, and the context of personal taste is only one possibility—and not necessarily the most important one.

3. The film industry, as a system, regards reviews as a minor form of free publicity—at best. The ideal setup is the TV review, which—even when it's not grotesquely favorable—employs clips and can thus function as a sort of trailer. There's bureaucracy that's well paid for managing reviewers—attempting to control when they review something as well as how they review it. (Of course, this wouldn't make any difference if editors weren't so committed to having something reviewed as soon as—or even before—it opens. I admit that, as a newspaperman, I've internalized some of this need to be out there early.) There are individuals in the film industry who are genuine cinephiles and who are interested in film criticism—sometimes surprisingly so. Over time, criticism helps create a climate where certain directors—Martin Scorsese is the best example—are perceived as critical favorites. Maybe this helps them get their movies made—I'm not sure. There's no shortage of self-important critical writing, particularly here in New York. I'd hope to come across as serious—not flip but not pompous. On an individual level, I don't kid myself about the extent of my influence. I think individual readers are motivated by reviews, but whatever impact a critic has on the industry is marginal. In my case, it's probably restricted to distributors of foreign films and makers of independent movies.

4. After twenty years at the *Voice* I have pretty much adjusted to the exigency of a weekly deadline. Of course, I'd like to have more space to elaborate on my ideas—and there are also some movies that interest me far more than others. Ideally, readers should have already seen the movie before they read about it. This is utopian—but maybe that's the difference between film reviewing and film criticism. Film reviewing is basically informational (but not too much so; you have to keep certain plot elements a secret); film criticism presupposes a certain familiarity on the part of the reader. So far as my own gripes, I'd like to have more time to write books and longer pieces in the *Voice* and elsewhere. I make no attempt to see all the current commercial releases. Life is too short and movies aren't my only source of stimulation. So, I too depend on other reviewers to alert me

to things I might otherwise miss. As a reader, then, I wish there were more coverage of certain films—particularly those considered avant-garde. I do think that it is crucial to attend film festivals to keep abreast of what's out there and help the interesting stuff get shown. It's also fun.

5. As someone living in New York City and working for the so-called alternative press, I have far less cause for complaint than I might have otherwise. At least I'm able to see and write about all kinds of films—and even get to pick many of those that I want to cover. Sure, I'd be happy if audiences were more adventurous and if magazines and editors were less obsessed with current commercial releases. I'm a product of 1960s cinephilia—and I miss it. I've learned from many writers, theorists, historians, and programmers. I probably write for the *Voice* because I was such a devoted reader of Jonas Mekas's column and practically memorized Andrew Sarris's *The American Cinema*. Susan Sontag was another source of inspiration—more than any other American, she suggested that it was possible to be a film intellectual. The critics who were most important to me, however, are two exemplary modernists, Manny Farber and Siegfried Kracauer—Farber because of his brilliant, idiosyncratic writing style and his ability to juxtapose all manner of cultural artifacts, Kracauer because of his concern for situating movies in a broader cultural and political context. It was Kracauer who wrote, "The good film critic is also a critic of society." I still think that's true.

J. Hoberman was senior film critic for the *Village Voice* at the time of this symposium, a position he held from 1988 to 2012, when the weekly fired him as part of its cost-cutting measures. Hoberman's writing appears regularly in *Film Comment*, the *New York Times*, and the *Virginia Quarterly Review*, and he has contributed to *The Guardian* and the *New York Review of Books*. His books include *The Dream Life: Movies, Media, and the Mythology of the Sixties* and volumes on filmmaker Jack Smith's *Flaming Creatures* and on the American film musical *42nd Street*. Two of his books, *Film after Film: Or, What Became of 21st Century Cinema?* (2012) and *The Magic Hour: Film at Fin de Siècle* (2003), address the recent dramatic changes in film art, politics, and technology. Hoberman is a professor of cinema at Cooper Union and also teaches at New York University. The San Francisco International Film Festival recognized Hoberman in 2008 with its Mel Novikoff Award for his significant contributions to film culture.

STANLEY KAUFFMANN, *NEW REPUBLIC*

1. For me, because I've been with the *New Republic* almost continuously since 1958, being a film critic is like having another residence. I go to that residence once a week to think about the films I've seen in that week, to investigate what, one way or another, they have done to me. This is what I try to convey to the magazine's readers who, I can now gratefully believe, are interested.

2. The essentials are perception and style, perception that freshens, style that breathes and lifts. Negative or positive tone depends entirely on the instance. For much of the last century a critic, of film or anything else, was thought serious only if he was mostly negative, if—as the phrase went—he said no to America's yes. This seemed to me as formulaic as the reverse, just as facile and (sometimes) cowardly.

A film's social or political aspects are inseparable from its cinematic qualities if it's a good work. The more separable a film's cinematic qualities are, the less good it is likely to be.

3. The relationship between the film critic and the film industry is, or ought to be, of interest only to the industry. If filmmakers care about a critic's work, for whatever reason, it will influence them without his taking thought about it.

4. There are no obstacles of any kind in my writing for the *New Republic*. Any limitations are my own. It is not difficult for me to keep up with all sorts of films because I don't try. I choose to see those films that seem possibly rewarding in some way. Of course, life being what it is, I'm often disappointed; or sometimes I find out that I've ignored a worthwhile film, in which case I try to catch up with it. But, in general, instincts and experience are good guides.

5. I'm too far along to address my frustrations. Without forsaking a hope for alertness and self-discipline, I'm pretty much stuck with myself as I am. If I have a credo, it is that the criticism of film, or of any art, can be a literature in itself. The reader can be enlightened by the best criticism and, additionally, can be glad that the art in question has brought about a corollary art.

Stanley Kauffmann was film critic for the *New Republic* from 1958 until 2013, when he passed away at the age of ninety-seven. For eight months in 1966, he served as drama critic for the *New York Times*. Through his writings, Kauffmann introduced the American moviegoing public to such European and Asian filmmakers as Bergman, Truffaut, and Ozu. He was an acquisitions editor at Ballantine Books in 1953 and later an editor at Albert Knopf, where he discovered Walker Percy's *The Moviegoer*, a novel he nurtured along to win a National Book Award in 1962. His own books include two collections on theater criticism and seven on film criticism, the most recent of which is *Regarding Film: Criticism and Comment* (2001); he also edited the anthology *American Film Criticism: From the Beginnings to "Citizen Kane"* (1972). Beyond his career as a film critic and editor, Kauffmann taught in the theater department at CUNY's Hunter College.

STUART KLAWANS, *THE NATION*

Film critics sometimes speak of publications as "vehicles" for reviews. We also call our employers a "berth." Apparently, we can't decide: are we the merchant or the cargo ship, the dispatcher or the product?

This ambivalence is a defining mark of today's American film criticism: a showy, self-advertising form of writing, whose main business is to whistle up customers for a publication, and whose allure is borrowed, sometimes guiltily, from the supposed glamour of the subject matter. I know how quickly a name (however small) can be made in journalism, once you've taken a bit part in the movie business, since I spent my early years in obscurity as a book reviewer. Did my prose improve with the change from literature to film; did my ideas deepen? Unfortunately, no. The modest repute I suddenly enjoyed, along with invitations to parties and festivals, was owed to my objects of study. So much for critical distance. Though I may profess disdain for "critics" who are mere puff writers, I recognize that my publication and I both use the movies—just as the blurb-o-mats do—and are used in turn.

For me, this confusion in identity and mission has been a happy one, because my berth (or vehicle) is *The Nation*, a magazine that allows its writers complete freedom within strict limits. On the one hand, *The Nation* has a dauntingly impressive (though discontinuous) history of publishing film criticism, going back to Siegfried Kracauer, James Agee, Manny Farber, and Susan Sontag—a history that the magazine honors today by letting its contributors run loose. The editors may occasionally question my diction or syntax; but they never interfere in my choice of films to review (the selection is left entirely in my hands), they never challenge my judgments, and they never expect me to serve as a reliable consumer guide. As for politics, broadly construed: should I venture an opinion that the editors and subscribers find reprehensible, the explicit policy is to let the effrontery stand.

On the other hand, I rarely venture such an opinion. I write for *The Nation* because no other publication will have me, but also because I am a typical *Nation* reader. We're not what you'd call movie brats. Though committed to an inclusionary politics and perennially hopeful of mass appeal, we are (relatively speaking) an old, pale, and academic crowd, who reveal our demographic skew through an elitist tone and taste. When we enjoy a big, studio-made movie, we rush to congratulate ourselves on being in touch with the people. But, more often, we're proud to be out of touch, preferring the small, the independent, and the foreign to anything that carries the scent of money.

A lot of the pleasure I've taken in writing for *The Nation* has come from toying with these prejudices, which are of course my own. For example, I have avoided writing about John Sayles's well-meaning and honorable films, except for *Lone Star*, which was a big enough hit that I could afford to give it a drubbing. (When artistic angels are lifeless, there's good fun in being of the devil's party.) An example from the opposite end of my reviewing might be the lengthy, enthusiastic notice I gave to *Bill and Ted's Bogus Journey*. Not even a *Nation* reader could score points for liking that one.

Does this mean I'm practicing a form of self-mortification? God forbid. I'm merely suggesting that criticism is a continual questioning of one's situation in the world: a situation that's always being rediscovered through one's relationships to a single film, to a body of films, to an industry, to a publishing business, to one's readers, to oneself. Is the situation often intellectually dubious and morally compromised? That, too, is part of life. One's job is to keep the questions in play—and I'm fortunate to work for one of the few publications that encourage such writing.

That said, the logistics aren't great. Because *The Nation* cannot afford to put me on staff or provide medical insurance, I subsidize the habit of film criticism by maintaining a demanding full-time job. My employer, though patient, sometimes suffers from my inattention; and so does *The Nation*, since paid work interferes like hell with moviegoing. I struggle to keep up even a pretense of following the new releases, and I write my copy in the minutes snatched between distraction and exhaustion. Fortunately, my editors allow me to file at the last possible moment (ten days before the issue mails), so long as the word count hovers between 1,400 and 1,600. The editors also put up with my wholesale rewrites on galleys; but even so, the great majority of my pieces come straight off the top of my head.

Given these circumstances, I don't look to Farber, Kael, Bazin, Daney, or any of the fashionable critics as my model. I think instead of Vincent Canby, who wrote extraordinarily well, on short deadline, for year after year, and never once felt impressed by himself. If you want to marvel at the insight he could bring to the most difficult pictures, look up his review of Aleksandr Sokurov's *Save and Protect*. But if you want to see what I value most in Canby's work, dig up the two hundred words he wrote about a little picture titled *Love Your Mother*: a heartfelt, thoroughly amateurish movie produced in Chicago by some people who had hired an industrial filmmaker to direct their script. Most other critics would have crushed this movie and moved on. Canby, while quietly letting his readers know that they would not want to watch this film, conveyed a sense that real human beings had poured themselves into *Love Your Mother* and that they deserved respect. I think his review, headline included, ran all of six column inches. It did as much as criticism could.

Stuart Klawans has been film critic for *The Nation* since September 1988 and also contributes to the *New York Times*, *Parnassus: Poetry in Review*, and the *New York Daily News*, where he writes a visual arts column. He was a selection committee member for the New York Film Festival from 1992 to 1995 and is part of the adjunct faculty of Columbia University, where he teaches a seminar on writing film criticism. His books include *Film Follies: The Cinema Out of Order* (1999), a finalist for the 1999 National Book Critics Circle Award; and *Left in the Dark: Film Reviews and Essays, 1988–2001*. Klawans's film reviews also appear in *Cinema Nation: The Best Writing on Film from* The Nation, *1913–2000*, for which he also wrote the introduction.

TODD MCCARTHY, *VARIETY*

1. In the simplest terms, working as a film critic means being in the forefront of the general public discussion of new films, presumably being one of the voices that shapes the overall perception of a picture. But specifically in the case of *Variety*, where I have written—with one eighteen-month

break—since 1979, the job fulfills the particular function of getting out the word on new films specifically to other people in the profession, to the "trade," be they filmmakers, executives, distributors, aspirants, film festival denizens, or other film critics. From the time I started reading *Variety* at age fourteen, I always liked its reviews for the way they seemed to inhabit the "real" world, to reflect the multiple reasons films get made, to equally weigh their artistic/cultural/commercial importance and to recognize the diverse hands that influence how a film turns out. As always, reviews of the big, self-evidently commercial Hollywood films are the most eagerly anticipated, but in the long run are usually less important than reviews that "discover" new and unknown quantities. The latter is by far the most consistently exciting part of my job, and the thing that can, in some instances, make a difference in the career of a film. Because of the comprehensive manner in which it has long covered film festivals and independent and international cinema, *Variety* can fairly be said to hold a unique position in the realm of "discovering" new pictures. Over the years, the English-language public first read about films from *Rashomon* and *A Touch of Zen* to *Berlin Alexanderplatz* and *Sátántangó* in *Variety*, and my twenty years on the beat have given me the opportunity to be the first English-language critic to write about many films—*Return of the Secaucus Seven, Chan Is Missing, White Dog, The Last Emperor, sex, lies & videotape, Slacker, Reservoir Dogs, The Thin Blue Line, The Crying Game*, and on and on. To see these films and others go on to their successful careers invests the critic with no special credit, but it does undeniably generate a certain sense of satisfaction that connects directly with why I write criticism, which is to communicate excitement (and, one hopes, insight) about particular films to others (which in my case includes distributors and other filmmakers), a function that might, in turn, lead to wider exposure and more significant lives for worthy films—as well as further opportunities for their makers.

2. Memorable criticism can place a work in a fresh light; plumb the depths of the real, or even just provocatively conjectural, reasons a film might have been made; situate the picture in the continuum of a filmmaker's career in a new way; illuminate political and possibly hidden or even unconscious motivations and aspects of the film; expose delusions, pretensions, and presumptions under which the filmmaker might have been working; revealingly place the film in the context of other films that have been made on the same or related subjects; effectively rebut prevailing opinion about a picture; or passionately convey the feelings that a film

has aroused in the critic. Unfortunately, there is far too little of any of the above being practiced these days. The artistic/entertainment values of a film remain paramount for me, but it is absolutely always interesting for pertinent political and social considerations to be raised.

3. Although most members of the film industry can afford to ignore film critics as much as they want, I find that most filmmakers have a desperate craving to be liked, by critics as well as by the public. Some filmmakers make a point of courting critics, and the smart ones recognize that they don't want to make enemies of them over a single negative review, for instance, since there is always, presumably, the possibility of another day, another picture.

Personally speaking, early in my life I had a great desire to meet and know filmmakers, particularly the great old Hollywood figures. But since they're now all but gone, I feel much less of that compulsion, and actually feel more comfortable reviewing films without ever having met the directors or knowing so much of the behind-the-scenes gossip and so on, even though the latter is much more prevalent now due to the celebrity-oriented nature of many magazines. All the same, a critic should be as knowledgeable as he/she can be about the filmmaking process. Ideally, the critic should not get too intimately involved in all the hype, marketing/PR shenanigans, and industry manipulations, but should also be as informed as possible about the influences at work behind the making of a film.

4. The demands of meeting *Variety* deadlines mean instant turnaround on most reviews, particularly if they are written at film festivals. At Sundance, Cannes, Toronto, and elsewhere, we critics often see three or more films per day and must file reviews at once for *Daily Variety*, so there can be no thought to such luxuries as multiple screenings, time to ponder, et cetera. During festivals, our work is daily journalism at its most intense. Obviously, the format of *Variety* reviews is quite standardized, but we do enjoy the freedom to review everything and don't suffer from the editorial constraints that bug so many critics at more mainstream publications, where thoughts of the lowest common denominator of interest seem to increasingly prevail.

5. My general view, shared by many, I'm sure, is that so-called serious film criticism, like serious films, seems to matter much less than it did two or three decades ago; that a collective sense of film history is on the decline, despite the paradoxical increase in the easy availability of thousands of older films; that the opportunities to see anything but the latest

pictures on the big screen are exceedingly difficult anywhere outside a handful of major metropolitan areas; that magazine/newspaper editors subscribe to industry-generated hype to the extent of effectively marginalizing or eliminating coverage of more interesting foreign/independent/ specialized fare; and that too many critics are oriented toward box-office views of film achievement. As a *Variety* critic whose job is partly to predict BO [gross box-office receipts] on every picture, this latter development is particularly ironic. When I started at the paper, *Variety* was the only publication that gave thought to the business prospects of films; now, everyone seems preoccupied with how a film will perform. When I happened to meet Warren Beatty recently, he said that he was always wary of critics, that (with certain obvious exceptions) they were not among his favorite people, and that he could never have imagined a time when he would actually be nostalgic for a certain culture of film criticism. But he now feels this way about the late 1960s, when critical debates raged and reviews of the new Kubrick, Godard, Penn, Bertolucci, Altman, et cetera, would be the equivalent of major news. He misses that intensity, and I do, too.

Todd McCarthy was chief film critic for *Variety* from 1979 until 2010. He went on to write for *IndieWire* and the *Hollywood Reporter*, where he became chief film critic. He has contributed to *Esquire*, *Film Comment*, *Cahiers du cinéma*, *Premiere*, and the *Village Voice*. Among McCarthy's books are *Des ovnis, des monstres et du sexe: Le cinéma selon Roger Corman* (2011); *Howard Hawks: The Grey Fox of Hollywood* (1997); and *Kings of the Bs: Working within the Hollywood System* (1975), coedited with Charles Flynn. Beyond his career as a film critic, McCarthy wrote the Emmy Award–winning documentary *Preston Sturges: The Rise and Fall of an American Dreamer* (1990) and directed several documentaries about film, including *Claudia Jennings* (1995), *Forever Hollywood* (1999), and *Man of Cinema: Pierre Rissient* (2007). His *Visions of Light* (1992), on the art and history of cinematography, received awards for best documentary of the year from the National Society of Film Critics and the New York Film Critics Association.

PETER RAINER, *NEW YORK*

1. I write film criticism because I enjoy the process of working out in print my ideas and confusions about a movie; I enjoy discovering what I think

about a film, not so much in the generalities as in the particulars. This sounds selfish; I suppose it is selfish, but I think that most critics who say they are writing for a specific audience and not for themselves are fibbing. You must, of course, bear in mind the audience who is reading you; but one's prose style and critical mojo should not have the changeability of a mood ring. I have written for women's magazines, alternative weeklies, film journals, big-city dailies, and weekly city magazines, and in all these cases I have always tried to write neither up nor down to my readership. I would like to think that, varying space limitations aside, I always speak with the same voice.

Critics must, I believe, posit for themselves a kind of ideal readership in order to bring out their best work. If you don't think that your publication affords you that readership, you must pretend it's there anyway. And so an imaginary—and, one hopes, at times, not so imaginary—rapport is set up between writer and reader. The subtext, of course, is that you can never be good enough for this ideal reader. Or for yourself. (Self-satisfaction for the critic equals death.) A critic may have the arrogance of his opinions, but he must humble himself before the demands of his calling. In writing criticism, I am not attempting, at least not directly, to lift the standards of readers or audiences or the film industry; this is a posture more suitable for a politician than a critic, although it is regrettably true that there is sometimes an overlap in these two professions. All I can expect to do is offer up my way of thinking, of expressing myself, and hope that this results in someone seeing a film with a wider eye. You want to offer up your passion—not always easy, or even appropriate, in an unpassionate era for movies such as ours.

2. Movie reviews can be memorable for all sorts of reasons—for as many reasons as movies can be memorable. They can be rigorous, impressionistic, acidic, voluminously funny, elegant. What all good reviews have in common is good writing; critics are, above all else, writers, and the best of them are artists. Criticism at its highest level is an art, not a science, which bothers many people who think that there must be a surefire way to calibrate excellence (hence, the continuing editorial emphasis these days on attaching letter grades and stars and thumbs to movie reviews). Judgments are important in criticism, but no writer's taste is infallible, and how could you even measure such a thing? It is less important to agree with a critic than it is to be challenged by a critic. I always find it a backhanded compliment when someone tells me that he likes my reviews because he

always agrees with them. In a way, the most flattering compliment a critic can receive is more like, "I loved your review even though I disagreed with everything you said!"

I began writing about movies in high school, in the mid- to late 1960s, when American movies weren't very good but films from countries like France and Italy and Japan and Sweden were, although I was too immature to appreciate most of them fully. I became a fixture at the New York revival houses and museum film societies and gave myself an education in movie history. I loved, still do, everything that movies can be; a good day for me back then would involve seeing *Dr. No* and *Potemkin* in one afternoon. Moviegoing must, before anything else, be a pleasurable experience.

At the same time that I was becoming serious about movies, I also grew to recognize what film criticism could be. James Agee's reviews were collected in book form in the 1960s, and they remain the most rapturous of discoveries for me; they are what made me want to be a film critic. Pauline Kael's first book, *I Lost It at the Movies,* also came out around then, and her passionate intelligence, the rowdiness of her writing, was unlike anything else; plus, unlike Agee's, her reviews were for the most part about the fairly recent movie scene, which made their immediacy even greater for me. Manny Farber's reviews, when they were collected, reflected a strange and beautiful mindscape, brambly as hell. Robert Warshow, especially in his essays on cultural trends in movies, was a revelation; and so, in their ways, were Otis Ferguson, Parker Tyler, André Bazin, to be sure, and many others, including writers such as Mailer, all of whom wrote extraordinarily well on the movies without being professional critics. I remember laughing uncontrollably at Dwight Macdonald's review of *The Greatest Story Ever Told* in *Esquire.*

Is it possible for great film criticism to be written in a bad era for movies? Probably, but what often happens in such situations is that the criticism becomes increasingly shrill or sociological in orientation. There is much to be said for the sociological approach, but sociology is not what brought me into the movies, and it's not what can keep me there either. I love the way movies can be discussed in a totality of ways, but if the essence of most of what I'm writing about is, even from a purely entertainment level, negligible, then why bother? I don't think movies are in quite such awful shape as some of my colleagues think, and discovering one good new movie in a rotten dozen usually recharges my batteries. But to keep going as a critic right now, one must be an optimist—a cockeyed optimist.

3. Film critics are being made somewhat irrelevant by the studio marketers, and maybe that's not entirely a bad thing. I don't think critics should set themselves up as tastemakers for the nation. The problem is that critics, as opposed to blurb-meisters, often can't be heard anymore above the din of the market; many of their outlets have become co-opted, subtly and not so subtly, by the studios, or by conglomerates or publishers cozying up to the studios. Wherever there is lucrative movie advertising money to be made, there will be problems. Some critics give up, become shills; others become unemployed.

The film industry isn't something critics can influence very much because few, if any, critics have the power to damage Hollywood in its pocketbook—which is the only real way to influence which movies get made. Critics can make a difference in the foreign film/indie arena, but for the most part the so-called independent cinema is just a lower-budgeted version of the big-budget studio stuff. I don't think it's possible, especially if one writes from New York or Los Angeles, to remain aloof from the business or from its filmmakers, nor do I think it necessary to be aloof. Sometimes you want to seek out a filmmaker you care about, and there's nothing wrong with that. It's a human response. But Hollywood can seduce a critic faster than a Pauly Shore movie can go to cable. What Lester Bangs advised the kid in *Almost Famous* holds true for movies, too: these people are not your friends (with very few exceptions).

4. I have the luxury these days of writing, for the most part, about the movies I want to write about, at a space that generally allows me to have my say. I usually can get more space to stretch out if I need it, although the extended essay, which is a format I enjoy, demands a different venue. I am not required to cover the waterfront the way that, say, a daily newspaper critic must, and that's a blessing when so much of what's out there is disposable. It seems like there are about three times as many movies opening throughout the year as there were when I started out as a professional critic in the early 1970s. It's very difficult to keep up with everything. Videocassettes of some of the smaller films are available, but seeing films on tape for review purposes is problematic. On the other hand, I don't know of a critic who hasn't done it. Sometimes it's the only way to see a film in time to make your deadlines. The weekly deadline routine is a good rhythm for me, but increasingly, the studios are screening their big movies, except for the junketeers, at the last minute, in order to minimize the damage from bad reviews. Any purported damage exists more in the

studio publicists' minds than in reality, but the end result is the same—no reviews from the weeklies on the week that the film opens. I like going to film festivals in order to scout what's coming up, but the time gap is often great between seeing the film and then writing it up for review upon its eventual release, and so usually I have to see it again. I'm not crazy about seeing films more than once in a relatively short space of time. I need time to air out my initial responses.

5. I don't fancy the phone call from a publicist asking me what my "reaction" is to the film I just saw. It makes me feel like an adjunct of the film company's marketing division. It's my policy not to give such "reactions," but the problem is that you have to keep reiterating that policy because the publicists are always moving around to new jobs and being replaced. My standard response now is to rank the film somewhere between *Plan 9 from Outer Space* and *Citizen Kane* and let them figure it out.

Peter Rainer was film critic for *New York* magazine at the time of this symposium and has since become film critic for the *Christian Science Monitor*. He reviews films regularly for National Public Radio's *FilmWeek* and is a Bloomberg News columnist. Rainer served as chairman of the National Society of Film Critics from 1989 to 2004, and he is editor of the anthology *Love and Hisses: The National Society of Film Critics Sound Off on the Hottest Movie Controversies* (1992) and author of *Rainer on Film: Thirty Years of Film Writing in a Turbulent and Transformative Era* (2013). He had been film critic for the *Los Angeles Herald* and the *Los Angeles Times*, where during his tenure he was nominated as a finalist for the 1998 Pulitzer Prize for Criticism. Rainer also wrote and coproduced two A&E documentaries, one on Sidney Poitier and the other on the John Huston family.

JONATHAN ROSENBAUM, *CHICAGO READER*

1. What does being a film critic mean? It means in my case having a forum to write about things that matter a great deal to me, including film—though by no means restricted to that topic. I hope to reach other people who care passionately about the same things, and what I hope to communicate above all is the passion and interest that we share.

We don't have to agree. "I like to think of myself as an airplane, not an airport," Jean-Luc Godard once said to me in an interview, and I feel the same way. In other words, I'd be happy in some cases if readers use me to travel somewhere—somewhere specified by them and not by me—and then get off, rather than just regard me and what I have to say as the final destination. Dialogue adds up to more than monologue—at least if it includes multiple viewpoints rather than simple assent.

It's also true, of course, that in my criticism I'm often proselytizing on behalf of certain films and filmmakers, which means that I hope some things will be more widely seen. But that doesn't mean that I always learn the most from the critics I agree with, or that I necessarily expect readers to take what I say without a discussion or an argument. As Manny Farber has suggested, evaluations often turn out to be the least important aspects of criticism, and I'm particularly fascinated by those moments in his own writing when you can't even tell whether he's ridiculing or celebrating something.

By and large, I'm most in favor of whatever takes film out of the realm of business, since just about everything in our life and culture seems bent on placing it exclusively in those terms, which I generally find both limited and monotonous. I realize it's important for business people to keep up with film as a business, but why anyone else should care how much money someone else makes is a total mystery to me. There's so much else to think and write about, although sometimes it becomes necessary to discuss certain aspects of business that get in the way of criticism—something I try to do in my recent book, *Movie Wars: How Hollywood and the Media Limit What Films We Can See.*

It's unfortunate, moreover, that film criticism is often thought to be about film and nothing else, and is linked as such to simple consumer advice—a fairly narrow and boring activity by itself. I considered myself a writer for many years before I ever thought about writing film criticism, and for me part of the challenge and interest of writing about a film at length is often to explore related topics, such as the subject of a documentary, the novel or story or play that a fiction film is based on, what a film might have to say about a particular time or place, and so on. As far as I'm concerned, the same applies to other kinds of criticism and, for that matter, other kinds of writing.

2. "What qualities make for a memorable film critique?" Provocation, originality, information, engagement, a sense of ethics and ideological impact, insight, attention to detail, humor, good prose, a wide enough context, a feeling for what a film does both while you're watching it and

afterwards, and energy—not necessarily in that order. In fact, I'm often inclined to place information first on the list; it's perhaps the most underrated and neglected single element in film criticism. One striking recent example among many: *Rosetta*, which won the top prize at Cannes in May 1999, inspired a new law in Belgium that passed six months later, "le plan Rosetta," altering the minimum wage for teenagers. To the best of my knowledge, I was the one who actually "broke" this story—which I heard about from *Cahiers du cinéma*'s Bill Krohn after he learned it from a Paris colleague—in January 2000, when the film opened in Chicago, because no journalist outside Belgium, or the film's US distributor, reported it.

One of the recurring limitations of leftist film criticism in America is its efforts to separate a film's social and political aspects from its cinematic qualities and its value as art and entertainment—a puritanical distrust of pleasure that is frequently accompanied by a lack of interest in form. In Europe, where I lived for almost eight years, I found that the critics with the most sensitivity to form were almost invariably communists. In this country, communists and fellow travelers are more apt to be philistines about form, aesthetically if not intellectually. This often seems connected with an impoverished sense of what pleasure consists of, which Latins often seem more proficient in identifying and appreciating—such as taking the radical step of finding that art is closer to play than to work, a relatively suspect notion in American culture because art is often needlessly confused with class. But as far as I'm concerned, the best criticism is the kind that shows me how to have fun. And contrary to some of our popular notions about entertainment, this doesn't necessarily entail shirking any moral concerns.

3. Existentially speaking, most individuals nowadays who call themselves film critics are controlled, if not literally owned, by the film industry. (Sometimes literal, or at least figurative, ownership also applies.) Given the industry's financial resources and the eagerness of the mainstream press to cater to these resources rather than to the interests of the public, this situation isn't likely to change. It means that the "decision" of most of the press regarding which releases of Miramax are relatively important (e.g., *Kids, Pulp Fiction, The Wings of the Dove, Life Is Beautiful*) and which are relatively unimportant (e.g., *Through the Olive Trees, The Glass Shield, The Young Girls of Rochefort*, the color version of *Jour de fête*) is made by the Weinstein brothers, not by reviewers. Moreover, the reviewers who think otherwise—and judging from the evidence, there aren't many—are likely

to be stymied by the reluctance or refusal of Miramax to rethink its own priorities in terms of advertising or making prints, clips, or videos available. Maybe if there were a bit more independent investigation—such as a better sense of what opens abroad, or what gets "picked up" but then is made virtually invisible for one reason or another—we might have a kind of film criticism and/or film journalism worthy of the name, not a simple rubber-stamping of industry decisions. I continue to be amazed that most reviewers implicitly accept and endorse the chaotic sort of reediting and even reshooting that is sometimes prompted by the studios' favorite form of voodoo science, test marketing. And of course if you don't or can't keep up with the particulars of this process, you're condemned in one way or another to become a part of it by accepting its operations as the final creative decisions that matter.

Much of the blame for this rests on editors and producers who choose promotion over investigation. In the mainstream press, most material about movies is advertising of one kind or another masquerading as news, and this situation shows few signs of changing or even of being acknowledged as such. But critics might be more influential in this relationship if we had something more closely resembling a free press. By and large, the American press is allowed to be free—i.e., pluralistic and independent of studios and multicorporations—regarding its assessment of what's important in cinema only when its influence is felt to be relatively inconsequential. Rightly or wrongly, I assume this is why Miramax hasn't raised any fusses over my campaigns against its practices, at least to my knowledge—when it already has so many more prominent reviewers in its vest pocket, why should it care?

4. At the *Chicago Reader*, I consider myself unusually and inordinately fortunate in having fewer restrictions regarding deadlines, space, and choice of films to write about than any of my colleagues—or at least any of my colleagues that I'm aware of who write on a regular basis for weekly publications. This is thanks, in part, to a tradition of writing about film for the *Reader* that was mainly established by Dave Kehr in the 1970s and 1980s, a precedent for which I continue to be grateful. Since then, it's a sad commentary on the evaluation of film criticism in the United States that every time Kehr has been hired to review films elsewhere—at the *Chicago Tribune*, at the *New York Daily News*, and most recently at *CityWatch*—his space has been cut in half at the same time that his salary has gone up. Presumably, then, the way one becomes rich writing film criticism is learning

how to speak in sound bites on TV—which in effect means to shut up and let the clips do most of the talking. (Even if what you say is thoughtful, it's the promotional aspect that mainly registers.)

A few years back, the *Reader* hired a second-stringer, Lisa Alspector, who currently reviews as many films for the paper as I assign to her, leaving me more time to work on my longer reviews. On the whole, I believe the biggest problem in film reviewing over time is a kind of combat fatigue that often makes one disproportionately grateful for movies that are slightly better than average. More generally, any reviewer is likely to see more releases than the average ordinary viewer, and this alters one's overall standards and responses enormously—a factor that is seldom taken into account.

5. Most of my pet peeves have been aired above. Here's a critical credo: the best film criticism almost always emerges from a critical community—which generally means a population of cinephiles who can hang out together and discuss movies, read one another, and/or communicate with others by phone or fax or e-mail. Some colleagues insist that they don't like to discuss films or read other criticism before writing their reviews, but it's my conviction that isolated responses tend to be relatively impoverished. And in the past, many critics have reflected the communities they emerged from and/or nourished: in an American context, think of James Agee's and Manny Farber's wide range of references to other arts and artists, Andrew Sarris's allusions to other auteurists, and Pauline Kael's use of the royal "we" and the ways she quoted friends and companions. I know that these practices are often treated negatively, but I tend to think of them as the soil from which valuable insights grow.

In a French context, there's André Bazin, the future New Wave directors, and Serge Daney—not to mention eccentrics like Henri Langlois and Noël Burch who also need to be seen as part of collective situations. Even Harry Alan Potamkin, a neglected American critic of the 1920s and 1930s, was something of a yenta, and so was Sergei Eisenstein, for that matter. Of course, a lone figure such as John Simon also gossips, but he's more likely to get his facts wrong—such as his recent assertion in *National Review* that Raúl Ruiz is a homosexual. (By the same token, it has to be said that the solitary expert is both a myth and a kind of cottage industry that needs to be retired, because it rarely leads to a healthy environment. Think of how much fresher things might be, for instance, if we had four or five books about John Cassavetes by four or five separate American critics instead of just one.)

Colleagues who say that they don't want their ideas stolen usually don't have many ideas to begin with. (It's a different matter, of course, for reviewers who for one reason or another don't want their opinions about movies leaked in advance—but opinions aren't the same things as ideas or criticism.) Personally, I sometimes love it if an idea of mine gets stolen—which admittedly doesn't happen too often—because it's one way of having influence. I also have to admit that a major influence in my writing is the feedback as well as the pieces of information I get fed by readers. As I put it in my collection *Placing Movies: The Practice of Film Criticism*, "Whether acknowledged or not, virtually all critical discourse is part of a conversation that begins before the review starts and continues well after it's over; and all the best critics allude in some fashion to this dialogue, however obliquely. The worst usually try to convince you that they're the only experts in sight."

Jonathan Rosenbaum was head film critic for the *Chicago Reader* from 1987 to 2008, when he retired. His work has appeared in *Cineaste*, *Cahiers du cinéma*, *Film Comment*, and *Cinema Scope*, among other prominent film publications. Rosenbaum's books include, among others, *Goodbye Cinema, Hello Cinephilia: Film Culture in Transition* (2010), *The Unquiet American: Transgressive Comedies from the U.S.* (2009), *Discovering Orson Welles* (2007), *Movie Wars: How Hollywood and the Media Limit What Films We Can See* (2000), *Moving Places: A Life at the Movies* (1980 and 1995), *Placing Movies: The Practice of Film Criticism* (1995), and *Movies as Politics* (1997). Beyond writing for print media, Rosenbaum regularly publishes on the DVDBeaver website and has launched his own website, www.jona thanrosenbaum.net.

ANDREW SARRIS, *NEW YORK OBSERVER*

1. Film criticism is what I do now, and what I have been doing for the past forty-six years, or ever since 1955 when I persuaded Jonas Mekas to let me review (and pan) George Seaton and Clifford Odets's *The Country Girl* in exchange for doing some editing on foreign manuscripts in uncertain English. I was paid nothing for both services, and so, at the outset at least, money was not my motivation, and I was too obscure to face the temptations of industry corruption. I liked movies. I liked to write and talk about

them. I still do. Perhaps it is the only thing I can do. As for whom I hope to reach with my criticism, I suppose anyone and everyone who can read. I hope to communicate how much I like and appreciate movies so that my readers and listeners can like and appreciate them too. Of course, belles lettres and rhetoric loom in the background as worthy goals in themselves. I would like to affect the way people look at movies and think about them. I tell my students, in the words of Oscar Wilde, not just to look at movies, but to see them as well.

2. "Memorable film critiques" can be either positive or negative in tone, though more often positive. All films, even the most escapist, have social and political aspects. I think a film's cinematic qualities and its value as art or entertainment take precedence over its inescapable social and political aspects. See Lionel Trilling on Dreiser versus James.

3. I suppose the relationship between film critic and film industry varies with the critic and the people in the industry. I have generally kept my distance from industry people, and they have kept their distance from me. I don't think that critics should try to be "influential" with filmmakers. Their first duty is to their readers and listeners. I have known a few filmmakers, but I doubt if I have ever influenced any. And that is as it should be, I think.

4. I don't recall any obstacles placed in my path by my publications. But I had to keep my editors and publishers happy to keep my jobs. Space is always limited in publications, and time to deadline has always been onerous. That is the curse of journalism.

5. I am now seventy-two years old, and it is much too late to complain about anything as I race against the final deadline. My credo is simple: Try to be fair and just, but try, above all, to be accurate.

Andrew Sarris was film critic for the *New York Observer* from 1989 until 2009 and for the *Village Voice* from 1960 to 1989. His most influential book, *The American Cinema: Directors and Directions, 1929–1968* (1968 and 1996), elaborates upon the auteurist approach to cinema that he introduced into US film critical discourse. Among Sarris's other books are *"You Ain't Heard Nothin' Yet": The American Talking Film: History and Memory, 1927–1949* (2000), *Politics and Cinema* (1978), and *Confessions of a Cultist: On the Cinema, 1955–1969* (1970). A cofounder of the National Society of Film Critics, Sarris is himself the subject of a book, *Citizen Sarris, American Film Critic: Essays in Honor of Andrew Sarris* (2001), and is prominently featured in the documentary *For the Love of Movies: The Story of American Film Criticism* (2009). In addition to his work as a film critic, Sarris taught film courses at his alma mater, Columbia University, until his 2011 retirement. Sarris passed away in 2012 at the age of eighty-three.

RICHARD SCHICKEL, *TIME*

A definition: critics write for people who have seen or read or heard the object they are writing about; reviewers write for people who are perhaps thinking about (but probably won't be) exposing themselves to the movie or book or symphony in question. The contributors to this symposium are, most of the time, reviewers, not critics, so your title is misleading—and perhaps a little pretentious.

I, for example, may have written a little movie criticism over the past few decades, but for thirty-five years I've mostly plied the humbler craft of reviewing. Over that time, it has become something of a habit with me. It's not quite as mundane as brushing my teeth every day. It's more like my Tuesday tennis game—something I look forward to, engage in passionately for a finite amount of time, and then pretty much forget until the next week. Another way of putting it is that you have to take the task seriously while you're doing it, but it's self-deluding—no, self-aggrandizing—to take it seriously after it's done.

Still, as jobs go, it's not a bad one. You get to shoot your mouth off without causing anyone any lasting harm—least of all yourself. Sometimes you even get to do a little minor good—bringing attention to a neglected film or advancing a worthwhile young career. I also value the work because it keeps me involved, week in, week out, in what passes for public life in our times. Without having to get out and see movies, I would probably spend a lot more time in bed with the covers pulled over my head. Also I like seeing my name regularly in print in a major American magazine, a privilege not vouchsafed to many. Finally, movies, being the capacious medium they are, provide a nice variety of socio-political-aesthetic topics to write about at least glancingly.

But that's about it. To make any larger claims for reviewing is to reveal yourself as a pompous ninny. This is a breed not entirely unknown in the trade, and it is one reason reviewing has always been a part-time job for me. It is an occupation that should not become an exclusive preoccupation.

To that end I have, from the beginning, spent more time writing books and writing, producing, and directing television documentaries than I have reviewing. Sometimes in these other jobs I make broader critical gestures than I do when I'm reviewing. I certainly think that making films for television has made me a better reviewer, more alert to the processes—and the often sly tricks—by which movies are put together. These other activities also serve a need I have to make things that are a little larger and more complicated to construct than a movie review, to express myself in ways that reviewing cannot fully accommodate.

Given my rather modest and solipsistic definition of the reviewer's job, the question of what makes a "critique" (a loathsomely pretentious word, by the way) "memorable" strikes me as moot. I can't think of a review I have ever read that I thought ought to outlive, in toto, the shelf life of the publication in which it appeared. Some old reviews (Agee's, Otis Ferguson's, Manny Farber's) are helpful to the historian and sometimes these writers spin some very nice aperçus. But when I go back to them I generally find myself arguing with them.

Politely, of course. Like me, these people were doing their jobs as best they could. That is to say, contingently, in a hurry. They undervalue films we now regard as masterpieces. And vice versa. They had no idea they were writing for the long run. Most of them, indeed, wanted to be doing something else—writing a novel, say, or painting a picture. They were not lifers. They thought there must be an existence beyond the jute mill. Which may, paradoxically, account for the wacky grace of the best prose. They often just grabbed a thought out of thin air and ran with it until the deadline or exhaustion stopped them.

I don't know that any of them particularly confronted the insoluble contradiction that lies at the center of movie reviewing. Which is that words are an awkward and frustrating tool with which to confront an essentially visual medium, a medium that usually creates its best effects through sub- and nonverbal means. All of us who review movies are trapped in narrative—the who, what, why, and whens of the plot—which is often silly and misleading, obliged for reasons of space (and literary logic) to skip the shot or the cut or the series of same where a movie's most profound, if flickering and accidental, logic lies.

Because of this, I am pretty much convinced that it is impossible to write sensible movie reviews—or for that matter art or music reviews—at a very high level. Logically, you would have to paint or compose a response to a painting or a symphony. Perhaps only literary criticism—words applied to words—is possible.

Doubtless, I'm exaggerating this argument for effect. But the thought is, I think, usefully instructive. At the least, it keeps one's own self-regard decently within bounds. All I try to do when I'm reviewing is to turn a nice phrase or two, make the pieces as pleasurable to read as I can, and offer an honest first word—not a definitive last word—on whatever movie I'm talking about, something that perhaps helps set the terms of any argument that may develop over a given movie—which these days are not many or particularly illuminating.

Eventually, if you are a reviewer who appears regularly in a significant publication, you establish yourself not by isolated acts of brilliant writing or thinking, but by a sort of reliability. People get used to your voice, grow accustomed to your quirks, and you become a source against which they measure their own taste: "If that guy likes it, I probably will, too." Or, conversely, "If he likes it, I know I'm going to hate it."

The best short definition of movies I ever heard was offered by Joseph Campbell, the scholar of myth, in a lecture he gave not long before he died: "The genial imaging of enormous ideas." I know, of course, that many great movies are short on "geniality." But even they offer the shimmer and sheen of their imaging, a quality that disarms and seduces us, makes us willing accomplices in their explorations of "enormous"—though often hard to define—"ideas."

I'm thinking now of pictures like *Bonnie and Clyde, Chinatown,* and *Fargo, Double Indemnity, Hail the Conquering Hero,* and *White Heat*—allusive, elusive movies that offer curiously subversive visions of American blandness and terror, permanently nourish our memories, and entirely evade firm theoretical and ideological definition. It's the duty of the reviewer to be alert to these rarities, to single them out of the endless rush of film passing before him. That may not be a big deal. But it is not entirely an inconsequential one, either.

For a movie must either live up to its first notices or live them down as it seeks such place as it may have in history. If we are responsible reviewers we must strive not to make too many egregious errors as we confront the new releases. You're bound to make some, of course, but you don't want to be a laughingstock after you're gone; it will embarrass your children.

Beyond that, what? Well, I think it is important to make it difficult for distributors to pull quotes from your pieces to adorn their ads. Who wants to be an unpaid adjunct to their marketing departments? It is also important to be intellectually flexible. Any reviewer who insists on approaching all movies from a fixed ideological perspective—Marxist, structuralist, feminist, auteurist, what have you—is by my definition, totally, and joylessly, wet. And bound to miss the delightful point most of the time.

I think reviewing is an instinctive occupation. We respond to a movie viscerally: we like it, we don't like it. Then comes the hard part: analyzing both the movie itself and our response to it. It makes it more interesting if that response is complicated by having seen lots of movies, by having a sense of the careers, the cultural exigencies, that have brought the anxious—not to say quaking—object to its moment of scrutiny. But the main thing is to stay in touch with your instincts. By them—largely—do we find out why a movie works or doesn't work, why it gives us pain or pleasure.

But movie reviewing, even of this modest sort, is in decline—perhaps even approaching that "crisis" the editors speak of in their invitation to contribute. In the 1960s and 1970s, when the literati—as usual well behind the cultural curve—discovered (or permitted themselves to admit) that movies were an "art form," more prestige attached to movie reviewing than it now enjoys. Movies, of course, were more stirring then. People were really trying to get a handle on the then-flourishing modern masters of the form—Bergman, Godard, Kurosawa, et al. Also the American movie was in an inspiringly unsettled state and was trying to expand and redefine its generic boundaries. The services of reviewers as mediators and explicators were more centrally interesting to readers then than they are now, when imported films struggle for attention and the American film has settled into largely vulgar display.

Other unpleasant circumstances have also arisen. I don't know if many reviewers have been, as Cineaste's editors darkly suspect, "co-opted" by the industry, but television has created hundreds of "critics," most of whom are what the publicists scornfully call "quote whores"—people who will give you something to run in the ads even before they have written the rest of their imbecilic notices. It is also true that the new pattern of release—2,500 or so prints of a major film going out on the same Friday, a movie's commercial future foretold in that first weekend—diminishes the role of the reviewer and enhances the role of pure hype in drawing crowds. By the time the public gets around to reading the few serious reviewers who are left (who also may have less space than ever for their views), the die has been long since cast. We are, at that point, playing catch-up ball,

Figure 1.3. *Chinatown* is among several "allusive, elusive movies that offer curiously subversive visions of American blandness and terror," according to Richard Schickel. © Paramount Pictures, 1974.

at best. The studios, we might note, are aware of this, and if, as I do, you write for an influential magazine, they make it as difficult as possible for you to see the film in time to publish before that first weekend. I suspect our views are irrelevant to the success or failure of the movies on which they have gambled the most money, are therefore most nervous about, but those birds aren't taking any chances.

I don't know if this constitutes an authentic "crisis." But then, I'm not at all certain that movies—let alone movie reviewing—have much of a future. I suppose theatrical distribution of films—almost certainly in some digital format—will continue, if only because adolescents will always require a dating destination. But whether movies for this audience will require attentive reviewers, I doubt. Whether movies in general will survive as a genuine art form—with products appealing to every element of a vast audience, some portion of which welcomed serious reviewing as a goad to their own thinking—is also dubious, I think.

The studios and distributors would, naturally, be glad to be rid of us—to turn movie journalism exclusively into a branch of celebrity journalism. And I think a lot of newspapers and magazines would be glad to be done with our gesturings (or are they merely posturings?) as well. It takes up valuable space and annoys some readers. Something punchy in the jejune dot-com manner—consumer guidance rendered in a superficially subjective, purely populist style—would do almost everyone just as well.

Will you miss us when we're gone, you rascals you? Maybe more than you know—the rattle of more or less informed, more or less cogently expressed opinion, appearing in generally accessible venues, has its mysterious, indefinable uses in societies that maintain the democratic pretense. It keeps people buzzing, hopping, stirred up in ways that an in-depth profile of Britney Spears never will. Maybe it's not much. But I'm bound to think, given the time I've devoted to this curious occupation—next to Andrew Sarris and John Simon I guess I'm the longest continuously serving reviewer around—that it is not nothing, either.

The late Richard Schickel was film critic for *Time* magazine from 1965 until 2010 and also wrote for *Life* magazine and the *Los Angeles Times Book Review*, with his most recent writings appearing on Truthdig.com. Schickel is the author of more than thirty books, including biographies of Marlon Brando, James Cagney, Cary Grant, D. W. Griffith, Walt Disney, Elia Kazan, Woody Allen, and Clint Eastwood, and he recently published *Keepers: The Greatest Films—and Personal Favorites—of a Moviegoing Lifetime* (2015). He has written or produced and directed dozens of television documentaries, including *Shooting War: World War II Combat Cameramen* (2000), *Life Goes to the Movies* (1976), and documentaries on filmmakers Vincente Minnelli (1987) and Elia Kazan (1994)—all four of which received Emmy nominations. Schickel has lectured at Yale and the University of Southern California and was awarded a Guggenheim Fellowship in 1964 and the National Society of Film Critics Special Citation in 2005.

LISA SCHWARZBAUM, *ENTERTAINMENT WEEKLY*

1. I write film criticism for readers of *Entertainment Weekly* so that they can compare how I see a particular movie—that's what I explain in my review—with how they see the same movie. Of course, I hope that my readers will be won over by my persuasiveness, or brilliance, or insights. But I'm just as happy if they disagree. I feel I've done my job if I've argued my position clearly, and I'm particularly happy if I feel I've suggested new ways for moviegoers to consider a particular film or filmmaker or actor or visual style, even if a reader ultimately rejects my approach. I want to communicate the excitement of the medium—but I also want to lobby in favor of high

standards, particularly since criticism is the only defense against the ever-, ever-, ever-escalating assault of hype and promotional bullshit through which potential ticket buyers must pass to decide what they want to see.

2. Good writing, good writing, good writing: without it, even the most erudite, most perceptive, most beautifully reasoned critique is forgettable, or impenetrable, or alienating, or dull. The reason Pauline Kael excited her readers (and inspired generations of guys after her—they're mostly guys—to write from her POV) was her voice, her language, the passion she conveyed with her words. Same thing with James Agee. Of course, style can be dangerous, sprucing up rotten aesthetics and arguable tastes and making them look solid. (Kael, again, and Agee—they could be so wrong about stuff, and sound so sure of themselves.) A memorable critique is one that elegantly, confidently analyzes a film within a context that allows a reader to enter into the debate. That context can be as global as the social and/or political issues a movie tackles, or as specific as the particular critic's aesthetic quirks, but the arguments need to unfold naturally, logically. Sometimes a memorable critique is one that can sensuously convey the actual cinematic sense of what the writer sees, so the reader feels like she's seeing it, too. I don't think either a positive or negative critique has the edge on being memorable, by the way.

3. The symbiotic relationship between film critics and the film industry is as compromised or as clean as one makes it, but always, the pressures and persuasions can be felt. We (the critics) need screening access to films in order to review; they (the film industry) control that access. They want good reviews (and want to fend off bad ones); we want good movies, and must hold the line against bad ones. Sometimes we're a necessary evil to the industry—a gauntlet of bad reviews to be gotten past, a subdivision of quote whores and junket jockeys to be serviced in exchange for a "what a thrill ride!" quote—but sometimes, they know, we can be of tremendous "service," championing a film or director or actor because we're impassioned. We really are impassioned, you see, except about crap, and then we're discouraged, sour.

There may not be big ways to be more influential, but there are small ones. Every critic, I'm sure, even the most rigorous, highbrow one, knows when she's writing a "blurbable" sentence; we could be more precise, more rigorous in our choices. And what if, for instance, quote whores stopped selling their souls? What would the whole "thrill ride" industry do then?

4. The publication each critic writes for determines the obstacles each faces. But I'd wager that unless one is writing for an alternative weekly (with relatively ample space in which to hold forth), or for a daily paper committed to comprehensive coverage of every film that opens, the biggest obstacle is selectivity. At *Entertainment Weekly*, we cover more and a greater range of new movies than any other national weekly, but we've still got to let many smaller films go unnoticed. We've got to weigh our coverage of small/indie/foreign-language films in limited release against larger studio movies (even if crappy) in wider release. I can push to cover the little Chinese or Iranian film, but I don't want to ignore the latest interestingly awful demonic-possession flick starring Kim Basinger or Winona Ryder.

As for quick deadlines or the constraints of single viewings, those don't bother me, not for the kind of writing I do. If I were writing for a scholarly publication or doing a larger critical analysis, this would be an issue—but not for a weekly pub.

5. There's a whole other question to be asked about viewing movies through male and female critical eyes—maybe a whole other symposium to be done, tied to "chick flicks" and "guy movies." But for the purposes of the question you pose, I'd say one peeve—don't want to dignify it with "pet"—is reader response that goes like this: "You didn't like Stinker X? What's your problem? You need to get laid." A good argument could be made that all film critics need to get laid, often—who'd say no? But I'm curious whether the aesthetic tastes of male critics are challenged so regularly along such lines.

Lisa Schwarzbaum joined *Entertainment Weekly* as a senior writer in 1991, where she remained until 2013, when she left to pursue other professional opportunities. She continues to contribute to the magazine's website, EW.com, and also writes for BBC.com, *Slate*, and Yahoo! Movies. Schwarzbaum reviews films regularly on CNN's *Showbiz Today* and other national and local TV and radio programs. Her book reviews, essays, and cultural criticism have appeared in the *New York Times Magazine, Time, DGA Quarterly, Vogue, Redbook*, the *Baltimore Sun*, and numerous other publications. A member of the New York Film Critics Circle and the National Society of Film Critics, Schwarzbaum also served on the selection committee for the New York Film Festival.

JOHN SIMON, *NATIONAL REVIEW*

Film criticism means coming to grips with an exciting art. By writing about a film, I crystallize my thoughts about it, express my feelings, achieve understanding. I write this for myself, and consider myself my toughest critic. Then I publish it, and hope it reaches the right people: those who feel they benefit from it, even if only to disagree creatively. But my fondest hope is that they will learn something from what they read.

A memorable piece of film criticism should delight, instruct, and stimulate independent thought. It should be as well written as a piece of literature and withstand the test of time. If negative, it should preferably be witty; if positive, it should glow with passion as well as light up with reason. Social and political issues should be dealt with, if relevant, at the appropriate length. The main thing is not to mince words, and tell the truth as best you can apprehend it.

The relationship between the reviewer and the industry is a sorry one. If the reviewer writes for a major publication, he will be wooed up to a point. If for a minor one, he'll get the odd bone tossed to him. If he is a tough and independent-minded critic, he will be ignored. I can see no way—or need—for this to change.

There is never enough space for the review you would wish to write. Still, you should value concision as a powerful virtue. I have been censored now and then for various reasons, but very infrequently. I review what I choose, but try to balance what the readership wants with what I think it needs. Deadlines are not that much of a problem, though I find it hard to write before my back is against the wall.

My credo was and is that the critic has to be as good a writer as the novelist or playwright; that he must be a teacher, perfectly lucid and comprehensible; and that he must also be a thinker and, as such, know about other things besides movies, notably about life. In a perfect world, there would be an intelligence test for critics, which would mercifully eliminate a large number now reviewing. The biggest problem for movie criticism today is that so many reviewers think that raising or lowering their thumbs is doing their job, and that most readers demand no more from it than one to four asterisks posing as stars to tell them all they need to know. Criticism of any kind is a process, not a commodity.

John Simon was film critic for the *National Review* and drama critic for *New York* magazine from 1968 to 2005. He currently writes for the *Westchester Guardian* and the *Yonkers Tribune*. Simon's film, music, book, and theater reviews have appeared in *Esquire*, *Opera News*, the *New Leader*, *Commonweal*, and the *Weekly Standard*, where he publishes a monthly essay. He is a member of the New York Film Critics Circle and a recipient of the George Polk Award in film criticism. Among his numerous books are *Acid Test* (1963), *Private Screenings* (1968), *Movies into Film: Film Criticism, 1963–1973* (1975), *Ingmar Bergman Directs* (1974), *Something to Declare: Twelve Years of Films from Abroad* (1983), *Reverse Angle: A Decade of American Films* (1983), *The Sheep from the Goats: Selected Literary Essays* (1989), and *Dreamers of Dreams: Essays on Poets and Poetry* (2001).

DAVID STERRITT, *CHRISTIAN SCIENCE MONITOR*

1. What being a film critic means to me is inseparable from what film itself means to me, and a key aspect of this is cinema's great diversity as an art form, an entertainment medium, and a cultural force. I originally became a critic because it would let me see lots of movies, get paid for expressing my opinions, and have an ongoing dialogue with other critics, general moviegoers, and any filmmakers who might happen to be paying attention. I was also drawn to film because of its intersection with other arts, and because thinking about film often led to thinking about other disciplines that interest me. While all of this still holds today, there's no single answer to the question of why and for whom I write, since I write different kinds of criticism for different purposes. I've spent most of my career as film critic for a national newspaper (and a secular one, despite its churchy name) that aims at an educated audience and is willing to publish reasonably thoughtful reviews. I still enjoy the daily-newspaper beat because it keeps me on the front lines and offers me a haven from the ponderousness of much academic writing. But even the best newspapers are journalistic enterprises, more interested in keeping up with events than in plumbing their depths; and the constraints that result from this—word counts are low, vocabularies are limited, snappy prose often crowds out serious analysis—have made me increasingly interested in writing books and contributing to film magazines and journals. This said, I can sum up

what I hope to accomplish by saying that I want to encourage the artistic qualities that most excite me—riskiness, spontaneity, audacity, intuitiveness—throughout the film community, from directors and producers to exhibitors and audiences.

One part of my job is to praise works that embody these virtues; another is to censure works that don't; a third is to help viewers appreciate the pleasures of being challenged and stimulated rather than lulled and coddled. Hollywood has spent decades brainwashing us into thinking cinema is defined by a narrow range of time-tested formulas, and the public's current aversion to such irksome phenomena as subtitles and avant-garde innovation shows the campaign is still succeeding. I find good and bad works at every point along the cinematic spectrum, from big-studio haymakers to esoteric abstractions. It's my responsibility to steer viewers away from the bad ones while sharing the excitement I feel over good ones of all kinds by spreading the word as widely as I can.

2. I'm no more eager to generalize about memorable reviews than about memorable movies—let a zillion flowers bloom! Bad pictures deserve devastating pans, good ones deserve illuminating raves, and any kind of critique can lodge in the memory if its ideas and clarity are in sync with the impact and significance of the work(s) being discussed. More broadly, reviews of lasting value are likely to go beyond individual films in order to make larger points. Consumer-guide criticism is unquestionably the least enduring kind, despite the high esteem it's held in by virtually every newspaper editor on the planet. I often tell students that the critic's opinion is important, but ultimately less so than the information or analysis that's conveyed along with it—that is, readers should be able to tell from a review that they might like the movie even though the critic disliked it, and readers should be able to profit from a review even if they know this is a picture they themselves aren't likely to see.

Addressing a film's social or political aspects is often an important part of this, and journalistic reviewing would profit enormously from more alertness to these areas. By the same token, much scholarly reviewing would improve if more attention were paid to the fact that film is an art form as well as a sociopolitical phenomenon, and that aesthetics are as legitimate a field of discussion as the niceties of social-science discourse. Finally, much memorable criticism is characterized by memorable writing, and in some cases—plenty of Pauline Kael's pieces come to mind—a punchy sentence or phrase can be recalled for years even when the idea it's expressing is dubious, doubtful, or downright wrong. Memorable reviews come in all shapes and sizes, but that doesn't mean they're of equal value in the long run.

3. I'd like to think critics have some degree of influence over the film industry, since I have tremendous respect for many of my colleagues and am convinced that cinema would be better if their ideas were heeded. Reality tells me that many awful films are as critic proof as Hollywood thinks they are, though, so there's no particular reason why the executives who green-light them should pay attention to us. Independent filmmakers are more starved for recognition and therefore more grateful when their work is discussed, but those who see themselves as partners in a genuine dialogue with critics are a minority.

For these and other reasons, my goal isn't to police the industry but to encourage the mavericks on the outskirts, hoping one more supportive voice might make a difference to their morale and confidence if not their dollars and cents. The biggest problem with the relationship between critics and the industry is that popular journalism has turned most reviewing into a form of advertising, focused primarily on big-studio products that already have huge promotional campaigns pounding their alleged merits into our heads. Editors don't want thoughtful discussions of interesting films, they want entertaining synopses of whatever releases have the big ads in this week's paper, decked out with glitzy photos, quote-laden sidebars, shorthand rating charts, ticket-window statistics, and other eye-catching junk signaling to the reader that movies aren't really worth reading about, much less thinking about. All this will have to undergo major changes if critics are ever to have a meaningful influence on the industry or on film culture at large.

4. Every critic has obstacles, and for years I chafed at a list of painfully common ones, from limited space and sloppy editing to infelicitous tilts in my paper's idea of what criticism is all about. I'm still chafing, but I've removed some of the irritation by entering other kinds of dialogue via teaching and writing for different venues. I don't think any single publication can accommodate every kind of writing an energetic critic would like to do, and this is a reality we've got to face. I suppose the best maneuver is to set up one's own website, thereby removing all obstacles in one stroke, and I mean to get around to that one of these years.

5. Pet peeves? The degree to which film journalism has become a branch of film advertising, and the fact that I abet this by simply doing my

job. Critical credos? Be as adventurous as you can, be as independent as you can, and look beyond the movie of the moment to the health of film culture as a whole.

David Sterritt was film critic for the *Christian Science Monitor* from 1968 until his retirement in 2005. His work has been published in *Cineaste*, the *New York Times*, *MovieMaker* magazine, *Film Comment*, *Film Quarterly*, *Senses of Cinema*, and the *Huffington Post*. His books include *The Films of Alfred Hitchcock* (1993), *The Films of Jean-Luc Godard: Seeing the Invisible* (1999), *Mad to Be Saved: The Beats, the '50s, and Film* (1998), *Spike Lee's America* (2013), and *The Cinema of Clint Eastwood* (2014). Sterritt has appeared on several television shows, including *Nightline*, *Charlie Rose*, *The O'Reilly Factor*, and *CBS Morning News*. A former chair of the New York Film Critics Circle, Sterritt is an emeritus professor at Long Island University and has taught at Columbia University, the Maryland Institute College of Art, and the S. I. Newhouse School of Public Communications at Syracuse University.

PETER TRAVERS, *ROLLING STONE*

1. "What does being a film critic mean to you?" Always, to shove my opinion down the throats of mere mortals who dare to imagine they have the right to think on their own. I'm kidding, but the snob approach can be nearly as destructive as the knee-jerk labeling of films with thumbs, stars, letter grades, and other consumer shortcuts that discourage "thinking" about movies. Punditry and puffery are the twin evils of film criticism since both cut off the conversation that the best film criticism inspires. For me, being a film critic means taking responsibility for thinking about film and for writing reviews that encourage readers to think as well. That's an enviable position, and a challenging one. A good film critic should inform, interpret, spark curiosity, provide historical perspective (from other arts besides film), and raise questions that stimulate a response. That's true whether you have five thousand words or five hundred words to craft a reasoned critique that is also reasonably entertaining, since you don't want readers dozing.

"More specifically, why do you write film criticism?" Because it would be unthinkable for me not to do it. Film criticism requires enthusiasm, not necessarily for the films themselves, since artistic success is increasingly rare in a marketplace dominated by commercial compromise, but for the job at hand. Many film critics today write as if they were condemned to the job. But to criticize film without passion for the medium—the kind of passion that can provoke praise and censure—seems a waste of time for the critic and the reader.

"Whom do you hope to reach, and what do you hope to communicate to them?" I hope to reach readers who are interested in the possibilities of film, readers not scared off by low budgets, subtitles and experimentation, readers who want to move beyond tips on what to see this weekend. "Is it fun?" "Is it worth nine bucks?" I hope to communicate that there is a world of film outside the boundaries of Hollywood, from American indies to the burgeoning cinema of Iran. I hope to communicate that even a failed film, say, Spike Lee's *Bamboozled*, is loaded with achievements and shortcomings worthy of discussion. I hope to communicate that there's more to movies than stars—that directors, screenwriters, DPs, editors, and designers all make contributions that contribute to a film's success or failure. I hope to communicate that movies have an afterlife, that the best of them can serve as artistic touchstones far more valuable than their box-office standing.

2. "What qualities make for a memorable film critique?" Negative critiques tend to win attention—for the critic not the film, which is the problem. It's easy to be smart-ass. Every honest critic knows that a positive review is far more difficult to write. A gush of adjectives won't do the job; neither will a purely academic deconstruction. For me, a memorable film critique communicates a critic's feelings as well as his standards of judgment. The notion that a true critic should remain a paragon of untouched objectivity strikes me as nonsense. Be ardent, be pissed off, be alive to what's happening on screen. Dealing with subtext, with social, political, and moral context, with what a film offers beyond entertainment or technical artistic value, brings out the best, I think, in the critic and the reader. Of course, I'm talking about movies with aspirations, however failed. A critic who uses the usual Hollywood swill to show his smug superiority is just showing off. His critique may be good for a few laughs, but it doesn't stay with you.

3. "How would you characterize the relationship between film critics and the film industry?" Contentious. The film industry, meaning the fat-cat Hollywood executives, see critics as assassins ready to skewer its coddled, vulnerable babies. Film critics, being coddled, vulnerable babies

ourselves, see film industry leaders as philistines ready to plunder their critiques for blurbs to use in their crass marketing campaigns, often distorting the meaning.

"Do you think film critics could be more influential in the relationship? How?" Sure. I once wrote off a slick, studio crowd-pleaser as an appalling romance that I feared would be a date night hit. "A date night hit," read the blurb until a cease-and-desist order was issued. The general public has the idea that studio executives sneak around screenings passing out large bills to critics in exchange for a good review. Never happened. And why should it? To the delight of the studios and perhaps with their collusion, a whole group of unknown critics from unknown media outlets seems to have sprung up to supply blurbs the producer's mother could have written.

4. I write on deadline for a national magazine that provides sufficient space and—pause here for a grateful sigh—no restrictions on which films I should critique. It's the short deadlines that rankle, cutting down my time to see the film more than once and reflect on its merits or lack of same. Keeping up with film releases can also be a problem when screenings are clustered and you must choose one film over another. But the greatest obstacle I face is a more insidious one. Many film companies, believing— often wrongly—that the film they are distributing is a dog, refuse to screen the film for critics or provide screenings so late that a timely review cannot be completed on deadline. It's a knotty ethical problem since studios, claiming they have no obligation to screen films for critics, are manipulating the press by effectively delaying critiques they believe will hurt the film's opening weekend box office.

5. "Do you have any pet peeves or personal frustrations as a film critic that you'd like to address?" Yes, the notion of critical consensus. I am struck by the proliferation of charts, like those found in *Entertainment Weekly*, that use statistical averages to grind opinions into a middle-ground, middlebrow "critical mass." Nothing like consensus to kill passion and provocation. Where's the benefit or the art in celebrating only what goes down easy? Some of the best critiques I read challenge my own perceptions. For that reason I welcome some of the new critical voices on the Internet, the so-called geeks who spew out uncontrolled gut opinion. Whatever they lack in writing skill and scholarship, the geeks help audiences to bust out of the preconditioned response to film set by marketers and traditionalists who think films and critics of films need boundaries. At their best, these Web critics look at films to discover the same things we print critics do: signs of life.

Years ago, I asked the director Arthur Penn what benefits, if any, he derived from reading a critique of his own work. "I like it when a critic takes a movie seriously, even when it hurts," said Penn. "I like it when a critic brings the same care and attention to the job that I bring to mine. When that happens you might get roughed up but you don't feel cornered. What happens is something more rewarding—it's an even match."

Peter Travers has been film critic at *Rolling Stone* magazine since 1989 and served as film critic for *People* magazine from 1984 to 1988. He has appeared as a film commentator on CNN, has hosted an ABC interview show, and can be found online, streaming video each week at rollingstone.com. He is the editor of *The* Rolling Stone *Film Reader* (1996) and author of *1,000 Best Movies on DVD* (2005). A member of the National Society of Film Critics, Travers also hosts the New York Film Critics Series, presenting live national screenings and featuring on-screen interactive broadcasts with filmmakers and actors.

KENNETH TURAN, *LOS ANGELES TIMES*

1. Like most critics, and probably most writers, I write both for myself and for an audience. The joy of this job, when there is joy in it, is twofold. First, it's the challenge of coming to intellectual and emotional grips with a given film, of trying to figure out what it's trying to do and then deciding if it's meeting its own aims. Second, it's communicating my passion to an audience, trying to get them to see what I've seen, to care about what I care about.

2. Again, like any other kind of written work, it's the quality of the writing and the quality of the thought that makes a review memorable. You can have one without the other, but both together are, obviously, best. Readers tend to remember and, frankly, enjoy negative reviews more than positive ones, but to me nothing is more satisfying than convincing people to go to a film they might otherwise have missed. A film's social and political aspects are important to me when they're important to the filmmaker and apparent on the screen.

3. Someone I know once said the studios view critics as unruly adjuncts of the marketing department, and there's a certain amount of truth to that. We can be helpful with certain kinds of films, irrelevant to others, and

always useful to blame if something with good intentions but bad execution doesn't succeed. The relationship is by its nature wary and not too close, because while the industry wants every film to be a hit, the critic is not invariably plumping for that kind of universal success. The best way for critics to be influential, though it's as difficult as it sounds, is by educating audiences and convincing them to patronize quality films. The industry, though there are exceptions, by and large listens only to the cash register.

4. I'm very fortunate in that the *Los Angeles Times* doesn't arbitrarily limit my space or dictate what I need to do. Yes, I sometimes have to write on tight deadlines, but that is typical for the newspaper business and more a function of studio reluctance to show critics films in a timely manner than anything else. The greatest obstacle I face in writing the best reviews I can is the great number of reviews I have to write, week in and week out. There are more weeks than I want to remember where a dozen or more films are scheduled to open, and though I obviously am not expected to review or even see them all, the constant pressure to turn out copy sometimes makes it harder for me to be as thoughtful in my writing as I'd like to be. Lost in the general enthusiasm about how new technology has made it simpler for anyone with determination to make his or her own film is the plain fact that a great many of these new films are not very good, a situation that doesn't look to be changing anytime soon.

5. Minor frustrations aside, this is too good a job to complain about. Over the years, I've made a habit of collecting maxims about criticism, and here are a couple of my favorites. I believe the first is from George Bernard Shaw, and I'm unsure about the second.

"Criticism written without personal feeling is not worth reading. It is the capacity for making good or bad art a personal matter that makes a man a critic."

"The task of the critic is not mainly to point out the faults of works of art or to discriminate good from bad. . . . The task, I think, is to articulate our most intimate responses to the work that moves us. And it moves us partly for reasons that are in us and partly for reasons that are in it."

Kenneth Turan is film critic for the *Los Angeles Times*, a position he has held since 1991, and film reviewer for National Public Radio's *Morning Edition*. He is also director of the Los Angeles Times Book Prizes and has been a book-review editor for the *LA Times* and a staff writer for the *Washington Post*. Among his books are *Not to Be Missed: Fifty-Four Favorites from a*

Lifetime of Film (2014), *Free for All: Joe Papp, the Public, and the Greatest Theater Story Ever Told* (2009, with Joseph Papp), *Now in Theaters Everywhere* (2006), *Never Coming to a Theater Near You* (2004), and *Sinema: American Pornographic Films and the People Who Make Them* (1974). In addition to working as a film critic, Turan serves on the board of directors of the National Yiddish Book Center.

ARMOND WHITE, *NEW YORK PRESS*

As hits go by—on a weekly basis, without sticking to the ribs or memory—film critics have become virtually useless. They no longer retain the culture, providing historical or aesthetic contexts for new releases or, more importantly, for younger, uninformed audiences. To be a mainstream film critic with popular influence, one is required to cooperate with the industry's manipulation of ignorant, gullible viewers for whom every chase film, every film noir, every sex comedy, every blockbuster disaster flick is a "new," "astonishing" experience (*Titanic, Armageddon, Gladiator*). As a result, "hype" is now the definition of what "criticism" means to most people.

Perfect examples of the process behind that perversion can be seen in the different media response to Alan Rudolph's *Trixie* and Neil LaBute's *Nurse Betty*. Most critics accepted the failed aims of the latter rather than trying to figure out the themes of the former. In plain terms, critics no longer attend to art. Instead of figuring out Rudolph's eccentric use of language as a key to how contemporary media-bred fantasies isolate us socially and politically, critics celebrated LaBute's castigation and sentimental condescension toward those who are unsophisticated media junkies. Conventional cynical pathology was preferred to politicized humanism; LaBute's crude mise-en-scène was praised while Rudolph's subtle visual elegance was ignored. Guile appreciated over sincerity.

There used to be two cinemas: commercial Hollywood, which overwhelms us, and another competing cinema, the art cinema we had to purposely seek out. *Pulp Fiction* (1994) signified the merging of the two. Since that moment, the increased self-consciousness of American movies (which had been happening since Hollywood swallowed the French New Wave whole) has turned everyone—journalists, filmmakers, audiences— paradoxically skeptical of craft and style yet more than ever susceptible to formula and technique. Serious critical approaches such as Pauline Kael's and Andrew Sarris's became part of mainstream film lingo, yet their rigor has been diluted—thus Ebert and Siskel and the Internet kids promote a film culture of consumption rather than inquiry and sensitivity.

But all this is prelude to the abyss.

In the May 13–19, 1999, issue of *New Times Los Angeles*, a help wanted ad appeared that blew the profession into oblivion.

Its entirety:

FILM REVIEWER WANTED

Are you sick and tired of the movie reviews you read in the *LA Times* or even in these very pages? Are you annoyed by reviewers who believe that movies must aspire to high art to be valid, that the auteur theory still pertains? Are you more interested in *Go* and *Very Bad Things* than *Titanic* and *The Truman Show*?

New Times is looking for a new voice to join our weekly mix of critics. If you think movies are the greatest form of pop culture we have, and if you can write with energy and wit, you are a candidate to become our newest film critic.

Please send (no phone calls) cover letter, clips, and resume to *New Times Los Angeles*—FILM, Suzanne Mantell, Arts Editor. 1950 Sawtelle Blvd., Suite 200, Los Angeles, CA 90025.

It's difficult to know what Ms. Mantell wanted, given her inane requirements (anti-aspiration, pro-validation) and contradictory requests (the "greatest form of pop culture" yet antagonistic to "high art"). But her ad's attitude, plainly, stinks. Like most people in the contemporary film-going audience, she's looking for someone to give her and her readers permission to go to the movies and not think. That ad doesn't seek a reviewer but a huckster in the guise of a critic—the latest evolution of that 1960s–1970s movie love and pop savvy into idiocy. And the attitude is rampant. Once, criticism was a practice that denoted Agee-Kael-Sarris intellection and literacy, now it's all thumbs.

Foolishness (film savvy that anyone can claim) explains the confusion of that *New Times* ad as it pits the flip cynicism of *Very Bad Things* against the flip cynicism of *The Truman Show*; as it imagines *Titanic*'s sentimentality was somehow less popular than the (now proven unpopular) humanist comedy in Doug Liman's *Go*. But these are not the major upsets in our cultural climate. What makes moviegoing uninspiring, repellent these days is the nonsense in pictures like *Leaving Las Vegas, The Sweet Hereafter, In the Company of Men, Affliction,* or *Payback*—all critical hits that destroy one's artistic and social and humane hopes. Bad critics who praised those films and then hold no responsibility for the bilge that follows have set a tone of gaseous criticism and dishonesty.

And there are practical difficulties to being a critic in this insane era—the treadmill effect of tending to the market's new fast turnover makes it almost impossible to cultivate an appreciation of film. Reviewers have altogether given up probing movies, so that even a race-and-religion-based hit like *The Matrix* lingers vacantly—like a going-out-of-business sign—because critics can't see anything in it beyond visual noise; they've stopped thinking of movies as expressions of social fear or desire. They're content seeing movies as product—as in the delimited response to *The Phantom Menace.*

Sigourney Weaver's threat in *Alien*—"Blow it the fuck into outer space!"—is what most reviewers tried to do to George Lucas. Trashing *The Phantom Menace* became "smart" critics' inglorious, pathetic way of salvaging integrity. But it was too late; the profession had already sunk under the weight of its own corrupt collusion. You know: going along with a manufactured zeitgeist, giving print space and airtime to something that is, primarily, of commercial interest.

Taste (what's that?) wasn't offended by *The Phantom Menace.* In Y2K desperation, critics needed a way to convince themselves they have not been had. (So Jar Jar Binks became the new Milli Vannilli.) Breathlessly straining on the hype treadmill, there's no time to make cultural significance of most films. Critics are stuck following the industry's dictates rather than encouraging erudition, thought. This *Star Wars* mess is especially saddening, not because millionaire Lucas is stuck addressing a degraded pop audience when he really wants to do abstract metanarratives, but because out of our entire critical constabulary no one understood his frustration. Critics reacted like unenlightened children, complaining *Phantom Menace* isn't exactly like the *Star Wars* movies before it, that the thrill ride doesn't go fast enough.

These turnabout disses implied that previous coverage of *Star Wars* was something else—news. But this is typically disingenuous. The release of a multimillion-dollar Hollywood film is never news. Yet collusive media workers continuously promote a brother industry, and in that sense a review, negative or positive, is just more promotion. Criticism thus loses its significance; that's why it doesn't matter what critics say about *Phantom Menace* (it eventually grossed over $600 million); the profession has conspired in its own paralysis. Media exists only to sell product; that's what *New Times* knows.

In an imaginary world, far, far away, the amount of money spent making and promoting a movie would not correlate to the media attention a film received; *Star Wars* would be treated as indifferently and inconspicuously as a film by Ira Sachs, a book by Richard Dyer, a CD by The Wedding Present. In other words, reviewers would operate on individual taste, not marketing. Maybe then a film could be appreciated on its own merits, and we could stop this heedless consumption frenzy.

It's hard to explain these things to generations born into hype, who think it's a normal process and not a pernicious outgrowth of capitalist indoctrination. To be a mainstream journalist has come to mean one's complicity with this system rather than a detached view of it. Today's young moviegoers (courted by Hollywood and the media) don't realize that even in an artificial, commercial environment some things are, if not unnatural, then culturally untenable.

Pop permissiveness, the new form of anti-intellectuality, was first apparent in the herd response to *Pulp Fiction*; and it has infected much neocon critical writing as a rejection of liberal sanctimony. But it most nefariously expresses libertarian license given to the ever-mounting corporate domination and monopoly that melds filmmaking, journalism, and marketing. Hypercapitalism. Criticism's downfall proves our culture's submission to insensitivity, the media's abdication of intellectual life. Perhaps that's why *New Times* shamelessly advertised its complicity. Editors who control film journalism do so to promote the film industry.

A common question in this era—"Does it live up to the hype?"—is not even a rational thought. A film ought to present itself—ideas, images, sensibility. Naïve moviegoers thus reveal their inherent gullibility. You can't talk them against hype; because they believe the hype actually has something to do with the film that was made. Conformity has become the law of cinema-land; people would rather get tattooed than admit that *Beloved* was the best film of the past year or that *The Phantom Menace* isn't that bad.

You may have noticed that in many newspapers, the label "reviewer" or "critic" has been struck from many bylines. Under hypercapitalism criticizing a product simply isn't allowed. Forty-five years after James Agee's death the badge "critic" has been retired. We have movie writers, staff writers—anything that won't be misconstrued "naysayer" or "thinker." No matter the new vistas digital-era film can create, this isn't a democracy that turns everyone into a critic, it's a bazaar. Though we all may have Internet access to mass audiences, making moviegoers, more than ever, their own critical experts, the fact is, we are lost in space.

Armond White writes film criticism for the *National Review* and *Out*. He was lead film critic for the *New York Press* from 1997 to 2011 and editor of *CityArts* from 2011 to 2014. He has written for numerous publications, including the *New York Times*, *The Nation*, *Film Comment*, *Slate*, and the *Columbia Journalism Review*. A member of the National Society of Film Critics, he chaired the New York Film Critics Circle in 1994, 2009, and 2010. White has been a jury member at the Sundance Film Festival, the Tribeca Film Festival, and the Mill Valley Film Festival. He authored *The Resistance: Ten Years of Pop Culture That Shook the World* (1995) and *Rebel for the Hell of It: The Life of Tupac Shakur* (1997). Beyond his work as a film critic, White has taught classes at Columbia University and Long Island University, and he received the American Society of Composers, Authors, and Publishers Deems Taylor Award for music criticism in 1992.

CHAPTER 2

International Film Criticism Today
A CRITICAL SYMPOSIUM

In introducing its 2000 symposium on film criticism in America, *Cineaste* editors bemoaned the fact that in many cases, film critics, "especially those writing for mainstream newspapers and magazines, . . . feel increasingly embattled in their efforts to write serious film criticism because of commercial pressure from publishers, publicists, and film distributors, all of whom are principally interested in using critics as marketing aids." Interestingly enough, responses to the 2005 symposium "International Film Criticism Today" reflect similar anxieties among critics working in Europe, Asia, Latin America, Africa, and Australia. Although few of the participants report being blatantly pressured to tailor their reviews to suit the interests of advertisers or bosses, many of the critics working for daily newspapers report that a number of their colleagues have capitulated to the consumer-guide, "thumbs-up, thumbs-down" approach to criticism that has plagued this country for some years now. As is true in the United States, critics around the world at independent film magazines (and independent Internet sources, which have grown in number significantly since 2005) have virtually complete freedom and a generous amount of space with which to express their opinions if they are willing to endure the relative (or, in some cases, total) penury that results from being unaligned with the corporate media.

In selecting the contributors to this symposium, *Cineaste* was interested not merely in geographical diversity but also in a variety of critical

Originally published in *Cineaste* 31, no. 1 (Winter 2005); copyright © 2005 by Cineaste, Inc.

approaches. Some of the critics included hew to a breezy journalistic style, while the responses of others reflect the influence of scholarly critics such as André Bazin and Serge Daney—a tradition that has thrived much more abroad than in an American context, where there is still, for the most part, a strict dichotomy between journalistic and academic writing. A few of the critics participating are much more interested in the aesthetic components of film than in political preoccupations, while others believe that political and aesthetic criteria are virtually indivisible. There is, alas, one motif that is apparent in both the American critics symposium and its international sequel: a dearth of female critics—an ongoing condition, unfortunately, in the world of film criticism that has recently received renewed scrutiny in a variety of print and online publications. Despite *Cineaste*'s best efforts, only two pieces by women appear in this survey.

In an interview that *Cineaste* contributor Bill Krohn conducted with Serge Daney some years ago, the late French critic defines criticism as an "eternal return to a fundamental pleasure." Nearly all the critics in this symposium emphasize that their decision to write on film was primarily inspired by an irrepressible cinephilia—as well as by their determination to disseminate their love of movies to attentive readers. Driven by both a passion for cinema and a desire to combat the more parochial elements of American film criticism, *Cineaste* editors expressed in 2005 the hope that this special section would acquaint readers with a wealth of critical voices that rarely appear in stateside film magazines.

Some critics formatted their thoughts as essays and others as point-by-point responses to correspond with each of the following questions posed. Next to each critic's name is his or her professional affiliation in 2005, when this symposium was first published. Following each response is an expanded, updated biography of the contributor.

For assistance with this critical symposium, *Cineaste* expressed special gratitude to Charlotte Garson and her equally generous colleague, Elisabeth Lequeret, of *Cahiers du cinéma*, and to *Cineaste* associates Roy Grundmann, Adrian Martin, Louis Menashe, Dennis West, and Deborah Young—all of whom also provided invaluable suggestions and much-needed contacts, as did Parag Amladi, Shelly Kraicer, Marie Losier, Charisse Louw, Mark Peranson, and Chuck Stephens.

1. What does being a film critic mean to you? (More specifically, why do you write film criticism? Whom do you hope to reach, and what do you hope to communicate to them?)

2. What qualities make for a memorable film critique? (Do you think such critiques tend to be positive or negative in tone? Is discussing a film's social or political aspects as important to you as its cinematic qualities and value as art and entertainment?)

3. How do you assess (or combat) the perceived globalization of the film industry? How much space does your publication allow you to devote to films produced by your own national cinema?

4. Are there critics, whether still working or from a previous generation, whom you regard as models or mentors? How have they influenced your approach to film criticism?

5. What pressures do you encounter that either constrain or determine what you can say as a critic or how you can say it?

ARGENTINA: EDUARDO ANTIN (A.K.A. QUINTÍN), *EL AMANTE CINE*

1. In principle, I write for the sake of it, because of the desire of doing it. Like any kind of writing, criticism shouldn't try to reach anyone in particular (not even moviegoers!) or to "communicate." That doesn't mean that I don't want to be read, or that I don't want people to like my writing. Being more specific, (writing or reading) film criticism is one of the best ways to protect yourself from the irritation brought on by other responses to the cinema (the main sources of this irritation are populist sentimentalism and academic authoritarianism) through trying to connect to some of its mysterious pleasures.

2. Discovery, illumination, kindness, passion, freedom, elegance, humor, independence, knowledge, irreverence are qualities that make for memorable film reviews. Positive or negative, who cares? It's the singer, not the song. On the other hand, I don't think there is a good film piece that can separate politics and aesthetics: good cinema is liberating. And I hate the word "entertainment" even more than the phrase "value as entertainment." Which is not the same as thinking that cinema is Art with a capital *A*. It's something different, and we still don't know what that is precisely; that's the thrill of the job. But cinema is definitely not "visual" culture, nor audiovisual or televisual.

3. Cinema has been global since day one. And American studios have had distribution offices in every country since day two. Of course, blockbusters are bigger and bigger, but now there are DVDs and the Internet, blah, blah, et cetera. In my opinion, the real new thing, the truly global

threat, is the triumph of the script. These pieces of paper are the true commodities in the film industry, and filmmakers are forced more and more to write for committees, for "expert" readers, and everything depends on their word, which is always conservative and stupid. This is true for Canada, for Australia, for Germany, for Argentina. That's why films are more and more uniform, adapted to those silly formulas for scriptwriting. Since I don't write regularly for a publication anymore, I might be the right subject for this poll. Up until a year ago, I used to run a film magazine and did what I wanted. But let me tell you that the true victims of criticism these days are not (at least in Argentina, although I don't think it's an exception) national cinemas, which are in general protected by patriotism or chauvinism, but non-American foreign films, increasingly less distributed all over the world and frequently ignored by the major media.

4. Serge Daney was a major influence—not only in my writing (I usually find myself trying to imitate him unconsciously) but also in my decision to become a critic. For many years, and because of the reviews I used to read then in the newspapers, I thought that I had to love Bertrand Tavernier's films to be a true cinephile. Once I read Daney's piece on *Coup de torchon*, I discovered what the whole game is about: "cinéma de qualité or academic film equals an apology for death." Jonathan Rosenbaum is the other great critic I would like to mention. On the one hand, reading *Moving Places* was a major inspiration, a book that achieves the miracle of making film and life the same thing. I subsequently met the author and benefited since from his wisdom and generosity.

5. As I said, I always had the chance to write what I wanted. I remember one exception—an occasion when I tried to write for an American newspaper. I found the editing process really bothersome: I am not used to that kind of intervention, of "polishing," in Spanish. We never did it in our magazine, by the way. On the other hand, film critics in my country are under a lot of pressure when it comes to dealing with Argentinean films. They are supposed to be treated as masterpieces. There is a lot of hypocrisy going on in that department, especially these days.

Quintín (Eduardo Antin) is former editor of the monthly film journal *El amante cine*, which he cofounded and directed until 2004, and former director of the Buenos Aires International Film Festival. Before working as a film critic, Quintín (whose pseudonym originated during his college days as a math major) was a computer programmer, a graphic design entrepreneur, a football referee, and a student of philosophy. He writes a weekly newspaper column and contributes regularly to varied blogs and websites. In addition to his work as a film writer and critic, Quintín has written a book on wine, *Más allá del Malbec: Conversasiones sobre vino sin dogmas* (2013).

AUSTRALIA: ADRIAN MARTIN, *THE AGE*

1. The idealistic part of me believes that writing film criticism is all about: (a) encouraging people to see (or seek out) films they might not normally see, to help incite that desire; and (b) encouraging people to think a little differently about whatever films they see. Film criticism is all about "finding an angle," suggesting a context, and illuminating a film in a way that is not the most immediately apparent way.

2. For me, any film review (whether a short piece in a newspaper or a long essay for a journal) should be a kind of a story—a story fashioned from ideas, bits of description of the film at hand, indices of social and historical context, and whatever else can be jammed in there. I do not feel that either extremely positive or extremely negative criticism "brings out the best" in a critic. It all depends—sometimes strong passion for a film can bring lucidity, and sometimes just murky assertion; sometimes the "kick 'em till they bleed" mentality can offer a powerful polemic, and other times it merely demonstrates the critic's own narrow-mindedness. I do not ask for a spurious "balance" of positive and negative in a review or essay; but I do ask for logic, argumentation, and backup—not just "gut reaction."

3. I am lucky in the respect that Australia—like many a comparatively small nation in the shadow of the Hollywood monolith—still has a little cultural nationalism left, at least in the "quality" (i.e., middle-class) media. Therefore, in the newspaper for which I write, a good, interesting, or worthy Australian movie will always be accorded decent space for critical discussion (positive or negative). Where the American dominance over exhibition and distribution is most keenly felt, at the level of media coverage, is in the treatment of "special events," like small film festivals, one-off screenings, cinematheque retrospectives, art-and-film gallery exhibitions, et cetera. When push comes to shove, newspapers (quality or otherwise) will always bow to the pressure to highlight the latest Hollywood blockbuster over the small, marginal cultural event that really needs the

publicity much more (because its commercial life is so fragile). Many critics I know have to constantly fight this battle over the "prioritization of space" in their columns, airtime, et cetera.

4. I look to critics who have combined a rigorous analytical logic (no matter how economically expressed), and a love of intellectual ideas, with the ability to write well and entertainingly. The French critic Roger Tailleur (less well known or evoked in English-language circles than André Bazin or Serge Daney, because of his *Positif* rather than *Cahiers* association), whose work spans the early 1950s to the late 1960s, is an inspiration to me: his stuff jumps off the page. At different times, I have also learned a lot from the Australian Meaghan Morris, the Japanese Shigehiko Hasumi, the British Judith Williamson, the Cuban Guillermo Cabrera Infante, the French Nicole Brenez, the Spanish Carlos Losilla, and the Americans Jonathan Rosenbaum and Manny Farber. In the field of cultural criticism generally, my current hero is Vilém Flusser (born in Czechoslovakia, he worked mainly in Brazil)—most of his remarkable essays on a "philosophy of culture" were written as newspaper columns.

5. Recently in Australia, there have been some insidious moves by film distributors—in the art house as much as the commercial sector, and in fact even more in the art house—to try to "regulate" critics out of speaking their mind. An appalling "code of ethics for film reviewers" has been floated at movie industry conventions, suggesting things like "critics should only review the film in front of them" (there goes sociopolitical comment) and "a review should predominantly tell the prospective consumer what the film is about" (there goes criticism, period). When all else fails, these industrial agitators can always smear critics by claiming that the "bad vibes" they put out are no doubt due to mysterious personal "vendettas" and "agendas." Even if such regulation does not come into being (and it probably never will—once again, the quality media likes to brandish its free-speech and fair-comment principles), its function is to create a climate of fear and trepidation among critics. And if one cliché about this reviewing game is true, it is that critics need to be fearless, so as to stick to that contract of telling their readers/listeners/viewers exactly what it is they truly think, and why they think it.

Adrian Martin was film critic for the Australian newspaper *The Age* and coeditor of the online film journal *Rouge* from 2003 to 2009. He is currently coeditor of the online film journal *LOLA* and serves on the editorial staffs of *Cineaste* and *Screening the Past*. Among his books are *Mise en Scène and Film Style: From Classical Hollywood to New Media Art* (2014), *Last Day Every Day* (2015), *Phantasms* (1994), and *Once Upon a Time in America* (1998). He is coeditor, with Jonathan Rosenbaum, of *Movie Mutations: The Changing Face of World Cinema* (2003) and has provided audio commentary for dozens of films on DVD. Besides working as a film critic, Martin has taught film studies at Melbourne State College, Germany's Goethe University (as a distinguished visiting professor), and Spain's Monash University.

AUSTRIA: CHRISTOPH HUBER, *DIE PRESSE*

1. Probably all serious film critics started out of the overwhelming need to convey the passion and relevance of cinema and/or the cinematic experience (the last factor may be dwindling these days). And of course there's always the hope that you have something interesting and worthwhile to say, despite the occasional drawback that occurs when films come along that may leave you no choice but to state the obvious. (Then you should attempt to make it funny, at least.) There's no real answer possible to a "why" stated on such general terms—just as the comforting thought, no matter how endearing it seems, also is unsustainable: that in your privileged position you're now writing exactly what the young film enthusiast you once were voraciously wanted to glean from the newspapers and film magazines. People change, and so do situations (and film politics). The idea is to try to effect changes for the better, plant seeds of thought.

2. A film critique can be memorable for many different reasons (including even awe-inspiring wrongheadedness), but whether it's positive or negative has nothing to do with it. Thumbs-up, thumbs-down has just become a marker because it's so easy to illustrate, and marketing assures us that's what's so important these days, but have you ever encountered someone discussing just the evaluation without its arguments? Still, it bespeaks the necessity of labels, which usually just tend to help compartmentalize, like the dichotomies between art and entertainment or cinematic qualities and politics in your question, which can be more of a hindrance than a help. Ostensibly, a critique that successfully manages to fuse the most important factors in the specific case would be the ideal, but, as film criticism is a work of compression, not the least due to limits of space, some factors can

be treated as negligible. Also, sometimes it may just be one unexpected, staggering thought in an otherwise not too interesting piece that's more lasting and important.

3. In Austria, the handful of outlets with actual film criticism have been working on a (mostly unspoken) give-take basis: certain film "events" (e.g., *Downfall, The Phantom Menace, The Passion of the Harry Potter*) are invariably featured prominently, but as an exchange, being the editor of the film section, I get a considerable amount of freedom otherwise, deciding almost always independently on how (big) to cover what—retrospectives, new releases of any kind, trying to get film festival reports into the paper. (The hardest part, still: I usually have the gratifying power to let, say, Takeshi Kitano kick Nora Ephron's ass.) Also, the Hollywood globalization model may rule in dollars, but during the last decade a sort of art-house globalization, filtering out what's obviously deemed "too risky," has been much more noticeable here: the huge percentage of fluffy bullshit releases is getting alarming, and while at least you can still count on getting to see the new films by, say, Martin Scorsese, Michael Mann, Richard Linklater, and the Farrelly Brothers (and recently even George A. Romero again!), you probably won't even get Arnaud Desplechin, Hou Hsiao-hsien, or Claire Denis, not to mention Jeff Lau and Takashi Miike. Which incidentally is the segment where weighing in would actually have noticeable effect. That is, of course, even more the case with national cinema: I'm trying to cover almost all Austrian releases, because, for these films, critical debate at home is most important and probably also most influential. Space is allotted mostly according to estimated relevance, regardless of national status. And, for example, with Michael Haneke, Ulrich Seidl, Gustav Deutsch, or Michael Glawogger, it's usually possible to get the opening page headliner of the arts section.

4. Manny Farber's criticism, for instance, conveys, probably more powerfully than anybody else's, how film writing is a thought factory and a poetic act. Equally important is another lesson it conveys: do not try to imitate, find your own voice.

5. The biggest problem may be space: it is usually only a fraction of what is possible in serious papers in the United States (or even Germany), and the trend to further reduce that space in favor of graphic design decisions has been noticeable in most places. Also, outlets where you can use more experimental and essayistic forms of writing are rare.

Figure 2.1. Austrian critic Christoph Huber explains that films by Austrian filmmakers, including the late Michael Glawogger, have been given prominent coverage in *Die Presse*. From *Workingman's Death*, © Lotus Film, 2005.

Christoph Huber was the main film critic for the Vienna daily newspaper *Die Presse* at the time of this symposium, where he continues to write, as he does for *Cinema Scope* and *Senses of Cinema*, among other newspapers and publications. Huber has contributed to books on Peter Lorre, Robert Frank, and Georg Tressler, and is curator for the Austrian Film Museum, which also sponsors Huber's blog, *Following Film* (blog.filmmuseum.at), devoted to cinema's past, present, and future, and to the ever-changing landscape of film criticism.

BRAZIL: PEDRO BUTCHER, *FOLHA DE SÃO PAULO*

1. José Carlos Avellar, a good friend and one of the film critics I most admire, says that being a film critic is no kid's dream. Have you ever heard something like, "Dad, when I grow up I want to be a film critic!"? I bet not. And he's right. There's no glamour, no "mystique" about the profession, and people tend to assume that every film critic is a frustrated filmmaker or a lazy journalist. However, even though I felt the need to write down something about the films that were transforming my world at an early

age, I never felt the same urge to grab a camera and make films of my own. All I wanted, from the beginning, was to share a passion, and that's what I try to keep in mind as a basic principle of my activity. Each movie experience gives birth to new feelings (more or less intense) that you want to share with other people. And that's what I try to do.

2. All memorable film critiques I can remember are passionate—therefore, they tend to be positive, even if the film is not a masterpiece. For example, I remember very clearly a text by Avellar about Jaime Hermosillo's *La tarea* (1991), one of the first films made with a video camera and in a single shot. Avellar's text is a masterpiece of observation, capable of extending the pleasure of the screening time. I can also remember that it was a very good text about *Andrei Rublev* (I don't remember the author) that made me leave home on a rainy day, despite a bad case of the flu, to see the film on a big screen. Since this forced me to reassess all of Tarkovsky's work, it was a decision I never regretted. I believe all good critiques tend to take social and political issues into consideration, but not necessarily in a traditional way, since the definition of "political cinema" keeps changing. A film like Karim Aïnouz's *Madame Satã*, for example, has no obvious political reference points but is extremely political in the way it deals with racial and sexual issues that are rarely discussed in Brazilian cinema.

3. After years of being treated with contempt by the media, Brazilian cinema started to regain its respect in the last few years. But, ironically, it was only after the international acclaim accorded to Walter Salles's *Central Station* that this cynical approach started to change. Now, the space devoted to national films is much better—if not in quality, certainly in quantity. It tends, even, to be bigger than the space dedicated to Hollywood movies, since TV Globo, the main open channel in Brazil (part of a giant national media corporation) started to coproduce movies. So, it's funny to talk about the "globalization" of films in a country where the most powerful television network is called "Globo." What we saw recently in Brazil was a "globalization" of the movies, each time more and more influenced by TV aesthetics.

So, I like to be cautious when evaluating the polarization between Hollywood movies and national cinemas because this point of view is usually banal and reductive. Is Sergio Leone, for example, a "colonized" filmmaker? However, there's no doubt that each country must find its own way of protecting its production against unfair commercial practices since we know that Hollywood is not kidding in the business of conquering the foreign markets, and its massive presence means a "monoculture of images"

Figure 2.2. The international critical acclaim accorded Walter Salles's *Central Station* brought renewed attention to Brazilian cinema both in Brazil and around the world, according to Brazilian critic Pedro Butcher. © Ministère des Affaires Étrangères, 1998.

that compromises the cultural diversity of the world.

4. In Brazil the critics I consider models or mentors: Paulo Emílio Salles Gomes and José Carlos Avellar. Foreigners: Serge Daney, François Truffaut, André Bazin, Bill Krohn, Peter Bogdanovich, Martin Scorsese. These are some that come to mind—and some of them, as you can see, are also filmmakers. I must say that Bogdanovich's book of interviews, *Who the Devil Made It*, and Scorsese's documentaries on American and Italian cinema constitute some of the best film criticism I'm aware of.

5. The practice of using "stars" to evaluate films is the worst plague to hit the media in recent years. In addition, during the last twenty years, all of the big newspapers in Brazil drastically reduced the space allotted to film criticism. A critic is usually forced to express his or her point of view in two or three paragraphs. I can see, however, that the Internet is emerging as a true space for film debate and criticism—be it through film lists or websites, most of them created by a new generation. I can recommend at least one excellent Brazilian website, www.contracampo.com.br, which features extremely thorough analyses of current and classical films.

Pedro Butcher is film critic for the São Paulo newspaper *Folha de São Paulo* and editor of *Filme B* (www.filmeb.com.br). Butcher has written for other Brazilian newspapers, including *Jornal do Brasil* and *O globo*, as well as the magazine *Bravo*. His books include *Rio, eu te amo: 11 diretores em ação* (2015), *Cinema brasileiro hoje* (2005), and *Abril despedaçado: História de um filme e roteiro* (2002). Butcher has served on the juries at several international film festivals, including those in Rio de Janeiro, Venice, Cannes, and Mar del Plata.

CHINA: LI HONGYU, *SOUTHERN WEEKEND*

1. My writing is, first of all, driven by my desire to evaluate; I cannot help but admire great films and criticize bad ones. I hope film critics have the power to pressure filmmakers to produce more high-quality works—films that are successful, whether commercially or artistically.

I want to make readers more interested in and passionate about cinema, so they can enjoy films as more than mere entertainment and develop their own critical standards. At the very least, I hope my writing will expand the reader's horizons beyond the regime of commercial movies, where many filmmakers are struggling to be heard. Art-house theaters have little chance of survival in China. Many films, although artistically worthy, can't be enjoyed by a mass audience since commercial movie theaters question their profitability and refuse to screen them.

2. A memorable critique must first have a sharp point of view. You have to uncover those subtle qualities that viewers aren't aware of—but will be when you spell them out. A critique can also be memorable if it provides some unknown but important information about a film.

Whether a review is positive or negative doesn't matter. People are fond of reading negative criticism, because it makes them feel smarter. However, if someone really loves a film, a positive critique can leave an even stronger impression, because it speaks directly to the reader's feelings.

In China, discussing a film based on its social/political aspects is equally, or maybe more, important than evaluating its artistic and entertainment values. I reviewed *House of Flying Daggers* for an art magazine and focused solely on the film's political background. My opinion was that Chinese officials want to see the commercial success of the film industry on one hand, but on the other will never allow filmmakers to challenge their censorship. Zhang Yimou's film was formulated as a model for this political system. For those struggling for creative freedom, however, Zhang's film is a bad model—the more successful it is, the worse the influence it has.

3. Globalization is actually not a bad thing for the Chinese film industry. Warner Bros. has built many cineplex theaters in major cities. Showbox, a Korean entertainment company, has entered the exhibition business as well. Capital from the United States (from Columbia Pictures) and Korea

(CJ Entertainment) has already been invested in the Chinese film industry. Not only does this help Chinese film productions financially, it also brings in advanced technologies and professional administration.

The biggest problem is still with China itself. Film import restrictions that are supposed to protect the domestic industry are still in place, so it hasn't yet been completely opened to the free market, while the lack of freedom in productions results in few films and a certain dullness. It almost sounds ridiculous that more than three thousand theaters all over the country are screening the same small group of films every year.

Unlike others, I'm not particularly worried about the Westernization that may accompany Western capital. Whenever international companies enter the business, they have to satisfy the specific tastes of the Chinese audience to make a profit. Simply importing Hollywood formulas doesn't always work.

"Globalization" in the cultural sense is a different matter. I used to joke that the MPAA shouldn't have problems with Chinese piracy; instead, the American government should subsidize companies whose profits suffer. It's through piracy that a great number of Chinese young people get access to the latest Hollywood movies, as well as popular TV series like *Friends* and *Sex and the City* (of course there's also cultural influence from Europe, Japan, and Korea, but primarily from America). From movies and TV shows, they learn more about American than Chinese society, as the representation of social reality is still a restricted subject in Chinese media. As Chinese youngsters get more familiar with, and accepting of, the lifestyle, consumer fashions, and even ideologies of America, traditional Chinese culture becomes less and less influential in the mass media. In China, as in many other countries, American culture is often considered the dominant one, in which cinema plays a very important part. The medium I'm working within provides me enough space to care about Chinese. After all, it is our own cinema, standing right beside us.

4. Film critics who began writing in the 1980s and early 1990s are not particularly influential anymore. Restricted by their historical background, their criticism focused on formal analysis and provided little reading pleasure. But today's films are dramatically different, making it difficult to find mentors from the previous generation.

Film critics who started to write in the late 1990s rely more on the Internet. Though passionate and fearless, they have their own problems—they lack systematic training and are often unfamiliar with some basic conventions (for instance, some of them describe the complete narrative story line in their reviews). Some may also lose their objectivity given commercial influence.

My favorite film critics are Sato Tadao in Japan and David Bordwell in the United States. I also like the work of Jacob Wong, the director of the Hong Kong Film Festival, who is my friend and also a mentor. I wish my writing could have Sato's honesty and generosity, and I admire Bordwell's intelligent formal analysis of genre films. Jacob doesn't write much, but his humor, wit, and sensitivity in his work are worth emulating. One magazine I often read is *Sight & Sound,* which I regard as a model for film criticism.

5. I'm a professional journalist, with frequent contact with filmmakers. It's not hard to imagine the pressures I encounter.

We recently did a series on Chinese cinema's one hundredth anniversary. A colleague tried to interview Xie Jin, a very famous old director, but was refused. According to my colleague, Xie said, "Zhang Yimou told me that I should never accept interviews with this newspaper—*Southern Weekend*—because they are too mean." In fact, I did an interview with Zhang when *Hero* was released, and published a long article. Zhang had no problem with my interview. But later, we published a full-page review harshly criticizing *Hero* (I wasn't the writer), which I guess is the reason why Zhang warned Xie to keep his distance.

I know most contemporary filmmakers in China. There are some whose films I don't think I could openly criticize in print. If I want to, I can use a pseudonym.

Li Hongyu is journalist and film critic for *Southern Weekend,* a weekly mainland Chinese newspaper. He also writes film criticism for Chinese journals, including *Life Weekly, Art World, Time Out Beijing,* and *Magazine.* Li has been widely quoted in a variety of English-language articles concerning censorship and Chinese film criticism.

FRANCE: MICHEL CIMENT, *POSITIF*

1. I have had a parallel professional life in teaching and writing film criticism and film history. For me, these two activities have the same functions: to communicate, or as Lindsay Anderson titled his essay on Humphrey Jennings (invoking E. M. Forster): "only connect." Since a humanist perspective is often missing in our modern approach to culture, I hope to reach a variety of readers, not just students and teachers. We have too many

specialists, who ignore the worlds of knowledge around them, including politics, the other arts, history, et cetera.

2. The qualities of a critic or a critique should be, in no order of preference or importance: (a) factual information (the context of the production, the background of the director, the economics, the history of the making of the film, some elements about the actors, and the creative contributors); (b) a sense of analysis borrowed from various disciplines (aesthetics, history, psychoanalysis, structuralism, etc.); (c) an evaluation of the quality of the film; I believe in a personal hierarchy which should force you to establish your criteria of appreciation; (d) a passion for your craft and for cinema; (e) a gift for elegant writing; (f) a curiosity and a will to discover new directors and national cinemas. Political and social aspects and considerations are important, but artistic considerations ultimately count the most. Otherwise, a film might as well take the form of a newspaper article or TV documentary.

I'd argue, however, that most of the great directors establish a connection between the individual and the society that surrounds them. The filmmakers to whom I have devoted books—Kubrick, Losey, Kazan, Rosi, Boorman, Angelopoulos, Lang, Schatzberg—exemplify this preoccupation in their work. And I would say the same about artists I would like to write about—Mizoguchi, Renoir, Bergman, Buñuel, Fellini, Ford, Altman, Hou Hsiao-hsien.

3. I think that the dominant position of Hollywood in the world market is a threat to national cinemas and tends to make international audiences aware of only one kind of storytelling. *Positif* devotes quite a lot of space to French cinema, but, of course, France is probably (besides India) the country where the local production has managed to create its own space in relation to Hollywood (from thirty percent to forty percent of the moviegoing public).

4. I have been nourished both by some writers of the *Cahiers du cinéma* school (mainly André Bazin, François Truffaut, Eric Rohmer, and Jacques Rivette) and from *Positif* (Bernard Chardère, Robert Benayoun, Louis Seguin, and Roger Tailleur), who tended to be more politically oriented (left) and keenly aware of the other arts and sensitive to the surrealistic influence with a taste for humor, eroticism, and fantasy.

5. Not being paid and belonging to a publication owned by its contributors, I never felt any particular pressures in my forty years of film criticism. But unconscious pressures I cannot determine!

Michel Ciment has been on the *Positif* editorial board since 1966. He has written books on Stanley Kubrick, John Boorman, Elia Kazan, Joseph Losey, Francesco Rosi, Theo Angelopoulos, Fritz Lang, and Jerry Schatzberg. Among his most recent books are *Éric Rohmer: A Biography* (2016), *The Berlinale: The Festival* (coathored with Peter Cowie, 2010), *Film World: The Director's Interviews* (2009), and *Kubrick's Cinema Odyssey* (2008). He participates as a film critic in two radio programs in Paris, has served as the president of the International Federation of Film Critics, and is an officer in the Order of Arts and Letters.

FRANCE: JEAN-MICHEL FRODON, *CAHIERS DU CINÉMA*

1. I write film criticism because I believe films offer both pleasure and an opportunity to better understand the world we live in. I think that film criticism is a way to combine these seemingly contradictory motives. I hope to reach anyone who is ready to use his or her own freedom of judgement to derive from cinema whatever he or she wishes: aesthetic as well as sociopolitical conclusions. And also, on a more private level, I write about films because I get paid to do two of the things I most enjoy in life: see films and write. I believe I am a very lucky person.

2. A good critique is one that opens up the reader's mind to a new relationship with a film. This can be done (and should be done) in many ways through many approaches that enable the critic to develop the most complex rapport between himself and a particular film. The departure point could be the story, the style (details that resemble inscriptions within larger ensembles as are often found in works of art), a specific scene, a political issue, the use of a color, the rhythm, one actor's performance, the relation between sound and image, et cetera. In any case, it largely relies on the quality and the imaginative richness of the writing itself. And, obviously, it has nothing to do with merely defending or attacking the film in question.

3. I can see two opposite and complementary movements. One is the salutary expansion of the cinematic planet, allowing us access to more styles, cultures, stories (and nonstories) than was ever possible in the history of cinema. At the same time, I see the globalization of mass entertainment reaching a level unparalleled in any previous era. In truth, what should now be called Hollywood is no longer the North American film

industry, but a globalized, and hegemonic, form of storytelling and representation. This sort of cinema will increasingly be made in various parts of the world, financed by money from many countries, and will feature actors and directors from various parts of the globe. This is a major threat—if not the worst ever—to our freedom of thinking and acting. Naturally (I guess), I'd do my best to accompany, support, and help to discover and understand the first movement, and fight the second.

At this time, the second part of your question does not make much sense for me, since being the director of *Cahiers du cinéma* allows me to dedicate as much space as I wish to topics I consider important. But I have been in this position only for a few years, after working twenty years in general interest publications (seven years at weekly *Le point* and thirteen years at daily *Le monde*), where I was not the boss—far from it. I must say that I am quite proud I was able, in both cases, to make way for criticism that was not mainly driven by the promotion of blockbusters and the star system. It was tough sometimes, though. Film critics also have to fight the tendency to use films as pretexts to write about something else—as opportunities to merely amplify social or historical debates while disdaining cinematic specificity—which should be the starting point of any approach to a film—even if it has, naturally and hopefully, social, political, psychological elements. Within the film pages of a newspaper, these issues, however, should only be addressed from a cinematic vantage point.

4. There are many critics that have made an impact on me. André Bazin, François Truffaut, Jacques Rivette, Eric Rohmer, Jean Douchet, André S. Labarthe, Jean Narboni, Jean-Louis Comolli, Jean-Claude Biette, Bernard Eisenschitz, Serge Daney, Alain Bergala, Pascal Bonitzer are among the critics who helped me ponder my relationship with the cinema. Pierre Billard, Jean-Louis Bory, Michel Cournot carried a more affective but very intense and generous relation with films and writing about them. Among the younger critics (younger than me), I have a great deal of respect for Jacques Mandelbaum's and Emmanuel Burdeau's work, and I often learn from them. Among foreign critics, I have an enormous admiration for Shigehiko Hasumi, Naum Kleiman, Adriano Apra, Jonathan Rosenbaum, Manny Farber, Víctor Erice (he is an excellent critic as well as a filmmaker). This answer addresses critics, not philosophers, scholars, or theoreticians. There are also a few directors whose written works have often been even more influential than their films.

5. My own weaknesses are the worst pressures. At *Cahiers*, the worst you

have to endure occasionally entails waiting to assess a film until the film is commercially released—if somebody in a position of power does not want you to see it beforehand. No big deal. In general interest newspapers, there are pressures of all kinds, from the boss who loved a film that you hated, to the advertising department, to your colleagues, friends, family who give you a hard time for defending films they don't like (discuss with them) or don't understand your attachment to the cinema (stop talking to colleagues, change friends, get a divorce). According to my own experience, all these pressures can be overcome if you take a firm enough stand. As far as friction with people in the industry goes, you're only endangered if you're an entertainment journalist, not a critic. As a journalist, you can be barred from access to information, but as a critic, as long as you can see the film, at least in a regular theater, you are usually shielded from the pressures of the industry. So the main task should be: convince your editor-in-chief (and reconvince him/her every morning) that film criticism is a singular kind of writing, different from regular journalism, different from advertising, different from gossip, and different from mass sociology. If you can achieve that, which is difficult, you can do your job.

Jean-Michel Frodon was film critic at *Le point* from 1983 to 1990 and at *Le monde* from 1990 to 2003. At the time of this symposium, he was editorial director at *Cahiers du cinéma*, a position he held through 2009. He writes regularly for the *Slate* blog *Projection publique* (blog.slate.fr/projection-pub lique). His many books include *L'âge moderne du cinema français* (1995), *Hou Hsiao-hsien* (2005), *Print the Legend: Cinema et journalism* (2004), *Conversations with Woody Allen* (2000), and *Cinema and the Shoah: An Art Confronts the Tragedy of the Twentieth Century* (2010). Frodon has taught film criticism at the Université Paris 1 Panthéon-Sorbonne, the École Normale Supérieure, and Sciences Po Paris.

GERMANY: OLAF MÖLLER, INDEPENDENT FILM CRITIC

1. I write film criticism because my German teacher in high school, a guy called Jochen Hufschmidt, told me to. He said that since I spent so much time with films—watching, thinking, and formulating opinions about them—and since I had a knack for writing, plus certain character traits that would probably make me a good journalist, I should become a film critic. Which is what, because I had his genuine support, I did.

He got me my first paid writing stints at an age when most people don't even think about life beyond school; he also arranged for my first trip to the Berlinale—during final exams! (If anybody wants to learn about this amazing teacher who has been a major influence on a lot of people from my high school, check out Sebastian Winkels's 2003 documentary *Sieben Brüder* [*Seven Brothers*]: half a century of German history as told by the seven brothers Hufschmidt, the youngest of whom is Jochen—an ode to Lutheran oral culture, as austere as it is fascinating.) My parents, with whom I lived till the age of twenty-five, were actually another major factor in my making. Their support enabled me to write without ever having to think about making money: I had time to forge my style, make my pres-ence felt, my attitudes/principles known—s/he who deals with me knows what s/he's in for. In essence, I write film criticism because I was very lucky and a lot of people were unconditionally supportive and kind to me.

But there's another way of looking at this: Why do I *write* about *cinema?* The answer to part one would be: every other way of living with cinema is, quite simple, not my way—making films is too masochistic an endeavor (at least in Germany) and distributing too mercantile, as would be running a cinema; on the other hand, I love putting together film programs, which, for me, feels like a sensible extension of my writing. Writing, again, on the other hand, is something I thoroughly love to do: writing about cinema is, for me, as much about the act of writing itself as it is about the thoughts and consideration that get out that way into wherever.

And part two: because cinema seems to be the only art worth writing about; it's the only art left that is—or at least still has the very real potential for being—truly popular culture in the best sense. I could also write about literature or fine arts but . . . what good would that do? And to stay with writing in general: I don't have the kind of mind you need to be a good storyteller—the only thing I could sensibly write fiction about would be sex. Who knows? Maybe there's a future for me as a pornographer, which would be interesting.

Finally, the reader-question: I write for whosoever wants to read it and might find something in it. I write to make my point (whatever it is) in the manner I consider adequate and just—some can relate to it, others can't, and for some it might take some time; and so be it.

2. I often have the impression that a negative review/critique/piece of writing is considered to be more memorable than something positive in tone, which is an attitude I don't necessarily share, for I prefer to love, praise, and illuminate. That said, this doesn't mean that I'm not also quite

willing to—as well as adept at—tearing into major offenders. If thrashing frauds/demagogues/demiurges like Moore, Kusturica, Park (Chan-wook), Meirelles, Altman, and who have you is what it takes, then I'll do just that, for "es hilft nur Gewalt wo Gewalt herrscht." Which probably means that the social/political aspects are as important as all that other stuff—fuck! Can, should, there be an art that's not in its essence political, and an entertainment that's not social? And why should there be something like an art that has nothing to do with our lives?

3. Let me answer part one with a set of questions: Which kind of globalization: the neoliberal-industrial kind or the conservative modernist-intellectual (i.e., the liberal consensus) kind? And what's more of a problem, the quasi crypto-fascist ways in which capital tries to protect its investment, make it work big time, or the universalism of the dominant discourse of contemporary film criticism? And aren't they but two sides of the same coin; don't they, in a certain manner, even depend upon each other?

Regarding part two: depends on which publication you mean, and what kind of national cinema. Let's say, there's a certain kind of German cinema I love to write about but which doesn't necessarily surface in the theaters that easily and often: our tradition of essayistic filmmaking—a cinema in-between of a rather austere sensuousness, defiant and positively progressive, devoted to questioning history and considering reality. It's sometimes difficult to persuade editors to publish something on a film that's maybe only shown once some place or other (including TV, for which a lot of this stuff is officially produced), or isn't shown at all (and is, one would think, therefore in dire need of having something written about it). But that, in essence, is not a problem of nationality but of availability/market presence: *Lai* by Nuria Aidelman and Gonzalo de Lucas is as "off" as *Malerei heute* by Anja-Christin Remmert and Stefan Hayn, two of the most beautiful films of 2005. Therefore, the real question is, do my editors break my balls whenever I want to write about something that's just not simply "there"?

4. Certainly there are critics I consider mentors or models: The *Filmkritik*-auteurs of the 1970s and 1980s, in particular Hartmut Bitomsky, Peter Nau, Helmut Färber, Harun Farocki, Wolf-Eckart Bühler, and Gerhard Theuring, most of whom are also filmmakers. The fact that those of this group that I got to know personally are quite taken with my work is . . . well, something that really matters to me: if they like it, I must be right about a few things. Something of an extension of this was the programming/commissioning of Werner Dütsch and the other people of the WDR

Filmredaktion: I learned a lot from them, the films they aired, and what they had to say about them (they often produced wonderful short documentaries to accompany their seasons).

Let me mention a few more names, even if none of them can be considered a model or mentor, for different reasons: there's Raymond Durgnat, who always felt like a kindred spirit to me (one of my first film books was actually his study of Franju); recently, I've started to feel the same way about Francis Lacassin, whom I would love to meet and whose films I'd love to see; Manny Farber is . . . let's say, out there, somebody to connect with; and finally, there are Hans Schifferle and Ulrich von Berg—when I started writing somewhere in the mid-1980s, I didn't feel completely alone and out of whack, because of them, what they wrote about, and how.

Regarding part two of the question, just let me quote from memory something Peter Nau once wrote me: that I am among the few who understand that writing film criticism has something to do with writing . . . (cf. question number one). There's much more, but that would take up quite a lot of space to describe—let's just say that they defined the intellectual essence of my notion about what's sensible about cinema and life, and what's not—the emotional essence came courtesy of Kurosawa Akira.

5. Well, one thing is that editors are rarely capable and willing to just leave my stuff alone—my pieces are always too long, my writing is too . . . different: guilty as charged, give me the noose and let's get done with it. Another thing is that I can't necessarily write about whatever I want, for two reasons: one, it happens that I occasionally hold a "different" opinion on things, and certain editors, well, don't want to confuse things. And two, I can rarely write about recent films considered to be "important," not only because I might have certain "antagonistic" notions about them, but also because there's always somebody who has seen this film but not something "smaller" and "obscurer" which I (Captain Maverick, champion of the ignored and dispossessed—ha ha) will probably have seen, so, I end up writing about the off stuff and somebody else about the on stuff, which effectively prevents me from engaging directly with our day's discussions. But what the hell!

Olaf Möller is a Cologne-born and based film critic and programmer. He writes regularly for international film festival catalogues and prepares annual reports for the film festivals of Berlin, Venice, Rotterdam, and Udine. He regularly contributes columns to *Cinema Scope* and *Film*

Comment, where he serves as European editor. Möller is on the selection committee for the International Short Film Festival Oberhausen, is curator for numerous film programs at the Austrian Film Museum, and is instrumentally involved with the Midnight Sun Film Festival. His books include volumes on filmmakers Thomas Heise, Dominik Graf, Michael Pilz, and Ulrich Seidl. He is also coauthor of *Gustav Deutsch and Hanna Schimek: Shirley, Visions of Reality: The Film/The Exhibition* (2014).

GREECE: ANGELIKE CONTIS, *ATHENS NEWS*

My eyes and brain are taking a rest. After five years of having to see anything and everything that came out in Greek cinemas as the film critic for the English-language *Athens News* paper, I stopped two years ago to finish my own documentaries and—quite honestly—take a break from the two-films-a-day overload. I now write about the most interesting new Greek films, thankful for being able to choose what I critique.

During my intense watching spree, the number of films released each week increased—making it harder to see everything that came out. Multiplexes spread and the summer increasingly welcomed new releases. (In the past, only films released earlier in the year and classics were screened in Greece's outdoor summer cinemas.) I also observed a shrinking in the time it took for blockbusters to arrive in Greece; today, huge Hollywood hits often make it to Athens around the same time they open worldwide, while some European films arrive in Greece before hitting New York. As for Greek film, a handful of state-funded movies struggled to be released each year—and were usually whisked out of theaters faster than you can say "Angelopoulos."

Being both a critic and a filmmaker, American and Greek, I felt very much an intermediary. My duty to my English-speaking public was to give them the best possible sense of what to expect when they walked into each film (the bulk of which were American). I also offered a user's guide to the Greek films. I aimed for objectivity—to try to see each film in the way it was intended to be seen. If it was an action film, I'd try to put myself in the shoes of a fourteen-year-old adolescent boy. If it was a hot new romantic comedy, I'd pretend I was on a date—instead of in a smoke-filled room with largely cynical critics. If it was a slow-paced Chinese film, I'd try to escape my conceptions of time. Later, in front of the computer, I'd try to transmit to the viewers my impressions of the language, atmosphere, and structure of each film.

My efforts at objectivity frequently broke down with the Greek films. When the film was good, I'd be extra elated—and eager to talk with the director. When the film was bad, I'd grasp harder than usual for its positive points—or at least its significance to Greek reality. This was usually not because I felt pressure to be kind to the directors (and never due to advertising or editorial pressure), but because I was conscious of being one of the few voices that spoke of these films in English. Along the way, I realized that Greek films don't always reflect Greek life, any more than every Hollywood film captures real American experiences. (I was disappointed that not a single Greek critic ever asked me—as someone who grew up in the United States—if the things we saw on celluloid were accurate reflections of American reality. Hollywood gives Greeks, like, I assume, most of the world, the misguided impression that they really know US life.)

While being in the odd position of writing about primarily Hollywood films in Greece, I felt "in the loop" of international dialogue surrounding films, thanks to the Internet. While researching films, I'd often visit the Movie Review Query Engine site (www.mrqe.com) and find like-minded or dissenting opinions on what I'd just seen. I often checked in with the sounding boards of the *Hollywood Reporter, Variety,* or Roger Ebert, while consulting with the *New York Post* or *London Evening Standard* for reliably funny "trashing" of bad films. With regard to the Greek films, I was on my own—except for the Athens critics, whose sun-deprived faces I saw more often than my closest friends.

The critiques I wrote that I'm proudest of are anything but a casual assigning of star ratings and fair descriptions. They are passionate and unmeasured—a result of entering the world of the film so completely that I'd forget it was my job, or of being completely barred from entering the film's universe by its clumsiness, hateful spirit, and/or dumbness. I got this excited about a film about once a month, if I was lucky. Along the way, it became apparent to me that film critics can't help but crave extremes—something new, different, innovative, and stunningly well crafted. If they aren't numbed by the sheer bulk of what they have to see, as a group, they can best flag new talent.

Meanwhile, no longer compelled to see *Pokémon 306,* I'm convinced my subconscious is still clearing out the junk land of movie images crammed into it.

Angelike Contis is a journalist and documentary filmmaker who, from 1997 to 2008, was based in Athens, where she wrote on film and other topics for the *Athens News* and *Odyssey* magazine, to which she continues to contribute. She had previously been on the staff of the *National Herald*, the leading Greek American newspaper in the United States, where she produced videos for the paper's website and also worked as a journalist. Contis is executive director of Mt. Mansfield Community Television in Richmond, Vermont. Among the documentaries Contis has shot, directed, and edited are *Lost and Found in the Flood: Richmond, a Year after Irene*, chronicling the effects of Hurricane Irene in Vermont; *Lights, Camera . . . Skype!*, a collection of interviews with filmmakers and cast members of films screened at the New York Greek Film Festival; and *Muttumentary*, the story of eight adopted stray dogs in Athens.

HONG KONG: LI CHEUK-TO, *HONG KONG ECONOMIC JOURNAL*

1. I started writing film criticism in order to communicate my passion about cinema and to express my views on those films I loved or felt strongly about. One is forced to rethink films and to make sense of one's gut reactions and feelings about them in the writing process, which is incidentally not a bad way to understand more about oneself. Other than this self-serving aspect, I also wrote for a while in the hope that some of my readers could be persuaded to become more adventurous in their moviegoing habits and, consequently, help some smaller films to obtain the appreciation from audiences that they deserve. With the passage of time, I am more and more aware that it is probably nothing more than wishful thinking. Nevertheless, I still believe that film criticism is a worthy endeavor as well as an integral part of film culture. As a programmer doing his research on a certain topic, I always feel grateful whenever I come across writings—often written decades ago—that shed light on films that may or may not survive to this day. I trust future researchers will feel the same and all is not in vain.

2. A film critique can be memorable for its insight, provocation, intellectual rigor, or wit and humor. I'm always drawn to reviews that are both sensitive to the specific properties of film as a medium and are attuned to what theorists term the "reception process." But, for me, the most memorable film reviews are usually written during eras when their subjects were making history. As a critic, I have witnessed the rise of the Hong

Kong New Wave (1979), the Taiwan New Cinema (1982), and the New Chinese Cinema (1985), as well as the rediscovery and reevaluation of old Chinese classics like *Springtime in a Small Town* (1948) in the early 1980s. The reviews of the major works of these film movements are vibrant with the thrill of discovery and the excitement in witnessing history in the making. They all bear the imprint of a bygone era.

3. Now the golden era of Hong Kong cinema and film criticism is over. But it was not too long ago that the local cinema occupied a larger market share in Hong Kong than Hollywood product. In fact, this was true for more than two decades: from the early 1970s to the early 1990s. This current reversal of fortune has a lot to do with the decline in creativity—as well as less lavish production budgets as a result of dwindling overseas markets, which have always been indispensable for the survival of the local film industry. Meanwhile, during the past five or six years we, in Asia, have witnessed the rise of South Korean cinema, which has not only successfully fended off the Hollywood invasion in its home market but has proved increasingly adept in carving out a potential niche in the overseas market. The lessons we can learn are:

a. Globalization of the film industry worldwide is neither inevitable nor desirable for a diversified world film culture.
b. Market factors play a crucial role in the thriving or not of a national/regional cinema.
c. As long as a national/regional cinema is popular with its audiences, the critics will not be pressured to devote more space to Hollywood films.

In general, the space for serious film criticism devoted to one's national/regional cinema is getting smaller and smaller. But it has less to do with globalization or Hollywood dominance than with the general vulgarization of the press and media in search of maximal profit by catering to the lowest common denominator. The drop in readership and diminishing levels of literacy are other global problems common to us all.

4. Since 1971—thirty-four years ago—the veteran critic Sek Kei has been writing a daily film column. He is a rare case in Hong Kong—a critic who has managed to gain respect and recognition from both readers and people in the film industry. He has an excellent grasp of the film review format, speaks to laymen in their own language—but from a critic's

perspective—and writes intelligently without being excessively intellectual. I've often disagreed with him, but have also felt compelled to contend with his sometimes hyperpopulist views. At first I learned a lot from him, and later I was constantly alerted by his writings to keep a distance from the mainstream and to be more supportive of all kinds of alternative cinema.

5. Things haven't changed much for me in this regard since Hong Kong's reunification with China in 1997. Probably it is because, while making a living from another job, I have been writing less frequently for a small newspaper that ably maintains its own independence. Film criticism, with rare exceptions, can never be a full-time profession in Hong Kong. In general, the pressures a film critic encounters here are those mentioned above, which are not that much different from our colleagues worldwide.

Li Cheuk-to wrote a monthly column for the *Hong Kong Economic Journal* and is artistic director of the Hong Kong International Film Festival, where he was a programmer for seventeen years. From 1995 to 1999, he was president of the Hong Kong Critics Society. His film articles have appeared in *Cinemaya*, *Sight & Sound*, and *Film Comment*, among other publications. Li was editor in chief of *Film Biweekly* from 1983 to 1986. He has served on the juries of numerous international film festivals, including those in Berlin, Rotterdam, Vancouver, Melbourne, Vienna, Busan, Sydney, Zanzibar, and Stockholm.

INDIA: MEENAKSHI SHEDDE, *DAILY NEWS AND ANALYSIS*

For over a decade, as movie marketing strategies and other factors increasingly influence audience choices, I've felt that film critics are practically Jurassic beings. I have a somewhat schizophrenic reputation as a critic: as someone who specializes in art-house cinema in India, and as a Bollywood expert overseas. I am comfortable with both mantles. In fact, I've been a film critic by default because I wrote film reviews in my newspaper, whereas someone else held the formal title. Doubts were laid to rest after I won the national award for best film critic—a gold medal conferred by the president of India—for my writing in the *Times of India*, India's biggest English-language newspaper (circulation 2.4 million).

Fortunately, I've never felt any pressures when writing—but that's partly because I was never the paper's official film critic. That person was traditionally expected to also ensure film stars' appearances at the annual film award show of the newspaper group. The conflict of interest caused the public to question the credibility of the person in that post. So fraught is the position that it has seen a rapid turnover in recent times. Today, India's biggest English newspaper has simply no film critic in Bombay, heart of Bollywood, India's biggest film industry—it simply reprints reviews by its New Delhi critic. Being a critic has been a sort of cat-and-mouse game: India's film industry is deeply riven, with the mainstream industry producing about ninety-five percent of films released, while art-house films, which comprise five percent of films produced, struggle to find a distributor. The official film critic reviewed only mainstream Hindi films that were released; I tended to write mainly about art-house films that found relatively minor, delayed, or no releases, so as to steer clear of his turf.

While I truly respect, if not thoroughly enjoy—with a few exceptions—most of today's mainstream Indian films, my heart really lies with the quieter, thoughtful, art-house films that stimulate, provoke, exhilarate, or wrench the soul. I have seen hundreds of interesting Indian films in several languages (India makes films in thirty-nine languages and dialects), many of which have trouble getting released, if they ever do. There are brilliant directors in regional languages who have won many national awards, yet have carved entire careers without a single film getting released outside their home state.

At the *Times of India*, the last paper where I worked, for thirteen years (I'm now the senior assistant editor of Arts and Culture at *Daily News and Analysis—DNA*), I was bluntly told that any article I wrote that didn't bring the newspaper advertising revenue was a waste of newsprint. Given that I mostly wrote about art-house films from India and all over the world, the editors had been remarkably tolerant.

I must admit that being a film critic has afforded me the privilege of taking millions of readers on a journey of discovery of interesting films, of being open to a cinema of realities (as against Bollywood's oppressive cinema of romantic fantasies), other cultures, surprises, flaws, and despair—as well as the traditional happy endings.

I like to believe that writing in mainstream papers and magazines about such films over two decades, along with like-minded film writers all over the country, has somewhat molded the tastes of the public. After being exposed to international films, television, DVDs, film festivals, and writing on alternative cinema, they are now willing to try nonmainstream films. And art-house films by debut directors, without stars, songs, or love triangles, in Indian languages other than Hindi, are increasingly finding theatrical release.

Equally, film festivals worldwide, including Cannes, Berlin, Venice, London, and Busan, have asked for my Indian film recommendations as an independent critic, and all of them have selected films I have recommended. So the value of independent film criticism goes well beyond the traditional print review. And films coasting on the festival circuit find it easier to find distributors back home.

Critics I have been inspired by include Roger Ebert, Pauline Kael, David Thomson, and Tom Shone, and in India, Chidananda Das Gupta, Iqbal Masud, and Maithili Rao. Through their writing, I've learned that a good film critic needs to be widely read in all the arts, that the best reviews put the aesthetics of a film within the context of the director's earlier work and a national/international framework in which to fairly assess his/her contribution. I've learned that trickiest of all is balancing passion with compassion, and how to rip an awful film without destroying the director's creative potential.

Above all, I am always drawn to a rapier wit. In reviews, as much as in the movies, it takes great talent to raise an honest laugh. The most memorable reviews—like Pauline Kael's or Tom Shone's—often came from a barbed wit, but those they lampooned rarely deserved mercy.

The Indian film industry is unique not only in being the most prolific globally—averaging about one thousand films annually—but also because Hollywood, which has destroyed national cinemas worldwide, has less than a crummy five percent of the Indian film market. The Indian industry has adapted well to globalization: entire films are being shot in Manhattan, Canada, and Australia to tap the overseas market, while at home, Hollywood is unable to compete, despite dubbing in three local languages. The fact is Indians adore their own films. Accordingly, Indian papers are full of articles on Indian films, with relatively fewer articles on Hollywood and world cinema. It is with unabashed schadenfreude that we point to India—one spot on the planet where Hollywood is small change.

Meenakshi Shedde won India's National Award for Best Film Critic for her work in the *Times of India*. She has contributed to publications worldwide, including *Cahiers du cinéma*, *Sight & Sound*, and *Film Comment*, and to the books *Au sud du cinéma* (2004) and *Bollywood: Das Indische Kino und die Schweiz* (2002). A jury member for numerous international film festivals, including those at Cannes, Berlin, and Venice, Shedde is also India/South Asia consultant to the Berlin International Film Festival and has been India/Asia curator and consultant to film festivals at, among other places, Locarno, Toronto, Busan, Dubai, Kerala, and Mumbai, as well as the International Film Festival of India. She is director of the documentary *Looking for Amitabh* and was line producer for several feature-length documentaries shot in India, including *Comrades in Dreams*, a German film nominated for the 2007 Grand Jury Prize at Sundance.

ITALY: TULLIO KEZICH, *CORRIERE DELLA SERA*

1. Film criticism is one of the many ways we attempt to explain the real world as seen in the infinite mirror image that cinema offers up. Many years ago, I chose that road and I'm not tired of it yet. It probably has to do with how in 1946 the Italian neorealism of Rossellini, De Sica, Visconti, and others was exploding upon the world stage. It was a privilege to pay the necessary critical attention to a cinema then in the avant-garde; and even when it seemed the mine was exhausted, Fellini and Antonioni arrived on the scene, and then Olmi, Pasolini, and so many others. Up to a certain point, we Italian critics were in a privileged position.

2. It is not important if a critic writes positively or negatively about a film. It's not even important for the reader to share his judgment. What is important is that the critic helps one to understand the work, revealing new and different points of view, teasing out problems of style and content. The power of cinema enters into the battle of ideas—even in the political sense—but the critic must always know how to recognize the quality of a cinematographic work independent of his agreement or disagreement with that work's perspective. *The Birth of a Nation* is an apologia for the KKK but also a masterpiece. *Battleship Potemkin* is based on a limited, propagandistic notion of the 1905 revolution, but no one would want to reject it for that reason. Of course, if the beauty of the form coincides with the soul of the film (as in *Modern Times* or *Stagecoach*, *Paisan* or *Schindler's List*), then the result is perfect. The critic's duty is to try to explain if the craftsmanship of a film corresponds to the filmmaker's intentions; it is much better if he does this in a well-written review or essay.

3. Cinema is beautiful when it is accessible to everyone, from the

blockbuster to the art film and film of ideas. A healthy motion picture market generally contributes even to the financial backing of experimental films. In a time of box office crisis such as we have right now in Italy and elsewhere, the first to suffer are the independents, the innovators, and the art theaters.

4. Among American critics, I like *Variety*'s Todd McCarthy for his ability to tie the discourse about artistic quality to the demands of the market. Roger Ebert of the *Chicago Sun-Times*, master of the Internet, is quite expert and witty. I detest Parisian criticism, contentious and chauvinist; and, in particular, I don't buy *Cahiers du cinéma* anymore. My models in criticism are, among the Italians, Francesco Pasinetti (one of the first great historians), Filippo Sacchi, and Pietro Bianchi; among the French, André Bazin; in the United States, Pauline Kael—more for her very vivid style than for her, at times, inconsistent ideas.

5. Right now, the Italian press continues to afford less space to criticism, preferring to publish a so-called variety of film writing: news, interviews, gossip. A short formula for the daily newspapers is recommended; and many ask that their writers supply votes and starred ratings, an unjust practice comparing producers and directors, completely undeserving of being called criticism. In this way, readers looking for a coherent, well-argued article that helps them understand and discuss a film go away disappointed. Among the progenitors of this war against criticism, the most radical was Goebbels, who abolished criticism in Germany in 1936. It is not a good precedent.

Tullio Kezich was film critic for the leading Italian daily newspaper *Corriere della sera* before his death in 2009 at the age of eighty-one. Kezich, who was a film critic with the Venice Film Festival for over sixty years, also published film criticism in *Settimana incom*, *Panorama* magazine, and *La repubblica*. Kezich was editorial director of the film magazine *Sipario* from 1971 to 1974 and has authored dozens of books, including works on the Western film genre; actors Jean Gabin, Humphrey Bogart, and Marlon Brando; directors Federico Fellini, Roberto Rossellini, Mario Soldati, and Dino De Laurentiis; and the films *Salvatore Giuliano* and *La dolce vita*. He also authored the annual Cento Film series, his collected reviews of one hundred important films released each year. In addition to working as a film critic, Kezich was an actor, playwright, screenwriter, and, in the 1960s, artistic director of the production company 22 dicembre, which he cofounded.

Figure 2.3. One of the classics of Italian neorealism, *Paisan* is a film in which "the beauty of the form coincides with the soul of the film," as Italian film critic Tullio Kezich observes. © Organizzazione Film International, 1946.

ITALY: ROBERTO SILVESTRI, *IL MANIFESTO*

Roberto Rossellini once wrote that the technological developments of the future would provide the solution to problems of survival—health and education—for all of the planet's future inhabitants. I don't think it is so simple. Using profits plundered over four centuries of aggravated, repeated, and continuous crimes against Third World nations (including genocide), we have built sumptuous public and private structures—cathedrals, grand banks, Lloyd's of London, the Louvre. Now, we attempt to make recompense, but nobody at the International Court of Democratic Justice wants to transform London into Harare or Ouagadougou into Paris, or vice versa. We are, however, in favor of a new/other global cinema of the underground. Cinema, intoxicating and dangerous, which now can even be downloaded on the Internet, is still the most powerful weapon, a stimulant for breaking the pall cast by centuries of inequity. And so there are the marine-critics who reduce the visual, close off the journeys of the imagination, collect masterpieces to hang on the wall, and conceal or confuse hierarchies and urgencies. And there are critics who, like shock troops, attempt to destabilize established patterns of image making and the accepted codes of commercial cinema. They do battle against that military-industrial complex made up of producers/distributors/festivals/filmmakers/ministries who diffuse not "images" but passwords throughout the world. The revolutionary movement of liberating the image disassembles and reassembles it, reframing the dominant modes. This kind of critic loves the unexplored and supports the producers of ecstasies, not of the status quo. Being a film critic is a little like being the night-shift executioner, but side by side with Clint Eastwood against Charles Bronson, and with Bruce Lee against Chuck Norris.

For my generation, trained to value the formal, to disentangle "complex content," criticism is meant to decode the often raw and unexpected form of modernist films in order to discern all that they mean to communicate. This engagement with the visual always delivers an emotional jolt: the sometimes cruel boomerang pleasure of art of criticism. When a film is working, you enter the movie theater in one manner and you exit in another. The act of criticism puts the film in another light, gives it a new rhythm, reveals a new way to think of other works that you had only considered in one way before. In other words, you see the film as an amalgam of iconographies, political ideas, ethical dilemmas, lucid insights, and energetic, sensual storytelling. It either doubles the power or else sets it back to zero, diffusing its impact and poisoning its effect. A critic makes a film something new, by opening up its internal mechanism and smashing its fuselage. "Take away the outside and you have the inside; take away the inside and you have the soul," to paraphrase Godard in *Vivre sa vie*. A good review, whether you are smashing the film to bits or raving about it, supporting the filmmaker's "intention" or remaining detached from it, must somehow match the force of the film's presentation and the creativity with which it was made. Otherwise you lose by a KO.

We like only underground films, possibly only ones made without the proper permits and documentation from outside of the European Union—nomadic or stateless cinema. Italian cinema is completely unimportant to us; besides because there are always two Italian cinemas, in conflict with one another, just as there are two Hollywoods perpetually at war and two Arab cinemas. We are interested in defending the history of only one part of Cinecittà against the other—Matarazzo, Bava, Freda, Cottafavi, De Santis, for example—against those like Scotese whom I'd like to remove from the history of cinema, but not Jacopetti; and we are not always on the side of those who have the right membership card. You cannot combat globalization by emphasizing "cultural differences," as France does today. Nor can you address it by valorizing your own Eurocentric production standards over those of Hollywood; ours are just as monolithic and are often imitated to gain access to the niche festival market. Earlier antiglobalist strategies and economic policies (screening and importation quotas) arguing for a "cultural exception" (as in France) in the name of protecting national cinemas were a means of allowing governments to control filmmaking through internal financing. This is accepted globalization, and not its antidote. We don't ask for any documents. A Don Siegel, Robert Aldrich, Jean-Marie Straub, Chris Marker, or Djibril Diop Mambéty will never come to be privileged and sought after simply because of where they were born, unless it is because of their criticism of their native regimes, be it in a cleverly commercial or joyfully didactic mode.

I like "critics and something extra." People who write and do. The shopkeeper, the director of the festival, the projectionist, the filing clerk, the philosopher, the feminist, the reinventor of a city's nocturnal pleasures, the professional Pan-African, the filmmakers. C. L. R. James, René Daumal, and Benjamin. Carlos Clarens, Henri Langlois, the boys of *Cahiers du cinéma* who became filmmakers, Giuseppe Turroni (who wrote on photography for *Corriere della sera* and skillfully wielded literature and painting), Serge Daney, whose emotional geography never failed to carry us elsewhere. And Enzo Ungari, who managed our Anthology Film Archive in Rome, Filmstudio 70—Aldo Moro was a member. Ungari died very young after having written *The Last Emperor* for Bertolucci, my master. He had the courage to bring us Syrian and Algerian films, as well as bring Meredith Monk and Patti Smith to Venice after the death of Papa Luciani, producing fertile synchronicities among music, dance, and film. He actually preferred Warhol to Morrissey. And, in a country like Italy, which has repressed its horrid colonial past, in the 1980s, Ungari was the first to scout around the Mediterranean and to track down Khemir and Gitai, *Les Dupes*, and Assia Djebar; the first to get excited over Ghatak, Masumura, and Chahine; to admire the porn of Damiano at Cannes; to consider Joaquim Pedro de Andrade to be like Dreyer or Disney; and to never be restrained by labels or pigeonholing films as "high art" or "low art." Furthermore, he invited the Tunisian Mahmoud Ben Mahmoud to present his masterpiece, *Traversées*, at the Venice Festival when Carlo Lizzani was the director. Only Ungari, the film's director, and the actor attended the film's screening, projected in the grand hall, at noon. The next day at the press conference, the critics were claiming even to have asked the filmmakers questions. It was the perfect snapshot of the cultural poverty of our country. It anticipated, in a single incident, the notorious "Bossi-Fini" anti-immigration law. Because thinking, writing, and shooting revolutionary films is not putting on a show. It is producing facts.

Roberto Silvestri has been film critic for the Italian daily newspaper *Il manifesto* since 1977, and he edits the paper's weekly cultural supplement, *Alias*. His books include an anthology of his film reviews, *Da Hollywood a Cartoonia* (1994); a collection of interviews, *Macchine da presa* (2002); and a film guide, *Cinema: Film e generi che hanno fatto la storia* (2012). He is cofounder of the Polytechnic cinema club and director of the Festival of Sulmona.

JAPAN: TADAO SATO, *ASAHI SHIMBUN*

When Japan surrendered to the Allies at the end of World War II, I was fourteen years old. I had to give up my trust in the Japanese educational system, which had taught me militaristic values until that time. Instead, I learned about democracy by watching American films and felt hopeful about the future of the world. Since then, films have been texts that have given me a vision of what the world should be. These texts could be occasionally wrong or mutually contradictory. Describing the process of how I interpret these texts is what I do in my film criticism.

Unlike in my youth, when I was able to simply learn democracy from American films, these texts are full of contradictions and confusions today. Therefore, the act of film criticism has become more difficult to pursue. I feel, nevertheless, that it's more necessary for me to understand these texts correctly. At the same time, the fact that we have been able to see many different kinds of films from all over the world has required me to solve many contradictions.

For example, take the following problem. In Hollywood films about the Vietnam War, Americans always proudly emphasize the fact that their soldiers fought bravely like real men, despite the fact that Americans did not win the war. On the other hand, in good Vietnamese films, we often see the question posed to the protagonist: "Why did I survive, while all of my good friends were killed?" This sentiment is often expressed as an expression of the debt that the characters owe to the dead.

This contrast is tremendously interesting. Why are the American film-makers obsessed by heroism? Is it because the Vietnamese are Buddhist that they are consequently more interested in portraying the spiritual interactions between the living and the dead instead of emphasizing their victory? If we compare the American and Vietnamese ways of thinking while watching their films and observe closely, our views of the world will be enriched through the opposing interpretations of the war. However, this will be difficult to achieve. We can see many Hollywood films throughout the world, while we are, unfortunately, extremely limited in our opportunities to see Vietnamese films. I believe it's better to increase opportunities for people to see excellent Vietnamese films so that they can easily compare the films from these two countries.

Many Hollywood films are based on the belief that they can please audiences by depicting destruction in a morbid fashion. Isn't it sinful to destroy things purposelessly and derive pleasure from waste? I believe that this impedes historical progress and promotes our own destruction. On the other hand, there are countries producing films that emphasize the importance of treasuring their cultural heritage. Mongolia, followed by Iran, head that list. Other Asian countries, such as Uzbekistan, Sri Lanka, and the Malayalam-language region of India, have been producing great films in which gratuitous waste and destruction are not celebrated. These films, however, have not been sufficiently appreciated.

Today, films provide people from all over the world with the opportunity to search for common moral values together. Yet Hollywood films dominate the market. Given the globalization of the film business, American films crowd out others, and the values and the worldviews promulgated by Hollywood have been invading the world. It may be almost impossible to stop this huge trend. I want to insist, however, that there are many excellent films based on different ways of thinking, from many countries, and I hope that viewers will express interest in such films. We must strive to appreciate the many valuable films produced by these countries.

To attain this goal, I have been working as the general director of the Focus on Asia Fukuoka International Film Festival. Fukuoka has been sponsoring this film festival every year in September to show films from around twenty Asian countries. A copy of many of the films screened at this festival has been preserved at the Fukuoka city library's film archives.

I'd argue that contemporary critics should not be content with merely writing on films available for distribution. It is the task of critics to prove to distributors that there are other kinds of films worth seeing, and I will continue to publish essays in order to persuade distributors and viewers that this is true. This is an important aspect of my work as a film critic.

Tadao Sato is one of Japan's most accomplished film critics and historians. He has authored over one hundred books on film, including volumes on directors Akira Kurosawa, Yasujiro Ozu, and Kenji Mizoguchi and on actor Toshiro Mifune. Sato's 1982 English-language translation of his collected reviews, *Currents in Japanese Cinema*, established him as a prominent critic on the international scene. Among his many honors was the 2010 Japan Foundation Award for his promotion of cultural exchange. In 1996 Sato became president of the Japan Academy of Moving Images, a private film school established by Shohei Imamura that has educated many of Japan's foremost filmmakers. Sato's writings have appeared in numerous publications, including *Asahi shimbun*, to which he contributes regularly.

MEXICO: LEONARDO GARCÍA TSAO, *LA JORNADA*

1. In the first place, being a film critic means making a living from one of the things I enjoy most, which is watching movies. Of course, besides that selfish concern, it also entails the responsibility of acting as an intermediary between a movie and its audience. But basically, I write film criticism to develop some sort of rapport with my own points of view. I don't have any clear idea of who my readers are, so, in essence, I write for myself as part of an internal dialogue I have between myself and the cinema. But I do take into account that I'm using a public medium to express my opinion, so I strive to be accessible and even amusing.

2. A memorable film critique is the one that enriches your experience as a viewer, while revealing formal strategies, meanings, and subtexts that weren't evident. I try to strike a balance in my reviews and touch upon the subject matter as well as formal aspects of a movie. Ideology was a mainstay of film criticism in my formative years, the 1970s, and it's still a valid preoccupation. Sometimes social and political matters are the most relevant aspects of a film, especially if it's a run-of-the-mill production with no artistic merit to speak of. In that sense, I think genre criticism is very useful.

I'm seen as a severe critic in Mexico, so maybe my negative reviews are more common than the positive ones. But I don't think in terms of "thumbs-up" or "thumbs-down." Generally, films are too complex to reduce to "good" or "bad" categories. What I dislike is reducing film critics to mere consumer guides.

3. In Mexico, about ninety percent of all releases are Hollywood films. So it's impossible to escape that globalization. However, writing for the only liberal paper in Mexico City, *La jornada*, allows me to emphasize other releases, whether domestic (one per month, on average) or the few European or Asian titles that are bought for commercial distribution. But blockbusters will get their due coverage even though it's usually skeptical.

Where globalization is more apparent is in the sorry state of today's film criticism in Mexico. Most colleagues nowadays are superficial "reviewers" that evaluate Hollywood mainstream movies through the usual impressionistic standards and clichés, with little knowledge of film history or even basic rules of writing in Spanish. Most of them seem to come up with hype-inflected phrases ("the best comedy of the year!") just so they can be quoted in the ads.

4. My generation was very much influenced by the first methodical film critics in Mexico: the Spanish refugees from the civil war, many of them sons of Leftist intellectuals, who became the first to convey a sense of a group with a collective interest in cinema. Critics like José de la Colina, Jomí García Ascot, and Emilio García Riera were in turn influenced by *Cahiers du cinéma* and therefore applied auteurist theories to their work. (Sadly, most of them have either died or retired.)

Although the magazines those critics published—like *Nuevo cine*— were short-lived, their influence was decisive, as they also expressed a very critical view of the ongoing crisis that has affected Mexican cinema since the 1950s.

5. After thirty years of writing film criticism, I've earned the privileged position of not being pressured at all. So far, in *La jornada*, I haven't experienced any kind of censorship and have been able to write freely about the films or themes I choose. Sometimes, my editor will suggest a current release or a theme, but I'm free to decide whether to write about it or not.

Leonardo García Tsao is film critic for the Mexico City daily newspaper *La jornada*. His work has also been published in *Variety*, *Sight & Sound*, *Cahiers du cinéma*, *Cinema*, *Images*, *Film Premiere*, *Nexos*, and the *Journal of the University of Mexico*. He has written books on Sam Peckinpah, Andrei

Tarkovsky, François Truffaut, and Orson Welles, as well as on Mexican film-maker Felipe Cazals and actress Diana Bracho. The head of programming for, and later director of, the Mexican National Film Archives, García Tsao was also director of the Film Festival Guadalajara and programmer for the Palm Springs International Film Festival, a position he has filled at other festivals as well. Beyond working as a film critic and programmer, he is a screenwriter (*Intimacy*, 1989; *Ponchada*, 1991) and an actor, as well as a film professor at the Film Training Center.

THE PHILIPPINES: NOEL VERA, *BUSINESSWORLD*

1. I want to address Filipino viewers, for one, to tell them what they're missing or what they don't quite understand. Our middle and upper classes suffer from a prejudice against Filipino films, seeing them as cheap sex flicks, sloppy comedies, endless melodramas, ultraviolent actioners. When the occasional good film comes up—given the greater media noise made by, say, a George Lucas fantasy feature—they're blissfully unaware of it.

Even when speaking to the rare Filipino who has an idea that we have a cinema, his views can often be blinkered: the classic line is that there has not been a good Filipino film made since Lino Brocka (our most famous director) died; that the best filmmakers are those who are most honored, or able to send their films to international festivals; that the keys to international success are large-budgeted projects with production values equal to Hollywood's. Truth is there have been excellent, even great, films made after Brocka's death—Mario O'Hara's *Pangarap ng puso* (*Demons*, 2000) or *Babae sa bubungang lata* (*Woman on a Tin Roof*, 1998), Lav Diaz's *Batang West Side* (*West Side Avenue*, 2001) and *Ebolusyon ng isang pamilyang Pilipino* (*Evolution of a Filipino Family*, 2004), Mike De Leon's *Bayaning Third World* (*Third World Hero*, 2000), Tikoy Aguiluz's *Bagong Bayani* (*The Last Wish*, 1995), and Raymond Red's *Anino* (*Shadows*, 2000) come to mind. It's also true that the Filipino films that do go to festivals are often the ones from filmmakers with enough political clout to pull strings to get funding for subtitles, et cetera. Maybe some of the best Filipino films made in the past twenty—even thirty—years haven't even been seen outside of the Philippines, mainly because no one is willing to spend the money to send them out (either that or the print has turned to vinegar). Then there's the fallacy of production value—every film I've cited (except, arguably, *Batang West*

Side, whose budget climbed because of delays) was made for $180,000 or less (sometimes much, much less), often in ten shooting days.

I'd also like to reach out to foreign viewers, with essentially the same message in mind. Why do I write? It's practically a mission, a crusade—I've got to get the word out.

2. My favorite critics can range from Pauline Kael to André Bazin to Donald Richie to Constantino Tejeros; pieces I like can range from hilarious satire like Lucius Shepard's pan of the latest version of H. G. Wells's *The Time Machine* (he writes it as a letter from the elder Wells to the younger Simon Wells, his great-grandson who directed the atrocity) to David Walsh's astute demolition of *Million Dollar Baby*, about as overrated a film as any I've seen.

I have prejudices (a weakness for humor, for one), but I try to be as open as possible to as many forms of criticism as possible, with an awareness that for each film there are many ways to attack, or approach, or at least open up the material for analysis.

3. Any objective viewer would say it's a losing battle, with Hollywood films growing larger and larger in both production and marketing budget and Filipino films growing smaller and smaller in number and stature. It's frustrating. I've always argued that we should simply tax the Hollywood films to subsidize the local industry, and if the upper classes object, we should tax their Starbucks cappuccinos in response. But I haven't quite lost hope; the latest development is digital video, and several filmmakers, Lav Diaz in particular, have ventured into it. There is a thriving mini-industry in independent video production—both in fiction and documentary.

4. James Agee, André Bazin, Graham Greene, and Cervantes are more inspirations than actual influences. Critics I read who are still alive include Lito Zulueta, Constantino Tejeros, Jonathan Rosenbaum, Mark Schilling, Tony Rayns (when I can find his stuff), Olaf Möller, and David Kehr. Oh, and Joe Bob Briggs.

5. I experienced censorship once—I left a periodical because the editor wouldn't allow me to write negatively about a Filipino filmmaker. Nowadays the biggest editorial constraint would be relevance (is it something currently showing, or would it be of interest to current readers?), in which case I write my response to a film on my blog. Otherwise, I have to admit I enjoy a huge range of freedom and space. Well, I don't get paid very much—but that's probably true of almost all critics.

Noel Vera has been a film critic for the Manila-based newspaper *Business-World* since 1995. He is a correspondent critic for *Cinemaya* magazine and has written for *Rouge Magazine Philippines, Film International,* and *Cahiers du cinéma España,* as well as for the San Francisco Asian American Film Festival and the film festivals of Singapore, Hong Kong, Udine, Cinema-nila, and Rotterdam, where he curated the Filipino film offerings in 2006. He served as a juror at the Jeonju International Film Festival, is author of *Critic after Dark: A Review of Philippine Cinema* (2005), and maintains a film blog, criticafterdark.blogspot.com. In addition to working as a film critic, Vera served as an officer at the Bank of the Philippine Islands and collaborated on the screenplay for Tikoy Aguiluz's *Rizal in Daitan* (1997).

RUSSIA: LEV KARAKHAN, *ISKUSSTVO KINO*

1. It's true. Readers are very important persons for a film critic. If you want to be a critic, you have to realize very clearly "whom you hope to reach" and "what you hope to communicate to them." Still, it seems to me that stressing the "critic-reader" relationship, as it is done in the first group of questions, is risky. Too often, the well-intentioned concern for the reader transforms itself into guardianship or even into ideological "diktats." The transformation starts with innocent attempts to guess what the reader wants; then the critic starts to feel unjustifiably confident of his thorough knowledge of the reader's wishes and interests; and then, finally, the critic determines what the reader has to want.

Unlike in politics, a transition to "diktats" within film criticism occurs peacefully, and for that reason, the transition seems painless, almost natural. However, such intellectual pressure deforms communication even more considerably than direct instructions from imposing authorities. Those directives always frighten the reader off with their aggression. The aggressive thoughts of critics can prove quite edifying. But it is easy to labor under a delusion: totalitarian regimes are not the only sources of ideological conformity.

Indeed, under Communism, critics (not only the most loyal ones) used to brainwash their readers and often participated in witch hunts where readers had to play the part of a furious, bloodthirsty crowd (the writer Solzhenitsyn, the actor and singer Vysotsky, the film director Tarkovsky—those are but the most well-known personae non gratae of the Soviet era—figures who were regularly castigated by critics influenced by a public influenced by critics). Under democracy, when authorities never or (as under the young Russian democracy) almost never interfere in aesthetic evaluations, critics are much less likely to ruin an artist's career with the support of a sympathetic crowd.

In a liberal society, film critics do not serve as a drive belt of the state's punishment machine. But, unfortunately, no democracy or freedom can save critics from the excessive focus on the reader or from a temptation to rule and command, thus drawing the reader to a specific critic's agenda. It is fine when, as the Chinese say, a thousand flowers bloom and many critics' colors proudly soar and none of them strives to persuade readers to turn into crusaders fighting infidel art trends. However, a critic's fixation on the audience can turn cinema into an ideologically fraught pursuit.

Only cinema itself can keep film critiques from becoming bloated. And assuming the triad of critic-film-spectator as an axiom, then the main power vector of the critic's interest and attention should be directed not to the spectator but, in the end, to the film. This very model of interaction seems most natural to me, and I never resist the magnetism of reality that is easy to feel in any film—even in a feature by "the world's worst director," Ed Wood. Only by striving for an almost absolute devotion to and confidence in the screen can the critic be safe from bias and prejudice—from everything alien or borrowed, which irremediably damages the nearly direct contact with the energy of the film itself, its hidden codes and meanings, and experiences that only cinema can provide. But that only proves that the critic has to be open and acutely sensitive when facing the screen. Even when watching the most desperate disaster of a movie, it will help the critic not to miss the feeling of immediacy that screen images, due to their aesthetic nature, convey—even while contradicting the director's intentions. Perhaps, cinema's price to pay for this amazing immediacy is the unusually rapid aging of films, including some acclaimed masterpieces. But that only makes it more interesting for me to seize the moment by plunging into the intriguing discovery of time's mysteries within the flow of images on film. Even if those mysteries remain unsolved, the process of exploring them makes the job of a film critic meaningful.

As far as the reader is concerned, for me it is more natural to marvel at the fact that I have readers at all. It's important to avoid feeling superior to them. The great Pushkin warned us against showing disregard for the reader.

Figure 2.4. Russian film critic Lev Karakhan describes filmmaker Andrei Tarkovsky as being among "the most well-known personae non gratae of the Soviet era." Tarkovsky's *Andrei Rublev*, suppressed by the Soviet government for twenty years, chronicles the persecution of a fifteenth-century monk who painted religious icons. © Mosfilm, 1966.

2. My reply to the second question directly stems from my reply to the first one. Any evaluation of the film, as well as an evaluation of its themes and the genre it belongs to, derives not from abstract, predetermined categories but from my actual viewing experiences.

3. I believe that fighting globalization is not one of the critic's immediate tasks. While opposition to these trends is definitely topical, it has no bearing upon the interaction between a film and the critic. The problems of globalization belong to the more immediate domain of film industry journalists, who are mainly interested in analyzing the economic state of cinema. Although I respect their job and help them in their research, I can say that the commercial dominance of American cinema, for example, on the Russian market, does not limit critical assessments of local cinema in any way. Russian critics, moreover, are inclined to write about our own films with much more interest and sympathy. Obviously, the time we face on-screen is local by its nature. And it makes no difference how much Coca-Cola we drink or how much popcorn we eat here: "American" time does not seem so intimate to the local audience as "Russian" realities. In that sense, globalization, at least, in this country, only helps to reveal and establish the framework of the nation's existence.

4. To a much greater extent, today I regard as models critics of the later, not previous, generations. It is because the main thing I am trying to learn

from them is the ability to grasp how contemporary reality is depicted on screen. In that context, the experience that young critics possess is much more useful to me than achievements of the idols of the 1970s, the years when I was acquainting myself with this occupation. But, certainly, such classic authors as Siegfried Kracauer (*Theory of Film*), André Bazin (*The Myth of Total Cinema*), or Victor Diomin (*A Film without Intrigue*) and Ian Bereznitsky (his essay on *The Godfather*, "Components of Success") in Russia gave me the sense of direction in cinema and inculcated in me a taste for substantial film criticism.

5. Fortunately, after the collapse of Communism, I feel no pressure, and the only thing that sometimes complicates evaluating films is my friendly relationship with some directors. My life in cinema constantly expands the circle of my professional acquaintances, but, especially lately, new talents appear in the Russian film industry much more quickly than my opportunities to meet them in person. That is why I do not lack film material for a free and open discussion.

Lev Karakhan is editor of the magazine *Iskusstvo kino* (The art of cinema). He is a member of the Russian Academy of Film Art, a lecturer in Moscow State University's Department of Journalism, and author of more than two hundred articles and essays for Russian and foreign publications, including for the *Frankfurter Allgemeine Zeitung* and *Cahiers du cinéma*.

SOUTH AFRICA: LEON VAN NIEROP, *THE CITIZEN*

1. Coming from a country where cinema literacy was at quite a low point when I started to write reviews in 1975, my aim was first of all to inform, to educate, and to inspire. I wanted to make my fellow South Africans aware of the immense possibility and provocative nature of film. While suffering under an extremely conservative censorship system for many years, we were denied access to most of Europe's top art films. In my reviews, I tried to demonstrate that film should also be perceived as an art form and not merely popcorn entertainment. In that way I tried to educate and inform readers, viewers, and listeners by writing reviews (as opposed to criticism) that were accessible, inspiring, informative, and, in a way, entertaining. I tried to open up film to a wider audience, analyze its subtext and purpose, draw the attention to hidden subtext, and place it in proper perspective. I

could later take my passion to universities where I taught students the art of analysis without bogging a film down with a heavy, academic load of often-irrelevant information simply to fill a page.

Film criticism (and also reviewing) means opening up a film to an audience and helping them to discover the reasons behind the message and the purpose of the director. It means seeing a film for a second time on paper with the luxury of time to leisurely enter into its hidden corners and fully explore it. It also means analyzing its themes in an effective way that connects to an audience and challenges them to participate in further debate. As we don't have any "serious" film publications in South Africa, the frustration is that critics here don't really have an outlet for challenging criticism and analysis except at a university level.

2. The irony is that a negative review often sticks in the mind longer than a positive one. It is also easier to write a negative critique and dwell on the flaws of a film in a cruel, witty way that draws the attention to the critic's sarcasm instead of the film's problems. The challenge is to write a critique in such a way that it opens up debate and challenges the reader to find his own truth within the review/critique. A good critique should be a serious analysis that inspires a reader to see a film and make up his own mind. It should therefore not be too heavy-handed, manipulative, or arrogant, but rather offer a clear view of the various themes and possibilities that a director creates. Also whether those themes have been fully realized and explored. A good critique should be objective (as far as that is humanly possible) and not intimidate its reader or manipulate him/her into accepting your point of view by bullying the viewer into submission. The fact remains that it is a personal opinion that can also be challenged and discussed. So a good critique should create the forum for debate or challenge a viewer to form his own opinion after being inspired by the film critic to see the film.

3. I write for several publications, among them general magazines in which my reviews (as opposed to critiques) simply reflect the film's potential to entertain. I also write for newspapers where a deeper analysis is required and where the editor allows for a more meaningful and vivid analysis. I also write and present radio reviews where I aim to inform and entertain while reviewing, which is quite a challenge. Remember that a heavy-handed review could fall heavy on the ear and could irritate rather than inform and entertain. I also write for a glossy quarterly magazine that allows an article/critique that blends analysis with information and

addresses certain aspects of world cinema such as globalization. This I find much more fulfilling as a critic. The daily newspaper allows me up to 1,000 words, while the quarterly magazine allows for 1,500 words. I also write a script for a television movie (as opposed to film) program aimed at a young market that simply wants to know whether they need to spend their money on a certain film where the aim is to simply entertain. In my more challenging articles I try to instill a sense of pride in our local film industry that, after eleven years of democracy, has finally started to come of age. As I also lecture in film directing and script writing, I try to encourage students to take pride in work with a distinctly South African flavor. I teach them to work towards excellence and to form an identity, and not to be swallowed up by the global perception of film as a medium of artificial entertainment. I try to inspire them to reflect the personality and current state of the people of this country and the challenges that lie ahead.

4. There are no local critics that inspire me. My inspiration came from the *New Yorker*'s great Pauline Kael. I didn't always agree with her, but was inspired by her provocative (and often infuriating!) essays on film and the way she opened up a film and fearlessly gave her opinion. She inspired me to become a film critic, as she seemed to enjoy the art of analysis and sharing her views with readers, even if they were negative. I sometimes found her getting too personal and often bitchy, but her best essays bordered on genius. I also read Roger Ebert's reviews, and although he may not be a mentor necessarily, I enjoy comparing my views with his.

5. No publication that I write for prescribes what I should say or not, so I have been very fortunate in that respect. My only frustration is that South Africa doesn't have a serious publication like Britain's *Sight & Sound* or your own *Cineaste* that allows film critics enough space to write an in-depth and serious analysis of a great (or bad) film.

Leon van Nierop is film critic for the South African daily newspaper *The Citizen* and also writes for *DEKAT*, *Huisgenoot*, *Drum*, *MaksiMan*, *Lig*, and *You* magazines. He is also an actor and the well-known writer of numerous South African radio and television series, including *Ballade vir 'n Enkeling*, *Stralejakkers*, and *Ratels*, and he was a coproducer of *DEKAT TV* on BBC Three. Van Nierop's film books include *Seeing Sense: On Film Analysis* (2000), *Movies Made Easy: A Practical Guide to Film Analysis* (2008), and *Leon van Nierop on Film Study* (2010). Additionally, he has written dozens of novels, some under the pseudonym Jacqueline Brink. Van Nierop lectures on film appreciation at the Tshwane University of Technology in Pretoria, where he is an Extraordinary Professor in film and has served as the head of the film school.

THAILAND: KONG RITHDEE, *BANGKOK POST*

It's easy to feel like you're toiling in a thankless job being a film critic in Thailand—not as thankless as the poor peasants who constitute the back-bone of this country, but thankless enough to wear one down to the point of throwing in a towel. Perhaps it's the same in some other countries, but here the reality is acutely simple: advertising speaks louder than reviews, even well-written reviews. Most people here never question a career in an advertising agency (which naturally employs all the mechanisms of lies and half-truths to plug a movie). But they raise their eyebrows to resemble a buffalo's ass whenever they hear that somebody can actually make a living as a film journalist.

In Thailand, there's no concept of film culture. Movies are dispensable entertainment, and the absence of film criticism wouldn't trouble anybody's conscience. In my humble capacity, though, I'm trying to convince people otherwise; it's not easy, but it's important to prove to them that film critics are interpreters of culture, that we're pulse readers who contribute to the state of well-being, or a lack thereof, of the country's cultural expression. Especially when movies have become the front man of popular culture that shapes the sensibilities of the world, I believe that film journalism deserves a better understanding. Most people glance at a movie column in a newspaper looking for basic clues regarding which film is "good" or "bad." But very few people read a criticism piece looking for reflections on how cinema has formed their perceptions and worldview.

A thankless job maybe, but I'm certain, too, that this is the best period to write about cinema in Thailand. Of course, Hollywood imports continue to bulldoze their way into the audience's collective perception. Yet during the past five years or so, there has emerged a new crop of able Thai film-makers who try to stretch the possibility of homegrown movies. And more importantly, there has also emerged a new crop of local audience members armed with the passion to discover those new possibilities with the filmmakers. It's this emerging audience, albeit small at the moment, that I believe can gradually reinforce the idea that cinema has social, artistic, anthropological, and political implications. Film criticism—good film criticism—should assist the formulation of this new agenda. I have fun writing about the latest Hollywood openings. But I have even more fun as I get the chance to share my opinion about a new Thai movie with readers, and to remind them that local people will always understand local movies better than they do American imports. Maybe that's the way to deal with the globalization of the film industry—to advocate our Third World pride and sensibilities.

The point of film criticism, for me, doesn't end when the writer hands down the verdict for or against certain titles; after all, the debate over what is good and bad, what is beauty and what is art, has been going on since Plato's time. Film criticism is in fact the beginning of a discussion, and because good, honest film criticism is always an indication that something has touched the writer passionately, either in a positive or negative way, his/her records of that feeling will enter into the national almanac of sentiments. (It must exist somewhere!) When read two, five, or twenty years from now, a piece of film writing can show, to an extent, how people see their society, how they read or react to the signs of change in ideas, politics, arts, taste, and in the direction of cinema itself.

What's funny about being a critic in Thailand is that Thai people historically equate criticism with disrespect. A disapproval of a film's quality often means a disapproval of the film's director as a person. That's the mentality: the Thais are too polite to say bad things about other people in public (though, like everybody else, we revel in doing it in secret). Again, new crops of filmmakers and audiences seem to have adopted a more open attitude towards the culture of criticism, though we critics still have to thread a fine line. Personally, most of my writing is in English, and I have the pretext of writing for outsiders (though in fact, the majority of my newspaper's readership is Thai) and thus being able to give an honest opinion on every film. Other critics who operate in Thai—and many of them are very good—write perceptive pieces though sometimes with one hand tied behind their backs. That's not necessarily a bad thing considering our unique culture of "kwam kreng jai"—which is roughly translated as being afraid to offend others. But I think the scene will become livelier and healthier if critics can perform their duties at full gear, especially when Thai films are now regular players in the world-cinema game.

In fact, critical opinions become more relevant as Hollywood's global dominance shows no sign of abating. Without the voice that reflects on the social and artistic values of movies, the movies themselves will probably face an uncertain future. Are we taking it all too seriously? Perhaps yes, but since most people who watch movies aren't, what could be so wrong about that?

Kong Rithdee has written film criticism for the *Bangkok Post*, Thailand's leading English-language newspaper. He has also contributed to *Cineaste* ("Filming Locally, Thinking Globally: The Search for Roots in Contemporary Thai Cinema" [36, no. 4]), *Film Comment, Cinemaya, Bio-scope*, and the Thai-language magazine *Nang Thai*, published by the Thai Film Foundation. In addition to working as a film critic, Rithdee is a filmmaker, having codirected three documentaries: *Gaddafi* (2014), about a fourteen-year-old Bangkok boy who deeply admires Colonel Muammar Gaddafi; *Baby Arabia* (2010), about a Thai Muslim rock band; and *The Convert* (2008), about a Thai woman who converts from Buddhism to Islam.

TUNISIA: TAHAR CHIKHAOUI, *CINÉCRITS*

1. A film critic is, to me, the opposite of a tourist guide. The latter guides strangers through a fixed itinerary, designed for the discovery of specific places in a particular country—the medina with its souks (markets), its mosques, its native architecture, or the desert with its sand dunes, its caravans of dromedaries, its oases. The tourist guide must speak to these strangers in their own language; he must follow a predetermined itinerary and bring them to places of which they are in theory ignorant (but may have heard of)—places belonging to the guide's own community. The film critic, in theory at least, speaks the same language as his readers; his topic is already familiar to them both. From this point of view, a film he writes about belongs to both equally but is not (except when the critic is also a historian) a fossilized element of the collective heritage. It is, rather, the original expression of a cinematic auteur. The job of the critic is not to introduce the work to the public, as one would introduce tourists to a place of cultural heritage. The roles are, in fact, almost reversed: the critic tries to bring the work, as he sees it, closer to the public; the singularity of his interpretation reveals the singular qualities of the film. These two singularities combined naturally call forth a third—that of the reader. The tourist guide's approach is descriptive, voluntarily superficial, and

publicity minded; the critic's analytical, obligatorily profound, and free of charge. The film critic is not an intermediary between a director and a public who turn their backs upon each other and must be reconciled. He is the third element of a dynamic threesome. He is not, however, a halfway house between the film and the spectator; film criticism has a particular dynamic all its own.

Why I'm a film critic I don't know; perhaps because of the twin pleasures of reflection and communication that it gives me: reflecting upon the image and communicating the resultant emotions. I see the job of the film critic as being one of relative autonomy (despite its close connection to the production process, i.e., proximity to the film's consumption, i.e., the audience)—when writing I don't necessarily take the reader into account. My discourse is determined primarily by what I think; I then try to adapt it for my public—not for an imaginary entity but for one filtered, rather, through the medium in which I am inclined to express myself.

2. The precise goal of my film criticism is hard to define (whether in general, or with regard to a particular film). My criticism results from the interaction of the film itself with my own expectations; the fruit of an encounter between the work's internal logic and my cultural outlook as an individual, it is always open-ended and has no predetermined logic. It is thus pointless to distinguish between form and content. The cinematic qualities of a film are decisive. The originality of a film, therefore, arises from that cinematic inventiveness which expands the concept of the film, rather than from futile formal experimentation for its own sake. When an old idea is expressed in a new form—and this expression is a success—the idea is no longer old; it is, on the contrary, renewed; it would otherwise be reduced to mere packaging—a disguise capable of seduction at best. To distinguish between activist and entertainment filmmaking, between the artistic and commercial, makes no sense to me; they do not constitute the criteria for serious evaluation.

3. It is readily apparent that the role of critic has suffered the same mutations as the world of contemporary cinema. It is, above all, the relationship between the film itself and its material qualities that have changed. Projection techniques (theater, television, or video) and the physical qualities of film (silver-based, magnetic, or digital) have become gradually dematerialized. Film has become increasingly volatile. This dematerialization is not a purely technical phenomenon. Its ideological and aesthetic implications are considerable. The greatest challenge facing any critical activity today

is that it is no longer anchored in a particular territory, but must take into account the increased mobility of its subject, as well as its new links with cyberculture. These frontiers, both in the concrete and figurative sense, are becoming more and more elastic. Not only does critical discourse move in an increasingly open and abstract space, but also its theoretical basis (especially when dealing with the relationship between filmic representation and reality) must change, of necessity. A critic like myself, writing for the Southern Hemisphere, cannot remain indifferent to the fact that the concept of national cinema makes less and less sense. The debate concerning the hegemony of Hollywood has been augmented (or replaced) by debates concerning the hegemony of format.

4. In order to fully comprehend these mutations, it is necessary to study the theoretical history of the image. The ideas of those who studied past moments of cultural change (Benjamin, Bazin, Deleuze, Rancière, and co.) are essential to the development of both a global and a relativistic vision of cinema. Rather than looking to these theories for a definitive truth, one must use them to develop a comprehension of the evolution of cinema. The contemporary critic's territory seems to me to lack a guiding light, its transformations too rapid to permit any reference to a particular critique as "guide" or "model." More so than in the past, it is necessary to keep up to date with all technical and economic changes in the world of cinema. This does not, of course, oblige an equal distancing from all cinematic critiques (notwithstanding their diverging points of view). I follow a deliberate path with a clear conscience, fully recognizing the formative influences of André Bazin's theories, of New Wave cinema, and of the ideas of Serge Daney, while at the same time acknowledging that this heritage belongs to an era and culture which is no longer that in which we live today.

5. I don't consider myself to be operating in a cultural, social, and political context devoid of constraints, but I do believe that the principal pressure to which I'm subjected (as a critic) is the lack of imagery from which my country (my Maghreb, Arab, and African cultural environment) suffers; it is difficult for me to define precisely of what this pressure consists and to what extent it depends upon my own interpretation of it. I must write about foreign (American, European, Asian) films in order to get ahead; the rarity of Tunisian-Algerian, Moroccan, Arab, or African films (and when they do exist, their invisibility in the local market) is disconcerting. Criticism develops through contact with films; my identity as a critic is undermined by virtue of this scarcity on the home front. This scarcity has

a notable and disturbingly violent effect upon my role as critic. The challenge, in any case that which presents itself to me, consists of developing my creativity as a critic, using these difficulties as a starting point; it consists of self-interrogation, of sharpening my self-interrogation in order to assume this deficit theoretically. The risk is great of falling into a discourse of resentment, a risk to be avoided at all costs.

Tahar Chikhaoui is founder and editor of the cinema review *Cinécrits*. He contributes to the Tunis-based daily newspaper *Le temps*, as well as to many other film publications in Tunisia and abroad. He is a lecturer in the Faculty of Arts, Letters, and Humanities of Manouba University, where he teaches French literature, film analysis, and film history. He also teaches at the Ecole des Arts et du Cinéma and is artistic director of the International Meeting for Arab Cinemas, in Marseille.

UNITED KINGDOM: JONATHAN ROMNEY, *INDEPENDENT ON SUNDAY*

1. Critics are always under pressure to align themselves with different positions. It's sometimes assumed that we represent the voice of our publication; or speak for cinema among the other areas of interest covered by a newspaper's arts section; or even voice the perceived tastes of our readers. Critics have to be independent of all these positions—but that only really means anything if we're also independent of our own prejudices. For that reason, I most enjoy my work when I somehow manage to surprise myself, to react to films in ways I wouldn't normally expect; since enjoying a Merchant-Ivory film recently, I wouldn't rule out any possibility.

Writing for a weekly Sunday newspaper, I'm not specifically addressing cinephiles (as I might in, say, *Sight & Sound*). I'd like to think my column might move some readers to see films that might not otherwise tempt them, or persuade them to rethink their views on a particular film. I'm not interested in giving a consumer guide, or saying, "Don't miss." I'd rather give a speculative spin to a review and raise questions. I'm relieved that I don't (at present) have to give films star ratings, which simply give a review the stamp of dogma, regardless of how it's written.

2. For me, it doesn't matter so much whether a critique is positive or negative in tone. What matters is some new insight, whether it's central

or marginal: even facetious observations can open up a film in a very bracing way. I really enjoy it when critics notice something that's eluded me entirely: after all, what you miss in a film says as much about the way you watch as what you see.

It's hard not to write in some way or other about a film's social meaning, even if you're not writing from a specifically political angle. Conversely, it's easy to concentrate on a film's "meaning" and entirely lose track of its cinematic nature, and of the ways it's likely to be perceived or used by its public. I once worked for a publication which insisted on giving films separate star ratings out of five for "entertainment" and "politics": it was an amusing game to play, but it felt pretty absurd.

3. Writing in British newspapers, you often have to persuade editors that the most important films to cover are not necessarily the movies making the biggest "news," which invariably would mean the big Hollywood releases. Very few newspaper critics in Britain get to devote much coverage to non-Anglophone cinema.

With my own newspaper, I've been very lucky in being able to cover a wide range of international cinema, including films that many British papers would simply regard as too recherché for a general audience (an argument which keeps these films underexposed and therefore perpetuates their supposed obscurity). There's no particular pressure on me to cover British cinema, and in any case I often prefer not to, because most high-profile British films tend to disappoint or even embarrass me—or worse still, to be Hollywood product by default. But I do like to go to town on the interesting exceptions, few as they are.

In general, though, I like to cover as wide a range of films as possible—I wouldn't want to be identified as strictly an art-house critic any more than I would as a multiplex one.

4. I was very inspired by the late Serge Daney, both for the complexity of his responses and for his ability to take a seemingly peripheral aspect of a single film and read it as an index of the state of cinema or of film language. Overall, I tend to be more impressed by American than by British critics, for their ability to engage with cinema in a way that's both enthusiastic and analytical. In Britain, film is still widely regarded as inferior to other arts as an object of criticism. So it's considered respectable to take a high-handed, facetious approach to cinema.

5. The worst pressure is always space. Writing in newspapers, you never know how much your column might get squeezed in a given week, and

sometimes you end up being more lapidary than you really want. I don't feel that in the *Independent on Sunday* I'm particularly constrained by any rules, except the ones I set myself—e.g., I don't like to reveal more than the bare minimum of plot, and I like to be as essayistic as space allows.

Currently, however, film writers are having to resist those restraints that distributors would like to impose: more and more, critics are regarded by many of them as an irrelevance that gets in the way of revenue, and major studios continue to pursue the ideal of the critic-proof film. Meanwhile, by the time we get to review a film, whatever we have to say about it—positive, negative, or indifferent—has often been defused in advance by the mass of noncritical press coverage that has been orchestrated around a release. This shouldn't leave us feeling powerless or superfluous: it simply means there's more reason to regard criticism as a gratuitous pleasure, and reviews can then be as playful, or as polemical, or as indifferent to market demands as critics see fit.

Jonathan Romney is chief film critic for the *Independent on Sunday*, the Sunday edition of the *Independent*. He was deputy film critic for *The Guardian* from 1993 to 2001, deputy editor for *Sight & Sound* from 1993 to 1995, and film editor for *City Limits* from 1989 to 1990. Romney contributes regularly to *Film Comment*, the *London Review of Books*, *Frieze*, and *Screen International*, among other publications. He is author of *Short Orders: Writings on Film* (1997) and *Atom Egoyan* (2003) and coauthor of *Celluloid Jukebox: Popular Music and Movies since the 1950s* (1995). A program advisor on French cinema for the London Film Festival and curator of the United Kingdom cinema retrospective at the 2011 Rome International Film Festival, Romney has spoken or participated in roundtables at film festivals in Edinburgh, Cambridge, and Estoril. In addition to working as a critic, Romney has taught at the University of Cambridge and has appeared as a guest lecturer at various other British and European universities.

URUGUAY: JORGE JELLINEK, *TIEMPOS DEL MUNDO*

1. The influential Brazilian film critic José Carlos Avellar once recounted a story about an Amazonian tribe. They used to gather around a campfire at night and, on one occasion, one of the elders told them his latest dream. The interesting thing was that another old shaman interpreted

the dreams for the rest of those present. In essence that's what critics do: they analyze the projected dreams that we call cinema. While trying to understand them—and going beyond regurgitating obvious platitudes—is our objective, this goal is not always attained. Yet by conveying our own enthusiasm or derision, we can also help people to better understand their own feelings about certain films. If by doing so we are able to enrich the experience, and awaken the curiosity of the public that read us, then we can be more than satisfied.

2. What I value most in a critic is the precision and usefulness of the information given, the insightfulness of the observation, and clarity in the presentation of the ideas. Naturally films are a product of society and reflect its ideology and culture. But as a language, films are also the best tool to understand our time, and to have a precise approach to the history of the last century. Political, historical, and social elements are always to be taken into consideration, although their relevance varies from film to film.

3. I don't "combat" globalization, which would be as useless as fighting television, but I favor all cultural diversity in opposition to the dictatorship of a unidirectional way of thinking. The problem is not Hollywood, but those who think that it's the only type of cinema that could and should exist. Throughout its history, the American film industry has always bene-fitted from foreign influences and talents and, if this disappears, the result will be an impoverished cinema. The public has the right to know about the richness of world cinema, and to taste different dishes.

4. In Uruguay, there is a strong critical tradition that began in the early 1930s and that established the basis of what is now considered one of the best traditions of film criticism in Latin America. Our first steps were guided with the work of people like Homero Alsina Thevenet, who was one of the first in the world to write about Ingmar Bergman, and is still active at eighty-four. I have also benefited from the work of British critics, especially those of the old *Sight & Sound*, and many of the French, from André Bazin to Serge Daney. Unfortunately, I can't think of any contempo-rary critics of equal importance.

5. Personally, I haven't been subject to any pressure at all in the media where I have worked, but I know of other colleagues who have experienced this form of censorship, which, of course, I totally reject. More and more critics are being relegated by newspapers to the function of a consumer guide, less concerned with helping people to think for themselves. Of course, we now have the freedom of the Internet, where anyone can write

and publish his own criticism. But, without discriminating and separating the wheat from the chaff, any opinion weighs the same as another. This may be good for democracy but is terribly confusing for the intellect.

Jorge Jellinek has been a journalist and film critic since 1982, writing for the newspapers *Últimas noticias* and *Tiempos del mundo*, as well as for several other Uruguayan publications and radio shows. He is vice president of the Asociación Críticos de Cine del Uruguay (FIPRESCI section) and artistic director of the International Punta del Este Film Festival. He has served on juries for several international film festivals, including those at Mar del Plata, Buenos Aires, and Rio de Janeiro. Jellinek also stars in Federico Veiroj's 2010 film *A Useful Life* (*La vida útil*), a Uruguayan drama about the closing of a movie theater and the protagonist's love of film.

CHAPTER 3

Film Criticism in the Age of the Internet
A CRITICAL SYMPOSIUM

Caught in the Web, print and new-media writers debate the pros and cons of writing on the Internet, where everyone's a critic.

In introducing the critical symposium "International Film Criticism Today" in its Winter 2005 issue, *Cineaste* maintained, with a certain resigned pride, that "critics at independent film magazines have virtually complete freedom, and a generous amount of space, to express their opinions if they are willing to endure the relative (or, in some cases, total) penury that results from being unaligned with the corporate media." In the spring and summer months of 2008, many American critics were fired, downsized, or bought out by a host of publications, as a result of the economic crisis of the time. Critics learned, unfortunately, that even making compromises with their corporate employers would not guarantee that they keep their jobs. This vacuum in the world of print film criticism soon was filled by online film journalism, already a part of the media landscape. A new group of online critics became increasingly prominent. There was also, at least in certain quarters, an intensification of friction between print critics and the denizens of the blogosphere. In an ungracious broadside in the *New York Press*, Armond White wailed that "Internetters . . . express their 'expertise,' which essentially is either their contempt or idiocy about films, filmmakers, or professional

Originally published in *Cineaste* 33, no. 4 (Fall 2008); copyright © 2008 by Cineaste, Inc.

critics. The joke inherent in the Internet horde is that they chip away at the professionalism they envy, all the time diminishing critical discourse."

Cineaste's goal in coordinating this symposium, "Film Criticism in the Age of the Internet," was to chip away at some of the hyperbolic rhetoric exemplified by White's jeremiad. Although the twenty-three survey respondents represent a host of critical stances, all consider the relative virtues and flaws of both print and Internet criticism from a nuanced perspective that is indeed alien to anti-Internet critics. Some of the participants in the symposium confess that they know little about Internet criticism, while a few bloggers take gentle jabs at their print brethren. Yet civil discourse prevails.

In addition, it soon becomes clear that there are very few critics who are exclusive inhabitants of either the print or Internet realms. This was true in 2008 and is even more the case today. A certain number of longtime print critics have been forced—or have chosen—to become full-time bloggers; writers who started out as bloggers or Web critics have found print jobs; die-hard Internet critics occasionally make appearances in film magazines; and even the most inveterate magazine and newspaper critics are pleased that their reviews appear on their publications' websites. It is also of interest to note that when it comes to embracing or critiquing Internet criticism, it is much too simplistic to speak of a yawning generational divide: veterans of venerable print publications often express undiluted enthusiasm for the possibilities of the Internet, while younger critics are far from hesitant to utter a few caveats concerning unrestrained cheerleading for the uneven quality of critical conversation on the Net.

Choosing whom to invite to this symposium was certainly daunting. Unlike the previous Cineaste symposia on American and international criticism, the terrain appeared almost limitless, and despite Cineaste's familiarity with the world of print criticism, its editors were engaged in the ongoing process of learning about the brave new world of the Internet. The editors could well have invited a totally different roster of critics and enjoyed an equally stimulating panoply of viewpoints. Nevertheless, they assembled here a lively and erudite (if far from comprehensive) group of seasoned critics, young bloggers, and writers who continue to oscillate between traditional and new-media venues.

Given the ever-changing and expanding Internet-scape, some sites that critics referenced in 2008 no longer exist—most notably GreenCine Daily, which symposium contributors praised for its comprehensive, up-to-date reports on the current cinema and on film criticism. Many useful new sites and blogs have also appeared (and disappeared) since the original publication of this symposium. As such, several of the websites listed in the responses below are either no longer active or have migrated to new URLs. We include the original references for the scholarly record. Paradoxically, however, in the all-inclusive digital age, whatever had been accessible on many now-defunct sites may be lost forever—an issue that resonates, in various ways, with themes raised in the chapters to follow on film programming and preservation. The archive of digital-age film criticism is perhaps no more stable than in the predigital days, for just as paper documents can be destroyed by fire, flood, or overanxious pets, so too can documents floating unmoored in cyberspace become inaccessible.

Some critics formatted their responses as essays and others point by point, to correspond with each of the following questions posed. Next to each critic's name is his or her professional affiliation in 2008, when this symposium first appeared. Following each response is an expanded, updated biography of the contributor.

For assistance with this critical symposium, *Cineaste* expressed special gratitude for suggestions offered by Steve Erickson, Jonathan Rosenbaum, and Girish Shambu.

1. Has Internet criticism made a significant contribution to film culture? Does it tend to supplement print criticism, or can it actually carve out critical terrain that is distinct from traditional print criticism? Which Internet critics and bloggers do you read on a regular basis?

2. How would you characterize the strengths and weaknesses of critics' blogs? Which blogs do you consult on a regular basis—and which are you drawn to in terms of content and style? Do you prefer blogs written by professional critics or those by amateur cinephiles?

3. Internet boosters tend to hail its "participatory" aspects—message boards, the ability to connect with other cinephiles through critics' forums and e-mail, et cetera. Do you believe this "participatory" aspect of Internet criticism (film critics form the bulk of the membership lists of message boards such as A Film By and Politics and Film) has helped to create a genuinely new kind of "cinematic community" or are such claims overblown?

4. Jasmina Kallay, writing in *Film Ireland* (September–October 2007), has claimed that in the age of the Internet, the "traditional film critic

. . . is losing his stature and authority." Do you agree or disagree with this claim? If you agree, do you regard this as a regrettable or salutary phenomenon?

ZACH CAMPBELL, *ELUSIVE LUCIDITY*

1. Internet criticism has absolutely made a significant contribution to film culture. Speaking personally, for one crucial example, the *Chicago Reader*'s film reviews archive (including its archived capsules) allowed me to first dive into the work of Jonathan Rosenbaum, Fred Camper, and Dave Kehr. (All three critics have a presence on the Web these days, too.) Before the Internet, a teenage cinephile like myself—circa 1998—could have scrounged back issues of various periodicals for some of their work, but here was a great deal that would have been inaccessible otherwise. Others could easily help me list quite a few more examples like these. So on that initial front—broadening the readership of writers who otherwise would have been contained to a certain geographical network—the Internet has been a giant boon. In terms of criticism, journalism, and discussion whose *genesis* has been online, however—LISTSERVs, blogs, sites like *Slant* (www.slantmagazine.com)—the issue is less clear cut. "Significant," yes. I think the jury's still out on all the ways in which it has been positively or negatively meaningful for film culture. But while there is a lot of "junk" in cyberspace, I am convinced that the blog and online discussion communities today, at their best, perpetuate the luxurious bloom of small cinema magazines and ciné-club chat that proliferated all over the world's film cultures in the earlier decades. Internet criticism, or online "film culture" more broadly, supplements more established print discourse. Sometimes, vice versa.

2. Blogs often lack a certain polish, technical or conceptual. When we don't have editors or other authority figures pressuring us on our writing, we can be very indulgent with our prose and our navel-gazing. Certainly there can be a workshop atmosphere from time to time, where online denizens critique each other's work rigorously and constructively. But in real experience I don't think this happens enough, and we tend to settle into routines of reading and thinking, not rubbing against each other in productive ways. (The Internet of course always allows *unproductive* conflicts.) I think of my own blog as a public notebook, and often post very unpolished or unreadable musings accordingly, in the hopes that people

will help me work through my ideas. In all honesty, though, many of my fellow bloggers and I would do well to become still stronger writers and researchers. I hardly mean to suggest that all blogs and websites must adhere to professional print standards. That would be unfeasible in any case. But we have certain freedoms that most professional critics don't have; for those of us who would like to be counted without snark alongside the pros, we must hold ourselves up to more of the same basic standards. I check a lot of blogs, film related or otherwise, but to name a handful of my favorites, there is of course the cordial and polymathic Girish Shambu's place (girishshambu.blogspot.com), which is the hub of my personal "film blogosphere"; Andy Rector's indispensable *Kino Slang* (kinoslang.blog spot.com); Mubarak Ali's *Supposed Aura* (supposedaura.blogspot.com); Kimberly Lindbergs's *Cinebeats* (formerly cinebeats.blogsome.com; now cinebeats.wordpress.com). That's just a drop in the bucket. And of course not all blogs are their proprietors' personal foray: let us spare a healthy review of sites such as *Serge Daney in English* run by one "LK" (sergedaney .blogspot.com) and *My Gleanings* by "jdcopp" (jdcopp.blogspot.com).

3. I am not sure how "new" the online communities of film culture are. A discussion group like A Film By (of which I was a founding member, in full disclosure) drew together a lot of people who already knew each other in real life, including people of generations older than my own who ran in the same circles in New York or Paris . . . in the 1970s. The sense of community discussion, I suspect, is not so new. It's now more a matter of articulations and scale. Aside from cinephilic discussion, the Internet has allowed for an altogether new spin on an old presence in film culture— bootleggers, collectors, and traders. Not all film culture is defined by talk!

4. What stature and authority did the traditional film critic hold before the Internet? It could be that the proportion of the bourgeoisie who once read reviews has shrunk; the name "Rosenbaum" possibly means less to the merely casual film fan than "Kael" or "Sarris" did forty years ago. I couldn't pretend to know. Among the crowd who devote attention to film criticism in a serious way, I don't think there has necessarily been a devaluation of the stature of worthy critics. We could consider the case of Rosenbaum, who would be an uncontroversial nomination to the spot of America's most important film critic over the last fifteen to twenty years. When he wrote his provocative piece on Ingmar Bergman for the *New York Times* ("Scenes from an Overrated Career," Aug. 4, 2007), multitudes online challenged him. Rosenbaum himself responded gamely and civilly

to some of these criticisms in discussion groups and blogs. Was this whole affair an instance of an unassailable figure being profanely attacked by the electronic unwashed? Or was it instead the healthy debate of impassioned viewers and commentators, propelled by the mutual capacity to respond across tremendous physical spaces in much more rapid succession and greater visibility than would have been the case had a similar article come up in 1978? I lean towards the latter (as I suspect Rosenbaum himself would). In certain respects, the Internet may not be as innovative and revolutionary as the hype proclaims. I suspect a lot of its usefulness and merit is in fact in keeping certain older practices alive.

Zach Campbell completed his PhD in 2015 at Northwestern University in the screen cultures program. His dissertation, "When Video Was New: From Technology to Medium, 1956–1965," explores the applications of video recording within television broadcasting of the period. In addition to his blog posts at elusivelucidity.blogspot.com, Campbell's film writings appear online at *Rouge*, *LOLA*, *In Medias Res*, and *Mumbi Notebook* and in print in *Krystalbilleder* and *Framework*.

ROBERT CASHILL, *CINEASTE* AND *BETWEEN PRODUCTIONS*

1. There are an estimated 113 million blogs out there, and 112 million seem to be about film. It's so big it can't help but have an impact, and so diffuse it's hard to gauge what that impact is. A lot of it is the usual piggybacking off print sources, which are invaluable for jump-starting online conversations even in their (presumed) twilight. The problem with print is that there are space limitations and formalities (like gobs o' plot summary) to be observed for the hoi polloi. What I like are writers who dispense with this, figuring you're in the know and up to speed, and dive right in to isolate key facets of a favorite film, either in a snappy paragraph or a deep-dish essay. It's an elastic medium, so the terrain can be as big or as small as the critic chooses.

Sites I have bookmarked include *Hollywood Elsewhere* (hollywood-else where.com), which gets my heart started in the morning; Tim Lucas's ruminative and eclectic *Video Watchdog* (videowatchdog.blogspot.com); the mysterious *Arbogast on Film* (arbogastonfilm.blogspot.com); Turner Classic Movies' idiosyncratic adjunct *Movie Morlocks* (moviemorlocks.com);

the invaluable DVDBeaver (www.dvdbeaver.com); and Glenn Erickson's informed and informative *DVD Savant* (www.dvdtalk.com/dvdsavant). I check in with these and others when not fiddling obsessively with my Net-flix queue.

2. Just as anyone who appears in a porn film is a de facto porn star, so, too, does anyone who blogs on film become an instant expert on the subject, just by showing up online. But there are professionals who write (and think) very amateurishly and amateurs who know more about the niches of this or that genre than any professional ever will. What I like is a professional who lets his or her hair down on the Web in a manner distinct from the voice-from-the-mountaintop style of print reviewing, as Matt Zoller Seitz was doing, and an amateur who conveys a stockpile of information with clarity, style, and wit. Then again, I'm more often drawn to the subject of a posting than I am to the writer; the opposite is true in print, where the name above the title has been the draw.

3. I learn a lot in the nooks and crannies, at the Mobius Home Video Forum (www.mhvf.net), the Home Theater Forum (www.hometheaterfo rum.com/community/), or at Dave Kehr's site, where the host throws out the red meat for auteurist death matches (polite, civilized death matches). And I try to give back. The online community is strengthened by the give-and-take at these more thoughtful sites. I'm not sure how it's weakened by the mosh-pit comments sections elsewhere, but they're mostly for rubber-necking. Interesting tidbits that bring you closer to a film or a filmmaker, which you might pass on to the community at large, pop up in unexpected places. The users' comments at the Internet Movie Database (www.imdb .com) are a lot of white noise; still, every so often, a commenter will rem-inisce about what it was like to have the film crew banging around his house on a location shoot, or how accurately a movie reflects a historical episode s/he lived through. Little, intimate gleanings that the Web makes it easier to share, if not always to find through all the rest.

4. Two things happened this spring. One was a distinct uptick in the number of newspaper and magazine critics becoming masterless samurai, looking for paying work in times of "old media" scarcity. Forget stature and authority: the traditional film critic is losing his or her job, period. And in the blogosphere, where some turn for meager sustenance (two and a half years in on my own blog, and the Google ads I should just shuck off have yet to return a penny), there was a new wrinkle: not blogging. Seitz's turn-ing over the keys to his site *The House Next Door* to someone else set off

a seismic ripple of soul-searching: why am I doing this, when I could be doing something more productive?

The answer: because we like the instant gratification. We get out what we choose to write about, when we choose to write about it, hit "publish," and for better or worse it's online. I am nostalgic for the horse-and-buggy days, when I had to go to the local library to catch up with Kael and Kauffmann, and distrust knee-jerk attacks on the old guard of print critics. Their reviews have much to tell us about the times they were written in, however dated or out of touch the opinions register today, and the old arguments still resonate.

In changing times, where critics try to maintain a livelihood, and relevance, in old media and the new bully pulpit, and question whether or not to continue at all, the most powerful person in the blogosphere isn't a critic. It's *GreenCine* editor David Hudson, for the hits he brings us when we are anointed for his daily aggregation. If he or *GreenCine Daily* decided to pull the plug, we would all be adrift until someone else with stature, authority—and the patience to wade through all this stuff—took over the rudder.

Robert Cashill is a member of *Cineaste*'s editorial board and film editor of Popdose.com. Cashill's work has been published in the *Wall Street Journal*, *MovieMaker*, *Playbill*, *Slant*, *Time Out New York*, and *Biography*. He is a member of the Online Film Critics Society and the New York–based theatrical critics association Drama Desk, on whose board he formerly sat.

MIKE D'ANGELO, *ESQUIRE* AND *THE MAN WHO VIEWED TOO MUCH*

Call me traitor. I was part of the initial wave of Internet film critics, way back in 1995, when pretty much the only people online were college students and tech nerds. The site I created had (and still has) no ads, no graphics, and no agenda—just endless text. The thought of somehow parlaying this hobby into a career in print media literally never occurred to me. I had zero ambition—and yet I was writing a 1,500-word column every single week, generally reviewing three to six films (all of which I paid to see in commercial release), simply for the joy of writing, and to entertain a readership that couldn't have amounted to more than maybe five hundred to six hundred people. Looking back on that era now, after ten years in the print trenches, it seems very Shangri-la.

And yet that degree of purity is now the norm. For every print critic who gets the axe, another dozen bloggers appear, many of them arguably more passionate and knowledgeable than the professionals they threaten to supplant (or at least render irrelevant). Granted, not all of these cats can actually write—one noted online critic, who seems to have quite a respectful following, wields a prose style so hilariously turgid that I can never make it past sentence number two; you need a machete to hack your way through his thicket of synonymous adjectives. But, of course, the glory of the Internet is that a voice more to your liking is only a mouse click away. What matters is the sheer number of ardent cinephiles out there getting all "ars gratia artis" on our asses.

The problem here, for those of us who'd like to continue being paid a living wage in the field, is that people willing to devote so much time and energy sans recompense are even more willing to accept any old pittance somebody might offer them. I was fortunate enough, when print media stumbled onto my site (which happened fairly quickly), to land ridiculously lucrative freelance work—my first regular gig, for *Entertainment Weekly*, paid two dollars per word. A decade later, one of my employers—a strictly online venture, significantly—decided they could no longer afford my (admittedly sizable) fee more than once a month, and shifted from a review format to a daily blog. I know and respect several of the folks who contribute to said blog, but I also know that they're being paid something on the order of one cent per word. (Literally.) And if talented writers are prepared to accept assignments for what's basically ramen money, clearly there's no earthly reason for anyone to shell out premium wages, much less a medical plan.

Yeah, I know, boo hoo. And there's no question that the recession we're all desperately pretending not to be mired in has been more responsible for the various layoffs and buyouts than has the Imminent Heat Death of Newsprint. Still, I do foresee a future in which the most gifted critics will wind up preaching primarily to a small, self-selected choir, while the average filmgoer—to the extent that he or she consults criticism at all—will simply check the aggregate results available on Metacritic and Rotten Tomatoes. It's inevitable that the more voices there are competing for your attention, the less valuable each individual voice becomes. And so a paradox: the advent of online criticism has simultaneously fostered greater diversity and greater homogeneity. Just like the expanding universe as a whole, if you think about it.

What I miss about writing online—and the reason I eventually started my own blog, though it's only updated approximately three times per annum—is the freedom to define your own audience, both in terms of what you choose to address and how you go about addressing it. If you have no editor, maybe nobody's catching your occasional lapse into self-indulgence; at the same time, though, neither is anybody shooting down your prospective ideas on the grounds that readers don't give a damn about Guy Maddin or Hong Sang-soo. And you can just assume a fairly high degree of cine-literacy, if that's the way you prefer to write. "Rivals *10 on Ten* as the longest DVD supplement ever projected in a theater to a paying audience," I wrote of *Captain Mike Across America*, Michael Moore's latest "effort" from Toronto last year—a comparison I simply could not make in print, because merely explaining who Kiarostami is would likely eat up all of my remaining word count. On the Net, even if a particular reference sails over your head, there's always Google.

Of course, on the Net, one needn't necessarily write at all. I'm sure I won't be the only one in these pages to single out the remarkable video essays of Kevin "alsolikelife" B. Lee, which permit a degree of shot-by-shot analysis that no amount of careful or dazzling prose could possibly convey. Perhaps the true issue here is that so many of us still insist upon "dancing about architecture" when such a blatant compromise is no longer necessary. But it's a struggle I continue to thoroughly enjoy, and one I can't imagine ever wholly abandoning. And as I began—writing primarily for myself and a tiny cadre of friends and fans—so I may well end.

Mike D'Angelo was chief film critic for *Esquire* magazine through 2008. He contributes regularly to Nerve.com and the *Las Vegas Weekly*, and his work has also appeared in *Variety*, the *Village Voice*, the *Salt Lake City Weekly*, and the *Nashville Scene*. He wrote for *Entertainment Weekly* from 1997 to 2000 and was chief film critic for *Time Out New York* from 2000 to 2004. He blogs at *The Man Who Viewed Too Much* (www.panix.com/~dangelo/) and is a member of the New York Film Critics Circle.

STEVE ERICKSON, *GAY CITY NEWS* AND *CHRONICLE OF A PASSION*

1. There have been a few examples of Internet criticism making an impact on American film culture. It's aided the rise of South Korean cinema and mumblecore. In the case of Korean cinema, Filmbrain's blog, among others, hosted interesting debates on the films of Park Chan-wook, Kim Ki-duk, and Hong Sang-soo. Bloggers like Tom Vick seemed to respond to the snobbery implicit in Tony Rayns's attack on Kim in *Film Comment*. In the case of mumblecore, the blogosphere's attitude was more hype driven; when the IFC Center launched its mumblecore series last year, every blog affiliated with *IndieWire* united to promote it. The only criticisms heard about the films related to their all-white casts, not aesthetics. I'm not sure what Korean film and mumblecore have in common, although the parallels between the latter and the blogosphere are obvious, but I think bloggers like making discoveries they can claim as their own.

Internet critics and bloggers I read on a regular basis include Glenn Kenny, Girish Shambu, Michael Sicinski, Mike Atkinson, Dave Kehr, Bryant Frazer, Theo Panayides, Dan Sallitt, and Karina Longworth. There are many more blogs I peruse on a more occasional basis, especially if I come across links to them on *GreenCine Daily*, which has become an essential resource. But I'm no expert on the field. I've never looked at most of the dozens of blogs linked by *Girish* or *Filmbrain*.

2. Blog writing tends towards informality and, much of the time, short bursts of information. At best, this can communicate an excitement that gets edited out of "professional" writing; at worst, it can lead to ill-thought-out gushing. In some cases, a dimension of anger has emerged from some critics' blogs that wasn't really apparent in their published work. The ability to incorporate links into text is a big difference from newspaper or magazine publishing, and it's sometimes useful. I don't really care whether blog critics are professionals or amateurs as long as their writing is strong.

3. I'm not sure that it's particularly new. I've seen similar kinds of community form during film festivals, at which one sees the same people at screening after screening over a week or more. The problem with the participatory aspects of online discourse is that they often attract people who value conflict and argument above all else. The Scylla and Charybdis of message boards are endless arguments and fading into apathy. I've only seen a few forums that have managed to navigate these successfully.

The Mobius Home Video Forum is the best example, but it's policed fairly heavily—discussions of Michael Moore films often get shut down for turning into off-topic, political name-calling.

4. The traditional film critic only had stature and authority within a very small circle, with a few exceptions, like Pauline Kael, as well as anyone writing for the *New York Times*. Amateur or professional, I think that anyone writing serious criticism is essentially talking to a niche.

Steve Erickson lives in New York. He has written for the *Village Voice*, *Time Out New York*, *Film Quarterly*, *Cinema Scope*, the *Chicago Reader*, and other publications. He also maintains his own website, *Chronicle of a Passion* (home.earthlink.net/~steevee/).

ANDREW GRANT, *FILMBRAIN*

Unlike the music world, which had a thriving zine culture, there weren't that many options available to cinephiles in the pre-Internet era. While there was no shortage of film magazines, there wasn't much of a DIY spirit, save for some independent publications on psychotronic or other cult cinema. The Internet provided film enthusiasts with a much-needed forum to share their opinions and, more importantly, to find one another. Unfortunately, the image of the film blogger was tainted early on by the rise of Harry Knowles, whose *Ain't It Cool News* became a Web sensation thanks to the legions of fanboys who embraced the "it's cool/it sucked" brand of film criticism (and discourse) found on the site. Yet lurking in the shadows were the dedicated film bloggers, motivated not by hit count, but by their own passions and a desire to share their enthusiasm with fellow travelers.

What separates the better film blogs from traditional print criticism is a greater sense of freedom, in terms of both content and style. There's no need to pitch an editor, or worry about adhering to a house style. Looking for an impassioned appreciation of Arnold Stang? You got it. Detailed coverage from a small, experimental film festival? Done. Film bloggers also tend to be more up-front about the subjective nature of their writing, and often you'll find the personal skillfully intertwined with the critical, which is less common in traditional print outlets. This, combined with the interplay that arises between critic and audience via comments, has unquestionably changed the landscape of contemporary film criticism. Girish Shambu, Lisa Rosman, and the anonymous Self-Styled Siren are perfect examples. On a personal level, Benten Films wouldn't exist if it hadn't been for the relationships established and opportunities afforded to me as a result of the blog.

As the popularity (and sheer number) of film blogs grew, the response from many paid critics was knee-jerk dismissal, while clinging to the same tired stereotypes; bloggers desperately need editors, they don't think before they write, this is opinion not criticism, et cetera. An established New York critic admitted to me a certain amount of bitter envy, for when he was coming up in the ranks, there were no outlets in which to express his opinion, nor means of finding an audience short of landing a job as a critic. That a blogger can, with little effort, find readership in the thousands must be somewhat vexatious to the old guard, particularly in a time when both readership and paid positions are on the decline.

At the same time, the profusion of online critics has given rise to some disconcerting trends that go far in providing fuel for the detractors. In an effort to increase readership, some bloggers will intentionally court provocation by tearing apart a classic for no purpose other than the linkage and pages upon pages of negative comments. (The old adage that there's no such thing as bad publicity seems tailor made for the Internet.) Even more troubling is the critic who feels the need to play the contrarian and/or trade in snark; lobbing semi-clever witticisms replete with PoMo posturing in lieu of any critical method. Lacking a proper sense of history, they are to criticism what Diablo Cody is to screenwriting. These squeaky wheels are masters at drawing attention to themselves, and some have managed to parlay their shtick into paying gigs, both online and in print. That such types can find work in a time when many qualified critics with years of experience are being sent packing is indeed cause for alarm.

While it's tragic that media conglomerates are cutting critics left and right, either through buyouts or outright dismissals, it makes sense when your only concern is the bottom line. The sad truth is that film critics matter far less today than they did years ago. I grew up a child of the film industry, and can recall just how important those Friday reviews were. At one time, strong praise for an art-house film in the *New York Times* or the *New Yorker* almost guaranteed its success; whereas, a pan would more than likely have a detrimental effect. Not anymore. Fewer people seek critical opinion, especially when they've been bludgeoned by aggressive (and effective, as it turns out) viral marketing campaigns that extend far beyond traditional means, and editors are conscious of this fact. Why pay salary and benefits for a single critic when you can hire three freelancers for less money, and syndicate their 250-word minireviews to boot?

The good news is that we haven't lost these critics—many have set up sites of their own, and have quickly become hosts to some of the most substantive and respectfully contentious dialogue in the film blogosphere. Blogs from Glenn Kenny, David Bordwell, Dave Kehr, and Michael Atkinson (to name but a few) find these critics writing in a somewhat more candid, unrestrained tone. The comment threads on these sites (where it's not uncommon to find Kent Jones or Jonathan Rosenbaum chiming in) have done quite a bit to further bridge the gap between bloggers, critics, and other cinephiles. Yet few (if any) are making money through their sites, which only gives credence to Matt Zoller Seitz's recent prognosis that film criticism may soon become more a devotion than a means of employment.

If that is indeed the case, what does the future hold for film criticism, particularly if only a select few can call it a profession? What steps can be taken to ensure its survival in the age of the capsule review? The first step is for all sides to throw down their arms, for pulling rank and taking jabs at each other is purely counterproductive. The argument that paid-equals-professional is all but dead, as is the traditional hierarchy that places old media over new. Collectives, such as *The House Next Door* (started by Seitz, now ably run by Keith Uhlich), have helped foster a sense of democratization by encouraging submissions, while at the same time maintaining a level of responsibility and professionalism that rivals any of the better film magazines. Yet the question remains—can this model be converted into something commercially viable, and do so without having to sacrifice content or quality?

Andrew Grant is a film blogger (*Filmbrain* and *Like Anna Karina's Sweater*) and film critic. He is president of Benten Films, a DVD distribution company that he runs with fellow critic Aaron Hillis, and he has been coprogrammer of Berlin's Unknown Pleasures independent film festival since 2011.

J. HOBERMAN, *VILLAGE VOICE*

1. The Internet has impacted on film culture, just as it has on all other aspects of culture. For me personally, it functions mainly as a technology of information. I use the Internet for research—Googling phrases and/or visiting IMDb scores of times every day—and, in general, my searches are more driven by specific movie than individual critic. There aren't all that many critics that I read on a regular basis—although it's certainly easier to find them online. The blog I visit most often is *GreenCine Daily*, which is really a means for gleaning information or opinions on whatever movies I'm interested in. Basically, I'm a print guy. I love newspapers. I love their social function—and as a workplace in which everyone contributes to a larger project. Before I loved movies I loved books and I still love them as objects. For me, a book is thought made material.

2. On the one hand, blogs are spontaneous and unedited; on the other, blogs are spontaneous and unedited. The strengths and weaknesses are identical—wild enthusiasm, outrageous rhetoric, ad hominem attacks. To the degree that film critics are self-important narcissists, those traits are only amplified by the Internet. I'm impressed by the seriousness of certain online journals (*Senses of Cinema*) and websites (*Moving Image Source*), but I'd rather read an essay on the page than the screen. Rants, however, are preferable on the screen. I suppose that if Proust were alive, he'd be a mad blogger. As someone who writes for a living (and might not otherwise), I'm amazed that people have the time and energy for their blogs.

3. Some people are better suited to message boards than others. I'm not much of a joiner. For me, a message board is a BYOB virtual cocktail party. You can lurk around eavesdropping until you get drawn into a conversation—then you might wish you never had or that you could go off somewhere for a private chat. It may be that communication is overrated—at the very least, it's time-consuming and addictive, although maybe not as much as computer games. As I said with regard to newspapers, I'm more interested in projects than communities.

4. Kallay's assertion pre-dates the Internet. James Wolcott said the same thing after Pauline Kael retired twenty years ago. I think that whatever stature and authority film critics have exists mainly in their own minds—and those of other critics, academics, and cinephiles, as well as a few overly sensitive or underappreciated filmmakers. It's also a factor of venue—with very few exceptions, critics are the institution for whom they

write. That's a challenge for the Internet critic. Of course, the traditional film critic is a hostage to the fortunes of two declining cultural forms, popular cinema and the print media. The real issue is that the movies have lost their stature and authority. I'm still susceptible to a utopian sense of technology—but remain skeptical. I really thought that cable TV would let a thousand flowers bloom, that Super 8 talkies and slide shows would democratize film production, and that music videos were going to be a whole new art form. I appreciate the Internet's potential for new forms of criticism involving linkage to or the incorporation of illustrational material. Perhaps I'm not looking in the right places but, outside of academic lectures, I haven't seen too much of that. The dispersion of dis-, mis-, and actual information aside, the most radical effect of the Internet has been its destruction of intellectual property rights. That's not necessarily good for writers, but to the degree that I'm an anarchist I have to appreciate it.

See biographical note on J. Hoberman in chapter 1, p. 51.

KENT JONES, *FILM COMMENT*

The Internet has made a significant contribution to film culture simply because it has allowed people from around the world to communicate with one another. When Jonathan Rosenbaum says, "I live on the Internet," I take him to be claiming citizenship in a community of shared passions and curiosities, free of economic imperatives or disputes—in other words, a utopia. It seems to me that criticism plays a secondary role in the composition and functioning of this community, in which someone in Bangkok can get excited by an Alexei Guerman film and instantly share his or her enthusiasm with someone in Canada. Isn't this the realization of Jean Baudrillard's "ecstasy of communication"? There is a compulsion to communicate, visible on any given day of the week in any city around the world as armies of people walk down the street or ride public transportation with cell phones or BlackBerrys in hand, chattering, texting, and e-mailing away. If I don't see this phenomenon in the dire terms outlined by Lee Siegel in *Against the Machine: Being Human in the Age of the Electronic Mob*, I do agree with him that it allows people to feel connected and comfortably solitary at the same time. Good? Bad? Something is always coloring our visions of ourselves and our fellow men and women.

The critical terrain of the Internet, thus far at least, is based in the immediate satisfaction of this compulsion. Someone has a position and they're able to make it instantly known, on a blog or their own website. This, for me, raises important questions about writing and civility. What is writing? Writing is rewriting, structure, argument, refinement. Is there a difference between criticism and writing? Of course not. Anyone who thinks there is, and there are many who do, is fooling himself or herself. There is a great deal of good writing on the Internet—from David Bordwell, Quintín, Lisa Rosman, Adrian Martin, the various contributors to *Senses of Cinema*, among others. But apart from the fact that you read it on your computer screen as opposed to a printed page, there's no property unique to the Internet that makes it special. The difference is one of dissemination. Internet criticism is instantly available all around the world and it is free.

Those who make claims for the greater democracy of the Internet are, I think, responding to the legions of writers in print who fail to work as hard at their writing as, say, Farber or Agee or Kael or Bazin worked at their writing, and who thereby misuse their authority and visibility. This mood of frustration with print criticism, even as it is dwindling away, is fully justified. Yet there are a great many bloggers who make the rhetorical leap of equating all print criticism with arrogance and abuse of power. The Internet affords opportunities that print journalism simply couldn't: it gives the members of the reading public multiple opportunities to "make their voices heard," so to speak. Is this a good thing? Of course it is. But, in a sense, the Internet also blurs the distinctions between the writer and the reading public. This, it seems to me, is neither inherently good nor bad, but simply a new wrinkle.

And here is where the question of civility enters. What kinds of obligations does democracy carry? On a very basic level, none at all. "It's a free country," as we used to say on the playground. But if we're exchanging ideas and opinions, don't we owe it to one another to respond thoughtfully from the privacy and solitude of our own homes? Aren't we obliged to behave on the Internet as we would in public? Don't we owe it to our fellow bloggers to read every word they've written with great care, as opposed to simply picking out the offending phrase or choice of words and going on the attack? And what happens when someone begins with a position that's carelessly thought through and argued in the first place? Does that give us the license to respond in kind? I don't think so. I've seen a number of scenarios played out around these issues, and some of them have been quite painful to witness—misunderstandings, dismissals, rejections, attacks, followed by wounded defenses. The most interesting exchange I've had was with a man who mischaracterized something I wrote about Pauline Kael. I responded as carefully as I could—or so I thought, since I began by mischaracterizing something he wrote about Nathan Lee. Unfortunately, this was followed by a post from a friend who congratulated me for "demolishing" this man's thinking, something I had neither the intention nor the inclination to do. This was followed by a fascinating response from the man himself. He unleashed a tirade against me, but what was most interesting was the overall impression he conveyed that I had intruded on his territory—in other words, he wanted to feel free to attack me, without having to suffer the indignity of responding directly to me. Why couldn't I have just stayed in the comfort of my elitist stateroom, and resisted the urge to stroll below decks and spoil the party in steerage? At which point, a fellow critic chimed in under one of his many Internet pseudonyms with the judgment that my response was both hysterical and overlong, and I opted out. In his essay on Ezra Pound in *The Gift*, Lewis Hyde wrote, "It is an easy power play to take a man's ideas and, instead of saying 'You're right' or 'You're wrong,' say 'You're crazy.' It impugns the status of the thinker and cuts off the dialogue." Which is exactly what happens all too frequently on the Internet.

There is no "new" form of criticism on the Internet. There is only a new delivery system (which occasionally yields some interesting byproducts: on many websites, you often begin with one topic and, through a thread of associations, arrive at something completely different) increasing the visibility of nonprofessionals and a new way for readers to respond almost instantaneously. As a "conversational forum," it leaves a lot to be desired—you miss nuances, subtleties, and, more than anything else, you miss the chance to breathe the same air and share the same space as your interlocutor. On this point, I am in full agreement with Siegel. Since we're talking about cinema, I believe that Godard is a genuine pioneer in this regard. His peculiar form of public discourse, a monologue that appears to be a dialogue, anticipated the most questionable aspects of blogging by decades.

I'll close by sharing my enthusiasm for two websites. Dave Kehr's site is the model of a good Internet forum: readers who share information and enthusiasms and passions, who occasionally disagree but take the time to clarify their positions. For criticism, it's difficult to improve on David Bordwell's blog.

Kent Jones is director of the New York Film Festival and editor-at-large for *Film Comment*. He is author of *L'Argent* (1999) and *Physical Evidence: Selected Film Criticism* (2007). Jones was formerly executive director of the World Cinema Foundation, a nonprofit organization dedicated to preserving and restoring neglected films from around the world. Inspired by the landmark interview book of the same title, Jones directed and cowrote the acclaimed 2015 documentary *Hitchcock/Truffaut*.

GLENN KENNY, *SOME CAME RUNNING*

1. "If cinephilia is dead, then movies are dead too," Susan Sontag wrote back in 1996. Cinephilia wasn't dead, it was undergoing a mutation—a mutation that miniaturized and privatized it, in a sense, while at the same time blowing it out. Between DVDs and other—some still emerging—video formats and the Internet, cinephilia went, and is still going, virtual. So I think that Internet criticism is in the process of making a significant contribution to film culture, yes. Among other things, it speeds the discourse and whets appetites. The tools the Internet provides do make a difference—just the fact that it's easy to get screen grabs or put up clips is a huge thing. Shot-by-shot analyses are far more common on websites and blogs than in most periodical-published criticism for that reason, I think, and that certainly adds a new dimension. Has Internet movie criticism yielded its own Bazin? I don't know, but if it has, he's probably David Bordwell.

2. *Filmbrain*, David Bordwell, Girish Shambu, *Cinetrix*, Jim Emerson, Jonathan Rosenbaum, James Rocchi at *Cinematical*; Dave Kehr, for the comments threads as much as anything else; *Self-Styled Siren* is, I think, the blog I'd point to if I were asked to justify blogs—movie blogs or blogs in general. Karina Longworth at *Spout* and Alison Willmore at IFC are good with both the opinion and newsy items. Of course I read the trade blogs, Anne Thompson's in particular. Jeffrey Wells is, for better or worse, sui generis.

I like a blog that has a strong individual voice, knows what it's talking about, and has a sense of humor; beyond that, I don't really care if it's by an amateur or a professional. Again, *Self-Styled Siren* can write rings around a large percentage of professionals in any specialty.

The House Next Door is a great multiwriter site that manages to host a bunch of strong voices, although I'm not crazy about every single one of them. I suppose that's part of the point.

Strengths and weaknesses of critics' blogs? I really am not sure I understand the question. Relative to what?

3. I think there's a great deal of potential there, but currently the Edenic qualities of the Internet are a little overrated, yeah. That said, my own experience in blogging has helped me find and communicate with a lot of kindred spirits who give me hope for cinephilia. With few exceptions, the dialogue I have with my readers in comments is incredibly productive. It was also enlivening to have put up a couple of posts last year on my *Premiere* blog speculating on the ending of *No Country for Old Men* and to have the thread on that extend to . . . well, I think people are still commenting, as there are links to the post on the official *No Country* website. So there's that.

And then there are trolls. It's like anything else, really.

4. Define traditional. Define stature. What or who are we talking about? If it's Peter Travers, that's one thing. If it's Peter Wollen, that's another.

Anne Thompson wrote about teaching a class somewhere and how her students didn't read movie critics because they didn't "trust" them. This sounded to me like about the most ass-backwards rationale I had ever heard. I grew up reading pop culture criticism in *Rolling Stone*, the *Village Voice*, *Creem*, and the thing about this stuff was that it was fun to read—whether I "trusted" any of it never entered into it. But if I was looking for a critic to use as some sort of consumer guide, I'd find one I enjoyed reading who had a sensibility close to my own. For music, back in the 1970s and 1980s, that guy was John Piccarella—we were both aficionados of a kind of squirrelly, slightly cerebral guitar rock. But again—first and foremost was that I enjoyed reading the guy, just as I enjoyed reading Robert Christgau, with whose taste my own did not correspond quite as closely.

But we're getting away from the question here. A lot of the time, when I hear my fellow colleagues wax rhapsodic on Pauline Kael, I get the feeling they miss not just her voice but an era wherein a film critic was something of a big shot, could successfully dress down David Lean, all that sort of thing. That power began to diffuse long before the Internet became significant.

Is it regrettable or salutary? Neither. It just is. My perspective is, finally, the same as that of Kingsley Amis: "[I]mportance isn't important. Good writing is."

Figure 3.1. The Internet provides fertile ground for extended debates, according to film critic Glenn Kenny, as evident in arguments concerning the ending of *No Country for Old Men*. The dissolve shot merging sociopath Anton Chigurh with sheriff Ed Tom Bell, along with Bell's monologue to follow, has helped fuel this debate. © Paramount Vantage, 2007.

Glenn Kenny is editor of *A Galaxy Not So Far Away: Writers and Artists on Twenty-Five Years of "Star Wars"* (2002) and author of *Robert De Niro: Anatomy of An Actor* (2014). He has written for, among others, the *New York Times*, the *Los Angeles Times*, *Rolling Stone*, the *Village Voice*, *Entertainment Weekly*, *Humanities*, RogerEbert.com, and *Vanity Fair* online. From the mid-1990s to the magazine's 2007 folding, he was senior editor and chief film critic for *Premiere*. He appeared as an actor in Steven Soderbergh's film *The Girlfriend Experience* (2009) and Preston Miller's *God's Land* (2010).

ROBERT KOEHLER, *VARIETY*

1. We're at a point where it's too early to judge if Internet criticism has significantly contributed to film culture in, I would add, a permanent and meaningful way. But it isn't too early at all to observe that it has moved and affected film culture, and that we're living through a time when the first movements are being felt. This is why any comments on criticism on the Internet have to be provisional; we won't have a clearer sense of its impact for at least a few more years.

The most direct way in which film culture and criticism have been affected is through the hugely beneficial imprint of globalization, which is surely the most misunderstood and absurdly demonized phenomenon of our time. Due to the Internet's global connections, the ways in which film lovers armed with a region-free DVD player (a beautiful product made in response to globalized demand, first spurred by fans of Asian/HK genre movies) can now access and purchase films from around the world in an instant—films that were either not accessible in a pre-DVD world (when the market demand prompting restoration and recovery of film titles didn't yet exist) and were virtually impossible to see in any form unless you lived in a major film center—have affected both the culture and criticism.

A site such as Masters of Cinema, which tracks current and upcoming DVD releases in all regions of great art cinema and reports on important developments in film culture, may not be strictly a place for criticism, but it's proven to be an immensely useful tool for those engaged in writing about film history and the cinema happening right now. I'm also pretty certain that the pre-Internet era couldn't have produced a site like *Rouge*, which is designed with the Web in mind and observes cinema from a certain international perspective that combines the Web and a view of things from Australia. (I would add that this is true of the *Senses of Cinema* site, also based in Australia, also quite global.) A site like *Rouge* illustrates how Internet criticism goes far beyond merely "supplementing" print-based criticism, but makes a distinct contribution.

We're now in a phase where many more sites, some of them created by individual critics and scholars (those by Dave Kehr, David Bordwell, and Jonathan Rosenbaum—ones that I visit regularly—are fine examples), suggest entirely new forums for criticism that are completely independent of, and very often superior to, what's available in print. To take my case for the beauty of globalization and its impact on film culture a step further, just observe how the global approach has visibly affected English-language print journals such as *Film Comment* and *Sight & Sound*—once much more inward and nationalist in perspective—and does so at the same time that younger, emphatically international journals like *Cinema Scope* and *Letras de cine* have developed into strong cinephilic voices. (Putting aside its current multipronged troubles, *Cahiers du cinéma*'s Web expansion and new availability in English and Spanish reflects this same film critical/cultural globalization, made possible only because of the Internet.)

There are more hacks among bloggers than there are fish in the sea—I believe that may literally be the case at this point—but among the good ones, I like to read Quintín and Flavia's incisive, strong, and amusing entries on lalectoraprovisoria.wordpress.com, Doug Cummings on film journey.org (Doug is a member of the Masters of Cinema circle, and his site is where I occasionally blog myself), and Karina Longworth's nicely written entries at Spout.com. To mention a few sites for interesting criticism which tend to be overlooked in the conversation, I would note d-kaz .com, chainedtothecinematheque.blogspot.com, Brazilian sites such as revistacinetica.com.br and critic José Carlos Avellar's escrevercinema.com and programmer Roger Alan Koza's ojosabiertos.wordpress.com. Also notable are sites that tend to blend what might be seen as certain bloggy writing with more formal criticism, such as cinematalk.wordpress.com.

2. As for the blogs I like to read, see above. As for blogs' strengths and weaknesses . . . this comes down to the writer's concept of what a blog is and what it should do. Blogging is blissfully free of rules and codes, which means it can attract messy thinking, but also creative and punchy writing—or longer musings—that traditional print can't accommodate. Blog reviewers tend to be, though not always are, the bottom-feeders in the film critical ecosystem; I'm thinking especially of the school spawned by *Ain't It Cool News*, which prizes badly written snap judgments by fanboys on commercial movies. To me, they're worthless since they're so poorly argued and written, yet they have had logistical impact, proving to be a real problem for determining print (and Web) dates for reviews at *Variety*, which, like all major trade publications, aims to review films at the earliest possible date, meaning, as close as possible to the film's first public screening anywhere in the world. (At the same time, I do enjoy the subversive effect that blog reviews have had on the studios' mania for controlling information—as a part of the Web's overall expansion of information liberty, this has been a delight to observe.)

Like every other kind of reviewing/critical writing, blogging can produce either empty notions or worthy ideas. While some bloggers, especially those hacking away at the American festivals, don't so much write as typewrite, others don't simply post their purely raw musings. Whether at *Spout* or in Quintín and Flavia's bloggings (to cite a pair), a certain self-editing has quite clearly preceded the posting. It's also, and always has been, the case that some critics are simply able to write well at a much faster pace than others, and for those who can, blogging is a natural form. I know that in my own festival blogging experiences, my tendency is to resist writing instantly, since this can often result in faulty readings. Rather, a few hours' worth of mulling, even another film or two seen subsequently, a meal, a conversation or lively encounter, a cup of coffee, all and any of these help the process of delivering a blog entry that retains freshness and immediacy with the essential weight of analysis and critical thinking. My blogs therefore tend to read not as blasts or miniposts, but worked-out though not extremely refined mini-essays; either form, or something in between, can qualify under the blog banner. And because of my own practice, developed by trial and error over time and in collaboration with a cinephilic website such as filmjourney.org, I tend to prefer blogs written by informed critics with a voice, and not by well-intentioned movie geeks. Geeks aren't without their moments, and their obsessions and specializations can be fun; usually, though, their sheer interest isn't balanced by good writing, and their reference points tend to be quite limited.

The primary weakness of the (in English) dominant fanboy bloggers is that their diet of cinema is so restricted and codified, resulting in work that suffers enormously from a nearly complete lack of knowledge or interest in international film tendencies. They're of essentially the same ilk as junket and quote-whore critics who watch and write about little more than American blockbusters. (These are people for whom a viewing of *Atonement* equals a weekend-long marathon of radical art cinema.) Since they lack the ability to draw upon film history, and since they effectively write in a reinforcing echo chamber of bloggers and readers who maintain the same strict viewing habits, their writing has no chance of expansion, reflection, internal revolution—precisely the sort of dynamics necessary to a vital critical practice.

3. Perhaps they're overblown, although I have witnessed several valuable exchanges of information and debates on both the UK-based Film/Philosophy forum site and at A Film By, which amasses a wonderful and often strongly opinionated group of cinephiles. (Neither site, incidentally, is actually dominated by film critics, with Film/Philosophy overpopulated by many jargon-heavy academics.) I know that the exchanges on Preminger that I've read over the past couple of years on A Film By have prompted me to revisit early and late Preminger with fresh eyes, and I know that I'm hardly alone in this. Sometimes, the sense of community is all too real, and reminds us that being in a community can often mean watching individuals in all-out conflict with one another. (The term "community" doesn't automatically equate with a peaceable assembly.) Some of the nasty spats among academics at Film/Philosophy are pretty amusing to witness, as the ivory-tower intellectual is brought down into the mud with a fellow

poster who disputes his/her view of Laura Mulvey or the all-holy Deleuze. Amidst the verbal noise and smoke, useful information can be gleaned, as can revealing cultural and political biases—biases the posters are often not aware they're exhibiting.

4. On its face, Kallay's claim is dubious at best; so are much of the gloom-and-doom pronouncements that are fashionably awash in our various artistic/political/economic cultures at the moment. The dominant mood is toward the dour right now; this will pass when most realize that we've been too gloomy. (This is the case in nearly every aspect of life I can think of right now, historically an indication that the mass opinion is wrong.) Without knowing the full context of her statement, her fear of the "traditional" film critic losing "stature and authority" sounds at least partly based on the fear that print-based, newspaper journalists have of losing their jobs. This is real, since the traditional newspaper business (where, presumably, "traditional" critics reside) is in a permanent state of decline, with many jobs (including those of arts critics) being eliminated. Conditions will force newspapers, not the most nimble entities around, to change, and this was predictable as early as the mid-1980s. I recall a conversation that I had with my *Los Angeles Times* theater critic colleague Sylvie Drake in 1986, when I noted that in a decade or two, we would be reading our news not on paper but on screens. Sylvie was skeptical, but then, so was almost every fellow newspaper person I discussed this with at the time. It was difficult for many to foresee the tremors and structural changes that the Web would trigger in the newspaper world, but anyone who had closely watched developments in the digital universe (I worked for the first Apple user magazine in 1980–1981 and saw the personal computer/Silicon Valley revolution firsthand) could envision enormous changes. Change engenders unease, unease engenders fear, fear engenders irrational conclusions. Kallay's film critic, assuming he/she is at a newspaper, must adapt to life on the Web, or fade away. This shouldn't be difficult, since writing is writing, and film criticism is film criticism, whether it exists on paper or on a screen.

Now, if by "traditional," Kallay means the typical critic that delivers weekly coverage of widely released commercial movies—no matter the medium—then I welcome their loss of "stature and authority." Particularly if this means a shift of authoritative stature toward critics who cover a wider range of the film world beyond the tiny portion that represents what is deemed "popular." (In this regard, the middlebrow critics in the newspaper world are afflicted with the same problem as the blogging fan-boy hacks and junketing quote whores—they regularly fail to see the films that matter.) Web versus print versus something else—this is no zero-sum game: readers of serious, thoughtful film writing will seek it out in a greater range of media, reflecting the increasing number of choices that (globalized) technology has ushered in—just one of a few nice reasons why we're too gloomy.

If I were to choose to work as a critic in the era of Kael versus Sar-ris—or, as I prefer to think of it, the era of Stanley Kauffmann—the era of Bazin, or our current era of a thousand flowering critical views, I will take ours in a heartbeat. Whether in print (and I'm thinking here mainly of film journals) or on the Web, a far more adventurous and creative critical envi-ronment, with extremely interesting writing, can be found now than in the days when a Kael or a Sarris dominated the conversation, and when access in all ways to international cinema was considerably more limited than it is today. In other words, a climate with critics such as Olaf Möller, Francisco Ferreira, Jonathan Rosenbaum, Quintín, Kent Jones, Diego Lerer, Jim Hoberman, Richard Brody, and Christoph Huber, as well as what I would call "critical programmers," like James Quandt, Berenice Reynaud, Nicole Brenez, Javier Porta Fouz, Mark Peranson, and Thom Andersen, is one that I want to live in, especially when I see younger, serious critics emerg-ing all over the place, from Toronto to Manila, as conversant on Lav Diaz as they are on Ford (and who see the connection between the two). The fact that I read many of these critics online (sometimes with Babel Fish helping with Chinese-menu-style translation, but no matter) as much as I do in print underlines the fact that the Web is helping make film criticism stronger, more interesting, more accessible, more vital, and more difficult to corral and define. Which are more reasons not to be gloomy.

Robert Koehler is a film critic for *Variety*, *Cinema Scope*, and *Cineaste*. A former theater critic for the *Los Angeles Times*, he has also written reviews, articles, and essays for a number of other publications, including *Cahiers du cinéma* and *Die Tageszeitung*. Koehler is a programmer and codirector for the Acropolis Cinema in Los Angeles and had formerly been director of cinematheque programming at the Film Society of Lincoln Center and a programmer at several film festivals, including AFI Fest, in Los Angeles.

KEVIN B. LEE, *SHOOTING DOWN PICTURES*

The (to my mind, overblown) debate over online criticism and its contentious relationship to more conventional forms of film discourse says more
about the fragmentation of the film community than about the relative
value of its different venues. When, in just a few years, the volume of criticism has expanded to mind-blowing quantities, how can anyone attempt
a blanket statement to characterize what's out there when no one can possibly keep up with everything worth reading?

At this year's Moving Image Institute, no less an icon of the film
critic establishment than Andrew Sarris acknowledged that online criticism was where the vitality and innovative thinking that characterized his
own groundbreaking writing of the 1960s could now be found. He also
expressed bewilderment at the overabundance of content and a lack of
knowing which sites are worth his while to investigate. This, I think, is a
much fairer critique of online film criticism than the broadside dismissals
I've seen in print or heard in person, which are symptomatic reactions to
the same vertiginous sensation of content overload. For established critics
accustomed to their opinion holding court, it's a radical landscape shift
amounting to an existential crisis. Hell is other critics. For them, three
simple words apply: get over it.

Solving this problem of online content navigation and aggregation concerns me insofar as it would allow older critics like Sarris (who still types
his reviews on a typewriter) to connect with his Internet successors, a linkage that could only benefit the future of film criticism. The closest thing
I have for a silver bullet (especially for those who can't manage an RSS
feed aggregator such as Google Reader) is the *GreenCine Daily*, the fruit
of David Hudson's countless hours crawling the Web for worthwhile cin-
ema-related content, which he summarizes and links for the ease of cinephiles everywhere. While there are dozens if not hundreds of other sites
worth mentioning (my own RSS aggregator tracks 112 sites and blogs), I
feel comfortable singling out *GreenCine Daily* for praise because it does
such a marvelous job at spotlighting everyone else.

Still, one website can only do so much to bring disparate sites together
into a semblance of a community. A beauty and a challenge of the Internet
is its spawning of virtual film communities collectively embodying a stunning array of cultures and interests, while also leading to enclaves of specialists engaged in lengthy threads of minutiae. While interests of all kinds

are part of what is necessary to push the boundaries of cinema culture, the propensity of some online discourse towards a kind of tunnel vision and loss of perspective bothers me. One thing that I've learned from my time spent online is that even the most respected and established critics can become embroiled in petty bickering and trifling discussions as much as anyone, poring over the trivial, mundane details of a film over dozens of posts.

For me, movies always have to come back to the world, which I suppose is why I've generally enjoyed conversing with everyday film buffs with lives outside the film world as much if not more than erudite film critics. I've enjoyed many exchanges over the years on forums such as A Film By, the Rotten Tomatoes critics discussion forum, and more recently, the visitor-friendly blogs of Dave Kehr and Girish Shambu, among many others, where name-brand critics and many more experts check in regularly.

But my ideal experience of a film community remains my time spent on IMDb's classic film message board, where people aged sixteen to ninety from around the world gathered to share and discuss what films they saw (contemporary as well as classics). Among my favorite peers were the director of a major city library in Tennessee; a film professor in the United Kingdom who professed not to be able to discuss films with her colleagues because it was too much academic shoptalk and not enough fun; the bored housewife of a *New York Times* journalist; a San Diego high school student with a penchant for Marguerite Duras; and a nursing home resident who attended the Kansas City opening night of *Citizen Kane.* Their collective insight on any number of films from all eras and countries (thanks to the age of DVD) was, in my view, better than any film school (indeed, the board was my film school since I couldn't afford a formal graduate education), especially in that it wasn't ensconced in a limited perspective of cinema, academic or otherwise.

This to me is the full potential of online cinema culture: to be expansive and connected all at once. This is one of the guiding principles of my own blog, and is a reason why I invite a variety of individuals to collaborate on my video essays, each one lending a different voice and perspective to a given film. This perspective is all the more important to nurture if cinema culture itself is to have a future beyond the specialized online cul-de-sacs to which many cinephiles have already migrated, and maintain its relevance within culture at large.

Kevin B. Lee is a filmmaker, critic, and the programming and acquisitions executive of dGenerate Films, a venture distributing Chinese independent cinema in the United States. He has written for the *New York Times*, *Sight & Sound*, *Slate*, and *IndieWire*. He blogs at *Shooting Down Pictures* and *Also Like Life*. Lee has collaborated with critics to produce nearly two hundred innovative video essays on films. He is founding editor and chief video essayist for Fandor's *Keyframe*.

KARINA LONGWORTH, *SPOUTBLOG*

Forgive me, *Cineaste*, for I have sinned. I wear the scarlet letter of the professional version of the home wrecker. I am a blogger.

One morning in June, I appeared on a panel at the Silverdocs Film Festival called "Main Street vs. the Blogosphere." On my right sat a friendly acquaintance who has worked as a reporter and a critic for both online and print publications. On my left sat a reviewer who, just two weeks earlier, had accepted a buyout from the newspaper at which he had been employed for twenty-five years. At a particularly heated point in the conversation, the man on my right accused me of "killing" the job of the man on my left. His tongue was clearly in cheek, and no one on the panel took the accusation at plain face value. But there was a kernel of authentic anxiety to the statement; that the panel had a "vs." in the title should be indication enough that the prevailing view holds that print critics and Internet critics can't coexist.

I've been working to combat that view every day of the past three and a half years. I started writing a film blog for a living in January 2005, when I was twenty-four years old. Through a combination of dumb luck, naïveté, misguided rebellion, and, very occasionally, shrewd calculation, I helped to plant the seeds for this debate, this rarely productive tug-of-war between, as it was worded in the invitation to participate in this symposium, "the cranky nay-saying of anti-Internet pundits and the undiluted enthusiasm of film buff 'Net Heads.'" For playing my part in this internecine war, I am truly regretful. But in my defense, I must say that it wasn't supposed to turn out this way.

When I got into this racket, there was a fledgling underground of interesting Internet film writers, whose generic interests and methods of approach had far more in common with highbrow mainstream media than with the so-called fanboy culture, at that time held up on one end by *Film Threat* and on the other by Harry Knowles's *Ain't It Cool News*. There was *IndieWire* for film news and festival coverage, *Reverse Shot* and *Slant* for sharp, unforgiving reviews of indie and indie-arm releases, *Twitch* for enthusiastic spelunking of obscure genre product, and a few handfuls of disparate blog voices, most of which languished in obscurity until swept up in the heroic collation efforts of David Hudson at *GreenCine Daily*.

That all of the sites named above are alive and thriving three years later should be evidence enough of their continued significance. But in 2005, when I was editing an early version of Cinematical.com and writing ten blog posts a day myself, the combined noise made by the established film websites in concert with us young upstarts seemed meek against the constant drone of corporate entertainment media. I saw very little material difference between what passed for film coverage in most mainstream outlets, whether it was *Access Hollywood* or the *New York Times*'s Sunday arts and leisure section. Maybe the latter earned (and deserved) credibility for extending their promotional efforts past the multiplex, to tiny films, foreign films, and retrospectives. But the available options failed to address what I thought (and still feel, perhaps now more than ever) was a major crisis for cinephiles. The bulk of entertainment "news" amounted to pure advertising (celebrity profiles, trailers as content, uncritical set visits . . . pretty much the entirety of *Entertainment Weekly*). Then there was a rarified, highbrow space (film festivals, big-city rep houses, and, um, magazines like *Cineaste*), but this space was often inaccessible to the average person who really cared about movies. I knew too many people whose personal tastes fell somewhere in the middle.

I've always tried to give voice to that man in the middle, to offer skepticism and passion in equal doses, to use my platform to steer the conversation toward films that deserve extra attention whilst at the same time questioning received wisdom whenever it seemed appropriate (and often when it didn't). At first, I felt like I could get away with anything, because no one was paying attention—the idea that I could have an audience as large and as dedicated as any newspaper critic seemed completely laughable.

But sometime in late 2005, things started to change. Page views, on my blog and others, soared. Publicists started calling me at home, usually angrily. And long before jobs for print critics began to disappear, people like Peter Bart were writing ill-informed editorials, bemoaning the blogosphere as an orgy without protections, trying to run us out of town. "They'll just publish anything!" the detractors moaned. Well, yeah, but what's your point? We never said we were going to play by your rules. We never said that what we were doing was pure journalism.

No, I'm not being entirely facetious: what I do for a living sometimes looks like journalism (in my case specifically, it often looks quite a bit like criticism), but on any given day, I also play the roles of activist, stand-up comic, camp counselor, therapist, and DJ. Above all, I think of myself as a hunter—it's my job to go out in the world and look for prey to feed to my hungry community.

Just as I wouldn't be able to do my job were it not for film festivals, publicists, and, of course, filmmakers, I wouldn't be able to do it without print film critics and journalists. Internet film culture needs mainstream/print culture to survive. We need something to push and pull against; we need the established media to set the words for our conversation. The best hope of the online film community is not to replace traditional film criticism, but to eventually earn enough respect from that establishment to be seen not as upstarts, not as a nuisance, not as a threat, but as partners in the common goal of keeping a public conversation about cinema alive. Every time either side drops a "vs.," an us-or-them binary opposition, we waste time and weaken both sides.

Karina Longworth is host of the podcast *You Must Remember This*, which focuses on the secret and forgotten history of twentieth-century Hollywood. She has authored books on George Lucas, Al Pacino, and Meryl Streep. At the time of the symposium, she was film and new-media blogger/critic for Cine matical.com, which she cofounded and edited. She was also editing the film-culture daily *Spout* and had contributed to the *Huffington Post*, *Film-maker* magazine, *NewTeeVee*, and *TV Squad*.

ADRIAN MARTIN, *ROUGE*

Over recent months, there has been an ugly war going on between the self-nominated "professionals" and the other-nominated "amateurs" of film criticism—with professional tending to mean "salaried" and, usually (if not exclusively), appearing in a hard-copy print newspaper or magazine, and amateur being equated essentially with self-publication on the Internet, especially in the blogosphere. Armond White, salaried critic for

New York Press, has put it most definitively and pugilistically in an online interview he gave to John Lingan in *Splice Today* (www.splicetoday.com /moving-pictures/interview-armond-white):

> I don't understand why an enthusiast also pretends to be a professional critic. That may just be a delusion proffered by the Internet where people can express their opinions without being required to demonstrate knowledge, experience or exercise intellectual rigor. . . . The differences between amateurs and critics are there to be observed. Think about it: professional publication (getting paid for it) used to imply a standard of knowledge and training. Now everybody thinks they can be a movie critic simply because they have an opinion.

This cult of professionalism—and the embattled defensive maneuvers that accompany it—seems to me a rather recent, and fairly puzzling, phenomenon. Did anyone reading Manny Farber's *Artforum* pieces on film in the 1960s bother to wonder whether he was "demonstrably" a professional of the film-crit trade, or merely a gifted autodidact? What about the great French-Algerian critic Barthélemy Amengual (1919–2005), of whom it is said that he wrote about cinema, passionately and eruditely, for almost sixty years—without, in the vast majority of cases, being paid for it? (See the tribute in *Undercurrent*, no. 1.) Writing and publishing on cinema as communal obsession or private vocation, subsidized expediently by other employment, or nursed along by the occasional, fickle government subsidy—isn't that the authentic history of film criticism, in all its amateur-driven glory? Whereas—certainly it looked this way to me when I was an Angry Young Man of the 1980s, and often still seems exactly the same today—it is the hard-to-budge professionals who (notable exceptions aside) appear to be the phonies, reactionaries, and blowhards of the scene.

It's time for a reality check. In the newsstands of my immediate vicinity in Melbourne, Australia, I used to be able to wander in and randomly buy the latest *Sight & Sound*, *Film Comment*, *Cineaste*—even the more specialized *CineAction* from Canada—all magazines that mix news, information, enthusiasm, good writing, a sense of film history, and in-depth analysis. But for around ten years now, there has only been the likes of *Premiere*, *Empire*, and their many glossy imitators—publications that are devoid of criticism, and full of shameless promotion for the products of the mainstream film industry. If I want to get deeper and read *Cinema*

Scope (Canada), *Screen* (United Kingdom), or *Positif* (France), I need either to subscribe or to have access to a university library. In this situation, there is absolutely no question where I, and most people with a serious interest in cinema, instantly go: online. And there's an added urgency to this situation: if I want to truly explore the films of Pedro Costa, Jia Zhang-ke, or Philippe Garrel, am I going to find anything more than marginal, token coverage of these relatively new, as yet uncanonized figures in even the best, most respected print publications? Again, it's online that the real, probing, extended work is to be found.

I tend to agree with US critic Kent Jones (as expressed in the comments section of Dave Kehr's blog, www.davekehr.com) that the "new amateurs" of the blogosphere are "neither the 'scourge' of cinephilia nor the heralds of a new democratic vista." Nonetheless, a new kind of vista is indeed appearing on the Net: one in which the well-known (such as David Bordwell, www.davidbordwell.net/blog/; or Bertrand Tavernier, www.tavernier .blog.sacd.fr) and the relatively unknown (such as Kimberly Lindbergs, a.k.a. *Cinebeats*, cinebeats.wordpress.com; or Andy Rector, kinoslang.blog spot.com) can be enjoyed and savored as they offer their rolling collages of notes, quotes, reflections, profusely illustrated analytical essays, and discussion with correspondents.

For many years, I encountered young people whose rather alienated fantasy was to be a "professional film reviewer"—where their models were the thumb-wielding Siskel-Ebert types on television or the tough-talking, tick-a-box scribes of *Variety* (on this point, Armond White is correct). One of the happiest results of the rise of the Internet is that, by and large, this particular adolescent fantasy is less prevalent. There is, of course, still plenty of that kind of reviewing—bad, summary, constipated, normative reviewing—that occurs online, in IMDb comments and on the Rotten Tomatoes site (and I try, for the sake of my daily sanity, not to read it). But since (it seems) one no longer needs to climb some punishing hierarchical ladder in the mass media industries in order to voice one's view of movies, a freer mentality has emerged: film critics in the blogosphere tend to think of themselves more as *writers* than as reviewers. That is, they pursue, literally from day to day, the formation of their personal voice, and the evolution of a general "discourse" on film, culture, and the world—rather than seeing their mission as the journalistic knocking off of identically formatted, bite-sized nuggets of rigid opinion. This trend is, I feel, a Good Thing.

Just before the onset of the Internet Age, the French critic-scholar Nicole Brenez described Serge Daney's posthumous volume *L'exercice a été profitable, Monsieur* (1993) as "an interior monologue where writing, speech and conversation, an intimate diary and a sketchy article are mixed together." For Brenez, at stake here was a certain *tone* or style of writing, "something proper to the analysis of cinema," which Daney had "accomplished with staggering facility" at death's door (see her essay "The Ultimate Journey" in *Screening the Past*). At its best, film criticism on the Net takes this mixed, writerly form and projects it into a better tomorrow.

See biographical note on Adrian Martin in chapter 2, p. 96.

ADAM NAYMAN, *EYE WEEKLY* AND *CINEMA SCOPE*

1. This is a question where the age of the respondent will go a long way towards determining the answer, beyond the obvious talking points that online writing is less encumbered by word counts and the need—ever pressing in the print world—for a "topical hook." If I were in my forties, I'd have a better sense of the "impact of Internet criticism on film culture"; as I'm twenty-seven, it's not so easy for me to separate the two. (I'm sorry, I hope that doesn't sound like a cop-out.) Anyway, I don't know how easy (or helpful) it is to draw cut-and-dried distinctions between print criticism and Internet criticism when so many "traditional" critics (great, good, bad, and worse) find so much of their readership online, or maintain or contribute to blogs in addition to their print gigs (like Matt Zoller Seitz did earlier this year, balancing his duties as the proprietor of the endlessly clickable *The House Next Door* with his duties for the *New York Times*). And this doesn't address the issue of freelancers who move freely between venues. Nick Pinkerton, whose work I first discovered through my association with *Reverse Shot*, has recently been contributing to the *Village Voice*. And then there are the likes of Ed Gonzalez (of the online magazine *Slant* and also the *Village Voice*), Michael Joshua Rowin (*Hopeless Abandon, Cineaste*), Michael Sicinski (*The Academic Hack, Cinema Scope*), and many other fine critics who navigate the Internet/print divide every week.

2. I prefer blogs written by good critics, period. If some happen to be "amateurs," in the sense that they don't blog for money or have a paid

byline elsewhere, it's not something that I think twice about. That said, the sheer space that an online venue affords can sometimes bring out the best in print critics accustomed to fighting for column inches.

3. I think the tone of the participation varies. For instance, Girish Shambu's site (www.girishshambu.com) is notable in that I don't think I've ever run across a sincerely antagonistic—or even mildly grumpy—exchange in the comments section. The people who congregate there strike me as being intellectually secure, and thus display no desire to pull out the sabers and start to rattling. The fact that I tend to see the same names posting over and over again in the comments section (and that these names—and/or pseudonyms—tend to belong to other film bloggers) could be used to support the argument that these "cinematic communities" are closed circuits, but the tone there is so generally welcoming that charges of insularity seem churlish. Of course, the same can be said of David Bordwell's characteristically affable homepage (www.davidbordwell.net), and he doesn't publish comments, period (that's one way to head 'em off at the pass). At the other end of the spectrum, there are blogs and websites that have been constructed as (sometimes pseudo-) intellectual hothouses and attract an accordingly combative group of readers, lurkers, and scab pickers. That's a kind of community-building, too, though what's being erected is really the Internet equivalent of fly-over country.

4. I disagree with Kallay's comment. If anything, the sheer volume of mediocre criticism (and noncriticism, from fanboy ramblings to Oscar handicapping) on the Internet (a lot of which, as I've mentioned before, is just traditional print criticism in a different venue) places genuinely good writing in sharper relief. If the traditional film critic is losing anything these days, it's his or her job—but that's a subject for a different and probably more apocalyptic symposium.

Adam Nayman is a film critic based in Toronto. He is the author of *It Doesn't Suck: Showgirls* (2014). He is a contributing writer for *Cineaste*, contributing editor for *Cinema Scope*, and writes frequently for the *Globe and Mail*, *Eye Weekly*, *Cineaste*, *LA Weekly*, and *Elle Canada*, along with such websites as *Reverse Shot*, *The House Next Door*, and *Moving Image Source*. Nayman also lectures on film at the University of Toronto.

THEODOROS PANAYIDES, *THEO'S CENTURY OF MOVIES*

First of all, a line should be drawn between "film culture" and "film criticism." The contribution of online criticism to the former can hardly be overstated—but mostly because it's part of the explosion in film talk produced by the Internet in general. Those of us in provincial towns or out-of-the-way places vividly recall predigital days, when it was literally impossible to be part of a conversation on nonmainstream cinema—except, if you were lucky, with a handful of fellow film buffs, and a few times a year when *Sight & Sound* or *Film Comment* (or *Cineaste*, though I never had access to the magazine) arrived in your mailbox. Cinephilia slowly atrophied, or at best retreated into hard, defensive, little kernels of nostalgic narrow-mindedness. All that has changed—and the situation is immeasurably better. Indeed, with film distribution increasingly closed off to adventurous fare—or just ill-equipped to deal with the boom in films being made—the abundance of websites calling one's attention to small, off-the-radar movies may be our single best way of preserving the culture.

So much for the Internet and film culture. When it comes to film criticism, however, the role of online writing is considerably murkier. The touted advantages—the new terrain potentially carved out—are well known: critics dispense with deadlines and word counts, write about whatever they want, allow themselves to go more in-depth, et cetera. Even with established names, however, freedom is a mixed blessing. Just as good teachers don't necessarily make good friends, a good critic won't necessarily make a good blogger; there are critics I actually think less of since they went online, due to snide remarks or strident political rants included with their (still perceptive) film analysis. As for going more in-depth, the sad truth is that Internet browsing—by its very nature—doesn't lend itself to sustained attention. For me, at least, the temptation to skim a piece and click on the next link is usually overpowering—unless of course (oh the irony) I print it out and peruse it later.

An even greater problem is the blog format itself. Blogs are searchable of course, but the diaristic approach means they live in the moment, each post implicitly superseded by a new one. Not only does this create a more superficial film culture, it makes it difficult, as a practical matter, to engage with a new critic. Reading a handful of arbitrary posts on whatever the writer happened to be watching that week seldom elicits a real sense of their voice or worldview. Emphasis therefore shifts on whether they're entertaining—and, crucially, whether you agree with them.

That's the fallacy behind all the talk of "community": yes, the Internet has made film culture more interactive and participatory—but communities form between like-minded people, leading inevitably to ghettoization and segregation. One sees it in bloggers' irritating habit of praising each other to the skies, as if confirming their mutual good taste. There's a simple but significant change in the dynamic between reader and writer: When Writer X appeared in the paper every Sunday (or in the film magazine every month), one may not have agreed with him but kept checking in, just because he was there. When one visits Blogger X and disagrees with his opinion—with no easy way of getting a handle on his other opinions—one simply stops visiting. Message boards are everywhere, but tend to be for aficionados. Who but a horror fan would visit a board where horror fans debate "suspense versus gore"? (On the other hand, I was first exposed to Mario Bava through an Andrew Mangravite article unexpectedly encountered in *Film Comment.*)

Speaking for myself, almost all the sites I visit on a regular basis are run by people I know personally—notably, Michael Sicinski, Mike D'Angelo, and Dan Sallitt—meaning I already have an interest in their opinions. They also tend to be sites rather than blogs, since I can use them for reference instead of sticking to the subject du jour (though I do check *GreenCine Daily*, just to see what people are talking about); I also read a few professional critics' blogs (Dave Kehr, Michael Atkinson) but often find them less satisfying than reading those critics in print. I'm sure I'm missing out on some fine writers—but there's just too much out there and no easy way to separate the wheat from the chaff.

In sum, I find Jasmina Kallay's claim slightly off target. The traditional film critic—viz., an expert offering authoritative opinions—hasn't been rejected per se. What people are doing online is indulging in film culture, not absorbing film criticism. There's no evidence that kibitzing with like-minded friends—which is what blogs and message boards essentially amount to—is viewed by serious film buffs as a substitute for reading a monograph, or essay, or indeed a specialized film magazine. The critic's basic function, to explain using expert knowledge, remains timeless—and a true critic, one who illuminates instead of just offering opinions, is as rare and valued in the Age of the Internet as he or she ever was. At worst, the online revolution may result in the newsprint reviewer going the way of . . . well, newsprint. That would be a shame. But then most of us provincials didn't get to read many print reviews before the Internet came along anyway.

Theo Panayides lives in Cyprus and cyberspace. He writes for the *Cyprus Mail* and has maintained his film blog, *Theo's Century of Cinema*, since 1997. He has written for *Senses of Cinema*, among other publications. A highly popular blogger, Panayides not only writes for his own blog but has himself been the subject of posts by other passionate film bloggers.

JONATHAN ROSENBAUM, JONATHANROSENBAUM.NET

1a. The Internet has made a significant and profound contribution to film culture. Because the changes it has wrought are ongoing and unfolding, it's still hard to have a comprehensive fix on them.

1b. The Internet can and does both supplement print criticism and carve out distinctive terrain. By broadening the playing field in terms of players, methodologies, audiences, social formations, and outlets, it certainly expands the options. The interactivity of almost immediate feedback, the strengths and limitations of being able to post almost as quickly as one can think (or type), the relative ease of making screen grabs—these and many other aspects of Internet discourse are bringing about changes in content as well as in style and form, shape and size.

1c. Here's just a sample: to varying degrees (some much more regularly than others), I like to read Acquarello, David Bordwell, Zach Campbell, Fred Camper, Roger Ebert, Flavia de la Fuente, Filipe Furtado, Michael E. Grost, Andy Horbal, Christoph Huber, David Hudson, Arianna Huffington, Kent Jones, Dave Kehr, Craig Keller, Glenn Kenny, Naomi Klein, Roger Alan Koza, Laila Lalami, Kevin Lee, Adrian Martin, Dave McDougall, Mark Peranson, Quintín, Andy Rector, Lisa Rosman, Alex Ross, Girish Shambu, Brad Stevens, Terry Teachout, Alexis Tioseco, and Noel Vera. Some of these writers don't have blogs of their own and some aren't even film people, but I've included them if what they've had to say occasionally relates to my film interests.

2a. The strengths and weaknesses of most critics' blogs relate to the fact that they aren't edited—apart from a few like the *Chicago Reader* blogs, whose strengths and weaknesses relate to the fact that they are edited (or at least the initial posters are edited, if not the respondents).

2b. The film blogs I read or consult most regularly at the moment are those maintained by three Davids (Bordwell, Hudson, and Kehr) and Girish. I tend to read Bordwell and Hudson more for content than for style;

among the bloggers whom I tend to read more for style than for content are Glenn Kenny, Quintín, and Lisa Rosman.

2c. I have no idea what differentiates "professional" film critics from "amateur" cinephiles, apart from the fake credentials dispensed by institutional bases—or the fact that "professionals," whether they're academics or journalists, don't have to be cinephiles, don't have to know anything about film, and don't have to know how to write or do research in order to be regarded as "professionals" within their respective professions. As for those with blogs, I prefer those who are cinephiles, know something about film, and know how to write and do research, such as Dave Kehr, even if he didn't make it into Phillip Lopate's *American Movie Critics* collection. I regret that many of the best film critics and film scholars that we have— including Thom Andersen, Raymond Bellour, Janet Bergstrom, Nicole Brenez, Manohla Dargis, Bernard Eisenschitz, Manny Farber, J. Hoberman, Alex Horwath, James Naremore, Gilberto Perez, Donald Phelps, and François Thomas—aren't bloggers, at least as far as I know.

3. Within my own experience, I would say that the "participatory" aspects of film writing, including criticism and scholarship, *have* helped to create a new form of community, and I would further submit that those who consider this claim overblown probably haven't been participants or members of this community, except indirectly. (I've written about this topic elsewhere, in "Film Writing on the Web: Some Personal Reflections," in the Spring 2007 issue of *Film Quarterly*—an article that ironically can't be accessed online.)

I hasten to add that my own recently launched website doesn't invite or allow other participants to post, which suggests that my feelings about this community aren't entirely or exclusively positive, by any means. Nor would I argue that the communities that have formed are always democracies, or that some of these communities wouldn't have been formed without the Internet. (A 2003 collection that I coedited and contributed to—*Movie Mutations: The Changing Face of World Cinephilia*, which is very much concerned with such formations—initially took shape before any of us had e-mail, but e-mail certainly helped us during its final stages.)

4. I agree and on the whole regard this phenomenon as more salutary than regrettable—especially after protracted exposure to more "traditional" criticism in both academia and journalism before the advent of the Internet. Even though I miss such invaluable outposts as *Cahiers du cinéma* during the 1950s and 1960s and Penelope Houston's *Sight & Sound*, not

to mention such eclectic scholars and critics as Raymond Durgnat and Jay Leyda, I can't think of any pre-Internet equivalents for *Senses of Cinema* in its early years, or *Rouge*, either. I also regret that some magazines as important as *Positif* don't have any online presence. Frankly, we get more of everything now on the Internet—including more that's worse than anything we had before as well as more that's better. I regret the way that some critical works that aren't available online have dropped out of our critical canons—Durgnat is a prime example—but this suggests only that we need to make more things available online.

See biographical note on Jonathan Rosenbaum in chapter 1, p. 67.

DAN SALLITT, *THANKS FOR THE USE OF THE HALL*

1. Some forms of Internet criticism, like blogs, have the advantage of having no fixed format. One can write an essay or a paragraph, focus on details or the big picture. Over time, we can hope that this informality liberates critics from the burden of padding and twisting their thoughts to fit established style templates.

The ease of integrating stills and clips into Internet criticism is perhaps as much a danger as a boon nowadays, but on the whole it has to be reckoned as progress.

I'm not a voracious reader of contemporary criticism, on- or off-line. Metablogs like *GreenCine Daily* and Girish Shambu's blog, which compile and recommend activity in the blogosphere, are invaluable. The bloggers I keep up with include established critics like Dave Kehr and David Bordwell, as well as many lesser-known but gifted film thinkers.

2. Any virtue in a critic is valuable. Brevity is certainly a desirable quality in any technological context! One of the best developments of Internet culture is the rise of the specialty blogger who serves a particular niche. Without meaning to single them out, I could cite as examples J. D. Copp's *My Gleanings*, which focuses on French film culture of the 1950s and 1960s; or Michael E. Kerpan's *Roslindale Monogatari*, which specializes in reviews of Asian films that are usually unavailable in the West.

The amateur and the professional each has his or her own demons to overcome. It is not clear to me that the professional has an edge in terms of scholarship or insight.

3. I would think it indisputable that participation in Internet film culture leads to a dramatic increase in real-life, off-line social encounters in movie theaters. I attended New York specialty screenings for many pre-Internet years without achieving much of a social network; now I can't swing a dead cat in a repertory lobby without hitting a few people I've met online. Obviously one needs to live where there are specialty theaters to obtain this effect; but even cinephiles from the sticks meet their online comrades on field trips and at festivals.

The quality of online society is an interesting topic. Mailing lists and forums inevitably recapitulate a rise-and-fall trajectory, passing through periods of great energy and camaraderie, and progressing to a plausible simulation of family life that drives out everyone who doesn't enjoy comfortable repetition and the license to express anger. In theory, I prefer the communal interplay of film groups to the soapbox approach of blogging. But so far the blogosphere has been far more cordial and supportive than any group I've participated in. Maybe the way to go is to give all film writers their little plot of land and hope that it calms them down.

4. The stature and authority of the critic, such as it is, is strongly connected to people's awareness that the critic is being paid and is prestigiously placed. The Internet hasn't destroyed those criteria—it's merely begun to shift them to a new terrain.

It's a toss-up whether we should want or need critics with stature and authority. Presumably some critics use their power for good causes. But power creates orthodoxies that obstruct the exchange of ideas. If the Internet actually manages to destroy the stature and authority of critics, I think I can live with that.

Dan Sallitt is a New York–based filmmaker and critic. He blogs at *Thanks for the Use of the Hall* and also contributes frequently to MUBI and *Senses of Cinema*. Also a screenwriter and director, he wrote and directed *The Unspeakable Act* (2012), *All the Ships at Sea* (2004), *Honeymoon* (1998), and the video *Polly Perverse Strikes Again* (1986).

RICHARD SCHICKEL, *TIME*

Movie reviewing has been a consequential activity in American journalism and intellectual life for less than a half century. Prior to the 1960s it was—at least in the mass media—largely the work of dullards and timeservers, the exceptions being James Agee and a few lonely voices in the little magazines. The rise of more or less serious reviewing coincided with another rise—interest in films imported from abroad (the New Wave, Bergman, Fellini, etc.), which demanded a more complex and knowing response than the typical film critic of the time offered. In this period a number of mass publications reached out to younger, more committed reviewers either to initiate or to upgrade their coverage of films.

The current demise of film reviewing coincides with the aging and death of the great foreign auteurs and with Hollywood's decision to concentrate on the production of blockbusters and tentpoles. I'm not saying that there are no interesting movies to review anymore, but I am saying that week in, week out there are very few of them that require the attentive interest of first-class critical intelligences.

I'm also saying that, instinctively, the editors of major publications, and the mass audiences they serve, understand that and are inclined to cut back on, or eliminate, serious reviewing. The movies that bring out the best in critics are nowadays of interest only to a tiny minority of the popular press's dwindling readership. The vast number of moviegoers—the people whose patronage make Judd Apatow movies or *Batman* sequels such huge international successes—need only know when one of those potential megahits is opening in a theater near them; they really don't give a rat's ass that it has displeased those remaining critical sensibilities that are still aquiver with the desire—the need—for art. Another way of putting this point is that critical opinion about mainstream movies has no capacity to affect the only thing that counts now: the grosses of movies on which the studios have bet a couple of hundred million dollars in production and marketing costs.

This is okay with most newspaper and magazine editors. Most of these people came up out of shoe-leather, reportorial journalism. They tolerated hoity-toity criticism when it seemed to support their needs, but mostly they never really liked us—or their music, art, dance, or book critics either, who are threatened species as well. Like most of their readers these editors wondered what right we had to our opinions, which were formed not by interviewing the masses, but by reporting exclusively on the state of our own minds, spirits, and historical knowledge. These people quite cheerfully believe that they are serving the needs of their readers by running star profiles, reports on visits to sets, and, most important to them, the economic news from showbiz.

I reluctantly suppose they have a point. There is easily understood drama in the box-office fate of high-risk productions; it's something that can be reported pretty much in the terms of a sports section story. That this drama's meaning is ephemeral in comparison to introducing readers to a film that may resonate for decades is of no consequence to editors looking for quick competitive fixes in their (as they see it) life-threatening battle with the Internet.

Ah, the Internet. To be honest, I know very little about it. I don't read a lot of reviews in print, and even fewer on the Net, though I now review—quite happily, I might add—exclusively for Time.com. I'm also aware that a number of my former print colleagues are now blogging, and good for them. But, as far as I know, no cinematic equivalent of Edmund Wilson has yet arisen on the Internet. On the other hand, I don't suppose these people are any more moronic than the "critics" who, until recently, popped up on the eleven o'clock news for their minute of fatuity.

I don't want to nostalgize the movie-reviewing scene as it was from—roughly—the 1960s through the 1980s. It was, at best, a bronze age, not a golden one. Certainly it was a time when aspiring movies, both foreign and domestic, could rely on getting a reasonably intelligent response from the critical community. And, speaking personally, it was fun to be a part of.

To a degree, that remains true. There are mainstream publications, ranging from the *Los Angeles Times* to the *New Yorker* that continue to provide worthwhile responses to the new movies. And there are, of course, intellectual journals, like the *New Republic* and *The Nation*, that remain true to their critical callings. For the foreseeable future, I think that a somewhat more limited critical dialogue about the movies will continue to take place. But I don't know how long it will continue. If American studio movies—the ones that (let's face it) most people are interested in—continue on their path to unreviewability (as I expect they will), that will diminish the need for, as well as the influence of, traditional reviewing. You cannot afford to keep people on the payroll awaiting the arrival of a new movie by Clint Eastwood, George Clooney, or Paul Thomas Anderson. The same will be true if American independent movies continue their descent into faux serious sentimentality—honestly, folks, *The Visitor* is not a movie that could possibly interest a reasonably alert viewer—it's just a nice, comfortable, totally inconsequential little picture that one is grateful for largely because it is not *The Squid and the Whale*. And this says nothing about the generally dismal quality of films from abroad. If the vulgarity of *La vie en rose* or the languid inspirationalism of *The Diving Bell and the Butterfly* are what is on offer from that quarter, then any hope for the innovations, both in style and content, that so stirred the 1960s is bound to be a chilly one.

I guess maybe I'm just ringing variations on a cliché: to have great criticism you need to have great art inspiring it—and we're not in a great movie age. But that endemic problem is surely exacerbated by the current tidal wave of technological changes and by the increasing vulgarity of the profoundly revised culture flowing from those changes. You think movie reviewing is endangered now? Wait until film's chief venue is the iPhone. OK, I'm just kidding. Or am I?

See biographical note on Richard Schickel in chapter 1, p. 74.

CAMPASPE, *SELF-STYLED SIREN*

The Internet has been a democratic revolution in film criticism, giving ordinary cinephiles an ability to be heard that didn't exist before. In terms of critical interaction, we are living in a golden age.

Even though I'm in New York, my odds of having James Wolcott respond to an opinion of mine, or exchanging views with Glenn Kenny, were slim indeed pre-Web. I never went to film school or took a cinema studies class. My qualifications consist of a lifetime of watching movies, reading, and thinking about them. But I started a blog and gradually acquired readers, and now I can go back and forth with people ranging from renowned academics like David Bordwell, to director Raymond De Felitta, to professional critics like Kim Morgan and Jim Emerson, to the self-taught and fiercely intellectual Girish Shambu. The Net gives me direct contact with Andrew Grant, Michael Guillen, Michael W. Phillips, Jonathan Lapper, Zach Campbell, Gerard Jones, Keith Uhlich, Peter Nelhaus, Dan Callahan, Marilyn Ferdinand, John McElwee, Andy Horbal, Nathaniel Rogers, and so many others, all of them strong, intelligent, and provocative writers. And I have knowledgeable commenters, many of whom aren't critics and don't blog, but who show up from places I've never visited (and in some cases have barely heard of) to discuss the movies they love.

Criticism at the big media outlets usually has been release driven, geared to reviewing a new movie in theaters or on DVD. Bloggers write about whatever we please, which I assume is why some professional critics blog on the side. In my case, the movies I care about are long, long past their release dates. At the moment there's no mainstream print publication that will pay me to write about Jean Negulesco or three *Titanic* movies because I happen to feel like it. They probably wouldn't even let me do it for free. That's the whole point. Good blogging should offer you something you can't get from the mainstream. The bloggers who interest me most aren't afraid to be idiosyncratic, like Noel Vera writing up Gerardo de Leon's vampire movies, Kimberly Lindbergs on pinky violence, Larry Aydlette doing a month of Burt Reynolds, or Dennis Cozzalio fearlessly working to resurrect *Mandingo*. Where in the big print publications are you going to find something like that?

One persistent complaint you hear from critics who dislike blogs is that blogs aren't edited. And yes, some bloggers are in desperate need of fact-checking, not to mention proofreading. Still, serious bloggers take care with facts and writing. I don't see errors in the blogs I've named here any more often than I do in print outlets. Another oft-cited drawback is the "post in haste, repent at leisure" phenomenon, where someone offends you, and you throw up a boiling-hot Web rant, and two hours later you realize you have started a fight you don't want. That's less likely to happen in an outlet where there is an editor to apply the brakes, but the Web system is self-correcting. When a blogger goes seriously off the rails there are usually commenters and other bloggers willing to shove him back on track. And those bewailing the persistent lack of civility in some comment sections can always change Internet neighborhoods.

I believe the "conflict" between traditional and Web-based criticism has been overstated. Most of us play nice and enjoy each other's company. Look at the survey of foreign-film favorites conducted last year by blogger Edward Copeland. The idea was to respond to a "100 Best" list from the American Film Institute that many of us found dull and predictable. The AFI list had been followed by a blogger-compiled list that in some ways was worse. Copeland handed out nominating ballots to both bloggers and print critics, some with small audiences and some with very large ones, then threw open the voting to anyone with enough interest to send an e-mail. The resulting list accomplished what all lists do best—it started an argument. But even better was Copeland's compilation of the comments from the nominators and voters. We wound up with a far-ranging survey of foreign film accompanied by remarks that were serious and jokey, erudite and lowbrow, exactly the kind of mix the Internet does best.

I think there are a lot of factors contributing to the traditional film critic's eroding influence, and the proliferation of amateur opinion on the Net is far from the only one. The quote whores, willing to paste up come-hither adjectives like "COLOSSAL!" at the drop of a junket, surely have done as much to make people suspicious of reviewers as some awkwardly written blog posts. More importantly, print is in deep trouble. It's painful to see an excellent critic like Glenn Kenny jettisoned from *Premiere*'s website, but what was worse was watching the print magazine decline in scope until it was shuttered. What we're seeing is a wholesale attempt to trim anything weighing down profits, like Gert Fröbe in *Chitty Chitty Bang Bang* throwing first the sandbags and then the employees over the side of the balloon. Obviously I love blogs, but I don't want to see them replace more traditional outlets. Does anyone? Coexistence would be the ideal, but for print, things are tough all over, and not just for film critics.

So in economic terms, I can't say this is the best of all possible worlds. There are a lot of Web writers producing a lot of good work, but few of us are getting paid for it. For any would-be professional critic, the Web is both godsend and nightmare—intense, endlessly varied, and renewable competition, offered free. I can't guess the end result of that, although I suspect it will end as most revolutions do, with a market-based counterrevolution. I'm just trying to enjoy this wide-open stage while it lasts.

Campaspe is the pseudonym for Farran Smith Nehme, who posts as the Self-Styled Siren on the blog of the same name. Her film writing has appeared in the *Baffler*, the *New York Times*, *Barron's* magazine, and *Cineaste* and on the websites *Moving Image Source*, MUBI, and Fandor. She has written essays for the Criterion Collection, including pieces on David Lean's *This Happy Breed*, Alfred Hitchcock's 1934 version of *The Man Who Knew Too Much*, Ingmar Bergman's *Autumn Sonata*, and, most recently, Lewis Allen's *The Uninvited*. She lives in Brooklyn with her husband, children, and a large collection of film books.

GIRISH SHAMBU, *GIRISH*

Internet criticism has inarguably made a significant contribution to film culture. Rather than merely supplement print criticism, I feel that Internet criticism complements it by providing new modes of thinking, writing, and talking about cinema. These modes are not without their limitations or problems. Then again, let's remember that it's up to us: the powerful and flexible technological paradigm of the Internet can be harnessed and used productively, or its potential can be wasted or put to ill use.

Figure 3.2. Salaried film critics are being jettisoned by print and web publications right and left, reminding blogger Campaspe (*Self-Styled Siren*) of "Gert Fröbe in *Chitty Chitty Bang Bang* throwing first the sandbags and then the employees over the side of the balloon." © United Artists, 1968.

What are some strengths of Internet film criticism? For one, it boosts the traditionally low ratio of writers to readers, allowing informed and valuable "amateur" voices to contribute to cinema discourse. This promotes a more "active" engagement with cinema for large numbers of film lovers. No doubt this also opens the floodgates and threatens to overwhelm us with a deluge of noisy assertion and less-than-useful criticism. But tools like RSS reader software—Google offers one for free—make it possible to tune out all the Internet film writing that one may find unhelpful and concentrate on a smaller segment of handpicked writers and sites (professional or amateur) that one wishes to follow. This software notifies the reader each time a site is updated with a new post or entry; and she can add or remove ("subscribe" or "unsubscribe") sites with ease. I cannot overstate that for the serious reader of Internet film criticism, this efficiency-enhancing tool is a godsend. It maximizes time spent reading a wide range of worthwhile film writing while keeping the loud chorus of Internet noise at bay.

The film blog I find most essential is the aggregator *GreenCine Daily* (daily.greencine.com), run by the Berlin-based David Hudson. He collects and posts the most significant news, links, and pieces of the day. Since I subscribe to and track a large number of film blogs (over one hundred—some are updated with new writing more frequently than others), let me cite, as an example, three or four indispensable bloggers who teach me something new each time I visit them: Kristin Thompson and David Bordwell (www.davidbordwell.net/blog/), Zach Campbell (elusivelucidity.blogspot.com), and Mubarak Ali (supposedaura.blogspot.com). And there are a dozen or more to join them in being especially valuable.

The potential for a new mode of film criticism exists on the Internet: a mode that has access to the formal resources of its very object of study (cinema). Images—both static and moving—and sounds can be pressed into potent and imaginative use to illuminate cinema. Some examples of such criticism include: the series of video essays authored or commissioned by Kevin Lee (alsolikelife.com/shooting/); the special "Image" issue (no. 5) of the Internet film magazine par excellence, *Rouge* (www.rouge.com.au); and the formal analyses of Bordwell/Thompson, Darren Hughes (www.longpauses.com/blog/), or Dan Sallitt (www.panix.com/~sallitt/blog/).

The Internet also holds great potential for communal interactivity and mutual teaching/learning about cinema. So why is it that sometimes the substance-to-noise ratio, the yield, for interactions on the Net can be dismayingly low? Here's a speculation: as children or adolescents, society (family, peers, educators, employers) "teaches" us, in a variety of ways, the social skills we come to possess. These skills become crucial for effective communication, for the social (and teaching/learning) processes we become part of every day. But new technologies bring new exigencies. Communicating on the Internet requires a whole new array of skills, a fresh set of "awarenesses" that must be learned for us to function with success. This is not an easy task. We know that electronic communication is less "rich" than face-to-face communication; greater "redundancies" and more care must be built into electronic messages to compensate for the lack of non-verbal expression, tone of voice, et cetera. Perhaps we should be looking to information/communications experts to teach us about how to create and be part of effective electronic "learning communities." One thing is clear: a cardinal prerequisite for each and every successful interaction on the Net is mutual respect. Without it, any community-building initiative is doomed to failure in ways both small (at the level of a single exchange between two individuals) and large (e.g., the success of a cinephile message board). The comments sections at sites like Dave Kehr's (www.davekehr.com) and *The House Next Door* (www.thehousenextdooronline.com) give us exemplary models of productive cinema discussion and interaction.

Let me conclude with some dreaming. My vision of an Internet film criticism utopia would be a large, international group drawn from three major cinema domains—professional critics, amateur/hobbyist cinephiles, and academic thinkers—engaged in a steady and mutually enriching dialogue. There are already pockets where we can see this happening; it's not an unrealistic hope.

Girish Shambu is a chemical engineer and associate professor of production and operations management at Canisius College, in Buffalo. At the time of this symposium, he identified himself as a cinephile who kept a film blog. His blog, *Girish*, has remained an active and important voice in the film blogosphere, establishing him as a prominent figure in the world of film criticism. His writings have also appeared in *Senses of Cinema* and *Cineaste* and on *The House Next Door*. Shambu is coeditor, with Adrian Martin, of the online journal *LOLA*, and author of *The New Cinephilia* (2014).

MICHAEL SICINSKI, *THE ACADEMIC HACK*

I think there is no question that Internet criticism has altered the terrain of film culture, but it's often frustrating to see just how much of the medium's potential remains underexplored. We are inundated with a lot of jargon designed to heighten our sense that new media are adopted and assimilated more quickly now than before, but this isn't entirely true. The Web is still very new, and in a lot of ways we're still in the "vast wasteland" period, and the so-called Internet 2.0 (which really just refers to the exponential privatization of cyberspace) has only made matters worse. I think back to the last *Cineaste* symposium, on international film criticism. The Internet should ideally provide the platform for a broader, transnational film discourse that accurately mirrors the global scope of film culture itself. This can be glimpsed on occasion, and people like Jonathan Rosenbaum and Mark Peranson have done yeoman work to make this happen, through publishing and symposia as well as forays into the Web. David Bordwell's young site is a wealth of insight into what's happening across the globe, in all realms of film culture. But there's still a long way to go. The US-based Internet film critical community, in particular, remains discouragingly parochial. Nevertheless, the tools are at our disposal to change this.

On the more positive side, one of the fundamental shifts that Internet criticism has produced in film culture (distinctive "critical terrain") is the ability for critics, both professional and amateur, to take it upon themselves to set the agenda for cinephilia, apart from the direct influence of capitalist imperatives. If you are writing for a for-profit publication, in print or on the Web, your weekly cinematic "talking point" will inevitably be decided by external circumstances. On the more benign side, this pertains to release dates, but come on—it's usually about the big honking corporate wannabe blockbuster of the week, as determined by one of the five international media conglomerates, one of which may well issue your paycheck. I am biased, of course, since experimental cinema is my bailiwick, and although I am blessed to have the support of some unusually progressive editors (*Cinema Scope*'s Mark Peranson, *GreenCine Daily*'s David Hudson, and the *Nashville Scene*'s Jim Ridley, in particular), I can't expect to make a living writing about the films of Lynn Marie Kirby, Scott Stark, or Michael Robinson. (And this is completely fair, by the way. No one I'm aware of is making a living by making avant-garde film. Why on earth should I earn my keep writing about it?) Since I can basically resign myself to operating as a semipro critic writing beneath the late-capitalist radar, I have the relative advantage of holding forth as much as I care to about a new video installation by Ernie Gehr, and ignoring *The Incredible Hulk*. This was possible before with DIY publishing and zines, but the Web broadens the reach and allows for indulgent column length beyond the ken of dead-tree distribution.

In addition to the aforementioned strength of self-selected content, the best film sites often have the advantage of personalized prose. I appreciate professionalism in film criticism, in terms of accurate facts, patiently accrued insight over crass hyperbole, and a basic consideration of audience. But when one writes for a broadly based publication, there is often the assumption that one must meet the reader more than halfway. This can take many forms, spanning from lengthy backgrounders on who Hou Hsiao-hsien is, to chunky plot summary of *Flight of the Red Balloon*, to a refusal to cover the film because your readership neither knows nor cares about Hou. (To paraphrase Negativland, "This guy is from China, and who gives a shit.") Since virtually all personal or group-personal blogs (like *The House Next Door* or *Auteurs' Notebook*) presume a specialized audience, a degree of shared language can be assumed, and a critic's individual voice can begin to emerge. This is the space where the critic can settle into her or his own skin and create critical art that transcends the narrow strictures of journalism as defined by a corporate capitalist press. In this regard, Web critics like Mike D'Angelo and Theo Panayides set the standard early on, and critics who've turned to the Web after extensive stints in print, such as Michael Atkinson and Glenn Kenny, have carried on this tradition. There's a "protagonist" at play in their prose, someone whose adventures in cinema you can follow with an interest apart from the gleaning of mere data.

Some of my favorite film sites, such as Vern's *Then Fuck You, Jack* or Victor J. Morton's *Rightwing Film Geek*, occupy niches (diametrically opposed, as it were) that no for-profit publication would support. Similarly, fine writers like Girish Shambu, Ekkehard Knörer, and Christoph Huber tend to use the Web to do what I try to do in my own more modest way, which is to tread that damnably unmarketable line between academic and popular writing, importing concepts while thinning out the jargon. Hell, even Bordwell has used the Web to cut loose a little, although he's thankfully refrained from bashing us Marxo-Lacanians. All of the writers I've mentioned maintain exacting, rigorous standards in their site work, and their critical acumen is present in every post. But I think the Internet has allowed these writers to explore their personal voice in a freer way, and this enriches film culture immensely.

Given the present environment of enforced journalistic mediocrity and corporate line toeing, I suspect that if Kael, Sarris, and Farber were producing their most influential work today, they would have had to start blogs to do it.

Michael Sicinski is a film writer and teacher based in Houston, Texas. A frequent contributor to *Cineaste, Cinema Scope, Moving Image Source,* MUBI, and, previously, to *GreenCine Daily,* he also maintains *The Academic Hack,* a film review site specializing in experimental cinema.

AMY TAUBIN, *FILM COMMENT* AND *ARTFORUM*

1. I use the Internet for research—to find factual information. I also check out *GreenCine Daily* and *Movie City News* as clearinghouses for criticism I might find interesting, and I glance at *IndieWire* for news (not always accurate and almost never contextualized or framed in analysis). The only blog I read regularly is William Gibson's, which these days is mostly photos and rarely has anything to do with film, although he has written wonderfully about movies in the past. Although I try to limit my reading of film criticism, I continue to read the same critics that I have for years: J. Hoberman, Manohla Dargis, Wesley Morris, Kent Jones and my other *Film Comment* colleagues, Rob Nelson, James Quandt and my other *Artforum* colleagues, Lisa Kennedy, A. O. Scott, Nick James and my other *Sight & Sound* colleagues. Although I now read them online, I don't believe any of them have blogs, and if they did, I probably wouldn't read them in that format. (I'll miss reading Paul Arthur more than I can express, and I can't imagine that anyone will take his place.) When a film opens that I particularly care about, I also scope out the responses of interesting critics at a couple of online publications: Ed Gonzales at *Slant* and Michael Joshua Rowin at *The L* magazine come immediately to mind, and I'll also link to anything written by a former student, Steven Boone, a terrific young film writer who sometimes blogs. It may be simply that I'm a loyal reader and that my film criticism queue has long been filled to capacity, but I have no inclination to seek out blogs.

2. See above. I should add that I am shocked at the conformity of style and content on most of the blogs I've looked at. As someone who read the *Village Voice* regularly in the 1960s and early 1970s, when first-person journalism was the rule, I find the use of the first person by bloggers nothing more than a self-aggrandizing reflex. As far as I can see, there isn't a fledgling Jonas Mekas or Jill Johnston among them.

3. I don't participate in the message boards you mention. I have to admit to being unaware of their existence. On the rare occasions I've read blog postings, I've noticed how insular bloggers' "conversations" are and how overwhelmingly the subject is blogging and bloggers (rather than whatever film or event is supposedly the subject of their writing). It's like an extension of the old-fashioned film-buff conversation. Where film buffs define themselves through the factoids they possess, bloggers define themselves

by their instantly formed opinions (this year at Cannes, bloggers were filing columns on their BlackBerrys during screenings—a new low) and by
access—to celebrities, behind-the-scenes news, festivals, et cetera. Ideas
and analysis are notable for their absence from the blogging conversations
I've observed, although this may not be the case at academic film blogs.

Since sniping at other bloggers and, in particular, at critics who don't
blog seems to be a major source of pleasure for the "blogging community,"
I expect to be torn to shreds for these remarks.

4. I never believed that film critics had much stature or authority in
our culture. If there is some kind of perceived loss of same, it probably has
more to do with the fact that the century in which history was written as
cinema is over, and film itself no longer has the cultural, social, and political importance it once did. The Internet has marginalized traditional film
culture. Employing the Internet as a means of distributing and exhibiting
movies will make more movies available to more people, but it will not
restore the status of film culture—neither the status of movies per se nor
the chatter that goes on around them.

Amy Taubin is a contributing writer for *Film Comment* and *Sight & Sound*
magazines and a frequent contributor to *Artforum*. She authored *Taxi Driver*
in the BFI Film Classics series, and her critical essays have appeared in
many collections. From 1987 to 2001 she was film critic for the *Village Voice*,
where she also wrote the Art and Industry column. Taubin was curator of
video and film for the Kitchen, a New York City nonprofit art space. Taubin
also teaches at the School of Visual Arts in New York City.

ANDREW TRACY, *CINEMA SCOPE*

As with most technologies, the dreams and fears that the Internet inspires
move faster and assume far grander or more dire shapes than the thing
itself. It's hardly necessary to rehearse once again the benefits and corresponding detriments for film criticism occasioned by the Age of the Internet. What is most difficult in discussing its "ultimate" effects is the sheer
vastness and mutability of the thing, which renders any judgments placed
upon it helplessly subjective and instantly refutable by counterexample.
The unmanageability of the field often means that what one wishes to find
determines—even more so than usual—what findings get aired.

The great boon of the Internet is that its seeming limitlessness will always necessitate partial judgments, which some will always like to pretend are grand conclusions. What this also means is that the dizzying horizon of possibilities the Net opens up, both positive and negative, are still circumscribed by our ability to deal with those possibilities. To me, those ever-present limits are a rather comforting thought, as it means that for all the changes that the online critical community has introduced to the nature of film discourse and the practice of film criticism, those changes are, on the whole, more ones of method than matter. The same positions, the same canons (however disputed), the same feuds are still being trumpeted by "amateurs" and "professionals" both. Indeed, the ever newness of the technology has given a second wind to past battles, and allowed newcomers to enter the fray heedless of the context or relevance of those battles today (O Kael, thy sting remains).

What has most decisively changed—to draw one of several possible grand conclusions—is that those battles are now undertaken with a far greater degree of informality, and with a corresponding (not inevitable) decline in the practice of film criticism as a literary, and essentially solitary, craft. The increased conversational traffic between critics and readers, which has been one of the great beneficial forces of online criticism, has also, to a certain degree, reduced focus on the critical essay (as per David Bordwell's recent taxonomy) as a sculpted literary object, as something that might be occasioned by an ongoing conversation but is also somewhat autonomous of it. The instant-response capability of the Net has allowed those conversations, arguments, or grudge matches to be played out in something approaching real time—and, at its worst, has had the adverse effect of personalizing film discourse to a truly uncomfortable degree, detaching it wholly from literary models and hurling it into the pettiness, snideness, knee-jerk irrationality, and fatuous posing of everyday speech.

The instant antithesis that such a declaration demands: the above qualities are, of course, not solely the province of everyday speech, nor can the personal ever be diametrically opposed to the literary—critics from Otis Ferguson to James Agee to Jonathan Rosenbaum have explicitly brought their own personal experiences to bear upon their critical practice. The discomfort I refer to is that of seeing writers' dirty laundry aired in public, whether intentionally or unintentionally. Crossing the thin red line between honesty and a rather seamy confessionalism is a proclivity that the Internet seems to encourage with abandon. The self-promotion, self-display, self-pity, and self-debasement on offer throughout the blogo-sphere is not exclusive to it, but it's certainly more abundant. "We don't want other worlds, we want mirrors"; so Stanislaw Lem (via Tarkovsky) informed us, and the New Solipsism of the Net—that world of a million niches, where individual hang-ups are so often narcissistically paraded as a badge of authenticity—often makes film-blog surfing akin to a tracing of pathologies: public diary keeping in the guise of film discourse.

What this (seemingly) infinitely flexible medium of communication has paradoxically encouraged is a relentless hardening of personality, a for-tification and exaltation of one's chosen public self and one's like-minded colleagues/acolytes. It's a strange dynamic, this simultaneous fusion and disconnect between the public and the private that online film discourse enables. Assured of an audience, however infinitesimal, the critic or would-be critic feels free to abjure any pretense of reaching that audience through argument, organization, and eloquence—through structuring prose rather than just employing it.

It's this quality that online criticism has most forcefully helped to degrade, or perhaps it has merely helped to accelerate a degradation that print media had already set in motion. The essay form, the form in which the best film criticism has always been written—even when it travels in the guise of a mere review—is at once a vehicle of personal expression and a means of distancing oneself from one's person; an attempt to define a common object or experience and to convey the reality of it to others through the sharable medium of prose. "My urge to write is an urge not to self-expression but to self-transcendence," said Susan Sontag—one of the best definitions of the essayist's task, and an imperative for the critic. Such generous intent rarely intrudes into the personality worship of the Net—personality in all its commonness and banality, stridently announcing its conviction in its deluded uniqueness.

Overstating the case, of course. Lazy writing and thinking and over-weening self-regard had infested print criticism long before the rise of the Net, and print media had already done more than its share to debase any essayistic critical tradition—which the Net, conversely, has been able to nurture through a relative absence of commercial imperatives. Yet it's pre-cisely because the Internet only accentuates certain dynamics that were already operative in film criticism that any distance we feel we've traveled is at least somewhat illusory. An expanded field of possibilities only throws us back upon our limits the more, and allows our faults a greater range in which to display themselves. What the partly genuine, partly faux "community" of the Net has fostered, however, is the felt sensation of being surrounded by others even when alone—an encroachment upon that solitude, however partial, which is still essential for any kind of literary pursuit. Like filmmakers, film critics always have their potential audiences in mind, but calibrating every line for instant reaction removes criticism from whatever realm of contemplation it inhabits and makes of it nothing but reflexology. It would be ungrateful to slight the impressive volume of film discourse that the Net offers, but sometimes the noise just needs to be turned down if anybody's going to get any damned work done.

Andrew Tracy is managing editor of *Cinema Scope*. He also manages publications for the Toronto International Film Festival and is a staff writer for *Reverse Shot*. His film criticism has been published online at *The House Next Door*, *Slant*, and *Senses of Cinema*, among other sites.

STEPHANIE ZACHAREK, *SALON*

Internet criticism has made a significant contribution to film culture in that it has opened the door for a wide range of voices. But as we're all seeing, it has opened the door too wide: there are so many film enthusiasts—if not actual professional critics, either former or current—writing on the Web that now we're faced with a great deal of noise. Let's not even talk about the zillions of film bloggers who aren't worth reading—who cares about them? The bigger problem is that many of the people writing about film on the Web are knowledgeable and have pretty interesting ideas. Unless you're really systematic about checking up on all of them regularly, there are too many to even read, so good people get lost.

There's something else, too. Even the smart bloggers, the ones who are potentially good writers, often don't shape their pieces. That's the nature of a blog: it's a quick take, a reaction. I don't know that the Internet has done much to destroy the process of thinking seriously about film, but it has had very grave consequences when it comes to writing about film. So much of what you read on the Web is reactive rather than genuinely thoughtful. There are Web publications that still publish longer pieces—*Senses of Cinema*, for example. But as far as blogs go, even though film bloggers are often "real" writers (or could be), what they're doing isn't "real" writing, in terms of rigorously thinking an argument through, of shaping a piece of writing into something that will be interesting, entertaining, informative, and possibly lasting—that is to say, worth reading ten or twenty years from now. That was the reason most of us wanted to become writers in the first place, or so I'd always thought: because we valued the craft itself. Now we're seeing a lot of "I have an opinion! I must state it NOW, before anyone else weighs in." There's a lot of "weighing in" going on, but not so much actual thinking. That's what I find tragic and disheartening.

As far as being a professional writer in this climate goes, of course, the jobs are drying up. And that's a tragedy too—not just for critics who are currently working, but also for serious bloggers who might otherwise dream of someday making a living at writing about film. Film criticism, as a profession, is disappearing. In print media, for years now a lot of editors have been saying, "We don't need a professional film critic—people can get all that stuff on the Web for free." First of all, it's not really "free"— someone's doing the work of putting it out there, at some cost to his/her personal life, if nothing else. Also, it means we have a lot of "information" out there. But information doesn't equal knowledge. And it doesn't equal good writing.

Even though I'm primarily an Internet critic, I don't look at blogs/film websites all that often. I really need to filter out noise rather than add to it, which means I'm sure there are good ones that I'm missing (and some, I'm sure, that I'm simply forgetting to mention here). But I do like to look at *The House Next Door* and *Senses of Cinema*. I like *De Palma a la Mod*, an example of a very specialized site that attracts and/or acts as a sort of clearinghouse for people with some pretty interesting (though sometimes wild!) ideas. I'm also very fond of *The Criterion Contraption* (criterioncollec tion.blogspot.com). I'm really not interested in obsessive loonies who need to prove how much they know about film. I gravitate more toward people who have genuine affection for film—a little obsessiveness is OK (we're all guilty of it), but even among film geeks you often find a kind of macho posturing, and that really turns me off.

In the early days of *Salon*, I loved the participatory aspect—the fact that people could write to me personally just by clicking a link to my e-mail address. And boy, did I get mail! A lot of wonderful, thoughtful stuff from people all over the world. I've made some dear friends for life, just by corresponding with *Salon* readers. Of course, I used to get—and continue to get—hate mail too. Things like, "Girls shouldn't be allowed to write about movies based on comic books." (Amazingly, even in 2008, I still get that one a lot.) When I panned *Titanic* I got a lot of heartfelt letters from teenage girls who accused me of having no heart, of being incapable of receiving or giving love. I came to realize that a lot of these letters had some very strange syntax and spelling issues—because they were coming from Japan! Apparently, there were lots of Japanese teenage girls who were nuts for that movie. They were very polite, but they were so upset that I hated it.

Now, *Salon* has an automated comments section, which means readers—I use the term loosely, because usually they read only the head and the deck of the piece—can post comments directly on the site. So you get a lot of people who have to be the first to post (generally with something idiotic or inflammatory), or people who are very transparently envious that I have a job writing film criticism and they don't. There are intelligent comments, but they're few and far between. It's mostly people who want to make themselves heard, even though they may have little worth saying. Very few people actually engage in discussion of the movie at hand. And so now I get fewer thoughtful, interesting, personal e-mails from readers (the real kind of readers, who actually read) and I miss them terribly. The idea of the Web as a democratic, participatory medium is very grand, but the reality is a total mess. Kind of like democracy itself, come to think of it.

Stephanie Zacharek is film critic for *Time* magazine. She was previously senior writer and film critic for *Salon* and principal film critic for the *Village Voice*. Her book reviews and pop-culture criticism have appeared in the *New York Times*, *Entertainment Weekly*, *Rolling Stone*, *New York* magazine, and *Newsday*. She is a member of the National Society of Film Critics.

CHAPTER 4

Film Criticism: The Next Generation
A CRITICAL SYMPOSIUM

Where have all the film critics gone? The simplistic assumption is that most of the more insightful critics, in both this country and abroad, have been downsized, have retired, or have been forced to migrate to the Web. Yet, what becomes clear in the *Cineaste* survey of film critics under thirty-five is that a certain number of talented young writers still either work exclusively in print or alternate between print publications and the many intelligent websites devoted to online criticism. For twenty- and thirtysomethings, sites such as *Reverse Shot* and *Slant* are, in many respects, their generation's equivalents of *Film Comment* and *Sight & Sound*.

Since 1998, the International Film Festival Rotterdam (IFFR) has nurtured talented writers under thirty through its Trainee Project for Young Critics (in 2013, five critics were selected from among eighty applicants). Among the graduates of the IFFR program are Dennis Lim, Mark Peranson, Gavin Smith, and Adam Nayman, along with Canadian critic Kiva Reardon, whose symposium contribution appears below. The trainees publish review assignments for the festival and often also file festival reports for their own local outlets. Since 2012, "critics' academies" at the Locarno and New York film festivals have offered an ambitious roster of seminars and writing gigs for a similarly high-powered contingent of young writers.

Cineaste editorial board member Richard Porton, who authored the original version of this introduction, suggested that the magazine organize a

Originally published in *Cineaste* 38, no. 2 (Spring 2013); copyright © 2013 by Cineaste, Inc.

symposium devoted to the vexing subject of contemporary cinephilia. After pondering the idea, *Cineaste* editors concluded that instead of polling the usual, albeit distinguished, suspects on the still-evolving nature of cinephilia, it might be more enlightening, and perhaps even more entertaining, to survey young critics, who might take for granted many of the developments graybeards grouse about (e.g., blogging, streaming video, the dearth of print outlets for serious criticism). In this respect, aspects of "Film Criticism: The Next Generation" continue the line of inquiry begun in *Cineaste*'s 2008 investigation, "Film Criticism in the Age of the Internet."

In the earlier "Film Criticism in America Today," in 2000, the participants were staff writers at magazines or newspapers. Contributors to "Film Criticism: The Next Generation" assume that staff positions are few and far between; the vast majority of our respondents are freelancers who supplement their writing with teaching or programming jobs. Many of the symposium entries also reflect this generation's predilection for the confessional mode; whether this penchant for autobiography is a product of blogging culture, the ongoing popularity of memoirs, or other extraneous factors is an open question.

As in the past, *Cineaste* invited an eclectic assortment of working critics to structure their essays around several questions concerning both the art of criticism and the state of contemporary film culture. While most of the contributors hewed closely to the questions below, several writers chose to take them as departure points for essays exploring their personal or aesthetic agendas. Since this outreach yielded many more compelling essays than the magazine could possibly have wedged into its print issue, additional responses appear as Web exclusives in the Spring 2013 and Summer 2013 issues on the *Cineaste* website (www.cineaste.com).

For help in the preparation of this symposium, *Cineaste* expressed thanks to Eric Kohn, Adam Nayman, Mark Peranson, and Bert-Jan Zoet.

1. What does being a film critic mean to you? (More specifically, why do you write film criticism? Whom do you hope to reach, and what do you hope to communicate to them?)

2. What qualities make for a memorable film critique? (Do you think such critiques tend to be positive or negative in tone? Is discussing a film's social or political aspects as important to you as its cinematic qualities and value as art and entertainment?)

3. What was your impetus for becoming a cinephile? How has the digital era redefined cinephilia for your generation?

4. It is often assumed that younger audiences and critics are unduly consumerist and are rarely interested in the nuances of film history. If you believe this is a stereotypical view, how does your own critical practice combat such assumptions?

5. Are there critics, whether still working or from a previous generation, whom you regard as models or mentors? How have they influenced your approach to film criticism?

BEN KENIGSBERG

1. For me, writing criticism began as a productive way to combine my cinephilia with my interest in journalism. Reading weekly reviews was one way in which I first learned about movies (see question 2), so it seemed natural that I might try to write them myself. I still consider reviewing a fundamentally journalistic discipline. I cover film as a beat, prepared to write about any title that's getting a weeklong run—a different skill from focusing only on the movies I'd automatically be interested in. This sort of ecumenical approach doesn't preclude advocacy, analysis, or engagement with film history. At *Time Out*, I write for a general audience. The hope is to get readers to consider films in a new way or, in some cases, to see titles they might not otherwise.

2. My cinephilia began early enough that it's hard to attribute it to a single source. One factor was certainly the availability of VHS, which allowed me to go on my first Hitchcock binge at age eight. But I think a large part of what drew me to movies was reading film criticism. Not canonical pieces, at least at first, just reviews every Friday in *Newsday* and the *New York Times*, to learn about what had opened and what I could see that weekend. I watched a lot of movies, and over time, I developed a better sense of what I liked and why. I had other, perhaps more obvious passageways to obsession: too many hours spent at Film Forum gorging on everything from Lubitsch to Siegel to Fassbinder; cinema studies courses as an undergraduate (including time I was honored to spend in the presence of the late Andrew Sarris); and an epic internship at the *Village Voice*'s film section.

Even early on, I suppose the dawn of the "digital era" played a role in my education. IMDb proved a far more useful resource than the perplexing judgments of *Halliwell's Film Guide,* and the Internet allowed me to read nonlocal critics like Roger Ebert and Jonathan Rosenbaum. (This was many years before I moved to Chicago.) There's no question that the Web and more recently Twitter have made it easier to share opinions. Interconnectivity has also allowed for a degree of specialized criticism, visual analysis, and conversation that could never have existed—or would be unlikely to be published—in print.

In terms of the medium itself, the digital onslaught has its drawbacks. Streaming services like Netflix and Amazon have increased the ease of access to movies—for those titles that make the leap, that is, and many (most?) will not. In Chicago, I still rent from two video stores, Facets and Odd Obsession, and it saddens me whenever this sort of institution is deemed anachronistic. The most alarming development is the loss of celluloid, particularly as it pertains to older films. As archives become reluctant to lend ever-more-fragile prints to repertory programmers, future cinephiles won't be able to take the path I took.

3. The notion that young critics are somehow more callow or consumerist than their older counterparts is a stereotype, possibly one perpetrated by each generation on the next. I see no shortage of young people when I frequent a Bresson retro or check out a 70 mm print of *Cheyenne Autumn*, and the man dubbed "king of the blurbs" in a December edition of the *Washington Post* has been a mainstay in the profession for decades. I don't think the myth of youthful doltishness is so pervasive that it requires conscious counteraction, but I hope my knowledge of film comes through when I write. I cover festivals, note influences, run pieces on major retrospectives and revivals, and promote awareness of prints and the physical medium. It's not as if there's some magic way to prove your credentials. Sensibility and seriousness will always separate cinephiles from boosters, regardless of age.

4. I'm a bit of an anomaly in my generation, because I've always been in print. Whether it was for the local pennysaver, the college paper, the *Voice*, or now *Time Out*, I learned to write on a weekly deadline schedule. I still practice the dying art of the word count. Of course, virtually all print publications are also Web publications now, and blogging adds a degree of speed and follow-up that I think improves the discourse on the whole—provided one treats it with the same standards one applies to a regular article. I'd be saddened not to work in print; nothing replicates the thrill of seeing your byline on a page.

The challenges of the current climate have little to do with age and everything to do with the changing nature of journalism. Online, your writing can reach more readers than ever before, but that's a double-edged sword. With more voices, it's harder to be original—and even if you have a scoop, there are sites that exist exclusively to poach Web hits from your work. The increased pressure to rush to judgment is also one of the more frustrating trends in film criticism. It sometimes feels as though if you haven't tweeted about the new Terrence Malick within one hour of its first screening, the blogosphere has moved on. That said, even in print, a review always functions as a sort of time capsule. Newspaper critics have traditionally written on short deadlines. The notion that judgments were less hasty or better considered in the pre-Web era may be a fallacy.

5. I have countless mentors and influences, too many to name here. I think Roger Ebert's credo ("A movie is not about what it is about. It is about how it is about it") is the most useful distillation of the profession ever devised, but I would single out, above all, the writers I worked with at the *Voice*, especially then film editor Dennis Lim and J. Hoberman. Hoberman's work is the first that taught me to view films not just as self-contained universes, but also as formal and social objects. That's an essential lesson in any cinephile's education.

Ben Kenigsberg is a frequent contributor to the *New York Times* and *Variety*. He was film editor at *Time Out Chicago* from 2011 to 2013 and served as a staff critic for the magazine beginning in 2006. Kenigsberg wrote frequently for the *Village Voice* and has also written for *Slate*, the *A.V. Club*, *Vulture*, *LA Weekly*, *IndieWire*, *In These Times*, and *Time Out New York*.

GABE KLINGER

My career as a film critic has been purely tactical. I've always loved the activity of watching films and at a certain point wanted to access as many and as ample a variety of films as possible. In the real world, this is difficult to do without a lot of money and time. As a teenager growing up in Europe, I went to cinemas every day and would end up with very little money to do anything else. Many of my peers at the uppity private school I attended took drugs and went out to clubs or on weekend ski trips or whatever rich kids do. I couldn't afford to do much of that, so I got stuck with movies, which were pretty cheap before the euro took over.

At a film festival, I got acquainted with some publicists who agreed to let me know when press screenings were happening. I think that's when it occurred to me to start writing as a journalist to be able to get on these lists and see movies for free. Since press screenings typically took place on weekdays, I skipped school to be able to attend them. Later, reading writers like Jonathan Rosenbaum, I had the itch to travel in order to see films that weren't showing near me. Unfortunately, I didn't quite have the bank for that yet. By this time, I had dropped out of school entirely and my parents cut my allowance. Rosenbaum told me I should apply for the young critic trainee program at the International Film Festival Rotterdam, which I did.

The festival wrote to say I wasn't accepted but happily granted me press credentials as a kind of recompense. At this stage I hadn't published in any legitimate outlets, and so I took the gesture from Rotterdam as an investment in my potential to become a real film critic. I saved up enough money, and it ended up being like a university film studies track compressed into ten very long days, where your teachers are Raúl Ruiz, Michael Snow, and Hou Hsiao-hsien. I've been going back to Rotterdam for the last eleven years and in 2012 got to cocurate an extensive retrospective for the festival. Rotterdam bet its resources on me when I was still a teenager, and over the years I have been able to reciprocate in many different ways.

Once I asked Peter Cowie who the ideal audience for a film critic should be. He shot back, "You write lucidly." The response has not satisfied me, and for the most part I do not feel read, understood, or made to feel that I've contributed meaningfully to the way that people understand or consume cinema, except occasionally from a small coterie of fellow critics. Is that enough? I think most of the time it is. I love my peers and they've helped me a lot, both personally and in the way that I'm able to derive pleasure and meaning from the culture around me. I've been able to sort out a lot of my own thoughts related to the kinds of films I like, and I've had a lot of (free) fun going to the cinema, traveling to cinema events, and meeting people who also love cinema.

At the beginning of my professional career, no one bothered to tell me that the new business model for publications didn't include a living wage for film critics. I invested a lot of time in developing my skill level as a film writer only to see few returns. I turned to other activities, like programming and teaching, in an attempt to make money. Ultimately, writing, curating, and lecturing all became part of the same pursuit in my mind, born out of the necessity to earn a living but then remaining so creatively and intellectually. Today I've kept the professional momentum going long enough that I only have to worry about money from time to time and can luxuriate in the activity of viewing films as part of a healthy cultural diet that also includes going to museums, listening to all kinds of music, and eating and drinking well. This is important. The qualities of a Brueghel painting or a bottle of quadruple-fermented Belgian beer can inform your view as a film critic as much as the audiovisual object you've been designated.

I resisted the autobiographical route here, but I think it's important to be clear about one's background and what kind of access one's class (upper middle, in my case) affords him. There are episodes in a privileged life that should give any individual pause about his position in the world. When I go to a film festival and get to watch an archival rarity on the big screen, I try to remind myself how extraordinarily lucky I am to be doing that. I guess then the idea is not to selfishly keep this experience to myself but to devise a way to share it with others through writing, programming, and teaching. I hope my generation agrees that it's important to impart as much as possible—or else it's all quite meaningless. I should say, almost as a footnote, that I'm generally appalled by the state of the world and hope more and more that my generation can turn people on to films that take a radical stake in the issues that concern all of us: the disequilibrium of wealth, the rights of immigrants, the environment . . . to be continued on this point.

Some influences (off the top of my head): Manny Farber and J. Hoberman taught me to be descriptive and not hastily evaluative. Serge Daney and Jonathan Rosenbaum persuaded me that it isn't enough to be satisfied with just what's in front of you. Manohla Dargis and Kent Jones showed (and continue to show) me a lot of humanity and kindness. Chris Fujiwara taught me not to use quotations. David Bordwell and Tom Gunning, pioneers, opened up so many analytical pathways that it's difficult to summarize their contribution.

And lastly, I'm always drawn to Jean-Luc Godard, the most inscrutable of mentors.

Gabe Klinger is a Chicago-based writer, film critic, programmer, and teacher. He teaches courses in cinema theory at Columbia College and is a visiting lecturer at the University of Illinois at Chicago. Klinger has written about cinema for numerous journals, including *Film Comment*, *Cinema Scope*, *Moving Image Source*, *De Filmkrant*, *IndieWire*, and *Undercurrent*. Beyond working as a critic and programmer, Klinger has consulted for various museums and festivals. He directed his debut feature film, *Double Play*, in 2013.

MICHAEL KORESKY

It's hard to say why I continue to write film criticism, but I can easily describe why I began to write film criticism. In 2001, when I was fresh out of college, the landscape for intelligent, thoughtful, cinephile-geared writing was limited. While working at *Film Comment*, it struck some of my fellow committed film friends and me that there ought to be something like that magazine, with its balance of academia and populism, for a younger generation. This was before the ascendance of blog culture; there were scattered websites devoted to more serious-minded film discussion but not much of a sense of community around it. So we decided to start our own magazine, *Reverse Shot*, which was, at first, a print endeavor, paid for out of our own pockets and distributed around Manhattan as staple-bound, 8½-inch by 5½-inch packets. Featuring reviews of new movies as well as "symposia" on themes that would encourage us to keep a dialogue going with film history, *Reverse Shot* was both a way to get our brash, twenty-something voices heard as well as an attempt to fill a perceived gap. As the years went on, and we, out of necessity and good sense, took it online, we realized we were part of a quietly growing nascent movement that would establish and confirm a cinephile community that remains strong and vibrant today.

Though this all seems tactical, it never felt so; rather it was just a logical step, an outgrowth of my cinephilic nature, which I had nurtured from a young age. Growing up in suburbia, I didn't have easy access to repertory houses, but thankfully I was part of the home-video age, and local libraries were stocking enough Bergman, Kurosawa, and Fellini titles to make the local Blockbuster selections seem paltry by comparison. Already I was drawing a line in the sand between the mainstream and the esoteric, and, as a child must, I chose sides. The bounty of titles seemed so great that it wasn't until years later that I discovered that, of course, this was but a tiny sampling of the world's important cinema. Today, access is the key word of the new generation of online cinephiles: even as film itself disappears, works, essential and non-, are more readily available, or potentially locatable, as downloads, torrents, or bootlegs. This has undoubtedly enriched the general landscape—with more access to films, the more writing on those films appears, and the more resources we have to keep film alive.

And "keeping film alive" is not simply a cliché, but now a call to arms. In the face of a culture that continually wants to bury the form (critics have been carping about the "death of film" for decades, and with the ascent of digital the doomsayers have only grown louder), the new generation of film lovers has become more wonderfully militant. Writing about cinema is not merely an act of passion but of persuasion—to convince others that film is vital and constantly evolving, not devolving. An engagement with cinema's history is the clearest way to combat such shortsightedness, and this generation of cinephiles is nothing if not constantly negotiating film's present with its past. There seem to be just as many websites and blogs devoted to classic and rare movies, Hollywood and beyond, as there are more contemporary-minded, review-oriented ones. And since these sites are easily accessible to all, not just cinephiles who once upon a time had to scour the film-studies shelves of libraries to find discussions of off-mainstream fare, it's arguable that cinephilia is less marginalized, and haler than at any point in the past. Though one is forced to use her or his good sense and taste to separate the wheat from the acres of chaff, the plurality of voices can only be deemed a positive development. Not only does the variety of strong writers naturally provide more support for good films that might otherwise fall through the cracks, it also creates a healthily competitive atmosphere in which critics step up their game and sharpen and fine-tune their voices.

The greatest drawback to this new culture of online criticism—most of it admirably, if unfortunately, written for no greater compensation than page views and words of encouragement from fellow writers—is the lack of editorial control and guidance. The relationship between critic and editor is an important part of the writing process, and its absence is keenly felt almost across the board. It's a reason why *Reverse Shot* has always been run on the traditional principles of a print publication, with a strong editorial hand. It's also why I continue to be influenced not by blog writers (though there are many capable and brilliant ones), but by those published writers who are not necessarily "online presences" and whose essays evince a certain amount of polish. Spontaneity and sophistication go hand in hand in the work of Kent Jones, Geoffrey O'Brien, James Quandt, Howard Hampton, Amy Taubin—some I know personally, others only by their writing, but all of them I consider guiding lights and mentors, and upcoming generations of film writers would do well to aspire to such reasoned, enriching prose.

The print and online worlds have been duking it out in an epic battle for supremacy most of the time I've been a film writer, and only in recent years do they seem to have come to a tentative reconciliation. Vanishing formats, like print and celluloid, have increasingly come to rely on the digital culture to survive at all, so it's silly for the two to remain sparring from opposite ends of the ring. That excellent writing is being done online from a wondrous variety of intelligent, engaged, and rigorous critics should be obvious to anyone who cares enough to look for it. Film criticism is alive and well, and as healthy as it's ever been, although due to the shriveling up of paying outlets it's increasingly become the pursuit of the passionate. So despite all challenges, it will continue to push ahead.

Michael Koresky became editorial director for *Film Comment* in 2016. Previously he was a staff writer for the Criterion Collection, cofounder and editor of *Reverse Shot*, and director of publications and marketing at Metrograph, a New York repertory cinema. His writings have appeared in *Film Comment*, *Sight & Sound*, *Cinema Scope*, *IndieWire*, *Moving Image Source*, and the *Village Voice*.

KIVA REARDON

1. As I came to professional paid criticism through starting a personal blog, I feel I must say I write for myself. This is, of course, both narcissistic and idealistic. Narcissistic, for it assumes anyone would care about my opinion on film (and, to my own [dis]credit, means I value my own thoughts enough to share them). At the same time, it is idealistic as I'm always aware of my audience or editor. While this doesn't dictate my evaluation of a film, it does shape how I write—the tone and scope. Thus, for me, being a film critic lies somewhere in between these two poles: writing about those stubborn ideas that lodge in your head while watching a film, while also aspiring to reach the reader and thus add something to the collective conversation about film. I have no one reader in mind, but with each review hope to communicate some nugget about the film, or film culture, which would cause them to continue to reflect beyond the review.

2. I find this question hard to answer without asking just what is meant by "cinephile." This isn't an evasive tactic but an honest quandary, as the word has many meanings. For me, the term means something like "passionate skepticism," where I'm deeply invested in thinking through the films I see, but hopefully never let myself be carried away by a blinding

fandom. The digital era has made this easier with increased access, as films that were once impossible to see can now be streamed on places such as MUBI or Festival Scope. While cult or foreign films were once harder to find, they're now often only a click away. (A few years ago, I recall struggling to find a copy of Menahem Golan's *Operation Thunderbolt*; now the entire film is on YouTube.) Some might argue the catch of this is the loss of the obscure, but I see it as broadening knowledge for those who seek it. Access doesn't always mean dilution. What this means for the film medium and viewing practices, is, however, an issue. (YouTube isn't an ideal way to watch most things.) Films will be watched in different ways, but to announce the death of cinema is preemptive.

3. I am wary of broad generalizations, especially concerning generations. As film and capital are inexorably linked, I would posit there has never been a time in which promotional film writing didn't exist. That said, there is a pressure that comes with increasingly short-form criticism, as page space (both online and in print) shrinks. The catchier the review, the more likely it is to be featured/promoted. In two hundred words, it's difficult to flesh out how any film connects to a broader historical trend. It isn't, however, impossible. In my own critical practice I like to think that I have respect for my readers; if I make a passing reference to another director, film, or historic trend, this may very well spur them to look it up. Film history, and indeed theory, need not be purposefully dense and elitist, and while I don't equate criticism and teaching, there is a place in a critical practice to share your own knowledge with the hope that it will expand the interests of those reading it. Perhaps I am idealist, but I share Mark Cousins's beautiful sentiment at the beginning of *The Story of Film: An Odyssey*, that it is not money that drives films, but ideas. Indeed, if the inverse were true, we'd have nothing to write about.

4. I am deeply indebted to, and ardently respect, the world of online film criticism. I find the sentiment to write it off as diluting the practice to be not only elitist, but also insufferable. For most, "online criticism" has become unjustly synonymous with—and I loathe using this sexist term—"fanboy" culture, the same consumerist form of writing that was addressed in an earlier question. This, however, overlooks the vast opportunity that writing for the Web has offered to other marginalized forms of criticism—feminist, Marxist, queer, genre cinema, to name a few. That said, a specific challenge, which I struggle with in writing predominantly online, is the lack of editing. This is partly due to the speed at which one

Figure 4.1. Menahem Golan's *Operation Thunderbolt*, about the hijacking of the Air France passenger jet forced to land in Entebbe, was a difficult film to find in the predigital, pre-Internet days. Thanks to greater digital- and Internet-era accessibility, film critic Kiva Reardon was able to locate it on YouTube—and outlets such as Netflix also began to make the film available. © Canon Film Distributors/Warner Bros., 1977.

is expected to turn around reviews—though print deadlines can be just as quick—but also is more broadly an epidemic of the laissez-faire attitude towards the Web. There is a need to shift how we view (or read) online criticism, respecting the medium itself as not being ephemeral. (And there are sites, *Reverse Shot*, for instance, which approach HTML-based publishing with the same rigor as pulp-based print.)

5. The writing on MUBI consistently motivates and inspires me (for instance, the recent "Tony Scott: A Moving Target" project). There is a certain pleasure in reading Armond White's hyperbolic criticism, which is often more revealing of the mode of criticism than any one film. I enjoy Manohla Dargis, the theoretical thinking of Vivian Sobchack, and revisiting Pauline Kael's old reviews. I'm also fortunate to live in a city (Toronto) with a thriving film community and admire the work in our two alt weeklies, *The Grid* and *Now*, as well as the *Globe and Mail*. As for mentors, I'm

very lucky to have been encouraged by Adam Nayman (*The Grid, Cinema Scope*). Although our friendship was forged in a dispute over *The Social Network*, he has always encouraged my writing. More importantly, while we disagree on films (what's the point of this whole field if we don't?), his evenhanded and respectful way of dissenting is something I aspire to. Never back down from your view, but make sure it can be eloquently backed up.

Kiva Reardon is a programming associate at the Toronto International Film Festival and founding editor of *Cléo*, a journal on film and feminism. Her writing has appeared in *Hazlitt*, the *Globe and Mail*, *Maisonneuve*, the *National Post*, and the *A.V. Club*, among other publications. She had previously worked at Qatar's Doha Film Institute and for the Hot Docs Canadian International Documentary Film Festival. She appears on Viceland's *VICE Guide to Film* and is biweekly cohost of the Toronto International Film Festival's *Yo, Adrian*, a podcast about life at the movies.

ANDREW TRACY

1. More and more, to me being a film critic means writing less and less—which is an advantage I have in that writing film criticism for a living is not, and has never been, my primary means of subsistence. Further, in my prematurely curmudgeonly view there is simply too much being written about too many (and too many unworthy) things too often by too many people—and many of those people, if you'll pardon me, have little business writing in the first place. And while, of course, there are many exceptionally intelligent people contributing to that great weekly critical clusterfuck, I often feel that their impressive efforts can be spread thin when trying to keep up with so much cultural chaff. This is not to say that I write about more "important" things when I choose to write, or that anything I write is necessarily more incisive, profound, thought through, et cetera. Rather, due to both my temperament and my limitations, I try to marshal my ever-shrinking intellectual resources to give as concerted and thorough an account of a subject as I can, and with enough mental space and time to iron out any contradictions, glibness, and debilitating conceptual weaknesses. Hopefully.

As for whom I hope to reach, I can honestly say I have no idea. I certainly don't write only to please myself—firstly because I'm rarely pleased with what I write, and secondly because if I'm going to sweat bullets to crank out a piece, it's damn well going to be read by someone. But whoever they are, the audience that does end up reading what I write is going to be a pretty self-selecting one, both by dint of the publications my work typically appears in and the incurable inside-baseball nature of my writing, which often assumes a more than passing familiarity with the subject(s) at hand.

2. To repeat some self-evident things I have written elsewhere on this subject, I think the digital era has allowed "my generation" (and older ones, I would say) (a) access to an astronomically wider range of films (in some ways, and not in others), (b) a wider appreciation of film history (in some ways, and not in others), (c) a wider, if not always wiser, definition of the canon, (d) a complacency about the vast amount of work that still remains unavailable for viewing, and thus about the perpetual limitations to our access to films, our appreciation of film history, and our definitions of the canon, (e) a corresponding complacency about the fundamental physical and existential transformations being wrought upon the medium by said digital era.

3. I don't really know what "unduly consumerist" means (can one be duly consumerist?), though I suspect it has some affinities with the "cultural chaff" gripe I aired in number 1. But that phenomenon is hardly exclusive to younger audiences and critics, and I would say that both their ignorance of and interest in film history is roughly proportionate to what it has been for that same cohort in times past. Like most passions, cinephilia is a choice, and the depth of each person's interest and knowledge is going to extend exactly as far as they wish to pursue it. As for my own "practice," many of the pieces I've been happiest with myself—e.g., my article on the Library of America's Manny Farber anthology in these very pages (*Cineaste* 35, no. 2 [Spring 2010])—are those which take advantage of my dilettantish former academic career in history in order to offer a more contextualized view of their often well-covered subjects. Again, hopefully.

4. As stated above, I'm unusually privileged in that I've now worked as a critic for almost a decade while never trying to make my living at this very difficult game, and also privileged in that my early affiliation with *Cinema Scope* has often opened doors to other publications and institutions to which I otherwise might have had to struggle quite hard to obtain entrée.

Re: part two, apart from my ongoing contributions to the great online journal *Reverse Shot* (happy tenth anniversary!), almost all of my infrequent work is limited to print publications. But as doubtless many other contributors to this symposium will point out, the boundaries between print and online are becoming increasingly porous: much of what I write for the print edition of *Scope* ends up on our website anyway (and for free, at that).

5. Jonathan Rosenbaum's fierce and dogged insistence on incorporating the social, cultural, political, and ideological positioning of films into his criticism was and remains an invaluable influence on me, even though I feel that of late he has sacrificed insight for a rather dogmatic stridency. David Bordwell, who is not technically a critic, writes some of the best film criticism out there: his attention to formal choices, his clear-eyed common sense, and his demonstration that there are indeed some verifiably true things about films are enormously refreshing in light of the nonsense that so often gets spouted under the guise of criticism. Bordwell's empiricism doesn't shut down speculation or interpretation at all, whether or not he's interested in doing those things himself—rather, for those of us inclined to undertake such activities, his approach allows us to do so from a more solid base of knowledge and reasoning.

But my chief, and very unfashionable, influence has remained constant for well over a decade. Stanley Kauffmann is one of the best and most underrecognized critics (at least among hard-core cinephiles) who ever plied the trade: in the unfailing elegance and wit of his prose, the breadth of artistic, cultural, and historical reference he brought to bear, his resolute levelheadedness, his belief that film is an art worthy to stand with all others, and his insistence that we do not need to bend, prevaricate, or otherwise degrade the aesthetic and intellectual standards established by those other arts in order to recognize film as such. I can't think of another writer who so finely and faithfully maintained the belles-lettristic tradition in the field of film criticism, and I can't imagine anyone since who could possibly maintain that tradition into the future.

See biographical note on Andrew Tracy in chapter 3, p. 201.

CHAPTER 5

"I Still Love Going to Movies"

AN INTERVIEW WITH PAULINE KAEL

Leonard Quart

Pauline Kael shook up the film critical scene with her controversial 1963 *Film Quarterly* article "Circles and Squares," which attacked auteurist critics for their attempts to promote hack Hollywood films as serious works of art. During the mid-1960s, she freelanced, writing for *McCall's*, the *New Republic*, *Sight & Sound*, and *Life*, among other magazines. From 1968 on, she wrote lengthy critical essays and reviews on film for the *New Yorker*, retiring in 1991. At the time of this interview in 1999, Kael was eighty-one. She lived alone in a large, handsome, book-filled stone-and-shingle house on the heights overlooking Great Barrington, Massachusetts. For a number of years she had suffered from Parkinson's, and she was no longer able to write. Though she was fragile, and age and disease had slowed her down, her passion for film and her intellectual combativeness, vitality, and independence remained intact when *Cineaste* spoke to her, two years before her death in 2001.

In her heyday Pauline Kael was arguably the most formidable and influential voice in American film criticism, as *Cineaste* contributing editor Leonard Quart pointed out in his original introduction to this interview (here somewhat updated and revised). Kael was awarded a Guggenheim Fellowship, and her fourth book, *Deeper into Movies* (1973), was the first volume on film to win a National Book Award. She was perceived then as somebody with the

Originally published in *Cineaste* 25, no. 2 (Spring 2000); copyright © 2000 by Cineaste, Inc.

power to make or break a film. It was her exultant reviews of films like Arthur Penn's *Bonnie and Clyde* and Robert Altman's *Nashville* (e.g., "It's a pure emotional high, and you don't come down when the picture is over") that made the critical reputations of those films.

Kael never permitted her readers to remain neutral—evoking either devotion or antipathy, whether from ordinary readers, directors, studios, or other critics. Her criticism was tendentious and at times outrageous, but never dull. One could find many of her critical judgments maddening, but her probing, idiosyncratic, and thoroughly original essays were always worth a careful reading. Her colloquial and pungent prose style was both accessible and exhilarating—the work of a gifted writer who saw criticism as an art, and cared as much about metaphors, witty barbs, and turns of phrase as about critical opinions.

Kael had a disdain for theory, eschewing abstraction and critical objectivity for the primacy of her subjective, gut response to the actors, performances, sociological import, and directorial style of a film. She embraced kinetic, unsentimental films and directors given to expressionist excess, like Peckinpah, Scorsese, and De Palma, but had a harder time accepting more meditative modernist directors, like Bresson. She had only contempt for big Hollywood movies like *The Sound of Music* (dubbing it "The Sound of Money"), for liberal, middlebrow films like *Coming Home,* and for studio executives who "love to play God with other people's creations" and mangle them. At the same time, she loved popular entertainment for the pleasure it provided. But, unlike many film academics, she never pretentiously discovered hidden meanings in schlock or inflated its significance by comparing a film like *Pretty Woman* to a Shakespeare or Shaw play. Nobody could ever call Kael's critical responses schematic or programmed. She was always unpredictable, and she had the gift of capturing the nature of a film in a single sentence.

For these many reasons, Kael inspired more than a few film critics of the generation to follow—both through her writing and, for some, through her personal encouragement. At a 2007 film criticism symposium moderated by *Cineaste* editors Richard Porton and Cynthia Lucia at Boston's Coolidge Corner Theatre, film critics Stephanie Zacharek, Owen Gleiberman, and others recalled—as they have elsewhere, in their writings—how thrilled they were to receive responses from Kael to their youthful letters expressing admiration and aspirations to follow in her footsteps. Some were fortunate enough to further receive Kael's generously active mentoring. The term "Paulette," in fact, was coined (sometimes in positive and other times in pejorative contexts) to describe film critics whose work reflected Kael's discernable, indelible influence.

Pauline Kael was a singular voice in the history of American film criticism. Leonard Quart interviewed Kael in the summer of 1999, discussing her critical career and early influences, her philosophy of criticism, great American films of the 1970s, her thoughts about retirement, and her provocative views on some contemporaneous American movies. *Cineaste* expressed thanks to Jim Schlachter for transcribing the taped interview.

CINEASTE: Who were your critical models?

PAULINE KAEL: When I was a teenage philosophy student at Berkeley, my friends and I were devoted to James Agee because he was the only movie critic who spoke to us. He reacted to movies the way somebody smart, honest, and knowledgeable would respond. Most of the other critics gave us blather about the virtues and defects of a movie, and all the good it was going to do. But he reacted emotionally and intellectually to what was on the screen, and we could recognize the feelings.

When I began writing I cited eastern critics (I was living on the West Coast then)—the best ones, such as Dwight Macdonald and Stanley Kauffmann—as examples of the mandarin solemnity that was sinking movie criticism. They didn't react personally to what was on the screen; they filtered the movies through a set of ideas. I tried in most of my West Coast pieces to differentiate myself from them. People on the West Coast saw the movies then in terms of what the eastern critics told them they should see, and often there were wonderful movies they didn't pay attention to or rejected.

CINEASTE: Did you think that your emphasis on a personal voice demanded that you be as much a writer as a critic?

KAEL: Leslie Fiedler once said something like, "A critic is an artist or he is nothing." I've always thought of criticism as a branch of writing, and if you don't honor the readers enough to write your very damned best, you're insulting them and you're insulting the work you're dealing with.

CINEASTE: Were there other critical models besides Agee?

KAEL: He was the dominant one for films. I felt an excitement reading Agee. Later, I also enjoyed reading Manny Farber—he's an amazing man, and a friend—but I don't feel a rapport with his responses to movie content. It's his analysis of the film frame as if it were a painter's canvas that's a real contribution. I also read people who were critics for a brief period, or who had an unusual slant, like Cecelia Ager and Vachel Lindsay and Robert Warshow, and who sometimes did wonderful pieces on film. I was more influenced, though, by literary critics, such as R. P. Blackmur. But I think it was more my friends' reactions and arguing with them about movies that got me interested—friends such as Robert Duncan, the poet, and another poet, Robert Horan.

I had no intention of becoming a movie critic; that was a surprise. The law school at Berkeley accepted me, but I got involved with Horan and lost interest. I started to write, and everything snapped together in my life when I wrote about movies. The pieces I submitted were accepted immediately, whereas my articles on books and other subjects interested editors, but I was told to try them again. Still, I didn't get a position as a movie critic until I was close to fifty. I put an awful lot of energy into crappy jobs, but I couldn't get a job as a critic. I did a movie review program on KPFA in Berkeley, and it got a lot of attention, but I didn't get paid. The one related job I had was running twin Berkeley movie revival theaters for five years.

CINEASTE: What is your opinion of academic film theory and criticism?

KAEL: I think much of it is useless. I don't understand how people get so far from common sense that they make difficulties where none exist. I tried to deal with some of that when I wrote about Kracauer's theory of film back in 1962. Contemporary theorists—feminist and deconstructionist—seem even more obfuscatory. So often the theories that are promoted are a way for professors to show off and be idolized by their students. Once this giant cloak of theory is placed over the movie-viewing experience, the students are at the mercy of the teachers because they are told that nothing they have felt is relevant.

It seems to me that the critic's task should be to help people see more in the work than they might see without him. That's a modest function, and you don't need a big theory for it.

CINEASTE: What audience did you aim your criticism for, and did you ever tailor your criticism for the *New Yorker*'s educated, upper-middle-class audience?

KAEL: I didn't aim it at any particular audience. Anybody who wants to read it can. I wrote the same way for *McCall's* as for the *New Yorker*, and I always tried to be as direct and plain as I could be. I got a terrific amount of mail at the *New Yorker*—an awful lot of it was from high school and college kids. You don't expect *New Yorker* readers to be that young, and sometimes they live in the Midwest or the South and they may be the only people in their small town who get the magazine. They often said that I had made them feel they weren't crazy—that they had read my criticism and it coincided with what they felt. When William Shawn first talked to me about writing for the *New Yorker*, I was dubious because of the swank look; the ads and the whole silky texture of the magazine was a real turn-off. I gradually talked myself into it, and was happy that I did.

CINEASTE: Do you see the rise of independent American film as a genuine alternative to Hollywood?

KAEL: Does that mean that Hollywood is the Great Satan? Generally, as soon as you make a successful independent film, Hollywood releases it anyway. What matters is that the movies reach an audience. I rather like Michael Almereyda's films, but does it matter where he got the money? You're always borrowing your money from someone. There have been good films, like *Flirting with Disaster*, *Chasing Amy*, and *One False Move*. I'm not sure which you would consider independent. I love *Vanya on 42nd Street*. It was certainly a small production. But I also loved the MGM musical *Pennies from Heaven*, and I preferred *Last of the Mohicans* to *Safe*.

CINEASTE: You have usually critically excoriated "middlebrow" films like *Chariots of Fire* and liberal, well-meaning films like *Coming Home*. How did your *New Yorker* readers respond to those critiques?

KAEL: The angriest mail I got was from disliking *Rain Man*, because people felt I was somehow putting down autism. It's the same problem I had when I said that *Shoah* was not a masterwork. They think you're being insensitive about the Holocaust, even though they themselves may have seen the movie in a blind torpor of tears and suffering. There's often confusion in the audience's mind between a movie's message and the quality of the movie.

Liberal moviegoers are so sweet on themselves, and liberal movies flatter them. I tried to make distinctions. For example, in *Coming Home*, the right-wing military officer was lousy in bed, and the mutilated boy wasn't just a liberal fellow—he was also great in bed. It's as if the liberals want to congratulate themselves in every possible way. The plot of a film like that is offensively convenient. It violates what you know about the world. *The Front* never came close to what we saw in the press, which was that the blacklisted writers looked like Woody Allen and the men who fronted for them looked handsome and distinguished. In the movie they reversed it. All I ask for is a little tough-mindedness. Can't educated liberals see that a movie like *American Beauty* sucks up to them at every plot turn?

CINEASTE: If you dislike films that project a facile, sentimentally liberal perspective, what is your critical response to two genuinely left, sometimes politically heavy directors whom *Cineaste* often interviews— Ken Loach and John Sayles?

KAEL: I agree that they're not facile, but their political content is heavy only in the sense of being often oppressive. Loach is no bundle of joy, and Sayles is a literal-minded director. His work is decent, intelligent, and filled with integrity, but he doesn't have a real instinct for making movies. There are kids who make movies when they're twenty-five, who know nothing about anything else, but who have a flair for the medium. He doesn't.

But to go back: I didn't dislike *American Beauty*—I hated it. It's not that it's badly made—it isn't. It has snappy rhythms and Kevin Spacey's line readings are very smart, and Annette Bening is skillful in the scene where she beats up on herself. But the picture is a con. It buries us under the same load of attitudes that were tried out in *Carnal Knowledge* and *The Ice Storm*, with the nice, trustworthy young dope dealers of *Easy Rider*. Maybe audiences are so familiar with this set of antisuburbia attitudes that it's developed into its own movie genre.

CINEASTE: Did you allow your political sympathies to intrude when dealing with right-wing films like Don Siegel's *Dirty Harry*?

KAEL: I don't know what you mean by "intrude." The movie was popular with people partly because of its right-wing attitude, but they didn't necessarily recognize it as right wing. Certainly most of the press didn't, not when it first came out. I felt it necessary to treat it as a political work because its politics offended me. Eastwood's films are right-wing in a way that doesn't get analyzed because they're not explicitly so. I'm amazed at the number of critics who let his attitudes slide right by them.

CINEASTE: If you're critical of the Eastwood films, why is Peckinpah such a favorite?

KAEL: I never said he was a good person. But he had a true gift as a moviemaker. I try to look at the quality of the work. That includes the quality of the perceptions.

CINEASTE: Was Peckinpah's machismo more posture than reality?

KAEL: Yes, but he lived the posture.

CINEASTE: What was the nature of your relationship with Altman? Cassavetes?

KAEL: I loved Altman's work, but I was never close to him personally. I've met him only a few times. He's a great risk-taking director, and *McCabe and Mrs. Miller* and *Nashville* are superb films. And I wouldn't leave out *The Long Goodbye*, *Thieves Like Us*, or *Vincent and Theo*.

I met Cassavetes one evening on the West Coast just as I was coming east in the mid-1960s. It's very strange that Cassavetes, who is identified with new directions in movies, had so little knowledge of movie history; he didn't know the experimental work of the 1920s and 1930s—I was flabbergasted to learn he had never heard of *Un chien andalou*. There was a naïve streak in a lot of what he did. I liked *Shadows*, but felt that he got into a trap with the films he made with Ben Gazzara and Peter Falk. I felt those movies were tediously overwrought and that he—out of love, no doubt—did the wrong things with Gena Rowlands, who had been wonderful in her pre-Cassavetes work. I felt she was acting all the time in Cassavetes's movies; she never relaxed. It drove me crazy. I don't fully understand why so many students and young directors made an idol of Cassavetes. But I could see that they were deeply affected by those movies in which men sit around joshing each other and being piggish.

CINEASTE: Few film critics have your capacity to capture the quality of an actor's performance.

KAEL: I think so much of what we respond to in fictional movies is acting. That's one of the elements that's often left out when people talk theoretically about movies. They forget it's the human material we go to see. A movie without actors is not, generally, a very compelling or memorable movie. There are great documentarians, of course, and directors who can make movies where we're fascinated by the whole look and feel of things, but generally we need an actor, or a group of actors, to involve us emotionally. Or just to pep things up—the way Christopher Plummer peps up *The Insider*. Or the way Mike Nichols brings something dazzling and original to *The Designated Mourner*. Or, to look back, the way that Debra Winger could be piercing. Movies give us presents: people like Judy Davis, a wizard at conveying neurosis and making it witty. They give us the sheer charm of Drew Barrymore.

CINEASTE: A film critic has written that Pauline Kael seems the most "un-self-doubting person I've ever met." Given that you write your pieces after only a single viewing, has your self-confidence as a critic ever faltered?

KAEL: I'm not a very insecure person. Maybe that has something to do with my having been the youngest in a large family. I was funny, so they liked me and always encouraged me to talk. Would you rather I studied a movie? I feel I get the movie on the first viewing more completely than I would get it if I labored over it. I like it best on the first viewing because it's got suspense and excitement. This is a personal thing that I should probably never have told people about.

I come from a generation that saw movies once. When 16 mm projectors and film societies started to become popular, and, more recently, when movie lovers got videos, they began to poke over the movies endlessly. I think that violates people's first reactions; they become scholars of movies instead of people who respond to what they see. I don't know why it would make those scholars feel better if I said I watched a picture five times.

CINEASTE: If you don't doubt your perceptions, did you ever doubt your talent?

KAEL: I doubted my talent when I first tried to write. I was very pedestrian at first because I'd had a lot of university and was a very good student. You learn to be pedestrian—to footnote everything and do all those damned things that they teach you to do at college that turn you into a bore. I doubted that I could ever loosen up enough as a writer, but I found I loosened up when I wrote about movies.

CINEASTE: Did being a woman present an obstacle to your career?

KAEL: I never thought of it as a career. It was more like a folly. Well, women then were gutsier than contemporary women think they were. And maybe I didn't think about obstacles because I never felt any pressure in the family to be any less than the boys.

It never scared me to be one of the few women critics in a male world. I found that many of the male critics could be quite stupid. But more often they were just scared people who wanted to be in the swing of things, and tried to please their editors and the advertisers. They were gutless, and they're still gutless. On the other hand, a lot of them lost their jobs by panning movies that had heavy advertising budgets.

CINEASTE: Some critics have asserted that your real genius is sociological, and that you are antagonistic to the European art film.

KAEL: That's a hostile question, especially with the sly "your real genius." Have you read me on Gillo Pontecorvo or Francesco Rosi? Have you read me on Bertolucci's *1900* or Truffaut's *Story of Adele H.* or Visconti's *The Leopard* or Tanner's *Jonah Who Will Be 25 in the Year 2000* or Bellocchio's *China Is Near* and *Leap into the Void*? Or do you think I should have written more about the draggy ones? I know there are people who fell in love with the high-art qualities of movies, but I can't fully account for that phenomenon. I understand that some people dismiss me as "the ultimate democrat" because I like a lot of popular movies. But popular movies got me involved in movies in the first place, so why deny them now? Many of us love the actors, the excitement, the trashiness, the pure pleasure, without feeling we need to justify that pleasure.

CINEASTE: Still, given your critical sympathy for the sexual energy and kineticism of films, isn't there some implicit antipathy towards art films directed by people like Dreyer and Bresson?

KAEL: You've got the wrong people for me to be antipathetic towards. I'm not generally drawn to the directors who make spiritual movies that seem to occur in slow motion, such as Ozu and Tarkovsky. But I loved Dreyer's *Passion of Joan of Arc* and *Day of Wrath*. As he got older, I didn't respond to his movies in the same way. They simply weren't for me. Bresson is the only director who made a film (*Diary of a Country Priest*) that put me to sleep twice. I don't understand why, since I think it's a great movie; I admired it while I was dozing.

CINEASTE: What about Godard?

KAEL: Oh, I loved writing about films like *La chinoise*, *Masculine/Feminine*, and *Weekend*. I was hired at the *New Yorker* partly because of a piece I wrote on Godard in the *New Republic*. William Shawn read it, and, having admired some of Godard's movies, talked to me about coming to the *New Yorker*.

CINEASTE: The 1970s were arguably the most creative decade in American film. What is your opinion of *Easy Riders, Raging Bulls*, Peter Biskind's account of 1970s Hollywood?

KAEL: It's a piece of semifictional fantasy. He puts me, for instance, in the middle of situations that I don't know anything about. And I've heard from other people that he treated them similarly. But it's his approach that's really sickening. Here's this great, heroic era in American films, when people were struggling against all sorts of forces to get their visions onto the screen, and they achieved it. It's the greatest period in our movies. Films like *Nashville*, and *The Godfather I* and *II*, *The Landlord*, *Shampoo*, *Mean Streets*, *McCabe and Mrs. Miller*—dozens of great films, or at least amazing ones, were made. And all Biskind does is try to make everybody look like a backstabbing egomaniac. However they may have misbehaved, those people had to have some commitment to the art of movies to do what they did. He's using our knowledge of how great that period was as a come-on to read about how swinish the people were.

CINEASTE: Would you say that the 1970s directors were able to harness their self-destructiveness into creative work?

KAEL: Their self-destructiveness sometimes worked against them. Ashby died young, and some of the others never did as great work again. Directors such as Wyler and Hitchcock who lasted for decades had a studio system supporting them. These guys had to pull it all out of themselves. It's miraculous, really, what they did. When you go to a movie now, it doesn't give you the tensions in how people live now in the way their movies did.

CINEASTE: What has happened to Coppola's career since the 1970s?

KAEL: I think people sometimes burn themselves out, particularly in making movies. He's done some respectable work since then. Some of his pictures have promising conceptions, such as *Peggy Sue Got Married* and *Tucker* and *Gardens of Stone*, but he doesn't fully realize them. He seems content just to put on a show. Still, if you have three or four great films to your credit, you shouldn't be called a failure. An author who cared about movies would be obsessed with what a director like Coppola put into his movies—not what (in Biskind's fancy) burned him out.

CINEASTE: You have written that you find films "a supremely pleasurable art form." Are there any contemporary movies that provide that kind of emotional and aesthetic charge?

KAEL: No, they don't offer that richness. The 1970s movies meant so much to young people. They argued, thought about, and were really upset by them. Movies affected audiences in so many ways. The kids who said "Wow!" when they came out of a movie and couldn't say any more were expressing some deep feeling. The kids who come out of *Twister* may say "Wow!" but it isn't the same "Wow!" It's a special-effects "Wow!" This doesn't mean that movies are finished; it means they're changing.

CINEASTE: In your critique of Kubrick's *A Clockwork Orange*, you wrote that Kubrick is "a clean-minded pornographer," that the film's sex "has no sensuality," and its characters are "frigidly, pedantically calculated." Isn't much of that critique also applicable to *Eyes Wide Shut?*

KAEL: Yes, the two movies have a spirit in common. The big difference is that *A Clockwork Orange* got to audiences. It works. While *Eyes Wide Shut* is a lousy movie, *A Clockwork Orange* is lousy in its attitudes and its thinking. Sometimes I hate a movie more when it works. The thuggishness of *Clockwork* is comparable to that of some of the Nazi films that worked. *Eyes Wide Shut* can be ignored. Scene by scene it's a howl.

Figure 5.1. "The thuggishness of *Clockwork* is comparable to that of some of the Nazi films that worked," Pauline Kael said of Stanley Kubrick's *A Clockwork Orange.* © Warner Bros., 1971.

CINEASTE: You've written that in *E.T.,* "Spielberg is like a boy soprano lilting with joy." What's your opinion of his ostensibly more morally and socially serious work?

KAEL: He's gone to the pulpit. Everything has gone flat in his directing. He had such flair in *Jaws* and his early movies. He seemed so sophisticated and intelligent—so sharp about what he was doing. There's still a little bit of joy in the *Indiana Jones* trilogy. But now there's a real simpleton's morality that he hands the audience, like when you hear him on television saying that everyone should be forced to see *Schindler's List.* Soon he and Benigni, director of *Life is Beautiful,* will be working up a doubles act.

CINEASTE: As a critic, were your relations with directors ever problematic?

KAEL: No one enjoys being panned, but what are you suggesting? That my relations with directors were improper? I don't think they were. How can you be involved in an art form and not know some of the artists? The important thing is to be honest about your responses to their work and not to profiteer off knowing them.

Directors or actors do often say horrible things about a critic in print or on TV, and then they may take the critic aside and try to square themselves. They may write you a little private apology—the apology is always private.

CINEASTE: Am I right that stylistically you prefer films that are looser, more improvisational and intuitive than those that are more calibrated?

KAEL: In general. But some calibrated movies work wonderfully. De Palma is not an improvisational director, and he's made several movies, such as *Casualties of War*, that are as good as anything done in this country in the last decades. Some of his very early films were improvisational. *Hi, Mom!*, for one, is whoopingly giddy about race relations. I don't mind elegant, careful filmmaking, such as Fred Schepisi's work in *The Russia House*. I mind the overly controlled film, one too bound by a classic structure. I like movies to have a little looseness and bounce.

CINEASTE: Are you particularly susceptible to films that aestheticize kitsch—movies like Sergio Leone's *Once Upon a Time in America*— that are vivid and vital despite having a second-rate script?

KAEL: Are you trying to nail me for something? I don't understand what. The Sergio Leone film was kitsch alright—lyric kitsch; its image of Lower East Side immigrant life is absurd. Leone's father worked in movies, and the boy literally grew up in the studio. All his movies are dream-plays. They derive from movies, and he didn't seem to have any experience outside of movies and studio life. So his movies are visions sustained from childhood of Hollywood's version of America.

CINEASTE: Do you feel that some of the younger American directors have been shaped by movies and nothing more?

KAEL: They sometimes make a smashing beginning and you think they're going to have a great career, but they lack the experience, the point of view, and the taste. They haven't read enough or seen enough of the other arts to grow as moviemakers. Movies by themselves are not enough of an education. Leone breathed a kind of visionary poetry into his epics, but most of the American film-school kids have a hard time projecting a strong enough vision to make their movies cohere. Then there are the very young kids who only seem to know hand-me-downs from Tarantino.

CINEASTE: You've also written about the special "aphrodisia" of films. Would you expand on what you mean?

KAEL: When we first begin seeing movies they have an erotic quality. It's one of the first attractions that kids feel for them. Part of the appeal of movies is the sensuality of the actors and actresses—their faces give us pleasure. The symmetry of their beauty is often very appealing. They're more beautiful than the people we see in life, and they give us standards of beauty and feeling. Their emotions transform us. Someone like Garbo opened up a generation of moviegoers to a kind of sensuality they didn't experience elsewhere. There's something about a great actress on screen that can be extraordinary. Garbo had something else plus beauty. When you watch her in the scene in *A Woman of Affairs*, where she inhales a bouquet of roses, you think you've never seen anyone inhale so completely. It's not comparable to what goes on on the stage. The closeness of the people and the darkness of the movie theater and the private quality of our emotions make us relate to the actors in a special way. I think people make a huge mistake when they become interested in film and don't give the actors and actresses more consideration. The popular audience reacts to a movie as a work with so-and-so. That really is the basis of our wanting to see more movies.

That's still the case. There's nothing comparable to the pleasure people get from soaking in beauty. Teenagers certainly go to movies to look at Leonardo DiCaprio, Keanu Reeves, and Brendan Fraser. Girls and boys want to look at Rachel Weisz, Jenna Elfman, Jennifer Lopez, and Gina Gershon, with her lovely warped smile—ideal for villainy. Even the special effects in *The Matrix* had a poetic quality—I don't think people were going to see that film for the story. There's something about watching Sigourney Weaver in *Galaxy Quest* that's like nothing else. It's fun watching big, strong women strutting their stuff. It's fun seeing talent reveal itself—I'm thinking of Amanda Plummer and Madeleine Stowe and Fairuza Balk.

CINEASTE: Do you have regrets about pieces you have written, and, more importantly, about retiring?

KAEL: I have regrets about retiring, and some of them have to do with extraordinary movies that I would have loved to review. I still love going to movies, and I feel a pang, sometimes, that I could have pointed out to readers some good ones that were passed over or disappeared. I would have liked to write positive things about Bertolucci's *Besieged*, Bertrand Blier's *My Man*, and Lasse Hallström's *The Cider House Rules*. Chris Marker's *The Last Bolshevik* is a great film that almost no one has seen. *Run Lola Run* I'd have enjoyed reviewing. *Being John Malkovich* kept me on my toes for about twenty minutes, but by the time it was over I felt no desire to write about it.

In any case, I no longer have the words; I hesitate. I loved writing about movies and I miss it, of course. But look: I was lucky, I lived in the century of pop. Or let me put it this way: culture without pop, to quote a phrase from McCabe, "freezes my soul." That's why I'm not so keen on Loach and Sayles. David O. Russell's political farce *Three Kings* is much more to my taste. I like the mixture of tones—*Gunga Din* and something of what Richard Lester was trying for in *How I Won the War*. It's got pop in it; it keeps you alive.

Leonard Quart is professor emeritus of cinema at the City University of New York, College of Staten Island. He is a *Cineaste* contributing editor and is coauthor of *American Film and Society since 1945*, fourth edition (2011), and *The Films of Mike Leigh* (2000). Quart has written numerous reviews and essays on film and other subjects for magazines such as *Dissent*, *Film Quarterly*, the *London Magazine*, and *Logos*, among others.

CHAPTER 6

Cult Films, Commentary Tracks, and Censorious Critics

AN INTERVIEW WITH JOHN BLOOM

Gary Crowdus

Just as devotees of foreign "art films" and Hollywood classics have long enjoyed deluxe DVD editions of their favorite films released by the Criterion Collection, fans of horror, sci-fi, exploitation, and cult films are now being catered to, Criterion-style, by Elite Entertainment's new Millennium Edition DVD releases of such genre classics as *Night of the Living Dead* (1968), George Romero's debut feature about a marauding army of flesh-eating zombies; Stuart Gordon's *Re-Animator* (1985), an H. P. Lovecraft–inspired tale of a mad scientist who brings the dead back to life; and Meir Zarchi's *I Spit on Your Grave* (1978), acclaimed or reviled, depending on your point of view, as the most powerful or repulsive rape-revenge melodrama ever filmed.

The Millennium Edition releases boast state-of-the-art visual and audio improvements, filmmaker commentary tracks and interviews, poster and photo galleries, deleted scenes, storyboards, and other features, as *Cineaste* editor in chief Gary Crowdus noted in the original version of this introduction (here slightly updated and revised). The 2003 DVD release of *I Spit on Your Grave*, with a commentary track by drive-in-movie critic and cult-film guru Joe Bob Briggs was the occasion of this interview. Joe Bob Briggs is an exploitation film connoisseur and the alter ego of writer John Bloom. Former host of the Movie Channel's *Drive-In Theater* and TNT's *MonsterVision*, Joe Bob is the author of, among several other books, *The Cosmic Wisdom of Joe Bob Briggs*, *A Guide to Western Civilization or My Story*, *Profoundly Disturbing*:

Originally published in *Cineaste* 28, no. 3 (Summer 2003); copyright © 2003 by Cineaste, Inc.

The Shocking Movies That Changed History, and *Profoundly Erotic: Sexy Movies That Changed History.* He is also the author of the United Press International columns "Joe Bob's Drive-In," "The Vegas Guy," and "Joe Bob's America." By 2003, John Bloom, as Joe Bob Briggs, had been working the exploitation-film beat for over twenty years and was the ideal film critic to record a commentary track for *I Spit on Your Grave.*

In fact, Joe Bob has long been a champion of this much-maligned film, which he feels was "destroyed" by critics, in particular by Roger Ebert and Gene Siskel, who wrote extremely negative reviews in their respective Chicago newspapers and then targeted the film for further abuse in their popular *Sneak Previews* TV program. Ebert, for example, called the film "sick, reprehensible, and contemptible . . . an expression of the most diseased and perverted darker human natures," while Siskel suggested that *I Spit on Your Grave* might actually encourage men to go out and commit rapes.

In his commentary track, John Bloom, as Joe Bob, makes a passionate defense of the film and contends with the statements of Siskel and Ebert, as well as some feminist critics, on a virtual scene-by-scene basis. He makes a convincing case to illustrate their misreadings of the film and their utterly wrongheaded condemnations of it. Lauding the film's stark dramatic simplicity—little dialogue, no music score, and an almost documentary-like visual style—Joe Bob argues that the film clearly privileges the female victim's point of view. There is nothing remotely sexual or titillating about the film, which, he claims, emphasizes the brutality of the rape scenes. At one point, he exasperatedly asks, "If Susan Brownmiller, Andrea Dworkin, and Gloria Steinem all tried to come up with their version of the nature of rape, wouldn't it look something like this?"

Joe Bob's commentary also provides engaging background information on the filmmakers and performers (e.g., the lead actress, Camille Keaton, is the grandniece of Buster!) and discusses *I Spit on Your Grave* and the rape-revenge melodrama within a broader social and cultural context. He compares the film to a variety of other rape-revenge films and at various points, belying his good-ol'-boy pose, makes references to Aristotle, Greek tragedy, Puccini, and Shakespeare.

Bloom's commentary as Joe Bob—which earned the Best Commentary Track award from DVDcentral—is as entertaining as it is informative, with many amusing observations about the film's aesthetic shortcomings, including the mediocre acting by the male performers, the numerous plot clichés and illogicalities, the cheesy special effects, and the film's inspired ad campaign. Commenting on the promotional poster's tagline—"This woman has just cut, chopped, broken and burned five men beyond recognition . . . but no jury in America would ever convict her!"—Joe Bob points out, "Actually she only killed four men, not five, and she didn't really burn any of them, but they don't call 'em exploitation movies for nothing, do they?"

Cineaste editor in chief Gary Crowdus met with John Bloom in 2003 to talk about the critical attacks on the film, Bloom's views on DVD commentary tracks, and why he is fascinated with exploitation films.

CINEASTE: What do you think of commentary tracks in general?

JOHN BLOOM: Most commentary tracks I find boring. Most directors aren't very good commentators on their own movies. They tend to assault us with trivia and with the mechanics of the filmmaking process. There are exceptions—there are directors who would make good critics or good public speakers—but for the most part I don't find them that enlightening. It could be partly the way they're put together.

CINEASTE: Do you think they often just go in and wing it?

BLOOM: Yes, they do, but they should be prodded to talk about specific things that are germane to the experience, not just trivia about the making of the movie.

CINEASTE: What's needed is a commentary-track director, someone who sets the agenda for the writer or director or whoever, to point out the issues they should be addressing.

BLOOM: A commentary-track director—it would be like a radio director.

CINEASTE: What sort of preparation did you do for your commentary track?

BLOOM: I've answered questions about *I Spit on Your Grave* for years from cult-film fans. It's always been of interest because there are very few films that are considered "too grisly for cable." When I was doing my show on the Movie Channel and later on TNT, especially when I was on premium cable, in the 1980s, they would show anything. But they would not show *I Spit on Your Grave* on pay cable. It was just considered beyond the pale. It's refreshing that we still have movies that are considered beyond the pale, because we were getting to the point where anything was acceptable on cable TV.

But any movie that's that despised becomes a matter of intense curiosity to everyone, and they want to know where they can get the video and what's the story behind the film. What also makes it particularly interesting is that nobody involved with the film ever did anything else. People always want to know what happened to Meir Zarchi. He eventually did make another film, *Don't Mess with My Sister*, which is not a very successful film. I never asked him directly whether *I Spit on Your Grave* ruined his career, but I get the impression that he did find it hard to work after the movie came out. And the fact that Camille Keaton was not seen much after that, and that none of the sleazy rapists ever did anything else, made it one of those . . .

CINEASTE: Career-ending movies?

BLOOM: Yeah, that was the myth, anyway—that it was the ultimate résumé killer.

CINEASTE: Have you spoken to Zarchi lately?

BLOOM: I have traded letters and notes and e-mails with him. He was a little hesitant to talk about the Siskel and Ebert attack on his film, so he was happy to know I was also doing a commentary track because he knew I would talk about it. It was fairly devastating for him at the time that the two most influential film critics in America had said his film was the best argument for censorship that they'd ever seen, that no one should ever see this film, and that type of thing. He honestly thought he was making a feminist film, and an antirape film, and he was just as shocked as anyone when Siskel and Ebert turned on the film.

CINEASTE: Both Siskel's and Ebert's reviews of *I Spit on Your Grave* seem to be reviewing the audience as much as the film itself.

BLOOM: Yeah, that was my problem with them, because it's the classic censor's argument that the film is not bad for you and me, but it's bad for those other people over there who will take it in the wrong way and will go off the deep end and commit some violent crime or something. As I've always said, whenever I'm asked to talk about this, there are no "other people," because we all relate to the screen image in the same way. What I thought was disingenuous about their argument was that they said there were people in the theater who seemed to be approving of the rape. Well, as you know, if you've ever gone to any grind house—a kung-fu house, or horror theater, or any of those great Times Square theaters of the past—people would talk to the screen. They wouldn't always talk to the screen in an honest manner. The scarier the film was, the more macho the guys in the theater would become, as a defense. People talk to the screen at the point where they are most uncomfortable.

CINEASTE: The phenomenon of nervous laughter.

BLOOM: So the fact that some guy in the theater, especially if he was with other guys, said, "Yeah, get her, get that bitch!" or whatever he said, you could take the same incident and argue completely the opposite, that the film made the guy so uncomfortable that he had to deal with it socially at that moment. I've never bought the argument that the things people do or say in theaters indicate that the film is having some sort of horrendous effect. There was a similar case in California a few years ago when some kids were suspended from school because they reacted "inappropriately" to an execution scene in *Schindler's List*. I'm sure they were reacting "inappropriately" because they were disturbed by that scene and because they were kids. They were using whatever defense mechanisms they had.

I also think *I Spit on Your Grave* was an easy film to pick on. It was a fringe film. It wasn't going to have any defenders at that particular time. Janet Maslin used to do the same thing in the *New York Times*. She would pick on films that none of her readers would ever watch, like *Dr. Butcher, M.D.*, and you'd read the article and wonder if she had watched it herself. Getting back to Siskel's and Ebert's reviews, though, I do think that men tend to be more disturbed by rape than women are. The reason you don't normally see rape on screen—even when it's depicted, it's not actually shown on screen—is that the filmmakers are men, and something about rape is more disturbing to them than murder.

CINEASTE: What is especially remarkable is that not only did Siskel and Ebert write these condemnatory reviews but they also called for and actually succeeded in having the film withdrawn from Chicago theaters.

BLOOM: Yeah, I've never heard of that before. I didn't know that film critics had that kind of power.

CINEASTE: One suspects that Ebert may not be quite as vociferous about the film today, some twenty-five years later.

BLOOM: I wouldn't expect him to be, but he made his comments about *I Spit on Your Grave* after he had written the screenplay for *Beyond the Valley of the Dolls,* which I don't think is the most pro-woman thing ever written [laughs]. During the 1980s there were a lot of organized feminist protests against slasher films as being antiwoman, but I never thought slasher films were antiwoman. They always featured a triumphant woman, usually the sole survivor was a woman, and there weren't any more females than males killed, so I never understood the protests.

CINEASTE: Doesn't Carol Clover, in her book *Men, Women, and Chain Saws,* offer a feminist defense of those films?

BLOOM: Yes, Carol Clover, who is a professor of comparative literature at UC–Berkeley and who somehow got interested in Joe Bob Briggs–type films, examined them from a feminist standpoint and concluded that they are strongly feminist. Now I'm paraphrasing and abridging her—and maybe she wouldn't put it in these stark terms, she might hedge it about with various disclaimers—but essentially she discovers that the audience for these horror films is mainly pubescent boys. The only formula that works features a female protagonist with male characteristics—they frequently have male names like Jamie or Stretch—so that the male audience sees the threat through a female persona who must triumph over the creepy male threat. Actually, it's not a male threat, it's a confused-gender threat, a transvestite usually, like Leatherface in *The Texas Chain Saw Massacre*—and Clover goes into great detail about how these are strongly affirmative statements about women.

CINEASTE: Do you buy it?

BLOOM: I absolutely buy it. Every example she uses—and I may be the only person who has seen every film that she cites [laughs]—was right on target.

CINEASTE: As I recall, you essentially characterize the film in your commentary track as a feminist version of the Charles Bronson *Death Wish*–type revenge melodramas.

BLOOM: What little exposition there is in the early part of the film does identify the Camille Keaton character as an independent woman, an urban woman, a professional woman, an artist who goes her own way. There are several indications that she is meant to be seen as a strong woman even before she is raped. In fact, it's her strength as a woman that irritates these slimeballs who live in the small town. In some ways the story is more of an urban/rural clash than a male/female clash. Just as in *Texas Chain Saw Massacre*, as soon as you pass into the countryside, everything becomes sinister and perverted. In the early days of our country, you know, the opposite was true—when you went to the city everything became sinister and perverted, and the countryside was wholesome and family oriented. At some point the redneck small town became the place of menace. The first shot of the movie, as she leaves her Manhattan apartment, is the only time when everything is in order—and she never gets back to the safety of the city.

There's another important difference between *I Spit on Your Grave* and the Charles Bronson films. In the Bronson films and even in the *Dirty Harry* series, the protagonists retain the slenderest thread of selfless justification for what they do, in that they don't fight for themselves. They fight for their dead wife, or their dead partner, and the revenge comes on behalf of someone else, often a woman. In *I Spit on Your Grave*, there is no one else, it's just her. It makes the film more brutal, more raw, more daring, in a way.

CINEASTE: It's interesting that in her revenge she plays on the sexual stupidity of her assailants.

BLOOM: If I had been making the film, I would never have done it that way. I would have had two girls go into the woods to spend the summer together, and one of them gets killed and the other seeks vengeance for the killing. That is the traditional way to do it. It's not as interesting an approach, but it's reassuring to viewers. The way Meir Zarchi did it—and I don't know if he just didn't care about that or if he was truly a pioneer in this area—makes you uncomfortable because it brings out what we might all be capable of on our own behalf, not as some act of nobility.

In fact, one argument you could make to say that *I Spit on Your Grave* is antiwoman—although I've never heard anyone make it—is that her revenge is out of all proportion to the original crime. Now

Zarchi justifies it as much as he can—I think the four rapes go on for more than a full reel of film—and although the final image of the film, with her going up the river in the speedboat, is enigmatic, I would tend to say that the image says she is strong and satisfied. If she's strong and satisfied, then he's just said that this level of violence can restore you [laughs]. And if he's saying that, he's proposing murder as the proper reaction to rape.

CINEASTE: In his commentary track, Meir Zarchi for the first time reveals the inspiration for his film, when he recounts how he came upon the aftermath of a brutal rape in a New York City park, and he drove the victim to a police station to report the incident. One wonders why he kept quiet about this all these years and why he was not more vocal at the time in defending his film and his intentions.

BLOOM: Well, we're talking about the late 1970s, before the age of video and before the age of cable TV, really. Cable existed but most people didn't have it. So a film had a life that was only as long as its theatrical release—that was its only market. The distributor, the Jerry Gross Organization, was taking their shot at how widely exposed they could get the film, but after it had made its impact, whatever that was, it was essentially over. People at the time regarded films as expendable, although *I Spit on Your Grave* played for years as a second feature at drive-ins and grind houses because it is one of the all-time great titles. I think Jerry Gross was responsible for that. I don't think Meir Zarchi's first title, *Day of the Woman*, would have had such a long grind-house life [laughs].

CINEASTE: Your commentary track alternates between a vigorous defense of the film—defending it in an almost scene-by-scene rebuttal of analyses by some feminist critics and especially by Siskel and Ebert—and making fun of the film for its scripting clichés, holes in the plot, and bad acting.

BLOOM: That's because I think Zarchi's concept for the film was brilliant. His decision to do it like a Greek tragedy—with really no explanation and very little dialogue, just the raw force of what happens—I thought was great. Now he was working with less than stellar actors, and he had never made a film before, and I kind of make fun of him for his really slow establishing shots and long tilts and pans. I think he's trying to be dramatic, but it just kind of tests your patience. While I don't think those things affect the overall impact of the film, one thing that does is the performance of the actor in the rape that occurs in the forest. The guy was just so goofy that it didn't look like a rape at all. As I point out on the commentary track, however, Camille Keaton's scream is so horrifying that it overcomes his acting and you kind of buy the scene.

CINEASTE: I thought a few scenes in the film seemed to be designed for their titillation factor.

BLOOM: I disagree. I've seen many of these films and I don't think there's any gratuitous titillation in the movie. Before the rape you see her looking cute. She's sexy because she's a sexy woman. In one of the early scenes of the film—this is sort of a late-1960s, early-1970s statement—she takes off her clothes and runs through the woods naked to go skinny-dipping in the river. Now Meir Zarchi could have done a lot with that, he could have done full-body shots, but you only briefly see some breasts and her back, so I think pretty much everything sexual in the film is justified.

I don't think you can ever identify with the rapists, so the points where she's naked, by definition, you are not identifying her as a sexual object because you are her—from the camera point of view you are her at the point where she's most naked and abused. Later she uses her sexuality to commit these acts of revenge, so it's a different thing entirely.

CINEASTE: I gather you recently completed a commentary track on *Jesse James Meets Frankenstein's Daughter*, the next in Elite Entertainment's Millennium Edition series. Would you give us a preview of that film and your commentary?

BLOOM: *Jesse James Meets Frankenstein's Daughter* was the final film of the most prolific B-movie director who ever lived, William "One Shot" Beaudine. It was the companion film to *Billy the Kid Meets Dracula*, which was his second-to-last film. Beaudine started working as a teenager for D. W. Griffith when the film industry was still in New York. He made a slew of silent films, moved out to LA with Biograph, and for a time in the 1920s and into the early 1930s, was making A pictures with Lillian Gish and W. C. Fields and other big stars of the

Figure 6.1. The final image of *I Spit on Your Grave* is enigmatic, according to film critic John Bloom, who sees the rape victim as "strong and satisfied." This reading of the image suggests to Bloom that the film might thus propose "murder as the proper reaction to rape." © Cinemagic Pictures, 1978.

day. Then, for some inexplicable reason, he chose to go to England for six years, where he made a lot of Will Hay comedies. When he came back to Hollywood, no one would hire him, so he plunged into the world of B movies, and he never left it. So, from about the late 1930s until the mid-1960s, he directed—we don't know the exact number because many of his silent films were lost—about five hundred films, including *Mom and Dad*, the classic sex-education movie.

His final effort was a combination horror/Western film that was shot down at one of the old Western ranches in Chatsworth, California. It's a pretty good little film and, once again, it had a title that assured it a long life as a drive-in second feature. People loved the title.

CINEASTE: What does your commentary track include?

BLOOM: There's a lot of history and a lot about the cast and the way it was made. It's half Western and half horror film, which has never been done entirely successfully, but it's better when it's a Western than when it's a horror film. Probably the reason is that Beaudine had directed hundreds of B Westerns and very few horror films, so he was uncomfortable in the lab. It's actually a very enjoyable film and includes a great performance by Jim Davis, who later played Jock Ewing on Dallas, as the good cowboy who comes to the rescue. It has a lot of those great old Western character actors in it. It's a fun film.

CINEASTE: What do you find especially appealing or enjoyable about exploitation films?

BLOOM: They appeal to your naughty side—it's probably from child-hood—they are the things your mother didn't want you to do or to see. Also a great many of the original ideas in film come from the B-movie world and then percolate up into the A-movie world. The filmmakers who work at the Roger Corman level tend to be the young—people in their early twenties, who are innovators. *The Great Texas Dynamite Chase* is *Thelma & Louise. I Spit on Your Grave* is *The Accused. The Texas Chain Saw Massacre* became many serial-killer movies, most notably *Silence of the Lambs.*

The whole premise of my new book—and I chose fifteen films, but I could have chosen a different fifteen—is that there are a lot of movies that are not that significant as films but they are important for how they interact with society. If *Deep Throat*, for example, had come out about one year earlier or one year later, it would be just another trashy film that happened along—there might not be an existing print of it, but it hit at a certain time when everybody was ready for that kind of insanity, and it changed everything. It changed actual laws, it changed theaters, so I'm especially interested in those types of films. *And God Created Woman*, although I think it's an underrated film, is not a great film, but because of what it was at a specific point in time, it's an extremely important film and everyone should see it.

CINEASTE: Exploitation films, including *I Spit on Your Grave*, often serve as lightning rods or vehicles for broader and often controversial social issues.

BLOOM: Yeah, they may not be that significant as films—you wouldn't necessarily ever write about them in *Cineaste*—but as social documents, as engines of some social change, they're enormously important.

Gary Crowdus is editor in chief of *Cineaste*, which he founded in 1967, editor of *A Political Companion to American Film*, and coeditor of *The* Cineaste *Interviews 2*. He has a BFA in film production from New York University's Tisch School of the Arts and has worked in film and video distribution for over forty years, with such companies as the Tricontinental Film Center and the Cinema Guild.

PART II

THE ART OF REPERTORY FILM EXHIBITION AND DIGITAL-AGE CHALLENGES

CHAPTER 7

Repertory Film Programming
A CRITICAL SYMPOSIUM

Like all serious film magazines, *Cineaste* prides itself on being a forum for film critics, scholars, and enthusiasts of all stripes—all of whom work tirelessly to sustain a vibrant and vital film culture by studying films and filmmakers in depth and by seeking out the best of world cinema, both past and present. Rarely represented in *Cineaste*, however, or in similar magazines around the world, is another breed of film devotee, one that often labors (sometimes happily) behind the scenes, curating and organizing film programs at repertory cinemas, film societies, and other screening venues. Film programmers are a vitally important but often unacknowledged part of the film cultural landscape—they labor not only to keep great films in circulation and to discover those forgotten or overlooked, but also to ensure that films are seen as they were intended to be seen. If viewing a movie on video or a computer screen means experiencing an approximation of the work of art but not the work of art itself, then the world's cinematheques and the men and women who program them play an indispensable role in keeping cinema's heritage alive.

With this in mind—and (full disclosure) fueled partly by Jared Rapfogel's dual role as both a *Cineaste* associate editor at the time of this symposium and film programmer at New York's Anthology Film Archives—the magazine devoted a 2010 critical symposium to the field of repertory film programming. By doing so, as Rapfogel states in the original version of this introduction (here slightly updated and revised), *Cineaste* hoped to shed light on the practical realities involved in organizing and presenting film programs. But the goal, too, was to call attention to some of the individual programmers who were, and in many cases continue to be, largely responsible for ensuring that certain films, filmmakers, national cinemas, and film historical movements do not sink into oblivion—whose work, in other words, constitutes an integral part of the process by which a coherent history of cinema is formed and maintained.

To survey the art and practice of film programming, *Cineaste* invited fourteen programmers from around North America to respond to the five questions below, addressing their experiences and philosophies as programmers and offering their reflections on the current condition and future fate of repertory film exhibition. (Sadly, space did not allow the editors to look further afield, though of course there are legions of great film programmers working around the world.) While, traditionally speaking, a "repertory film house" denotes a commercial institution devoted to screening classic films, *Cineaste* wields the term more broadly to mean simply those film-exhibition venues that do not primarily focus on first-run releases.

With the classic rep house generally having fallen victim to the rise of home video, the exhibition of classic films has fallen to a broad range of institutions: museums whose public programs include film screenings, theaters attached to universities, cinemas that are encompassed within larger cultural organizations, and other independent nonprofit institutions. Almost all of these venues depart from the classic repertory model in featuring films both old and new, with retrospectives and historical surveys alternating with programs on filmmakers or movements in contemporary film that rarely, if ever, surface at first-run commercial theaters. In his original introductory remarks, Rapfogel points out that the goal at Anthology Film Archives—one most certainly shared by all the venues represented in this symposium—is to give exposure to films that might otherwise fall through the cracks. Given the inadequate state of theatrical distribution in the United States, where truly challenging new work, both foreign and domestic, often struggles to be seen, this inherently means screening neglected contemporary films as well as lost or long-unscreened classics.

It's true that repertory cinemas are far from the only means by which films are discovered (or rediscovered) and presented in contemporary film culture. As these cinemas become increasingly outnumbered by other avenues of exhibition—home-video distributors (aside from the studios, valuable work is being done by labels such as the Criterion Collection, Masters of Cinema, and many others), websites (Auteurs, now MUBI, has pioneered the presentation of films online), cable channels (Turner Classic Movies holds an important place in many a film buff's heart), and video-on-demand providers (IFC, among others)—the film programmers of the world are increasingly finding a home outside the confines of the movie theater. Fueled by the conviction that preservation of the traditional moviegoing experience is a crucial part of the role played by repertory film programmers, however, *Cineaste* limited the focus of this critical symposium to those whose primary experience, past or present, is at good old-fashioned movie theaters.

If there's one overriding theme that emerges from this symposium, it's an assertion of the invaluable role played by repertory film programming in placing films in context, along with an underlying conviction that this context matters—the context represented by the quality and nature of the experience (seeing a movie projected from a film print, onto a large screen, in public), but also that established by a creatively and perceptively curated film series, an in-person appearance by a filmmaker, or a lecture by a visiting film scholar. The consensus here is that film programming, at its best, helps start a conversation, putting different films in dialogue with each other and fostering an awareness of individual works as part of an oeuvre, a tradition, an historical era, or a nexus of relationships and interconnections—something that is easily lost when shopping among the hordes of films available on video or online.

While the value of repertory cinema is (naturally) universally affirmed by the contributors here, the question of the fate of these theaters, of the experience of watching films projected theatrically, is left unresolved. The contributors express a guarded optimism, predicting that a small but passionate audience will continue to exist, even if the experience is destined to become ever more specialized. As a programmer and an inveterate filmgoer (admittedly in a city with an unusually large number of repertory cinemas), Rapfogel attests that the community of avid cinephiles in New York, who are fully (often obsessively) committed to seeing movies projected in public and on their proper format, seems to be constantly replenished with new, younger faces—people who are passionately taken not only with the art of cinema but also with the transformative power of moviegoing.

This proliferation suggests that the experience of seeing movies projected does indeed remain (potentially) transformative, retaining the power to convert even (or perhaps especially) those growing up glued to their iPhones. The trick is to ensure that venues remain where these transformative experiences can take place. This may increasingly mean museums, archives, and university-affiliated screening series, but it's worth calling attention, as John Gianvito does in his contribution below, to the phenomenon of microcinemas, whose small scale gives them a remarkable versatility and vitality. (In New York, where several microcinemas passed out of existence in the last decade, Light Industry and UnionDocs, among others, triumphantly picked up the mantle.)

Like several other venues featured here—the Harvard Film Archive, the Museum of Modern Art, and the George Eastman Museum (formerly George Eastman House)—Anthology Film Archives (Rapfogel's own professional home) is an archive as well as a cinema. As an institution, Anthology's mission encompasses the protection and preservation of film prints that are in constant danger of disintegration and decay. And in some sense, its film programs are increasingly becoming an extension of this spirit, preserving not just particular films but the ritual of filmgoing itself. From this perspective, all the venues represented in this symposium are committed to the preservation of cinema and to ensuring that the art form remains—not just a collection of individual, consumable works, but also opportunities for dialogue, discussion, and debate—a basis for community interaction, and, above all, an experience.

Some repertory programmers formatted their responses as essays and others as point-by-point replies, to correspond with each of the following questions *Cineaste* posed. The critical symposium is extended online with additional responses from Robert Cargni-Mitchell (International House Philadelphia), Gary Meyer (Landmark Theatres), and Jackie Raynal (cofounder of the Bleecker Street and Carnegie Hall Cinemas), available at *Cineaste*'s website (www.cineaste.com). Next to each programmer or curator's name is his or her professional affiliation in 2010, at the time when this symposium was first published. Following each response is an expanded, updated biography of the contributor.

1. Is there a future to repertory programming, given the momentous changes over the last decade in technology and viewing habits? How would you characterize the impact on theatrical exhibition of home video, Internet streaming, downloading, et cetera? Are the consequences entirely negative, or are there collateral benefits (e.g., new

prints struck for video releases, more informed audiences, etc.)?

2. How would you characterize your programming philosophy, with regard to the variety of films selected, preferred formats (retrospectives, thematic series, national surveys, double features, etc.), your attitude toward audience expectation, or other considerations?

3. Do you find that good-quality prints continue to be available? Do you think film prints will continue to be struck and distributed, or is this a dying exhibition format? And if projecting from film is destined to become obsolete, how great a loss do you think this is? Are you open to screening video or digital formats?

4. How have your audiences changed over the years? Are they increasing or decreasing? Have their demographics changed, in terms of age or background? Have they become more or less receptive to challenging and innovative programs?

5. What are some of your formative memories of repertory filmgoing? Do you have stories of particularly unforgettable experiences, inspiring series, or legendary venues?

JOHN EWING, CLEVELAND INSTITUTE OF ART

1. There is definitely a future for repertory programming on cable TV, in museums that regard cinema as a visual art, and for home screening rooms. But is there a future for repertory programming in movie theaters? I want to say yes, but the cost of showing a 35 mm print of a classic movie these days (around $500; $250 to $350 for the film rental, $150 to $250 for two-way print shipping) is often prohibitive. And that doesn't even include staff and publicity costs and theater overhead. The availability of new and classic films on TV, DVD, Blu-ray, and the Internet has certainly undercut the urgency of seeing movies when they play theatrically, and attendance at the Cleveland Cinematheque has suffered accordingly. On the plus side, the availability of films in other formats has allowed many people to discover movies that would otherwise be unknown to them, and resulted in a certain level of film literacy not seen previously. (Now that they can be recorded, bought, owned, and loaned, movies are the new books.) And sometimes when people discover a film on TV or DVD and like it enough, they catch it in a theater when the opportunity presents itself. The growing ancillary markets have resulted in a profusion of new prints of classic titles that repertory theaters can show theatrically. But less remarked upon is

the fact that films shown in theaters become a hotter commodity in the extratheatrical marketplace. It's a two-way street, with repertory theaters separating the wheat from the chaff. But, still, the future of 35 mm repertory cinema may reside only in the largest cities, where people will pay a premium and where subsidies will fortify the bottom line. The era of bargain double features that change every few days is over.

2. The Cleveland Cinematheque shows about 250 different feature films every year. New films (American and foreign) that otherwise would not play in Cleveland make up forty percent of our offerings. Newly rereleased prints of classic films make up another twenty percent, and thematic series (director retrospectives, surveys of genres or national cinemas, etc.) comprise another twenty percent. The remaining twenty percent is devoted to worthy second-run films, to visiting filmmakers, and to other special events. We show almost everything on 35 mm film. The Cinematheque's diverse programming offers something for everyone—or at least something for everyone who cares about classic and contemporary cinema. With only one six-hundred-seat auditorium, we show two or three different movies every night that we are open (generally Thursday through Sunday) for separate admission fees (no double features). Since the Cinematheque is the last resort for a movie to play theatrically in Cleveland, I don't preview most new films, relying instead on national reviews, directors' reputations, and the perceived "want-to-see" quotient. If a film is getting good reviews or doing decent business in other large American cities, then I believe Clevelanders deserve a chance to see it, no matter what I personally might think of it. I'm more a conduit than a curator. But, obviously, I can't show everything, so I do prioritize. And being a dyed-in-the-wool auteurist, a director's name trumps everything—that, and the availability of the movie on 35 mm.

3. There are still enough good-quality 35 mm prints available that we can present thematic film series and director retrospectives. (Our ability to project reel-to-reel on two machines gives us access to archival and library prints that are not available to platter-only houses.) And there are enough new prints being struck that, starting this year, we are presenting one per week in an ongoing series entitled "Revivals & Restorations." This is not a thematic series but a collection of stand-alone classics united only by their fame, their merit, and their availability in a new or restored 35 mm print. Our first installment of this series contained titles as diverse as *Amarcord*, *Bye Bye Birdie*, *Odd Man Out*, and *Araya*. A major reason for doing a series

like this is to keep 35 mm product flowing through the distribution pipe-line. By playing new prints and paying a share of the cost to make them, I feel I'm holding up my end of a bargain that other exhibitors in other cities are also party to. Since I object to showing a video or a DVD of a movie that was shot on 35 mm film (just as an art museum won't hang reproductions on its walls), I pray that 35 mm prints will continue to be made. And I think they will—at least for a while. As far as I know, no digital format has been recognized and accepted as an "archival medium," which film is. As long as film is archival, then prints should continue to be made and maintained by studios—if only for their own libraries. I wish exhibitors would say no to DVD or video exhibition copies of films—especially studio films. Thir-ty-five millimeter is what sets movies in theaters apart from movies on TV, Blu-ray, and the Internet. And if we compromise, there will be no impetus for studios to strike new distribution prints.

4. The audience at the Cinematheque has definitely grayed and aged over the years as the 1960s through 1970s heyday of art-house cinema has receded into the past. And this audience's embrace of the cutting edge seems to have loosened into a regrettable preference for the mid-dlebrow—a trend accelerated by the *Masterpiece Theatre*-ing of "art" films that started during the 1980s and hasn't let up yet. Yet there are still bright and curious young people—and many non-Americans—truly interested in new trends in world cinema, in challenging work, and in the "antique," cumbersome, but gorgeous medium of 35 mm film.

5. I have attended repertory cinemas my entire adult life. And I have been inspired by many of them—including one I never visited, the long-gone Movies in downtown Cincinnati. During the early 1980s, Movies showed five or six different films a day in true repertory rotation. Each film ran for a few days or a week in a different time slot every day. I received the Movies jigsaw puzzle of a film calendar in the mail, and their wide-ranging offerings and complicated scheduling certainly influenced the Cleveland Cinematheque. I continue to monitor, and draw inspiration from, the best repertory cinemas, museum film programs, and cinematheques in North America—from New York's Film Forum and MoMA (where I interned in the early 1970s) to the Pacific Film Archive, the Harvard Film Archive, and the Cinematheque Ontario, among others.

Since 1986 John Ewing has served as both director of the Cleveland Insti-tute of Art Cinematheque (formerly the Cleveland Cinematheque, which he cofounded) and curator for film at the Cleveland Museum of Art, where he programs more than 250 different feature films annually. From 1975 to 1983 he was director of the film society of Canton, Ohio. In recognition of his significant contribution to French culture through his work at the Cleveland Cinematheque, the French Republic awarded Ewing the Order of Chevalier of Arts and Letters in 2010.

JOHN GIANVITO, LIST VISUAL ARTS CENTER, MASSACHUSETTS INSTITUTE OF TECHNOLOGY

What film education I possess is unimaginable had I not had the privilege of growing up in New York City amidst a plethora of repertory, art-house, and museum choices. At the time—the 1970s (and perhaps still)—New York was second only to Paris in terms of the number of individual films screened each week. This was the era of such memorable venues as the Thalia, the New Yorker Theater, the Elgin Cinema, Fabiano Canosa's First Avenue Screening Room, Jackie Raynal and Sid Geffen's Bleecker Street and Carnegie Hall Cinemas, the Collective for Living Cinema, Anthology Film Archives (whose latest calendar is itself evidence that great repertory programming is very much alive), Millennium Film Workshop, and many, many more. I also had sufficient economic privilege to avail myself of these riches, which I did with voracity. No doubt part of my impetus in later years to curate springs from the desire to share and keep alive the memory of so many wondrous and exotic visions.

With the burgeoning of video distribution, Internet streaming, cable downloading, et cetera, a measure of that class and geographic privilege has thankfully been erased, and, whatever its impact on those cities that sustained repertory programming, this remains a good thing. In many more places now, if you suddenly find yourself curious about Ozu or Akerman or cinema of the African diaspora, you can go to your library and check something out on DVD. And while many things are lost in transmission (scale, resolution, the social dimension, etc.), I think most cinephiles, if they're honest with themselves, can count among favorite films some they may have only seen once on a small TV, interrupted by commercials, maybe even panned and scanned, or viewed on a mediocre VHS dub traded via the "underground"—and yet enough got through to bowl one over and indelibly impress itself upon the spirit. That acknowledged, I think it should be obvious that it remains a worthy aspiration to present each film as closely as possible to the way in which it was originally intended to be seen. Is it heretical for a repertory house or film archive to project a digital copy of a film print when the alternative may be screening a scratched or faded or heavily spliced film print? In a curious twist on Benjamin's embrace of film for its reproducibility and, thus, its capacity to dispel the "aura" of the unique work of art, film's own "aura" appears to be at stake.

Not entirely a digital-age phenomenon. I am reminded of the ache, still felt by many, at the loss of the "sparkle" of silver-based nitrate print projection. I am also reminded of Jean Rouch's reactionary remark that "video is the AIDS of cinema." And while one may accept a less than exacting copy when looking at a film at home, will repertory audiences be as accepting of digital projections inside a theater, and should they? Would it be okay to walk into the Louvre and see exacting digital duplicates of master paintings or to go into the Isabella Stewart Gardner Museum and see a replica of Vermeer's *The Concert* since, for now, there's no other way to see it?

How much is lost and how much is gained by digital projection of films? Can we afford to ignore the fact that projecting from digital files is more carbon-neutral than shipping and projecting petroleum-based 35 mm prints? While I don't feel I have definitive answers to all these questions, it does seem to me likely that for the indefinite future, classic repertory cinema will continue to be a rarefied experience. If so, this will have less to do with winnowing audiences than with the ongoing scarcity of quality prints (this is where film archives will continue to have the advantage) and the business-as-usual gangland tactics of studios and exhibitors (so even if the owner of a twelve-screen multiplex wanted to experiment with repertory programming on one screen, and had reason to believe that it would be profit making, that owner would likely be pressured to play a run-of-the-mill studio film instead, rather than face the threat of not getting the summer or holiday blockbusters upon which the theater's existence depends). Going digital is not going to solve the dilemma and is more apt to exacerbate things. Worth reading is Dave Kehr's recent article in the *New York Times*, "The Ballad of Blu-ray and Scratchy Old Film," in which he points out the progressive diminution of film releases as we've moved from VHS to DVD and now to Blu-ray, a format that, Kehr predicts, in spite of (or perhaps because of) its dazzlingly superior image and sound quality, will see even fewer overall releases due to the high cost of resto-ration and digital transfer. And I certainly know that when I was growing up in New York I could see infinitely more films, and of a wider spectrum, on the nine or ten channels of reception we got than one can find today with 250 cable channels. All of which I suppose attests even further to the need for a revival of revival houses.

Still, there are some signs of life. One is the continuing cropping up of microcinemas (well chronicled in Rebecca M. Alvin's "Cinemas of the Future," *Cineaste* 32, no. 3 [Summer 2007]), which can circumvent a num-ber of the economic roadblocks that have squeezed traditional rep houses. Here where I live in Boston there is still no shortage of opportunities to see a breadth of cinematic expression any day of the week, with the still-surviving Brattle Theater, the Coolidge Corner Theater, Museum of Fine Arts, and MassArt Film Society, among other venues. And though I no longer program films at the Harvard Film Archive, I attend regularly and can report that attendance is as robust as I've ever seen it, thanks to the fine curatorial work of Haden Guest and David Pendleton—and while they draw from a generally moneyed and informed clientele, this alone, as we know, cannot guarantee turnout.

But how to achieve not only the widest breadth of programs but also the widest breadth of audience? I recall an interview years back with the director Peter Sellars after he'd taken a new managerial post somewhere and was pressed on whether he believed there was a sufficient audience in that community to support the kind of work he was undertaking. Sellars responded, "If not, it is our job as artists to create one's audience." As many have taught me through the years (Don Levy, Amos Vogel, Edith Kramer, and Mark McElhatten, among others), curating itself can be a form of creative expression, can be an art, can even be a political act. If repertory cinema survives, it will be due to the inventive, passionate efforts of individuals capable of invitingly persuading us that the memory of the past is not a luxury but a necessity.

John Gianvito is a filmmaker, curator, and teacher based in Boston. A for-mer film programmer for the Harvard Film Archive, Gianvito is a professor in the Department of Film and Media Arts at Emerson College. His fea-ture films include *The Flower of Pain*, *Address Unknown*, *The Mad Songs of Fernanda Hussein*, and the documentary *Profit Motive and the Whispering Wind*. His documentary *Subic* appeared on the 2015 Top 10 lists in *Sight &*

Sound, *Senses of Cinema*, and *Artforum*. At the time of this symposium, he was adjunct film curator for the List Visual Arts Center at the Massachusetts Institute of Technology.

BRUCE GOLDSTEIN, FILM FORUM, NEW YORK

1. As Film Forum's repertory programmer, I can speak only from a New York City perspective (even though I'm also involved in the national distribution end of the business with my company Rialto Pictures). New York has a long tradition of repertory movie houses, but by the time I first joined Film Forum in 1986, they were nearly extinct—victims not just of the VHS boom, but also of booming NYC real estate. Film Forum's director, Karen Cooper, hired me to book the second screen with no specific mandate—the understanding was simply that I'd offer an alternative to her own programming of first-run independent films. I decided from Day One that we'd devote the second screen exclusively to classics—a policy we've stuck to ever since.

At the time, the perceived wisdom was that home video would make the revival theater obsolete. But our rep screen took off immediately and, almost twenty-five years later, is still going strong. One reason for this is that we've built a loyal audience over the past quarter century, and we're still extremely aggressive with promotion and publicity (and, yes, we're in New York City, but contrary to popular belief, that doesn't guarantee instantaneous success)—and we're also reliable in terms of programming and the general quality of film prints. But I also believe that the new technology and viewing habits—DVDs, streaming, TCM, et cetera—have actually helped build a new interest in seeing films in a movie theater (just as television was the wellspring for my own generation's budding cinephilia). As evidence of this, some of our biggest rep hits of the past ten years have long been available on DVD—*Rules of the Game*, *The Red Shoes*, *In a Lonely Place*, *The Third Man*, et cetera. So the answer is, yes, there is a future to repertory programming. But it's important that both the organizations running it and the audiences are committed to it.

2. We put out a quarterly repertory calendar, and I try to offer a wide variety of movies on each one—the films and series are juxtaposed graphically on the calendar to pique the reader's interest and excitement over the lineup. On our Winter–Spring 2010 calendar, for example, we've got a new

print of Kurosawa's *Ran*, followed by a return engagement of the restored *Red Shoes*, followed by a new restoration of *Five Easy Pieces*. Then a series on director Victor Fleming (including Hollywood megaclassics like *Gone with the Wind* and *The Wizard of Oz*), a new 35 mm print of Joseph Losey's offbeat film noir *The Prowler*, new 35 mm prints of Abbas Kiarostami's *Close-up* and Murnau's *Sunrise*, a miniseries on Scottish director Bill Forsyth, and a four-week series on the newspaper movie, including films from the pre-Code era (another of our hallmarks) and a sidebar on fast-talking actor Lee Tracy. This is a very typical calendar: two festivals (one a director retrospective and the other a thematic series) and six long runs of new 35 mm prints (including two new 35 mm restorations). This calendar also reflects many of my own special interests—and those of our audience: pre-Code, film noir, silents, rediscoveries, et cetera. The only thing missing from this particular calendar is French films.

It would take an essay in itself for me to explain my "programming philosophy." I do think, though, that it reflects less on critical consensus than on my own taste—I want to keep the films that have meant a lot to me in the repertory—but I also pay close attention to what's popular with our audience. And I continue to be in contact with distributors, studios, and archives about new film restorations and still initiate many new 35 mm prints.

3. When I began in the business (which pre-dates my tenure at Film Forum by fifteen years), the quality of film prints was hit or miss (mostly "miss," as I recollect). I would say that over half of the films shown were in 16 mm. Thirty-five-millimeter prints were often riddled with splices and scratches (especially at the beginnings and endings of reels)—on some Marx Brothers movies, for example, I could recite the dialogue, splices and all (since there was only one print in circulation). Color films were, more often than not, faded to magenta. Most movie-buff audiences put up with this because "that's all there was." (I remember a sign at a Paris *cinéma d'essai* box office saying, in essence, that bad prints were the nature of repertory cinema, so take it or leave it.)

It was just as bad, if not worse, by the time we began Film Forum's rep screen in 1987. I realized that we couldn't keep an audience by offering the same old bad prints, especially as pristine copies of some classics were now available on video, so we began to offer distributors longer runs for classic films, thus higher film-rental guarantees, as incentive to strike new prints. (Prior to our long-run policy, most rep houses played films only for a day or

Figure 7.1. Although many films are now available on DVD and Blu-ray, 35 mm prints of *The Red Shoes* and many other classics remain popular with repertory film audiences, such as those at New York City's Film Forum. © The Archers, 1948.

two and most often on a split bill.) A Film Forum run will often cover the cost of a new print, and in this way we've put over seven hundred new 35 mm prints in general circulation. So from the very beginning, we've tried to raise the standard of film presentation with better prints, which I think has benefited the entire rep community. Film Forum is still the showcase for most new 35 mm prints and restorations (and we are very careful in differentiating). And our 16 mm projector is rarely in use anymore.

We're privileged to have access to prints from the studio archives—in particular, Sony, Twentieth Century–Fox, Paramount, and MGM—all of which, in the past fifteen years or so, have done outstanding work in film preservation. We also work closely with the Library of Congress, UCLA (University of California, Los Angeles), the Museum of Modern Art, George Eastman House, the BFI (British Film Institute), and the Film Foundation—all major players in the film preservation world.

It's important to note that not all of the prints we show are available to every venue, but a growing number of film distributors are making classics in excellent 35 mm prints generally available. I founded Rialto Pictures in 1997 in order to distribute (mostly) foreign classics unavailable in this country. Other independent distributors who've made classics a specialty are Janus Films, Kino International, Milestone, and the Film Desk.

Not all films are available in great prints, especially for a series when our aim is to show all of a subject's major work—but it's very rare that we play anything in less than fair condition. The overall quality has improved dramatically over the past twenty years. In fact, I consider this a golden age for cinephiles.

As for the future of 35 mm, I like to say that we'll stick to that format until the last projector part is unavailable, though I believe 35 mm is a long way off from dying (I don't even think it's seriously ill). But digital restorations have made tremendous advances in the past ten years. In fact, most of the major restorations today are done digitally and then outputted to film (the recent restoration of *The Red Shoes*—the most gorgeous I've ever seen—was done this way; the extraordinary work would have been impossible to achieve photochemically). So it's inevitable that we will be seeing more and more digital projection within the next five to ten years.

Since "new 35 mm print" is one of our hallmarks, we've avoided digital projection for the rep screen, apart from a few documentaries. Thus far, we've not shown a classic feature this way (since most independent films are now shot digitally, our first-run screen frequently uses digital projection), but we will be getting our feet wet in May with the complete version of *Metropolis* (discovered recently in Brazil), which we'll be showing in a high-definition format. But I've got an emotional attachment to 35 mm, as does our audience, so we will continue to be extremely discriminating when it comes to digital.

4. Film Forum's membership (who join for both the first-run and repertory programming) has been steady over the past quarter decade, and our overall audience numbers have increased. We also benefit from hits on the first-run screen, and vice versa, when new audiences discover the theater.

Regarding the age and demographic, that, of course, depends on the films being shown—and the time of day. We have a very loyal senior audience for matinees, but if you come at night, you'll see a very young audience for a lot of our classic screenings. But I can't tell you what our exact demographic is—I don't think we've ever done any kind of survey.

As far as what's considered innovative in repertory programming, on each calendar I try to feature a well-known classic in a new print as an opportunity for new audiences to discover it. But on each calendar we also try to include a long run of a film that's not a classic—in other words, rediscoveries, to which our audience is extremely receptive. Losey's *The Prowler* is a good example of this.

5. To this question I could write a book—if anyone would read it. My first rep houses were Channels 2, 5, 9, and 11 in New York (all I remember about Channels 4 and 7 was that their afternoon movies were cut to ribbons). My first rep screening was a double feature of *The Umbrellas of Cherbourg* (decades later, I'd promote its restoration) and the forgotten *Sundays and Cybèle* at the Thalia. When I picked up the Thalia calendar (which I still have) and saw all these double features of films I'd never heard of, I was hooked. I then discovered that another revival house, the New Yorker, was only a few blocks away (for more on the New Yorker, see Toby Talbot's wonderful new memoir). Later, Theatre 80 St. Marks was the place to see obscure Hollywood movies—films from the early 1930s that rarely appeared on television. In my twenties, I moved to London, where the programming at the National Film Theatre was a huge influence on me. (I began my own New York career at the Carnegie Hall and Bleecker Street Cinemas, and later the Thalia.)

Some of the major revival events when I was growing up weren't always at rep houses: the reissue of *The African Queen* at my local movie house; the 1969 reissue of *Gone with the Wind*, which had been out of circulation for seven years—though for this rerelease it was blown up to 70 mm and therefore cropped top and bottom; and, most important of all, the reissue, in the early 1970s, of all of Chaplin's great features. If you can imagine growing up reading about *City Lights, Modern Times,* and *The Great Dictator* all your young life, with no opportunity to see them, and then suddenly they're all announced at your local movie house, you may be able to channel some of my euphoria. This is the kind of cinephilia that I miss and still hope to recapture.

Bruce Goldstein is director of repertory programming at Film Forum in New York City. During the past thirty years, he has programmed over 250 film series and retrospectives and unveiled over seven hundred new 35 mm prints. In 1997 Goldstein founded Rialto Pictures, a distributor specializing in classic reissues. He has been the recipient of awards from the New York Film Critics Circle, Anthology Film Archives, the National Board

of Review, and the San Francisco Film Festival. In 2004 the French government named him a chevalier in the Order of Arts and Letters for his
promotion of French film and culture at Film Forum.

HADEN GUEST, HARVARD FILM ARCHIVE (HFA)

1. The troublingly uncertain future of repertory film programming in the
United States today is augured by the notably thinning ranks of supported
cinematheque programs across the country and, among those remaining,
a diminished commitment to original, in-house programming. As institutions lose support, or interest, in their film programs, increased calendar
space is being given over to all manner of visiting "festivals," which have
the cumulative effect of diluting the type of distinct curatorial identity and
autonomy that is the heart of cutting-edge cinematheque programming.
The loss of carefully articulated, argued, and focused film programs in
favor of loose, celebratory surveys is a dangerous and alarming trend.

I am convinced that repertory programming will survive, but only
within a limited number of dedicated and increasingly specialized cinematheques. Seeing classic or experimental films, correctly projected and
carefully contextualized by intelligent program notes, spoken introductions, and postscreening discussions by or with a curator or filmmaker,
will undoubtedly become something like going to the theater or opera, a
rarefied "live" event understood and supported by few institutions. Silent
cinema is today experienced in precisely this way, as always a special event
unto itself, sought out only by an experienced and knowledgeable audience. And one day, sad to say, 35 mm projection will go the same way.

The incredible range of films now available on commercial DVD and—
illicitly or legitimately—on the Internet has actually defused previous fears
that audiences would eventually prefer simply to stay at home. There are
now such a staggering number of films to choose from that filmgoers
appreciate the important work of curatorial selection, of being told what
they should see. The same audience whose increased discrimination and
appreciation of image quality fuels the analytical ratings of DVDs by their
bit rate also understands the unique qualities of 35 mm projection. These
passionate and deeply knowledgeable filmgoers will continue to seek out
repertory programs and the enhanced viewing experience offered by select
cinematheques.

2. The programming philosophy of the Harvard Film Archive is guided by the Miesian mantra that *less is more*. In recognition of our limited staff and budget, we recently cut back on the number of evening shows, since not doing so would have compromised the quality of our presentations. We believe passionately in innovative and original programming and the importance of developing and maintaining a distinct and consistent curatorial voice. For this reason we very rarely work with outside programmers or festivals, although we gladly and frequently collaborate with artists and fellow film scholars and curators. We invite a great number of filmmakers to present their work—up to forty a year. This is very hard but deeply rewarding work and, we believe, one of the most effective ways to engage and entice audiences. We also treat each of our evening screenings as live events, introducing almost all films and always providing original and thoughtful program notes to contextualize and provide crucial information about the film being screened.

The majority of our programs are monographic and auteurist, focused upon a single director or historical movement and, in most cases, organized as complete retrospectives. We are also deeply interested in innovative programs that engage the relationship of film to the other arts—such as our recent program of films curated with poet John Ashbery and our live tour of Chris Marker's Second Life museum, led by Marker himself. Recognizing the several distinct audiences who regularly attend HFA screenings, we try to be as creatively eclectic as possible, presenting a range of narrative, documentary, and experimental cinema from around the world and across film history. We are cautious not to ask or expect too much from any one of these audience groups exclusively. Instead, we delight in the dialogue that sometimes emerges felicitously between the radically different modes of cinema presented in the HFA calendar—between, for example, our recent showcase of Stanley Donen's films in the same calendar as a visit from Tsai Ming-liang.

3. While photochemical processes are most certainly endangered, I believe that 35 mm exhibition prints will continue to be made for longer than many expect. Yet new prints will depend upon increasingly specialized labs whose prices will most certainly increase. The future of film projection lies in the hands of archive-cinematheques such as the HFA who are working hard to collect prints and preserve films and who are fully aware of the urgent task at hand. In the future, film prints will only be made available to a network, most likely of International Federation

of Film Archives member archives, of organizations able to maintain the highest standards of archival projection and committed to screening work in its original format. It would definitely be a serious loss if film became completely obsolete, projected only on the rarest of occasions, just as historic magic lantern slides are today. But even when this does happen, the art and culture of cinema will continue to grow and even thrive as we go further and fully into the digital era.

4. With regards to audience, the case of the Harvard Film Archive is perhaps something of an exception. Situated as it is within a university and within Cambridge/Boston, one of the ultimate college towns, the HFA audience tends to be evenly split, on average, between undergraduate and graduate students of the eighteen to thirty-five age range and the older audience of fifty-five and up. The graying of the audience notable at many cinematheque venues is really not a factor at the HFA. We also witness enthusiasm and audience numbers for some of our more challenging programs—an almost sold-out Larry Gottheim show, for example—that I know you would be hard pressed to match elsewhere.

5. Some of my fondest and most vivid memories of repertory film going were of the glorious last years of the American Cinematheque in the late 1990s, when it was at the Raleigh Studios in Hollywood and programmed principally by Dennis Bartok. Each weekend my wife and I used to race across town to buy our tickets before they inevitably sold out. Squeezed into a studio screening room, this small, intimate venue was almost always filled to capacity, and the excitement of getting there and getting a seat somehow seemed to intensify the experience of the films. Or maybe I was especially excitable in those days. At the Cinematheque, in its golden age, I had my first and truly revelatory encounters with some of the directors I admired most—Sam Fuller, André De Toth, Lina Wertmüller, Monte Hellman. I shook Fuller's hand and stuttered my admiration for *Forty Guns* and I can still see his smile. Those were the unbelievable, delirious nights when I began to understand and appreciate film as I never had before, dutifully watching my first complete retrospective, of Anthony Mann, no less, and always craving more.

Haden Guest is director of the Harvard Film Archive (HFA) and is in charge of the HFA's cinematheque, preservation program, research initiatives, and renowned collections. A film historian, curator, and archivist, he is also a senior lecturer in Harvard's Department of Visual and

Environmental Studies. He was a producer for Soon-Mi Yoo's *Songs from the North*, which won major prizes, including a Golden Leopard at the Locarno Film Festival, the Best First Feature award at Doclisboa, and the Jury Prize at the Buenos Aires International Film Festival. In 2015 the Portuguese government awarded Guest the Medal of Cultural Merit for his curatorial work on Portuguese cinema.

JIM HEALY, GEORGE EASTMAN HOUSE, ROCHESTER, NEW YORK

1. My feeling is that there will be a future for repertory film programming but a diminishing number of titles from the past that an audience will show up for. As Dave Kehr pointed out in his *New York Times* column and on his blog, with each new home-video format that was embraced by mass consumers (VHS, DVD, now Blu-ray), fewer titles have been made available than on the previous format. This has limited the discussion about film history. How can you talk about what you can't see? My feeling is that the more that is available, the more interest there will be in seeing movies, including via theatrical repertory programming.

So far, we're not seeing a flood of previously unavailable stuff available for instant downloading or streaming, but if the studios release their entire catalogues online, I think it will only create more interest in seeing films in a theatrical venue. I can't be sure of it, but I would guess that Internet streaming and illegal downloading of movies has most affected audiences for new films that we show that would otherwise not have a venue here in Rochester. If someone would rather watch *The Night of the Hunter* on Hulu or YouTube instead of a restored 35 mm print on a big screen, then I'd argue that they're not really interested in seeing the movie (and probably mentally deranged).

2. Over eight years, I've favored a vertical calendar model that allows us to show series of films over one month or two months of Tuesdays, Wednesdays, or Thursdays. We're usually dark on Mondays, and the weekends are reserved for premieres of new films that would otherwise have no other theatrical venue in the region, or for one-off screenings of popular classics or centerpiece screenings of films related to the weekday series (e.g., the new print of *Mr. Hulot's Holiday* will screen on the weekend, whereas Tati's other films will screen on Wednesday evenings this coming March). Sometimes weekend screenings feature filmmakers or scholars in

person. This model allows us to show something different every night and attract potentially different audiences from one evening to the next. While some people will come every night, it relieves audiences of the pressure of coming night after night to see all of the Korean movies or car-chase movies. It's easier to make a commitment to a month or two months of Wednesdays than three nights in a row.

Though I've persevered with some auteurist-based series, I usually find that audiences will only show up for those films that have an obvious reputation (e.g., *Gone with the Wind* and *The Wizard of Oz* draw the most for a Victor Fleming series, and *Rebel Without a Cause* will draw the most for Nicholas Ray). There are only a handful of directors that audiences will show up for every time: Hitchcock, Kubrick, et cetera. I've enjoyed doing smaller national or continental surveys, especially when they're supported by a country's cultural embassy and there are only negligible shipping costs. For a long time, I would program a lot of films that I was interested in seeing myself—sometimes we'd get curious audiences and other times no one would show up. During the first five or six years I was programming here, I think you could call a lot of my selections "esoteric" or "obscure."

But since my daughter was born sixteen months ago, I've had less time to hang out at the theater and watch stuff, so I've relied on screening a lot of things that I predict will draw big crowds, while I stay at home a lot and watch Blu-rays and DVDs. Lately, for budgetary reasons, I've been relying on our own archival holdings for selecting series, and I've programmed a lot of popular things, like Marilyn Monroe and Audrey Hepburn movies. We're usually able to bring in big audiences for things like this, especially during the summer months and around the holidays at the end of the year. Though I still manage to see nearly five hundred movies a year that I've never seen before, it feels good to rely on what I've seen in the past as programming material. Plus, it's naïve of me to think that a large part of the audience is willing to follow me down so many obscure cinematic trails. There are always going to be large numbers of people who have never seen *Casablanca* on the big screen, or at all, for that matter, and screenings of this sort are the kinds of moments that create cinephiles.

3. In order to hype screenings, I've been guilty of thinking and saying that seeing films on 35 mm prints is the best way to view them because "it's the way they were originally meant to be seen." But, of course, 35 mm film used to have a nitrate-based stock, which gave the image a specific

Figure 7.2. While director Nicholas Ray's oeuvre is rich and varied, the largest crowds come out (at the George Eastman Museum, in Rochester, New York) for Ray's more recognizable classics, such as *Rebel Without a Cause*. © Warner Bros., 1955.

luminosity that's proven difficult to replicate—especially without arc-light projectors, which also used to be the standard. The Dryden Theatre at George Eastman House is one of the few venues in the country that can still show an original nitrate print, but only a handful are available to us, and even then, we don't use arc-light projectors anymore. So much for seeing films the way they were meant to be seen.

As far as studio titles go, Universal, Sony, and Fox have done a more than admirable job making new 35 mm prints available. Their work is exemplary. Speaking as an employee of an archive that's a world leader in film preservation efforts, I can also say that these particular studio archives understand the importance of preserving film in its original element and formats, at least until we better understand digital technologies and their various life spans. That said, I'm more impressed all the time with video and digital formats, especially Blu-ray and the way it's been able to replicate film grain. With improvements in DLP video projectors, I've allowed screenings of a handful of features and shorts on DVD or Blu-ray. As a viewer, however, I still prefer the look and feel of film, and I've always been able to tell the difference between a 35 mm print and any other digital or video format.

4. I've been able to increase our annual attendance about thirteen percent since 2001, through additional screening times and more screenings of recent features that would otherwise have no other theatrical venue in the area. These latter types of movies are more consistently well attended, usually because of the attendant hype that comes with them from reviews

in other cities and festivals. We've also been able to develop a more cohesive and easy-to-follow website that provides more content (like links to trailers and other reviews). We don't have a daily newspaper film critic in Rochester anymore, which means that a lot of films that would normally play weeklong or longer runs in larger cities won't even open at the local five-screen art house because there's no advertising and no chance of getting any sort of review, positive or negative. This means we often have the option of picking them up for one or two screenings just before they appear on home video. Consequently, in order to draw audiences to these films, we've had to rely on our website and an Internet-savvy audience who might have heard about the things we're showing on other international and national sites. Hopefully, we've been able to develop a following of people who might take a blind chance on seeing something just because we're showing it and because they've liked what we've shown in the past.

5. One summer, when I was thirteen and living in New Jersey, my mother bought the two of us a series pass for four Garson Kanin–scripted films at the Metropolitan Museum of Art in Manhattan. This is how I saw *Born Yesterday* and *Adam's Rib* for the first time. Kanin spoke before and after each screening, and one week the actress Ruth Gordon, Kanin's wife, sat right in front of us! The screenings were held over four consecutive Tuesdays, I think, and it was exciting to go into the city every week. This probably opened my eyes to what was available to a movie lover in a big city, and though I obsessively thereafter reviewed the listings in the *New York Times* and the *New Yorker*, I only begged my parents to take me back to the city once for a repertory screening, and that was, coincidentally, to see a Ruth Gordon double feature of *Harold and Maude* and *Where's Poppa?* at the Theatre 80 St. Marks (which used rear-screen projection).

We only lived for three years in New Jersey. Before and after that, I grew up mainly in the suburbs of Chicago, and though I was a movie fanatic from a young age, it took relocating to the city at age twenty-two to open my eyes to the thousands of titles that I never realized before were "essential viewing." Most of the formative viewing experiences I had were at the Film Center of the School of the Art Institute of Chicago (now the Gene Siskel Film Center) and the Music Box Theatre. I spent ten days in a row at the Music Box in 1994 watching double and triple features of Warner Bros. pre-Code movies, twenty-four titles in all, including my first ever viewings of *Gold Diggers of 1933*, *Public Enemy*, *Baby Face*, and *I Am a Fugitive from a Chain Gang*. I also remember seeing almost everything in the Jean Renoir and Ken Loach retrospectives at the Film Center in the mid-1990s.

Jim Healy is director of film programming at the University of Wisconsin's Cinematheque. From 2001 to 2010, he was assistant curator of exhibitions in the Motion Picture Department of the George Eastman House, now the George Eastman Museum, in Rochester, New York. At the Eastman House, he oversaw 340 individual programs annually in the historic Dryden Theatre. A former programmer for the Chicago International Film Festival, Healy is currently a programming consultant for the Turin and Moscow film festivals.

KENT JONES, WORLD CINEMA FOUNDATION

1. The future of repertory programming is obviously the question. The immediate answer is that repertory will become ever more specialized, an increasingly rarefied pleasure. The problem, of course, is that people will continue to expect that rarefied pleasure at good old moviegoing prices, but I wonder how much longer that will remain feasible. For instance, how much longer will the studios continue to service rep houses when so few of them remain? As it is, booking a studio print is expensive. It's even more expensive when you go to an archive holding a print of a studio title, which means you have to pay both. Meanwhile, procuring a print from Europe or Asia is exorbitant.

Then there's the print versus HD/digital question. Very few people care about that distinction outside of the small, tight circle of cinema devotees, some of whom, fortunately, work at the studios. But what's to stop the studios from sending HD tapes instead of prints? Cheaper all around.

On top of which, home entertainment is getting better and cheaper all the time. For every one person who would prefer to sit in a theater watching a 35 mm or 16 mm print, there are about five thousand people who would prefer to stay home and watch their DVD or Blu-ray on their big screen (their DVD will be "upgraded" in their Blu-ray player from 480 to 720 p). True, not everyone can afford this kind of hardware, but it is getting less and less expensive. Of course, Dave Kehr offers a useful corrective to the notion that "everything is now on DVD"—it's just not true, and that is where the underground community of collectors and file-share sites (not that there are any, mind you) enter into the picture.

Moreover, we are now confronted with a generation with a different relationship to images—a generation for whom, as a film director I know has put it, "size doesn't matter." David Lynch may think it's pitiful that people watch movies on their iPhones or their computers, and many of us may agree, but it's a reality. My sons are growing up in a world where they're confronted with moving images everywhere, at all hours of the day and night. That's a big difference from my own experience. I also want to mention a story that Chris Marker told. When *An American in Paris* came out, he and Resnais went to see it in the cinema over and over again. Years later, when it came out on VHS, he watched it and was completely unimpressed, no matter how big the screen. Then, when the DVD came out, he watched it on his laptop and found that it had regained its magic. I must say, I know what he means. The relation to the image is completely different from, say, watching TV or staring at an iPod Touch.

Having said all that, people do keep going to repertory houses, and even starting them. It's an uphill battle, and it is not a growth industry—if I were just interested in making money, I would not open a movie theater or start a distribution company. But it's possible that rep houses of the future will flourish in the spirit of green markets.

2. I always believed in a dialogue with the audience. That means thinking about time of year, or whether it's the right moment, historically speaking, to show this or that film. Doing a Hou Hsiao-hsien retrospective meant one thing ten years ago, and it means something completely different now. It also means: who is the audience? I think thematic programming means more in Europe than it does here—although, I think that Anthology Film Archives' brilliant "One-Eyed Auteurs" series did pretty well.

Essentially, when programming is at its best, the programmer is telling a story to the audience. I'm thinking of two vastly different programmers, Bruce Goldstein and Mark McElhatten, both of whom I admire, but who are so vastly different. Mark's programs are so meticulously thought through and realized that you feel like you're seeing a real *work*. Bruce, on the other hand, is telling an ongoing story through his programming, thinking about time of year, levels of familiarity, how short or long a time this or that artist has been in or out of the spotlight. What's common to both of them is the all-important personal connection. In both cases, you feel the presence of an individual behind the choices.

Regarding national surveys, I only think they work if there's a story to tell, i.e., an actual national cinema as opposed to a selection of movies from a certain country—two different things. I love double features, but that's something you really have to get behind now (in the conceptual sense) if it's going to work.

3. Let's face it: the future is not bright for celluloid. And if you're programming now, that means that somewhere down the line, you have or will have to project digital or HD. That is an economic reality.

4. I shouldn't be answering this question since I'm not programming at the moment. In my experience at Lincoln Center, younger audiences tended to pour in for certain events. Gavin Smith (another great programmer) and I once did a horror weekend, and it brought in a whole different, younger crowd.

5. I have many fond memories of sitting in incredibly uncomfortable conditions and watching lousy prints. At the old Thalia, for instance, where the rake was up and the floors were tilted. Once I went to see a 16 mm print of Sjöström's *The Scarlet Letter*, which looked dupey and splicey and which had a loop of Scott Joplin piano rags for a score. After the third round of "The Entertainer" (which we all had to listen to all summer long, blasting from ice cream trucks, as it was), the audience revolted and the projectionist cut the sound.

Once I was in Vienna for a show put together by Alex Horwath (who belongs in the programming pantheon with James Quandt). Monte Hellman was present for a screening of *Cockfighter*. Back in those days, Peter Konlechner and Peter Kubelka ran the Austrian Film Museum, and Konlechner's policy was to show everything full frame: 1.66 or 1.85 meant nothing to him, they were industrially imposed affectations. After the screening, Monte and I got up on stage, and he said, "Thank you all for coming. I'm glad you enjoyed it. I just want to say that it was not my intention to include the microphone at the top of every shot. Any questions?"

When I was a kid, I went a lot to two theaters where I grew up. One of them, Toad Hall, is long gone; the other, Images Cinema in Williamstown, Massachusetts, is still alive. It was located on the grounds of Wheatleigh, right near Music Inn, which was eventually shut down by Lenox residents because of the noise (Bob Marley, the Kinks, the Who, and countless other people played there). Toad Hall was slightly less comfortable than the old Thalia, and the prints were a little below the standard of Theatre 80. But that's where I saw a double bill of *The 39 Steps* and *Psycho*, films by Herzog and Bertolucci, and where I bought my first copy of Manny Farber's *Negative Space* (the paperback edition, called *Movies*). It's also where I took my mother and her friends to see *Zabriskie Point*, for which I was never forgiven. Images was a nicer, bigger place, and I saw many, many films there throughout the 1970s. As far as legendary venues, the Bleecker Street Cinema, programmed by Sid Geffen and then the ever-beautiful Jackie Raynal, will never be forgotten. Anthology Film Archives, another legend, is still very much alive, and for that we should all be thankful.

All of Bruce's pre-Code shows at Film Forum were revelations, as was the Naruse show, which originated with James Quandt in Toronto. I have vivid memories of the Oshima show Dan Talbot did at the Metro back in the 1980s. And I went to every single screening of Fabiano Canosa's Renoir retrospective at the Public Theater.

See biographical note on Kent Jones in chapter 3, p. 164.

LAURENCE KARDISH, MUSEUM OF MODERN ART (MOMA), NEW YORK

1. At MoMA we believe that many viewers who experience film seek a communal larger-than-life experience in which they gather in a darkened nondomestic semisacred space, paying full attention to the screen in front of them while being aware of those "around" them. This experience is integral to a certain type of moviegoing experience and has nothing to do with the personal delivery of information, whether on computers, iPods, or other devices. One provides a transporting experience, the other delivers information efficiently. There has been no diminution or growth in the audiences for our exhibitions—it all depends on what we are showing.

2. At MoMA we cover the whole history and culture of cinema—our art is young enough for us to be able to do this, and also to keep abreast of the fast-moving changes in the field of the moving image. As a museum we prefer to screen or present the work in the medium in which it was made, but more and more filmmakers are asking us to show "enhanced" or "improved" digital versions rather than 35 mm prints, particularly when the only analogue material is worn or faded. The artist's wishes always take priority at MoMA.

Our exhibitions may be monographic—Agnès Varda, Tim Burton, Roberto Rossellini, Mike Nichols, Julien Duvivier, Jia Zhang-ke, for instance—or synthetic, as in our current series, "Nuts and Bolts: Machine Made Men in Films from the Collection," and these thematic exhibitions are often more difficult to achieve because the works often come from many different sources. We also mount several national surveys, some annual (Brazil, Canada, Germany), some biannual (India), and some when we feel the need to introduce a certain nation's cinema to New Yorkers, such as our recent survey of Lithuanian cinema. We are, after all, an educational institution. Unless the works are short we tend not to present double features.

Those who attend our screenings are museumgoers, and we assume they are intelligent, curious, and receptive to film as both an art and a medium of personal and social engagement.

3. Good-quality prints are a sometime thing: some studios have repertory divisions, and some small independent distributors are headed by men and women who care about the quality of the work they handle, while others do not. The quality of the print now seems to be contingent on the concern of the individual in charge, and it is no longer a given. As long as we have some people who have the authority to make new prints, and organizations such as MoMA that request them, the exhibition format will not die out speedily. But the art is also an industry, and as film companies become absorbed into large companies indifferent about the medium itself, it will become more difficult to find good prints.

I think the chemical medium, which reacts to light, and the electronic medium operate with two different aesthetics, and how the information is delivered to the viewer's sensory system alters the reaction of the audience. I believe experiencing film is a deeper, richer, and more dreamlike experience than absorbing the electronic image, but I believe the digital image will play a primary role in our popular culture.

4. See my answers to the questions above.

5. When I first came to New York in the late 1960s there was a wealth of "repertory" theaters in Manhattan—there were great films in lousy cinemas (meaning they all needed repairs, and had seen better days), but somehow the seedy ambiance (the Thalia, the Apollo on W. 42nd Street, the Charles, the Film-Makers' Cinematheque in the Wurlitzer Building, also on 42nd Street, the New Yorker) and the absolute passion of the filmgoers made moviegoing memorable. But my favorite double feature ever was when I snuck into a really "dangerous" theater as a kid in Ottawa (and "dangerous" in Canada would be a joke in New York) to see a double bill that blew me away (and still does), since I was not prepared—Don Siegel's *The Lineup* followed by Robert Aldrich's *Kiss Me Deadly*. I was about twelve. An inspiring series for me when I first came to New York was a Preston Sturges retrospective held, of all places, within Trinity Church downtown.

Laurence Kardish has been curating film exhibitions for decades. He founded Carleton University's film society in 1963. From 1963 until 1966, when he moved to New York, he helped program the Canadian Film Institute's National Film Theater in Ottawa. An MFA graduate of Columbia University, Kardish worked for the New American Cinema Group before joining the staff of the film department at New York's Museum of Modern Art in 1968, when he became senior curator at the museum. He retired in 2012.

MARIE LOSIER, FRENCH INSTITUTE ALLIANCE FRANÇAISE (FIAF), NEW YORK

1. I am old school in a way, but I feel that there is always the same crowd running into movie theaters to see a great old film on 35 mm, with a good or even not so good print. I'm still very bad at technology and downloading films from the Internet, so I believe we're still a long way from the day when 35 mm films and repertory cinemas disappear or change completely. *Playtime* was shown in a brand-new 35 mm print last week at MoMA and it was still sold out, even though this film screens frequently. The repertory series at Film Forum are still filling the theaters—you have to buy tickets online way in advance to get in.

It is true that there are more films available online and on DVD, but the experience of watching a film at home and that of going to a theater is still not comparable. Life is busy, especially in New York, so of course I do both to save time; but in Paris, for example, people go to the movies a lot more—there are so many movie theaters, so many films screening, and so few good video stores, that the experience of going to the movies is still very vital.

I think Netflix and film downloading is good for some things—for finding rare films, films you missed, or films you don't want to pay twelve dollars to see in the theaters. In a way it does spread, and many people have more access to films in the same way that there are more people who can afford making films and editing on their own with home editing programs and affordable video cameras.

2. The films that I show at FIAF have to be in French, with English subtitles, so of course it is a very particular kind of programming and is

limited in a way because so many rare and wonderful films are no longer available in good quality prints or with subtitles. I have to invent series that will not be too repetitive and use what is being restored, or coming to New York, or know what filmmakers or actors are available for a series or retrospective on their work. Also, the audience at FIAF requires certain kinds of films—I can't go too far in showing experimental or obscure or difficult films. I leave that type of great programming to Anthology Film Archives and Lincoln Center's Walter Reade Theater, as well as BAM (Brooklyn Academy of Music).

Also I have to program in the face of competition from great theaters like the Walter Reade, MoMA, Anthology Film Archives, Film Forum, and BAM, which show films daily, all year round, while FIAF is open only on Tuesdays.

A great treasure for FIAF is the library of prints that the French government makes available—the Ministry of Foreign Affairs (MAE) owns a ton of incredible films, on 35 mm, and on Beta for a lot of their documentary selection. I know the number of new acquisitions each year is declining thanks to diminishing budgets, but there are still many treasures to borrow and show and share with NYC audiences, thanks to the MAE and the help of the French embassy.

3. FIAF's theater is equipped to show 35 mm without platters, reel to reel, so we can show archival films. We can also show 16 mm, DVD, and Beta. I always try to show films on 35 mm and have no idea how to organize DVD screenings since that involves a totally different way of clearing rights, not to mention attracting an audience (people are not going to pay twelve dollars to go see a movie on DVD when they can just as easily rent it and watch it at home). Also programming with DVD formats is too easy, in a way—it takes away all the hard work of a programmer, which is to track down prints and rights, a process that's often so difficult it makes you feel like Sherlock Holmes. Seeing an old film on celluloid is still, to me, a wonderful and magical physical experience, and no video format has replaced the emotional substance a print can convey.

Of course there are now films that are shot on HD and shown with HD projectors that are often of great quality, but that is more for newer films than for repertory cinema. Also, since this type of HD equipment is still a very expensive investment, only a few theaters have it. Of course, HD films are super cheap for shipping, which is certainly not the case for 35 mm films and which is often a huge concern for programmers with limited budgets.

It is harder today to find good-quality prints because the theatrical rights to many films have lapsed and the distributors do not always pay to have those rights renewed. But also the prints that are circulating are often old and scratched, and it costs so much to restore a film that fewer and fewer are restored, while existing prints are simply archived and, sadly, are not accessible. I can only hope and dream films on celluloid will continue to be exhibited for a while—hopefully this will only change when I am already dead so I don't have to argue and debate about preservation and formats and the rise of digital media!

I feel much will be lost if film formats like 16 mm or 35 mm disappear. A true lover of old-time cinema, I am very attached to the experience of seeing films projected, with all that it brings to one's senses. Of course, I adore cinema so much that I would be open to other formats, including digital ones if that is destined to come to pass. The shipping of prints and preservation are very expensive—if it becomes easier to get films and show them, if the whole system of programming and tracking down rights and exhibition copies becomes simpler, then I will follow, of course. But it will be a very different experience for me as a programmer and lover of cinema, and for the audience. Of course, new generations of young people going to the movies do not have any of this nostalgia for and love of the materiality of films—they know well the digital world and that is what speaks to them, so I guess there is space for all generations and desires in the cinema exhibition world.

4. I don't feel the audience at FIAF has changed too much, though there are more young people coming. But Cinema Tuesday remains the one constant activity of FIAF and creates a wonderful stability of audience. Cinema continues to speak to everyone; it is such a universal form of entertainment and remains relatively inexpensive today.

5. I remember that at a very young age I was touched by the discoveries I made at the Cinémathèque Française, in the classes of Jean Douchet, who led me to discover all the films of Franju, Ozu, and Renoir, which really changed my life. Or going to see *The Bitter Tears of Petra von Kant* by Fassbinder and *Winchester '73*, which played every day for twenty years in the same theaters—it was quite magical to me to experience cinema that way. Then I arrived in NYC and felt like I fell under a spell, spending a lot of my time at Anthology Film Archives and discovering incredible films like those of Jack Smith, the Kuchar brothers, and Robert Breer, plus some great repertory film series of rare campy films, which were unknown to me before.

I also remember feeling that cinema was truly alive at venues like Ocularis and the Robert Beck Memorial Cinema, two very experimental theaters—long gone today—where you would meet the filmmakers, spend the evening with them, talk, see their work, and experience films in a very personal light.

At FIAF I have a few cherished moments and series that I will never forget because of the artists who were invited and the films and aura they presented. The most memorable moments for me have been my week with the wonderful Raoul Coutard and his two-month film series, as well as Jackie Raynal and her wonderful wit and approach to film. Some repertory series that have stayed with me as great discoveries at FIAF were the ones on Jean Eustache and Albicocco.

Marie Losier, a filmmaker living in Paris, was film programmer at the French Institute Alliance Française in New York City at the time of this symposium. She has also programmed experimental films at the Robert Beck Memorial Cinema, Ocularis, and other venues in Europe and the United States. Losier's films are frequently screened at museums, galleries, biennials, and festivals around the world. Her many short experimental films include several made in collaboration with George Kuchar (actor and subject): *Bird, Bath, and Beyond* (2003), *Electrocute Your Stars* (2004), and *Eat My Makeup!* (2005); and she collaborated with Guy Maddin (actor) in *Manuelle Labor* (2007). Her feature documentary, *The Ballad of Genesis and Lady Jaye*, won the Teddy for Best Documentary at the 2011 Berlin Film Festival.

RICHARD PEÑA, FILM SOCIETY OF LINCOLN CENTER, NEW YORK

1. I do believe there is a future for repertory programming; despite the great success of *Avatar*, I wonder more about the future of commercial cinema. But just as I think there will always be theater and opera and ballet companies, I do believe that there will always be audiences for publicly projected moving-image art. Obviously, the new outlets are competition for repertory programs, but they do, or at least can, lead to more informed audiences.

2. I sometimes see myself in the "film history" business; sometimes I ply my trade as a teacher, and sometimes as the organizer of film series

and festivals. At best, or at my best (perhaps), I can help to plug in some "black holes" in film history by bringing to light certain films, filmmakers, or national cinemas that have been overlooked or which have been forgotten, broadening and ideally challenging our established notions of the development of film art. As a teacher, on the other hand, there are also classic films that are important to teach each year, as I'm hopefully educating new generations of students, just as for me as a programmer there are a number of national or regional cinemas (France, Africa, Italy, etc.) that we revisit every year to take the pulse of what's happening.

3. Thirty-five-millimeter prints are great when you can get them, which we can't always for all our series. Restorations are increasingly being done digitally, and unless you can get someone to pay for transferring the material to celluloid, they're most often available in digital formats. Thirty-five millimeter will of course continue to exist, but will, I think, decrease in availability over the years.

4. How have your audiences changed over the years? Audiences, I think, are much more atomized nowadays. We have an audience that will come out for Japanese films that doesn't come out for other series we do—but they're very faithful to our Japanese programs.

Are they increasing or decreasing? We've just had a very good year (2009), one of our best, in terms of attendance. But as anyone in exhibition will tell you, it's a crapshoot.

Have their demographics changed, in terms of age or background? As I said, audiences are more atomized. We do get a significant older audience because of our location, the fact that older people feel safe at Lincoln Center, and perhaps because of what we show. But some series or events draw significant younger audiences. Certain "new" ethnic groups, Koreans or Iranians or Indians, have also been strong supporters of series of films from their countries.

Have they become more or less receptive to challenging and innovative programs? I think they've largely been receptive, but then again, the people who like what we show come back, while those that don't, don't. But overall I feel audiences are more conservative nowadays and resistant to formal experimentation. It's hard to imagine films such as L'eclisse or Muriel getting commercial releases nowadays.

5. During the summer of 1975, just about the time I decided I would devote my life in some way to cinema, the Carnegie/Bleecker complex ran retrospectives of Howard Hawks and Jean-Luc Godard practically

simultaneously—a great education in cinema! MoMA has presented a number of crucial series in my cinematic education: their Brazilian Cinema Novo shows, the "Before Neo-Realism" show, "Film India" in 1980—the list could go on.

I can remember going to the Thalia with my then girlfriend, now wife, to see David Cronenberg's *The Parasite Murders* (a.k.a. *Shivers*, a.k.a. *They Came from Within*) and having the four original Ramones come in and sit behind us. I felt vindicated.

Richard Peña was program director of the Film Society of Lincoln Center and director of the New York Film Festival from 1988 to 2012. At Lincoln Center's film society, he organized retrospectives of Michelangelo Antonioni, Sacha Guitry, Abbas Kiarostami, Kira Muratova, Youssef Chahine, Yasujiro Ozu, Carlos Saura, and Amitabh Bachchan, as well as major film series devoted to African, Chinese, Cuban, Polish, Hungarian, Arab, Korean, Soviet, and Argentine cinema. He is a professor of film studies at Columbia University and is cohost of *Reel 13*, a weekly show on New York City's public television station Channel 13. He is also author of *Cinema without Borders: The Films of Joris Ivens* and coeditor of *New York Film Festival Gold: A 50th Anniversary Celebration.*

JAMES QUANDT, TORONTO INTERNATIONAL FILM FESTIVAL

1. It's little wonder that film programmers joke about our imperiled profession and our future as door-to-door consultants for home-cinema owners. I recently wrote an article on the "new cinephilia" for *Framework*'s fiftieth edition, which will probably be lambasted for its defense of such outmoded notions as original format, and for its critique of our tacit acquiescence to a film culture that is an abasement of the art we supposedly serve. As many of us attempt to nurture, defend, and promote the traditional modes of exhibiting and viewing cinema, we also participate in a faux film culture, by pretending that we have "seen" (and heard) a film when we have merely consumed a degraded version of it, in the delivery systems you identify in your question. Recently, an "onliner" rejected my claim that our touring Nagisa Oshima retrospective was "rare," arguing that most of Oshima's work can be easily streamed from the Internet, so is readily available to all. (He helpfully offered the necessary links.) Aside from the legal and ethical

issues involved, how can anyone actually claim to have seen and heard an Oshima film in that diminished manner? Is cinema art or is it information? And why do we as critics, scholars, commentators, and curators do our visual and sonic analysis of films from such approximate (and often misleading or inaccurate) materials, and blithely present it as though we have worked from the original? What other art form allows such dissimulation? (I am as guilty as the next one for relying on screeners, but try to abide by the rule that they act as an aide-mémoire rather than a substitute for seeing the film on screen.)

Two of Tsai Ming-liang's recent films, *Goodbye, Dragon Inn* and *It's a Dream*, are requiems for the classic cinema-going experience. Tsai has suggested that technology and aesthetics increasingly exist in inverse proportion, the advance of one diminishing the urgency of the other: "I am not happy about the whole DVD medium, in fact. The quality of film experience is crashing. People are now satisfied just watching a film to find out what the story is. The experience is almost being reduced to a kind of information gathering. What is going on? Who is it? My films are really for the big screen only." But Tsai's films will be seen mostly via the medium he decries, their enigmas rendered all the more mysterious by visual illegibility.

As someone who had the good fortune of making a career of giving others the opportunities I had as a developing cinephile to see, say, Godard's *Deux ou trois choses que je sais d'elle* or Oshima's *Night and Fog in Japan* for the first time on screen, and thereby attempting to foster the same "film love" that once consumed me—the immersive kind of cinephilia rather than the collector-cultish experience, as Thomas Elsaesser construes the two—I rue the thought of anyone's initial encounters with these Scope masterpieces on a computer or television monitor, no matter how large or deluxe.

Complications arise from the counterargument, which assigns ultimate value to access. Is the proliferation and ease of access to cinema from every period, every country, not a miracle of "open museum" cultural democracy? Do the extras on Criterion and Masters of Cinema DVDs not serve as the kind of film education I would have cherished as a geographically isolated, self-taught cinephile? Hard to argue otherwise, but I think we have to be cognizant also of what we lose in the process. Regarding your second question, it would be dishonest and ungrateful not to point out that there have been immense benefits from the DVD boom of the last decade. The many restorations, undertaken by the studios for DVD release, often result in new prints being struck and distributed. I would never have been able to accomplish organizing the Oshima retrospective without the immense involvement of Janus Films, which made new prints of many of his films, including some rather esoteric ones, which I assume will eventually appear on Criterion DVDs. Mainstays of our Sunday afternoon series of classics are Schawn Belston's amazing restorations of Fox titles. And so on.

2. I envy those who do thematic programming! Over the twenty-five years or so of presenting film series in Toronto, at four or five different venues, I have foundered on one immutable fact: audiences here much prefer narrowly defined and strictly cohesive film series to multifarious and complex ones. In other words, directorial retrospectives are much preferred to thematic series. As much as the latter elicit a programmer's creativity, knowledge, and reach, and therefore are the most rewarding to curate, the few successful examples I can think of in the cinematheque's history include a series that sounded like a graduate thesis: "Spirituality and Sacrilege in Medievalist Cinema." Indeed, it was almost completely sold out, and brought an extremely varied audience, not just cinephiles: theology students, early-music aficionados, historians. Two of the very first series I did in Toronto, almost thirty years ago, at the Art Gallery of Ontario, when it still had a film department, illustrate the fact. The series that did extremely well paired each of Bresson's films with one he influenced, the double bills sold as a single ticket; the one that did disastrously was the cinema sidebar of "The European Iceberg" exhibition of recent German and Italian art, because it mixed many disparate elements: masters and newcomers, experimental and narrative cinema, et cetera. Heady on paper, flummoxing in experience. The "through line" was difficult to discern for an audience: how do Kluge and Fellini "work" with Rebecca Horn and Carmelo Bene?

Double bills also function better as concept than actuality. (A confession: I have often been congratulated for double bills that were mere accidents of scheduling.) It may be a cinephilic parlor game to match films by thematic or stylistic kinship, or to illustrate influence and homage, but the occasional hunch can pay off on-screen. I thought it interesting to pair *Blowup* with *Bunny Lake Is Missing* in our recent Preminger retrospective. No suggestion of direct influence at all, simply hints of affinity: they're both puzzle movies set in swinging 1960s London with "whiter shade of

pale" protagonists (David Hemmings, Carol Lynley, Keir Dullea); one features the Yardbirds, the other the Zombies. Much to my surprise, it worked
splendidly. A counterexample from the same retro was programming Clouzot's *Le corbeau* after Preminger's remake of it, *The 13th Letter*. Not only was
the mystery solved and thereby "spoiled" for those staying for both films,
but the acidulous Clouzot also made Preminger's version look even weaker
than it is. National surveys are legitimate, especially when a country's cinema suddenly emerges or resurges. The most obvious recent example is
Romania, but also Argentina, the Philippines, Belgium. (I have been wanting to do a historical Belgian survey for some time, in light of recent developments.) It's one thing to examine an emerging trend, but on an annual
basis these surveys often become egregious, perfunctory. We used to do
yearly "showcases" of contemporary Spanish and Greek cinema, which
were extremely popular, but they became increasingly untenable because
of a paucity of good films to warrant an annual event, so I let them go.

3. I am shocked at the number of companies, and the growing number
of film directors, who instruct us to show DVDs when we find it difficult to
secure a good print. Projected DVD is the worst instance of digital delivery,
of course, and I often regret that I resorted to this shortcut when organizing the Rossellini retrospective. At the time, and I think the case has not
changed; it was the only way a few of the key history films could be shown,
so I slid down that slippery slope. But, to extend the metaphor preposter-
ously, that slope is all mud, and I think it is best to maintain, for as long
as possible, the high ground of original formats. We debate digital projection a great deal in our organization—especially as we are set to open Bell
Lightbox, with five cinemas—and I remain a staunch defender of film qua
film, celluloid qua celluloid, much to the distraction of those who see that
purist attitude as archaic, reactionary. But I think at some point it will be a
losing battle. In the meantime, I think it behooves us to educate audiences
(and each other, for I learn something new about digital every day, and eat
crow for breakfast sometimes) about such matters. Until the difference is
made apparent, it won't be the urgent issue it should be.

A Toronto film critic once claimed that the role of a cinematheque
was to show works that were not available on DVD, implying that the
latter replaces the former, while countless others have pointed out that
most DVDs have fewer visual flaws than a worn film print. (Digital has
indeed ordained the pristine, much to the chagrin of cinematheques.) The
phrase "in-cinema experience" has recently entered the discourse of film

curation—to differentiate traditional film going from gallery and installation presentation of "moving image" works, videotheques, et cetera—a marker of the rapid move of cinema's realm from the social and ceremonial to the insular and domestic, the analogue to the digital, the hard won to the easily accessible. Many film archivists now envision the day when a Fritz Lang retrospective, presented in its original formats (i.e., 35 mm film, the silents at proper fps projector speed), in the best possible prints, would be the equivalent of a Matisse or Bellini exhibition, the rarity and authenticity of which make it a destination blockbuster. That might restore a Benjaminian "aura" to cinema.

4. The question becomes do you attempt to shape an audience's taste, or cater and respond to it; do you have the luxury (and temerity) of the former approach, or do box-office concerns dictate the latter? We're fortunate in having maintained a large, dedicated audience, though its taste has changed markedly since our cinematheque first opened two decades ago. In the early years, it was much easier to sell out a screening of an Angelopoulos film than to get more than Pastor Ericsson's congregation to a new print of a John Ford classic. Everyone assumed that I had a prejudice against Hollywood cinema because we showed so little of it, but that was a totally specious inference. Our audience was more likely to pack out a Harun Farocki or Werner Schroeter film than to be caught dead at Hawks or Hitchcock.

That has gradually changed, and though I can't say the obverse is now true, a Preminger retrospective certainly does far better than Rivette. Which perhaps answers your other question about receptiveness to challenging programs. A show that proved quite successful in the cinematheque's early years, of documentaries about Japan by outsiders (e.g., Chris Marker, Kim Longinotto), would probably now have a tenth of the audience it did then. In the area of classic Japanese cinema, which is one of our mainstays, audiences much prefer Ozu and Naruse to Hani and Oshima, and not just because the latter are less known.

(Important caveat: attendance should not be the sole or defining marker of a series' success. We're all a little number crazy these days; I swear we'll soon be using terms like "weekly nut.") Regarding demographics, I think that, as with all the arts, our audience skews older than it once did. Though I get a little tired of cultural organizations' fetish with youth and desperation to avoid appearing uncool—the consequence of so many arts administrators' midlife crises—it's always gratifying to see a completely new audience turn up, as happened with our Hong Sang-soo retrospective.

5. A Gray Old Man of the Mountain response. An autodidact and hope-less movie lover from a village in northern Saskatchewan with no television (so no late-night movies, the provenance of so many nascent cinephiles), and long before video recorders, much less DVD players or the Internet, I took my holidays in New York or Toronto to see films. I traveled hundreds of miles, made a master schedule of all the things I needed to see, and ran day and night—in shoes with yellow Lucite heels!—mostly to venues that no longer exist: the Bleecker Street Cinema, the Public Theater, the Thalia. Formative series were the Mizoguchi retrospective at Japan Society; a trib-ute to New Yorker Films at the Bleecker, where I saw my first Bressons; and my first shattering encounter with *Red Desert* at the Thalia (even when shown in a battered, faded print—*Cerise Sand* was more like it). Would that any of the series at our cinematheque have the same overwhelming effect.

James Quandt is senior programmer at the Toronto International Film Fes-tival Cinematheque, where he has curated several internationally touring retrospectives, including ones dedicated to Naruse, Mizoguchi, Bresson, Imamura, Ichikawa, and, most recently, Oshima. A regular contributor to *Artforum*, Quandt has also edited monographs on Robert Bresson, Shohei Imamura, Kon Ichikawa, and Apichatpong Weerasethakul.

DAVID SCHWARTZ, MUSEUM OF THE MOVING IMAGE, ASTORIA, NEW YORK

1. I'm feeling very sanguine about the answer to this question, because the Museum of the Moving Image is opening its expanded, renovated building this fall with two brand-new theaters for repertory programming, along with gallery space, an education center, and much more. With new the-aters coming for the Film Society of Lincoln Center, a new theater already opened at the Museum of Modern Art, and the ongoing vitality of Anthol-ogy Film Archives and BAM (Brooklyn Academy of Music), the future in my immediate vicinity looks quite bright.

And beyond a New Yorker's provincial perspective, there's plenty going on around the world; the best place to check out the global scene is the *Moving Image Source* calendar section, with links to more than two hun-dred international venues. So as much as people talk about the demise of repertory programming, the scene looks quite vital. It was encouraging to see the overwhelming response to the threatened demise of the Los Angeles County Museum of Art (LACMA) film program (a response which took place, perhaps ironically, via Facebook), and along with the LACMA program's proud history, it is encouraging to see new venues emerge—see the lively programming in Los Angeles by REDCAT and Cinefamily (at the Silent Movie Theatre!).

As for new technologies, it's true that people will be watching movies on computers, handheld devices, on demand, but the theatrical experience will survive for three key reasons: the desire for a communal, social experience; the fact that the demand for online content will indeed fuel the creation of new prints; and most importantly, the fact that a movie can't truly be experienced on a small screen (you never feel like you're in the world of a film when you're watching on a video monitor or laptop screen).

2. Well, first of all, it's not so much a question of my personal philosophy as it is the philosophy of the museum. Moving Image's programs are characterized by a broad scope that moves between historically grounded programs and vanguard work (from silent films to interactive installations), always focusing on the highest quality presentation, as much as possible with a live element (guest speaker, live musician, etc.). To get a little more specific, I tend to favor in-depth director retrospectives—as a die-hard auteurist, I'll always see the cinematic world through the lens of Andrew Sarris's *American Cinema*, updated and expanded in my mind. Thematic series are irresistible to intelligent programmers, but often of less interest to the audience. And national surveys tend to be of most interest to sponsors. I also tend to program by double feature for the simple reason that the museum usually shows two films on a weekend afternoon, so it's critical to think of how those two films work together. No matter what the format of the program, the key thing is always to focus on the quality of the individual presentation of a single film. Still, the context in which a film is shown is very important, and *Rear Window* as part of a Grace Kelly retrospective would read differently than *Rear Window* as part of a Cornell Woolrich series.

3. To use a phrase that evokes another dying format, the handwriting is on the wall; to borrow the idea stated by Paolo Cherchi Usai at the last Orphans Film Symposium, the entire celluloid output of the twentieth century will one day be known as the predigital age. To look on the bright side, take the example of *The Rules of the Game*, which for many years was not available in a passable 35 mm print in the United States. The Criterion Collection's work on digitally restoring the film for DVD release led

directly to the creation of an impressive new 35 mm print. Also, it was interesting to see how well the touring 35 mm film version of the Janus Essential Art House collection did; the fact that these films were all available on DVD didn't diminish audiences. DVD releases generate publicity for specific films, which will only help boost theatrical attendance.

4. I think the real problem at the moment is the lack of enthusiasm for repertory film going among undergraduate college students. At a time when there are more cinema-studies programs than ever before, the thriving campus film society—or the notion that an outing to a local repertory cinema is the thing to do—has severely faded away.

5. Two indelible memories among many: during a trip to London when I was ten, I badly wanted to see *The Aristocats*. My mom forced me to see a revival screening of *Steamboat Bill, Jr.*, in a large, nearly deserted movie palace, accompanied by live organ music. I laughed so hard I literally rolled in the aisles . . . and started seeking out screenings of Chaplin and Keaton films. Even more important was a trip to Manhattan on July 10, 1978 (I was seventeen). I had read John Simon's book about Ingmar Bergman's movies, which brought the films to life with lavish illustrations and crisp prose. The Bleecker Street Cinema was presenting a double feature of *Persona* and Altman's *Three Women*. The Bergman film was overwhelming, and its reflexive modernism enthralled me with the possibilities of the art form. The Altman film struck me as a pretentious albeit quirky rip-off (the music score is almost identical), but I guess I was intrigued by the way the films were programmed.

These moments are two among many; the whole point of repertory film going is precisely that it provides memorable, formative, enthralling, entertaining, provocative experiences.

David Schwartz is chief curator at the Museum of the Moving Image and was editor-at-large for *Moving Image Source*. He has written for *Senses of Cinema*, is a visiting assistant professor in cinema studies at Purchase College, and hosts the Westchester Cinema Club.

ADAM SEKULER, NORTHWEST FILM FORUM, SEATTLE

1. Despite the increased accessibility of films in the home via the Web, DVD, and on demand, and paying little attention to the cries that the sky is falling, I believe that if anything, the last few years have proven that

Figure 7.3. As a result of a request from Anthology Film Archives, Paramount agreed to strike a new print of Jerzy Skolimowski's *Deep End*. According to Adam Sekuler, this is another example of a potentially forgotten film that, through the efforts of programmers and curators, has been rediscovered and given both new recognition and a new life. © Paramount Pictures, 1970.

repertory cinema is alive and well, and perhaps a little more interesting for the programmer. With so much of the canon available on DVD or streaming, it is important for the programmer to remember that a large body of repertory cinema is still awaiting discovery or rediscovery. And while prints for these titles remain harder to find, it is also possible for programmers to work collaboratively to encourage new prints to be struck.

A wonderful example of this can be found in the rerelease of Jerzy Skolimowski's *Deep End* just a few years back. Anthology Film Archives was presenting a retrospective of Skolimowski's work when they inquired about a new print being struck. As Paramount hadn't considered this title of significant importance in their collection, it was one of many neglected films that, as programmers, we could allow the audience to rediscover. Anthology requested a new print, assuring Paramount that they could find enough venues interested in screening the film, which indeed they did. As a collective, we programmers were able to bring this film back to the attention of the film-going public. As this example shows, it has become increasingly important for us to work collaboratively in preserving the future of repertory programming, but also for us to look towards those films forgotten or fallen by the wayside.

2. Programming for me is always about discovery, avoiding redundancy, collaborating, and remaining nimble. As Seattle is a city with many art-house options, I find it's important to define our identity as distinct from many of the other cinemas. For thematic series or national surveys, I program titles that are hard to find and unavailable on DVD, and often bring prints into the country. I want the audience to always find the unexpected. When screening canonical titles, I insist on adding an element to the programming that the audience wouldn't receive in any other context, whether that means providing substantive background in the form of program notes or blog posts, or arranging introductions from a local critic, an academic, or those involved in the production. We find it's also important to work with other organizations in the city. This brings us new audiences and often allows for nonfilmic introductions about context, et cetera. When events arise that suggest an unexpected screening, I don't hold rigidly to our calendar. I leave enough room for flexibility to assure our audience that we're providing the most nimble programming in the city.

3. As I discussed in my response to the first question, through a collaborative approach I find the studios are still open to striking new prints, but need a critical mass in order to do so. This puts the burden on us programmers to create a demand for new prints. Often, good-quality prints are also available, but we prefer newly struck prints. As for projection formats, we're open to screening titles on video, but usually only when those titles originate in a video format. Only on a rare occasion will we screen a movie digitally if it originated on film.

4. It may sound strange, but there are two audiences that we can count on: middle-aged men and young women. Yet all films provide us different demographics. These two core audiences are rather loyal and are willing to attend most of our programs.

5. I was fortunate enough to have worked early in my career for the Oak Street Cinema, a venue that still exists but hasn't programmed consistently for years. One year we launched an exhaustive Eric Rohmer retrospective, which received a scathing critique from the local press. Our executive director, Bob Cowgill, began a several-week-long printed exchange with Matthew Wilder, the critic most biting in his criticism. It made the series feel more vibrant and proved to me that an engaged intellectual response to negative criticism could push programming in more public directions.

Also, a site-specific program that was inspiring was a screening of *King Kong* on the top floor of the Empire State Building.

Some of my favorite venues, in no particular order, are Vancity Theatre (Vancouver), Lantaren (Rotterdam), the Castro Theatre (San Francisco), and Oak Street Cinema (Minneapolis).

Adam Sekuler was creative director for Seattle's Northwest Film Forum until 2013. He cofounded Search and Rescue—an ongoing effort to present and preserve discarded archives of 16 mm films—and is owner and founder of m'aidez films. He has contributed programming to the Minneapolis St. Paul International Film Festival and Sound Unseen. Sekuler organized the touring retrospective "A Man Vanishes: The Legacy of Shohei Imamura" and has organized North American tours for Serge Bozon's *La France*, Albert Serra's *Bird Song*, and Lisandro Alonso's *Liverpool*.

DYLAN SKOLNICK, CINEMA ARTS CENTRE, LONG ISLAND, NEW YORK

1. I could certainly be prejudiced by my background, but I remain convinced that people still enjoy going to the movies, whether the latest releases or classics. Most of the consequences of new technology in this case have been negative. Attendance is down for ordinary repertory screenings. I wish I could say that audiences are more informed, but I actually find that audiences raised on home video are generally less knowledgeable (and less well-behaved) than those who grew up in the theater-only era. The Internet is an immense resource of information on film, but it is also the bathroom wall of the new millennium, and it often seems like the latter is a more popular use of the medium. For us, new prints struck for video release are the main benefit of these technological advances.

2. Home video and downloading have suppressed attendance for plain-vanilla, no-frills repertory programming, but we have had a great response to programs that include a "value-added" element, like guest speakers, receptions, silents with live music, et cetera. Programmers have to be more imaginative to grab the attention of our audience. I love classic repertory programming where each day features a different unrelated movie (or two), but that kind of schedule simply can't generate enough publicity to attract contemporary audiences. We don't have a single audience; we have numerous audiences. I try to offer something for all of them with regular series focusing on documentaries, art, silent movies with live

accompaniment, LGBT, music, cult movies, classics, as well as countless one-shot screenings and first-run art-house flicks.

3. Finding good prints is an ongoing challenge, but they are out there. In particular, I want to single out the remarkable role played by private collectors in preserving prints that would otherwise be discarded by film companies. I think there is a future for 35 mm film. No video format can yet capture the unique texture of film. Thirty-five-millimeter repertory prints will continue to be made for as long as theaters like us provide a financial basis for their being struck. The loss of this format would be an enormous loss. Having said that, we do screen from video when it is appropriate. Most of those digital screenings are films that were shot on video, but we do screen classic films from digital formats when that is the best-possible option. I'm not one of those people who would show a crap 35 mm print rather than an excellent digital transfer, but I probably would choose to show a decent film print instead of a perfect digital copy.

4. We have no choice but to admit that the theatergoing audience for specialized cinema (repertory, foreign, independent) has shrunk. Movies are no longer the dominant cultural force that they were in the mid-twentieth century. In the 1960s, no self-respecting intellectual or hipster would consider themselves culturally aware without having a knowledge of Bergman or Godard (even if it was just to impress potential mates), but that time has passed. Older generations are undoubtedly our largest audience, but I find that every successive generation has a core group that falls in love with watching movies on the big screen. The audience for "challenging and innovative" programs has always been a minority, and that remains true, but it is always a passionate minority. It is up to us to provide programs that attract and inspire them. We also offer more popular films that help subsidize programs that attract smaller audiences.

5. My parents started taking me to movies before I could speak. My first spoken words were "The End." I grew up at the New Community Cinema in Huntington, now known as the Cinema Arts Centre. I was a fill-in projectionist at age seven, and spent countless hours watching movies. Excepting a brief flirtation with filmmaking, and the usual panoply of teenage jobs, I have spent most of my life working at the Cinema Arts Centre. I also used to love going to the Thalia Cinema on New York's Upper West Side. Owner Richard Schwarz ran a classic repertory schedule with new double features every day. I later worked for Richard at the Cinema Village in downtown Manhattan, and discovered that his programming grew out

of a personal passion for movies that is unmatched by anyone I've met since. He enjoyed talking about movies all night long, and would be disappointed when you wanted to go home simply because it was two in the morning. The amazing variety and creativity of Schwarz's programming remains an ongoing inspiration to me.

> Dylan Skolnick is codirector at the Cinema Arts Centre, Long Island's leading venue for alternative film. Skolnick has also been curator of the East Meadow Public Library's acclaimed Independent Film Series and coordinating programmer for the Lake Placid Film Festival. He is a graduate of New York's School of Visual Arts.

TOM VICK, SMITHSONIAN INSTITUTION, WASHINGTON, DC

1. Even with all the choices available to viewers, repertory programs still provide a vital function because they are curated by professionals, and therefore remain the gateways through which audiences discover new films and filmmakers and rediscover classics and forgotten works. Many of the foreign and classic films now available via these new technologies are there because people first programmed them in repertory theaters. A touring retrospective, for instance, can be the first step toward a director's work being released on DVD.

Before the proliferation of new technologies, this curating or tastemaking function of repertory programmers was pretty much taken for granted. Now that we have become just one choice in a sea of moving-image options, we need to recognize and emphasize the human expertise that makes repertory programming unique, and the importance we have as entrance points for new and restored films.

Judging by the heavy investment Hollywood is making in 3-D technology, they seem to be as concerned as we are that people no longer want to leave the house to see movies. Their way of creating a unique moviegoing experience is to make the spectacle bigger. Ours might be to emphasize the human element that makes repertory theaters unique, not just through creative, thoughtful programming and screening good-quality prints, but through informative film introductions, hosting visiting filmmakers, live accompaniment for silent films, and other elements that aren't available by download. In other words, maybe we need to think of ourselves less like movie theaters and more like concert halls or playhouses—trusted destinations in our communities that provide a distinct cultural experience.

2. My primary goal is to emphasize cinema as an art form, and to present films from as much of Asia as possible in any given year. In practice, I try to strike a balance between championing films that I think are important to show, responding to the culture of the Washington area, and creating programming that complements our museum exhibitions. Because Washington is a center of diplomacy and politics, regional surveys tend to bring in the largest audiences (our long-running Iranian and Hong Kong film festivals are our most popular annual events), but I also program retrospectives and thematic series whenever possible.

3. While I hope that there will always be a place for 35 mm repertory screenings, projecting on video and digital formats has become a necessity. For political and economic reasons, a lot of the most interesting work coming out of places like China and Southeast Asia, for instance, is being made on video.

The bigger challenge is in adapting to how these technologies have altered the way moving images are presented and received. The line between filmmaking and video art has become blurred. Filmmakers like Abbas Kiarostami and Tsai Ming-liang now also make video installations designed to be presented outside the traditional theater environment. Wang Bing and Lav Diaz use digital video to experiment with extremely long durations. Video artists like Yang Fudong and Fiona Tan incorporate cinematic aesthetics and references into works designed to be presented in gallery spaces. Rather than seeing these changes as a threat to traditional exhibition practices, perhaps the future lies in using them to open up a dialogue between film programming and contemporary art through collaborations with curators, museums, and galleries.

4. Our core audience of devoted cinephiles—the ones who come to just about everything—is definitely an older crowd, but certain programs, like genre films and anime, do bring in young people. Because of Washington's diverse ethnic population and large diplomatic community, the demographics tend to vary depending on where the film being shown is from. I haven't noticed a big drop in attendance over the last few years. In fact, the economic crisis boosted attendance for some programs because we don't charge admission.

5. My earliest memories of seeing repertory programming—though I didn't know that's what it was at the time—involved going to Kurosawa

movies on family trips to New York when I was a kid. When I moved to Los Angeles for film school, I loved going to the Silent Movie House, which at the time had live organ accompaniment and, in keeping with tradition, screened cartoons and shorts before every feature. Later, when I worked as an assistant programmer at the Los Angeles County Museum of Art, the programs I found most enlightening were retrospectives that either introduced me to filmmakers I wasn't familiar with (Gregory La Cava comes to mind) or, as was the case with a retrospective of Fritz Lang's American films, gave me a new perspective on a director's work.

Tom Vick is curator of film for the Freer and Sackler Galleries of the Smithsonian Institution, where he oversees year-round screenings of films from all over Asia. Vick has written articles on Asian film for numerous publications and is author of *Asian Cinema: A Field Guide* (2008). He was formerly coordinator of film programs at the Los Angeles County Museum of Art, is a consultant for the International Film Festival Rotterdam, and has served on the juries of the Korean Film Festival in Los Angeles, the Fantasia Film Festival in Montreal, and Filmfest DC.

CHAPTER 8

Utopian Festivals and Cinephilic Dreams
AN INTERVIEW WITH PETER VON BAGH

Richard Porton

Something of a cinephilic omnivore, the late Peter von Bagh (1943–2014)—archivist, academic, film historian, author (of more than twenty books), publisher, film-magazine editor, filmmaker, television presenter, and film-festival director—was one of the most distinguished figures on the Finnish film scene for over fifty years. To those outside the region, however, von Bagh was probably best known for serving as director of Finland's Midnight Sun Film Festival since its inception and, for the eleven years prior to this 2011 interview, as artistic director of Bologna's Il Cinema Ritrovato (Cinema Rediscovered)—a festival devoted to cinematic restorations and rediscoveries that has a well-deserved reputation as a film buff's paradise.

Von Bagh, who considered himself merely an "amateur" filmmaker, was the subject of a comprehensive retrospective at the 2012 International Film Festival Rotterdam, as *Cineaste* editor Richard Porton mentions in his original introduction to this interview (here slightly updated and revised). The retrospective, curated by Olaf Möller, included eleven features and four shorts and highlighted von Bagh's two most recent documentaries: *The Story of Mikko Niskanen*, a portrait of one of Finland's most important film directors; and *Splinters—A Century of an Artistic Family*. In the several years prior to his death, von Bagh won acclaim at numerous venues for two dexterously edited and frequently moving compilation essay films on the relationship between history and the cinematic medium: *Helsinki, Forever*,

Originally published in *Cineaste* 37, no. 2 (Spring 2012); copyright © 2012 by Cineaste, Inc.

which employs stunning footage from myriad films in order to explore the onset of modernity in Finland's capital city (a film lauded by, among others, Chris Marker, Jean-Pierre Gorin, and Jonathan Rosenbaum); and *Sodankylä Forever*, an inventive assemblage of footage from over twenty years of panel discussions at the Midnight Sun Film Festival, interspersed with von Bagh's own pungent voiceover commentary.

Sodankylä, a village 120 kilometers north of the Arctic Circle, in Lapland, lends a special ambiance to an event that has nothing but disdain for the glitz and superficiality endemic to the famous international megafestivals. The 261-minute *Sodankylä Forever* (originally broadcast on Finnish television) is divided into three segments that chronicle a wide variety of cinematic revelations and epiphanies, augmented by a feature-length supplement. The autonomous film, *Century of Cinema*, focuses on the impact of the often-traumatic events of the twentieth century—particularly the ravages of war—on a range of filmmakers from both the West and the former Eastern Bloc countries. What might seem like biographical minutiae actually yield some startling insights into the way cinema and the history of the twentieth century became intertwined. For example, the fact that both Miklós Jancsó and Vittorio De Seta (guests of the festival in 2002 and 2007, respectively) were prisoners of war undoubtedly suffuses, however subtly, their films. John Boorman's account of his childhood exuberance during the London Blitz is a useful adjunct to the fictionalization of his memories in *Hope and Glory*. Mario Monicelli describes how *La grande guerra*, his antiwar masterpiece, interweaves comedy and pathos, while his compatriot Ettore Scola reveals that viewing the shooting of *The Bicycle Thief* in a Rome still healing from the scars of war inspired him to become a director. A seemingly innocuous Midnight Sun screening of *Battleship Potemkin* inadvertently crystallizes Cold War tensions as two seminal Eastern European directors, Dušan Makavejev and Krzysztof Zanussi, decide to boycott the Eisenstein chestnut.

"The Yearning for the First Cinema Experience," *Sodankylä Forever*'s official first part, traverses more personal, occasionally nostalgic cinephilic terrain by collecting memories of the first films viewed by festival guests. More than a mere navel-gazing exercise, von Bagh's montage of anecdotes of childhood cinematic rapture goes beyond random reminiscences to reveal large-scale cultural trends and biases. Perhaps predictably, a wide array of filmmakers mention that a Chaplin film marked their first exposure to cinema. More surprisingly, Abbas Kiarostami cites a Danny Kaye film, and Agnès Varda's dismissal of Disney's *Snow White* as boringly insipid looks forward to the plucky feminist films of her mature years.

Sodankylä Forever's final segments, "Eternal Time" and "Drama of Light," intermingle the allure of Midnight Sun's distinctive milieu—a film-intoxicated subculture where the sun never sets as dreams and movies coalesce—with lyrical ruminations on cherished films and iconic movie stars. A question posed by von Bagh to guests that might seem trite in other circumstances—"Which film would you bring to a desert island?"— allows us to peer into various directors' psyches. It might not be particularly shocking that an art-house director such as Chantal Akerman names Murnau's *Sunrise* and Bresson's *Pickpocket*. It's a little more perplexing that Roger Corman, known for once-reviled and now-cherished exploitation films, enshrines *Battleship Potemkin*, the film that caused a good-natured Midnight Sun contretemps. Paeans to stars elicit even more passionate responses. Roy Ward Baker, director of *Don't Bother to Knock*, confides that everyone who encountered Marilyn Monroe, the film's star, felt a need to touch her. Vincent Sherman, still dashing in his later years, looks back on his affair with Joan Crawford with a mixture of glee and melancholy.

Cineaste editorial board member Richard Porton met with Peter von Bagh in October 2011, during von Bagh's visit to the New York Film Festival, which presented *Sodankylä Forever* as a special event. Von Bagh proved a witty and frank interviewee, whether empathizing with Porton concerning the fickleness of modern recording devices or offering his astringent views on the contemporary film-festival scene.

CINEASTE: How did the Midnight Sun Festival come into being in 1986?

PETER VON BAGH: This is the legend. In 1985, a Finnish director named Anssi Mänttäri was in the village of Sodankylä in Lapland. It was November and completely dark and depressing—nothingness. And then, he's in his hotel room—completely drunk—and looks into the darkness and has this revelation at four o'clock in the morning: why don't we start an international film festival here? Then he goes south and contacts the Kaurismäki brothers, and I agree to become the festival director. Finally, six months later, we have a festival where the four guests include Sam Fuller, Bertrand Tavernier, Jonathan Demme, and Jean-Pierre Gorin. Also, the tradition of having a two-hour discussion in the morning began at the first festival. Some members of the press interrupted to ask questions, but I quickly established my "dictatorship" to become the sole questioner. That established the unity of the event. It's an intensely personal thing for me to be close to these people.

CINEASTE: Was the idea from the beginning to have an informal, non-competitive festival that was something of an antidote to huge events such as Cannes?

VON BAGH: I don't think any of us cared about film festivals. I still don't care about film festivals, even though I run a few of them— Bologna as well as Midnight Sun. I had been going to Cannes for some years and, around this time, Kaurismäki began to show his films at a number of international festivals. But we went to festivals only to learn what pitfalls to avoid. As a result, there's no red carpet, no business negotiations, and, of course, no prizes. Still, we can get any new film we want, and part of the program consists of new films, which are always very good. During our discussions, there's absolutely no talk about deals. Coppola is very eloquent in the film about how these moneymen try to crush him.

CINEASTE: And was it that after more than twenty years, you had enough material for a film?

VON BAGH: Well, it took more than twenty years to find a form for the material. But there was also the idea that by editing all of the material we could come up with, we could create a "dialogue," say, between Abbas Kiarostami and Michael Powell, who were there during different years. Or Joseph H. Lewis and Dino Risi.

CINEASTE: So the process of editing allowed you to come up with what could be termed a utopian festival.

VON BAGH: Yes, it's utopian and also incorporates the finest human elements of any film festival. Ninety-five percent of film festivals are worthless, concentrate on the wrong things, and don't have any respect for filmmakers.

CINEASTE: And the major festivals rarely focus on film history.

VON BAGH: Yes, and even when many film festivals feature retrospectives, they're termed "sidebars." I remember being at San Sebastian in 1993 during their William Wellman retrospective. It was a fantastic retrospective featuring thirty-five films. At the same time, Robert

Mitchum was in town to get a prize and was being interviewed by all of the local magazines. But, despite the fact that he's the star of Wellman's *The Story of G.I. Joe* and *Track of the Cat*, it didn't occur to anyone in the festival leadership to invite him to the retrospective. It shows how film history is treated as a joke and a sideshow.

CINEASTE: And although Cannes annually programs classic restorations, very few people attend.

VON BAGH: Yes, and that becomes a way of claiming that people aren't interested in classic films. I also don't like the fact that Cannes projects these films digitally. We would never do that.

CINEASTE: So you have a policy of screening only 35 mm prints?

VON BAGH: Although it took me years to understand, it's a policy connected to the philosophical point of the festival. The festival deals with two types of light. There's the natural light and the fact that there's still full sunshine when we come out of the cinema at three o'clock in the morning. Then there's the natural light of film. Aki Kaurismäki puts it beautifully when he says that film is poetry plus light. Digital, on the other end, is electronic. By comparison, it's an almost deadly process. So we would never show digital prints of classic films. Last year we showed a 35 mm restoration of *Taxi Driver* because Michael Chapman, the cinematographer, was in attendance. It was a little faded, but it still worked beautifully.

CINEASTE: And it's true that screenings go on for twenty-four hours?

VON BAGH: Well, only on the weekends.

CINEASTE: So some people might be arriving for screenings as others are going off to bed?

VON BAGH: Exactly. But you sleep a little less there because of the constant light.

CINEASTE: One of the film's segments focuses on the influence of war, particularly World War II, on filmmakers. Is this a particular interest of yours?

VON BAGH: Yeah. It's the most structured of these four films. It emerged naturally from the material and didn't come out of any previous intention. But it was irresistible since I immediately noticed, while working on the film, that directors from both the East and the West had this shared experience. I didn't expect that this would be a determining factor in both the East and West, just as Western money and the terrible political history of the East coincide.

CINEASTE: Perhaps this is also related to the fact that Finland is on the cusp of the East and the West.

VON BAGH: Yes, because of our position in the world, we might be in a privileged position to view these conflicts. It's also true that my generation often saw the films of Jancsó, Forman, and Skolimowski in Finland before they were screened in Warsaw, Budapest, and Prague. And Soviet films were always screened in Finland. It's important to be aware of these films because these people lived such difficult lives. Bob Rafelson makes a beautiful point in the film when he says that his life in the West was relatively easy.

CINEASTE: Your film also drives home the fact that the reception of various films depends on specific contexts. When Roger Corman expresses admiration for *Battleship Potemkin*, one assumes it's for formal reasons. But when Dušan Makavejev and Krzysztof Zanussi refuse to attend a screening of *Potemkin* at another juncture in the documentary, there's of course a political animus.

VON BAGH: Corman is such an enigma, though, that I wouldn't be surprised if he actually had a revolutionary side. Just as with Michael Curtiz—you can't forget that he was a revolutionary in Hungary in 1918, then went on to direct *Casablanca*.

CINEASTE: Of course, he directed *Mission to Moscow* as well. But perhaps he was embarrassed about that later.

VON BAGH: I think they all must have been—except Joseph Davies, the guy who wrote the book. He seemed to be the only truly stupid person involved.

CINEASTE: In any case, Zanussi and Makavejev seemed quite genial while declining to attend the *Potemkin* screening.

VON BAGH: Yes, they were quite relaxed about it. For them, it was a humorous situation. They really disliked the film and they formulated it nicely and there wasn't a quarrel. And it wasn't only them; Otar Iosseliani also said that it was a terrible, reactionary, Stalinist film. But what I like about this sequence is then you see the crowd cheering *Potemkin* and finally have the testimony of Andrei Smirnov, the Soviet director who actually defends that generation of filmmakers. He illuminates the real human situation of people in those extraordinarily difficult circumstances who could still produce incredible artistic work. He presents a truly dialectical argument, and you have to recall that Smirnov, after making some really brilliant films, chose to quit filmmaking in the Soviet Union in 1979. He was in the same class as Tarkovsky and Konchalovsky. Coming from him, it's very beautiful that he observes that it's very easy for us from the next generation and different circumstances to criticize people who made films under dictatorships. It's very superficial, from the perspective of our very easy life, to simply condemn them for being slaves to Stalin.

It was one of the great blessings of my life that, when I was programming films at the Finnish Film Archive, in the 1960s and 1970s, I was able to invite one master of Soviet cinema to Helsinki every season. So I was able to spend a week with filmmakers such Mark Donskoï, Grigori Kozintsev, Alexander Medvedkin, Josef Heifitz, Roman Karmen, and so on. They spoke a very coded language at a time when it was impossible for them to speak openly. But it was clear that they thought it possible to convey truth amidst all the lies.

CINEASTE: Jay Leyda, whom I studied with at NYU, seemed to understand this. Although certainly not a Stalinist, he had great respect for Eisenstein and Vertov.

VON BAGH: He was a dear friend of mine and I used to visit his classes and recall, for example, a screening of Marcel L'Herbier's adaptation of Pirandello's *The Late Mathias Pascal*. He certainly wouldn't slide into simplistic condemnations of Soviet directors, which would be idiotic. But that's perhaps a habit borrowed from writers such as Solzhenitzyn, and others, who made rather aggressive jokes about Eisenstein. They thought he was a dupe.

CINEASTE: Did the section dealing with the first films viewed by filmmakers during childhood come together naturally?

VON BAGH: Yes, it wasn't intentional. But this is always the first question I ask and, as I say in the text, these films took on very complicated, personal meanings. It's a real global time trip.

CINEASTE: It's not much of a surprise that Víctor Erice talks about *Frankenstein!*

VON BAGH: Yes, Erice is wonderful because he's so eloquent. Among filmmakers working today, he has one of the most complex and nuanced views of the medium. He's really a philosopher. He needs years to develop themes slowly, since he's not making conventional, narrative films. Kaurismäki is now going in the same direction since he takes about five years to gather material. It's a very complicated, sometimes painful process.

CINEASTE: Did you know the Karuismäki brothers before becoming involved with the Midnight Sun Festival?

VON BAGH: Yes, they both said that my book on world cinema was the inspiration for them becoming filmmakers and cinephiles. Mika went to the Munich film school and Aki tried to get into the Finnish film school, but failed. It was a happy accident in a way, since it enabled him to start with a clean slate.

CINEASTE: He's one of a number of filmmakers who failed to get into film school.

VON BAGH: I'm very disturbed about the influence of film schools because they tend to produce a hopelessly formulaic type of cinema. One of the joys of the festival is that most of the directors were born and raised before film schools, although of course there are exceptions, such as Coppola.

CINEASTE: Do you think there's a possibility that your book on world cinema will be translated into English?

VON BAGH: No, I don't think so. But there's also a companion book to *Sodankylä Forever.* Readers have told me that it's useful. It covers the same territory as the film, but at greater length. In the film, the montage approach means that no one talks for very long. But, in a book, there's room for longer anecdotes. In addition, about a year ago, I published a small book on cinema and trains, a subject that comes up in the film.

CINEASTE: How would you compare your work at the Midnight Sun Festival with your programming at Bologna's Il Cinema Ritrovato Festival?

VON BAGH: They're complementary festivals. Midnight Sun is designed more for young people and others discovering film than for cinephiles. At first we thought that the only audience would come from Helsinki. But they come from every corner of Finland. It becomes more poignant every year since there are fewer and fewer chances to see true cinema. They're in the dark for most of the year. Since the beginning we also had great critics—Peter Wollen, Jonathan Rosenbaum, Raymond Durgnat, Guillermo Cabrera Infante, José Luis Guarner.

CINEASTE: Do the critics participate in discussions at the festival?

VON BAGH: A critic usually introduces one film during the festival. It's called a "master class." Of course, it's something of a misnomer to call it a "class."

CINEASTE: I suppose a certain camaraderie develops among the young people who attend the festival.

VON BAGH: Yes, there's also camaraderie between the filmmakers. It may sometimes be difficult to get a specific filmmaker to socialize with the others. But usually it works and there's a beautiful sense of community. I remember, with affection, how close Robert Wise and John Sayles became during the festival; they discovered they shared a true democratic spirit.

CINEASTE: To return to Il Cinema Ritrovato, I was intrigued by a series you curated for the last edition entitled "At the Heart of the 20th Century: Socialism between Fear and Utopia." What was the initial impetus for this series?

VON BAGH: It probably started from wanting to assemble some of the very significant films of my youth that influenced an entire generation in Finland—films like *Kuhle Wampe* or *Native Land*. They were virtually unknown to our very well-informed audience. Even if they were familiar with all of Raoul Walsh's films, they didn't necessarily know *Kuhle Wampe*. The counterforce—right-wing films such as *Hitlerjunge Quex*—proved equally impressive. We included some important films from that political tendency.

CINEASTE: Although I've seen many of the titles you included, there are some more obscure titles, such as *Kämpfer* and *Song of the People*, that I'm not familiar with.

VON BAGH: They're obscure, and those proved much less impressive than the memories I had of them from my youth. The Bologna audience is wonderful since they're the best-informed audience in the world. They don't mind viewing mediocre films since they can "read" them in an interesting way. They're not always after mere pleasure. But that's a factor as well—that's why we've featured CinemaScope films for many years. Since there's a wonderful screen, why not use it? We've screened all of the notable CinemaScope films from the 1950s with the use of rare, usually excellent prints.

CINEASTE: James Quandt has told me that Bologna is his favorite festival.

VON BAGH: Since James Quandt is an incredible programmer in his own right, the king of programmers, it's nice to hear.

CINEASTE: When you speak of your "public," are you referring to locals or out-of-town professionals?

VON BAGH: It seems to be almost a rule of thumb at all festivals, whether film, music, or whatever, that the locals seldom participate. The Bologna public does often come in the evenings when we screen films for five thousand people in the piazza, and the offerings are a bit more "popular" than the films screened during the day. But for the most part the audience is composed of professionals—the historians and critics whose books I am reading and people responsible for the best programming and restoration in the world. It's an incredible bunch. Many of them are very glad to view some enormously obscure films, even if they're not particularly good. David Bordwell has been one of our most enthusiastic visitors and has promoted the festival tirelessly. He writes frequently about the festival in his blog, and we should thank him for attracting so many Americans. He's a prototype of our good audience since he's a model cinephile who never misses anything, no matter how obscure. He's tremendously knowledgeable.

CINEASTE: And Olaf Möller, a critic and programmer I know slightly, wrote a rave review of *Sodankylä Forever.*

VON BAGH: You don't even know the full truth of Möller's interest in the obscure. He wrote a glowing review of an obscure Finnish comedy of the mid-1960s, a film that everyone regarded as trash, for a Finnish film magazine. Nobody took it seriously. But Olaf Möller was there at three o'clock in the morning to see a print of this film without subtitles and enjoyed it enormously. It was great!

CINEASTE: I don't understand how he has the time to see all of those films!

VON BAGH: I don't understand it either. How can you see everything? In a way, he belongs to a lost race of cinephiles. This was more common in the 1940s, when critics and historians like Jean Mitry tried to see everything, even films from obscure national cinemas. To a certain extent, they failed miserably, since in my book on world cinema I spent some time discussing all of the lies that had been perpetuated concerning Finnish cinema. I saw how certain film historians from big countries such as France could get away with being completely arrogant despite enormous gaps in their knowledge.

CINEASTE: Most of us have enormous gaps in our knowledge. But recently, for example, the Brooklyn Academy of Music screened a series of films by the Finnish filmmaker Teuvo Tulio and he's suddenly considered a great discovery. His films were a great influence on Kaurismäki, weren't they?

VON BAGH: It's complicated with Kaurismäki since he's assimilated so many influences. But I think Tulio was one of his favorites. And the outrageous aspect of Tulio's work certainly influenced Kaurismäki.

CINEASTE: But even though there's an outrageous quality of Tulio's work, he seems more earnest than the more heavily satirical Kaurismäki. What was the response to Tulio's films at the time? Were they considered scandalous?

VON BAGH: Partially, yes. They were also seriously underrated. When you understand the Finnish dialogue, it's really ridiculous. And he couldn't really handle actors. So I think those elements made it difficult for people to recognize his visual genius.

CINEASTE: So you might compare him to the case of Douglas Sirk, a filmmaker who was first appreciated by foreign critics who didn't focus on the dialogue in his Hollywood melodramas.

VON BAGH: Yes, maybe. And there's this outrageous element to Jerry Lewis, which is very difficult for American audiences.

CINEASTE: Of course, the Edinburgh Film Festival, which in the 1970s published a monograph on Sirk, helped to burnish his reputation in the English-speaking world.

VON BAGH: Unfortunately, I never got to that festival during that period. But I have wonderful personal memories from that era since Jon Halliday came from Edinburgh and told me that Douglas Sirk had seen, and liked, *The Count*, my only fiction film. He called it "a wonderful film by a born filmmaker." So I've carried that praise from Douglas Sirk with me during the bitter years of my later life.

CINEASTE: Like *Sodankylä Forever*, your film *Helsinki, Forever* also deals with important chunks of film history.

VON BAGH: I consider myself a kind of amateur filmmaker, since I direct when I can take time from other projects. But these two films are part of a series (and there are two others that screen at festivals) that deal with exactly the same subject: the relationship between memory and the medium of film. So *Helsinki, Forever*, which is a totally different type of film composed exclusively of old footage from Finnish films, addresses exactly the same questions that are considered in *Sodankylä Forever*.

CINEASTE: A few years ago, Guy Maddin made a film about his hometown, *My Winnipeg*, that was partially fanciful and freely invented "facts." That's another type of city tribute.

VON BAGH: I think Guy Maddin has a point. There's also a utopian quality to my Helsinki film. Even though it's entirely old footage and nothing's invented, there's also a fictional element. To find an essence of the thing you must also invent part of it.

CINEASTE: You've spoken of a previous generation of cinephiles with a certain amount of nostalgia. Do you think that a new cinephilia has developed with the current generation discovering films on DVD?

VON BAGH: I feel hopeful when I read certain books like Gary Giddins's wonderful collection, *Warning Shadows*, based largely on films available on DVD. I knew him as a jazz critic and wasn't even aware until recently that he wrote on film. The best American writing on film is currently on a much higher level than what's available in Europe. It's a very bad time for European film writing. I think here the germ of real, essential cinephilia is still in the air. In Europe, it's easy to lose all hope. To a certain extent, I'm longing for a utopian cinephilia that never existed, imaginary conversations between people who never met. I'm also interested in defending cinephilia. There's a cliché about movie-crazy people that I'm trying to refute. They're regarded as the *arrière-garde* of the arts, mentally retarded in comparison to theater or music fans. I have the opposite view. The film people I respect the most have an extremely lucid view of history and of the last, damned tragic century. They must balance their understanding of the overwhelming cinematic riches of the twentieth century with its tragic historical legacy.

Richard Porton is an editor at *Cineaste* and has written on film for *Cinema Scope*, *Sight & Sound*, and the *Daily Beast*. He is author of *Film and the Anarchist Imagination* (1999) and editor of *On Film Festivals* (2008). He is completing a revised version of *Film and the Anarchist Imagination* for Verso, as well as a book on the career of Adam Curtis for the University of Illinois Press.

CHAPTER 9

The (Cinematic) Gospel According to Mark
AN INTERVIEW WITH MARK COUSINS

Declan McGrath

In the late 1990s and early 2000s, former Edinburgh Film Festival director Mark Cousins was the enthusiastic and passionate face of knowledgeable film criticism on British television. Cousins introduced late-night cult movies on BBC Two's *Moviedrome* program and conducted in-depth interviews with respected filmmakers and actors in *Screen by Screen*. Cousins's 2004 book *The Story of Film* (reviewed in *Cineaste* 31, no. 2 [Spring 2006]) tells the global history of cinema through the story of innovation in the form. *The Story of Film: An Odyssey* is the film adaptation of that book—"film" because although it played on British TV, Cousins intended it for the cinema. *The Story of Film* is one of three films made near the time of this 2013 interview with which TV expert and critic Cousins established himself as a filmmaker. Over an epic fifteen hours, *The Story of Film: An Odyssey* covers the major directors, films, and movements of cinematic history, refreshingly treating voices from Africa, Asia, and Latin America with the same attention and respect as those from the United States and Europe.

Much of this story will be familiar to the knowledgeable cinephile, who may well note omissions and disagree with certain emphases, as *Cineaste* contributor Declan McGrath points out in his original introduction to this interview (here slightly updated and revised). But just as an art aficionado would celebrate a gallery where the best paintings in the world are gathered and expertly arranged to please and to provoke the viewer, so should the knowledgeable cinephile find much to appreciate here. Clips from the very best of cinema are juxtaposed (in a way that may indeed both please and provoke) to illustrate visual rhymes from throughout film history and the evolution of cinematic language. The intensity of so many film extracts placed together, each one triggering a memory of the viewer's initial reaction to that film, allows a cine-literate audience member, like the art aficionado in that imaginary gallery, to personally reevaluate his or her opinion of works, directors, and movements within the context of the broad sweep of cinema history. Quibbles with the curator are part of a pleasurable engagement with the material.

To help tell his history, Cousins sparingly uses interviews with practitioners and critics. He also intermittently interweaves archives of real-life horrors, such as world war and fascism, to establish a context and remind viewers that the evolution of cinematic language did not occur in isolation. Along with this skillful assemblage of film clips, interviews, and archival footage telling the story of cinema, Cousins includes a fourth element: his own footage depicting the locations where this history unfolded. As well as establishing context, these images reveal a filmmaker on "An Odyssey." Cousins starts the story in his native Ireland (he informs us that the opening images from *Saving Private Ryan* were shot there), and through his own visuals he travels on a parallel personal odyssey that is both an evocative pilgrimage around the physical shrines and relics of the cinematic story and also a metaphysical meditation on the relation of cinema to our transitory lives and its place within wider society. But unlike Homer, Cousins does not return to the location where the story began, but ends in Burkina Faso. In the film's closing images he places himself in front of the camera for the first time, at a ceremony remembering filmmakers who have recently passed away—a fitting end, considering the often elegiac tone of his own odyssey— and on a continent whose cinema he champions.

Cousins's personal exploration concerning the nature of cinema's relationship with its viewers and with society is more fully developed in his two feature documentaries that bookend *The First Movie* (2009), *The Story of Film* (2011), and *What Is This Film Called Love?* (2012). In *The First Movie*, Cousins documents his visit to the Kurdish village of Goptapa in northern Iraq, where he creates a makeshift cinema for children who have never been to the movies before. Motivated by his own childhood experience of growing up in Belfast in the 1970s, when imagination and movies provided him an escape from war on the streets, Cousins shows how much enjoyment the children get out of watching movies. He then hands them small flip cameras, inviting them to film their own stories. The footage they record includes a retelling of a Kurdish folktale and honest, open accounts by adults of the genocide. But Cousins is most impressed by one young boy's imagining the inner life of his friend, observing that the camera in skilled hands is an "empathy machine." *The First Movie* amounts to an unashamedly romantic celebration of the power and importance of cinema as a means both to stimulate our imaginations and to share our stories in an often brutal world.

In *What Is This Film Called Love?* Cousins is like the kid in *The First Movie*, using a small, one-hundred-dollar camera to depict his thoughts and dreams during a three-day stopover in Mexico City. The result is a candidly self-indulgent exploration of the meaning of life, happiness, time's passage, and cinephilia, as all are interlinked in Cousins's mind. The film makes visual references to ideas featured in *The Story of Film* and plays with form to explore how film enables viewers to see the world more intensely. Its audacious, transcendent ending, in a nod to *The 400 Blows* and Thai filmmaker Apichatpong Weerasethakul, suggests that cinema can transport us out of ourselves and into a mythological, almost spiritual world where all stories are shared and where each viewer can possess any story.

This evangelical advocacy of cinema is not confined to Cousins's filmmaking. In 2012, he issued a manifesto calling on the New York Film Festival directors to change the form of festivals in order to make them be less dictated by business and no longer "an alternative shop window for film industries." Cousins practices what he preaches, curating "alternative" film festivals with actress Tilda Swinton. In 2009, for example, patrons were invited to join Cousins and Swinton for six days of travel through the Scottish Highlands, at times accompanied by a mobile cinema, and each night camping and screening films in small villages without cinemas. Swinton and Cousins have also established the 8½ Foundation, which encourages children to have a "film birthday" at the age of 8½ and screen a film recommended by the foundation (recommendations include Kurosawa's *The Hidden Fortress*, Cocteau's *Beauty and the Beast*, and Tati's *Jour de fête*).

Declan McGrath, a regular *Cineaste* contributor, met with Mark Cousins in January 2013 at Cousins's flat in Edinburgh.

CINEASTE: *The Story of Film: An Odyssey* encompasses what are seen as the most important films, directors, and movements in cinematic history. Would it be fair to say you are covering the canon of cinema with some additions?

MARK COUSINS: I wouldn't say that. This is not the canon plus a bit more. It is decentering Hollywood. Hollywood is not the center of this. And it is decentering Bollywood. Bollywood is not the center of this either. If you look at the canon as it is in film magazines and popular discussion, there is almost nothing on African cinema. There is almost nothing on Taiwanese cinema. We have ninety minutes on African cinema in the film. The purpose was not to be revisionist for revisionist sake, but we do say that the canon is racist by omission and blind to the great women directors.

CINEASTE: But do you agree with the principle of having a canon?

COUSINS: Yes. I think it is extremely useful. Particularly in the digital age, when there is so much to know and to see, it can work as an aide-mémoire. A canon can also be useful as a Trojan horse to smuggle information into popular discourse. In an ideal world we wouldn't need canons—everything would find its own position according to its own merit. But that is not how it works.

CINEASTE: You have spoken about how as a teenager you painstakingly searched out music and films you read about on a recommended list. It must be reassuring to know that the teenagers watching *The Story of Film* today will find it much easier to watch the films you have included.

COUSINS: Yes. We are living in an age of plenitude when everything is available. An awful lot featured in *The Story of Film* is on YouTube. But you can argue that is both worse and better for young people today. Better in that they no longer have to wait five or ten years to see something, but worse in that they can become blasé and don't have that delicious longing. I was brought up Catholic and I was a Pioneer. That meant I pledged not to taste alcohol until the age of eighteen. When I eventually did, it was so much better! The problem today is not the problem I had, when first discovering film, of an appetite generated but forcibly deferred. The problem is that there is already a smorgasbord of choice and people don't know what to eat. So what we need are tasting menus and signposts.

CINEASTE: In putting together the list, the tasting board that is *The Story of Film*, were you aware that it is a subjective list, and did you fight your subjectivity?

COUSINS: I think so. I think it is objective in one way and subjective in another. It is objective compared to a lot of film history written by white men in Paris, Los Angeles, or New York that is overly Atlantic centered. They do not cover Ethiopian cinema, for example. I have tried to be geographically much more objective than those histories of cinema. But once you decide you are going to go to Ethiopia, which films do you look at? That is where the choice becomes subjective. For example, I had seen Dorota Kędzierzawska's film *Crows* (1994) at the Berlin Film Festival and I was amazed by it, so I knew I had to get to her, even though it meant swerving the story back to Poland in 1994. That is quite subjective.

CINEASTE: Refreshingly, there is no nostalgia in *The Story of Film* for any particular period. There is, however, nostalgia for the format of film.

COUSINS: Yes, I talk about the Last Days of Celluloid! Actually I am absolutely pro-digital at the cinema. I always sit in the front row of the cinema. If I see it is on film, I think this could go out of focus or this could weave.

CINEASTE: But you do contrast an old clip of a biplane stunt filmed by a real person in real danger with the manufacture of a CGI digital effect at a computer desk over "long hours with plenty of pizza." You imply digital technology has affected the creative process.

COUSINS: Absolutely. There is a big shift in the creative process. Creativity can involve physical courage like getting on a plane and filming a shot like that one. Some of that perhaps quite macho daredevilness has gone from filmmaking. Creativity in modern, big-budget digital cinema is a much more sedentary process. The kind of dreaming that happens now is in front of a computer screen rather than with a crew in Monument Valley at dawn. But the art of cinema hasn't really changed. If, at the beginning, cinema had a reality function and a dream function, this new era, when people are sitting with pizzas at computer screens, is no different. In the digital era there are more documentaries than ever before, and fantasy cinema has become more fantastic. The art of cinema may be stretched or even polarized a little bit, but those two poles remain. I really disagree with people who feel that digital has brought a shift towards the fantastic. They are just not seeing enough cinema.

CINEASTE: When we come to people like Charles Burnett and Gaston Gaboré, you talk of people starting to use cinema to tell their own stories. You present this as an important development in the story of film.

COUSINS: That is one of the biggest things that I realized when I was making it. The sense of people, nations, identities claiming the means of production, saying, "Here it is from our point to view." In the last third of The Story of Film, I focus on those new voices, and often they are innovative by their very newness. John Sayles says he and Maggie Renzi asked themselves, "What kind of lives are we not seeing on screen, and let's put them on screen." That echoes Robert Bresson's great statement: "Try to show that which without you might never have been seen." Showing things that might otherwise never have been seen is one definition of innovation. That is what Charles Burnett could do, and that is what Woody Allen could do.

CINEASTE: When we reach that cinema of Sayles and Burnett, and then the political domination of Reagan and Thatcher in the 1980s, you say that while "conservative ideologues tell false stories about life and love, the most innovative filmmakers speak back at those false-hoods." It could be said at this point that the story of cinematic inno-vation becomes more overtly political.

COUSINS: I don't agree. I don't back that horse. I have pretty strong political views myself, so I loved it when people like John Sayles and Charles Burnett came along. But look at what I covered in post-1980 American cinema. I did not stick with the lefties thereafter. David Lynch is right of center; he voted Reagan. I followed the innovation. There is nearly an hour looking at innovation in the mainstream cin-ema of the 1970s, including the American films Jaws, The Exorcist, and

Figure 9.1. According to former film-festival director Mark Cousins, film-makers such as Charles Burnett are "showing things that might otherwise never have been seen," which for Cousins "is one definition of innovation." Burnett's *Killer of Sheep* presents the daily rhythms of life in the Watts neighborhood of South Central Los Angeles, where the filmmaker grew up. © Charles Burnett, 1978.

The Godfather. For me, it was really important not to say that every-thing was building up to Godard and then Godard finally smashed the system. I wanted to show that innovation and talent appears every-where, not only in the arty edge. That is why the biggest chunk on any film is on *Sholay*, the most popular film ever made.

CINEASTE: You shot the footage between the film clips and interviews throughout the world in locations relating to the narrative of film his-tory. It is mostly made up of still, locked-off frames that seem to owe something to your hero Ozu. To me they not only create space in the narrative but also allow real life to intrude and contrast with the sealed world of the movies.

COUSINS: That is exactly right. I wanted stillness. I didn't want in any way to fight with the film clips, and I also knew that I would be talking over those images. That is why the camera often doesn't move. I kept imagining I was making a magic-lantern picture show. The shots are still like in magic lanterns and that's why new shots push in from the right all the time.

CINEASTE: Often in those shots you have bits of peeling paper or weathered concrete. There is a sense of impermanence and decay like you get in the Japanese aesthetic of wabi-sabi. There is a sense that all we are seeing, and all you are filming, is passing by.

COUSINS: Absolutely. The sadness of time passing. The ongoing moment. Wabi-sabi. All these ideas are definitely there. If you go to Los Angeles, you can feel that sadness, you can see what was once a great place of the movies isn't anymore and it is half forgotten. There is a touch of melancholy in it.

CINEASTE: And that melancholy bleeds into the film clips. You start to think of the sadness that those moments, captured and preserved on film, are long over.

COUSINS: Definitely that is there. But paradoxically that is also the great thing about cinema. When you look at Garbo's face, she is long gone but that luminous, momentary beauty remains.

CINEASTE: Adding to that mixed sense of both sadness and celebration that is inherent in cinema is the way your own footage is at times like a "pilgrimage" around the important shrines and relics of cinema's history. We are respectfully shown the "sacred" places or "shrines" where the directors directed, the writers wrote, the actors acted, and so on, as well as "relics" of the physical props used in the process.

COUSINS: You are spot on. Looking back, it is probably a Catholic thing. I no longer have any religious belief, but I am still fascinated by reliquaries and the idea that a physical object has a real presence. Because cinema is so flickering, I am interested in what remains, whether it is Dietrich's hat or Fellini's scarf or whatever. Pilgrimage is exactly the right word to use. It is not only that you want to see the object but also you have to suffer a bit before you get there, because you'll appreciate it even more. I felt that strongly when shooting, especially going halfway round the world to Ozu's grave only to find it pissing with rain when I got there!

CINEASTE: Although the historical story must ultimately follow a chronology, it is never predictable. Very quickly we realize that at any moment you may make a visual connection between films that will suddenly move the story to another country or forwards or backwards before returning to the narrative timeline. Did that require a lot of work and planning?

COUSINS: Yes, it was all planned. I made up charts. It was like an oxbow lake and I always knew where I had to swing back to. Those kinds of visual connections were very important, not only because it is fun but also because that is the way visual thinking works. Scorsese can recall movies from fifty years ago and think, bang, that would work in something he is making today. So many of the great film-makers think that way, and I wanted to try and capture some of that.

CINEASTE: You suggest the story of film did not unfold in isolation by intermittently using archival images to show us the horrors of the last century. Indeed, your opening images from *Saving Private Ryan* depict the visceral horror of the Omaha Beach D-Day landings. Inter-cutting that archive with the film clips gives me a sense that cinema has been used not only to reflect but also to escape from that horror.

COUSINS: That is exactly right. Pasolini said cinema is recovery. There is a sense of cinema being an escape and in denial about how tough life can be. I actually like the fact that cinema is happier than life. But at the same time cinema allows people who have had rather sheltered lives to experience a degree of sadness or tragedy safely on the big screen.

CINEASTE: You more thoroughly explore those two sides of cinema, as an escape and as a means to portray or experience the tragedy of life, in *The First Movie*, your film about bringing cinema to a group of children in a Kurdish village who have never seen a movie before. The town has suffered genocide. You bring them cinema. Are there not a lot of other things you should be bringing them first?

COUSINS: For me, growing up in Belfast during the war in the 1970s, cinema was an escape, a warm embrace, a place where you could unwind. Then, as I mention in *The First Movie*, when I was still in my twenties I went to Sarajevo during the appalling siege where one hundred thousand people were murdered. I was invited there to bring movies. People dodged the bullets to come and see them. Why? Because movies are magic and myth. They don't just make you forget your troubles, although they do that to a certain extent. They make you feel alive. That time in Sarajevo made me realize strongly that cinema is not just the icing on the cake of life. It is the cake as well.

CINEASTE: It could be argued that the people in Sarajevo, or Belfast, or those Kurdish kids in *The First Movie* really need political change and political activism rather than movies.

COUSINS: Well, it is not either/or. I am obviously not saying cinema is a replacement for political change. You need both. I have a quotation at the end of *The First Movie* from Ousmane Sembène, where he says, "We do not tell stories for revenge but to find our place in the world." So, as well as the whole political process of finding equality and safety for the people of Northern Ireland, Bosnia, Kosovo, Iran, and Iraq, those same people also need to use their art, and particularly this fantastic, luminous, popular art of cinema, to try and help them get their bearings again.

CINEASTE: After you screen the films, you give the children small flip cameras to make their own films. One makes a story about a boy talking with the mud; another kid relates an old folktale, while others record adults' memories of the genocide. It reminds us how film lets us share our stories with a wider audience, something that seems particularly important for that Kurdish village.

COUSINS: It is witness bearing. Coming from Belfast, I know the importance of monuments, the importance of being able to point to something and say, "That pain we went through was not in vain, because there is a physical thing that remembers it." You can point to a film and say, "That tells our story. It is outside me and it is in the world. I don't have to keep telling it now because it is there." I think that is part of the recovery process.

CINEASTE: You explore film, and indeed life, in *What Is This Film Called Love?* by recording your thoughts and dreams during a three-day stopover in Mexico City. You describe it as an ad-libbed stream-of-consciousness response to *The Story of Film.*

COUSINS: Exactly. I was working for six years to a plan, and now this was the joy of improv. I had been reading Virginia Woolf's diaries about her capturing her stream of consciousness. My wager was that as a man in the middle of my life, if I tried to portray my experience of having a fantastic three days on my own, but also thinking of sad stuff as honestly as I could, at least some people would see themselves in it. That was the idea.

CINEASTE: And it is possible to realize that idea, a personal stream-of-consciousness film, because of changes in technology. You shoot it on a small, one-hundred-dollar flip camera.

COUSINS: The only cost was getting a picture of Sergei Eisenstein laminated for $5.80. I had complete freedom. No plan, no script, no producer, no budget, no schedule.

CINEASTE: You begin an imaginary conversation with that picture of Eisenstein. As you explore framing and montage with him, the film becomes, in one sense, a recognition of how we can see differently and experience our lives more vividly through film.

COUSINS: That is crucial. I have always enjoyed the world through the pure pleasure of looking—scopophilia. There was a big debate in France in the 1860s and 1870s about why Manet, Delacroix, and Courbet were better than, for example, boring old Bouguereau. It was because they enjoyed looking and they were looking differently. If you have a camera and if you choose your frame carefully, then everything becomes electric within that frame. It is like having a cup of coffee in the morning. Suddenly the world sparkles.

CINEASTE: That conversation with Eisenstein then sends you thinking about the meaning of ecstasy. You discover its etymology is "ex stasis: movement out of stillness." You then realize that cinema generates ecstasy because it can move us out of ourselves.

COUSINS: Indeed. I always quote Joseph Campbell on the rapture of self-loss. If you are watching a movie, it is not that it is denying reality, it is more like you become part of myth. It is like dancing; you can get out of yourself although you are still yourself.

CINEASTE: And at the end of *What Is This Film Called Love?* you literally lose yourself. After musing over both the meaning of happiness and the value of cinema, you change into something else. For me it was as if your soul has entered an enchanted place where we can be part of any story we want, where all stories are one. You seem to suggest cinema can be that place.

COUSINS: That is why for me film is such a great art form at capturing what it is like to be alive. It is precociously good at that. I say precocious because I think cinema is still in its infancy or childhood, and it has already come up with this remarkable ability to capture these things that we are talking about: self-loss, change, and soul.

Declan McGrath is a filmmaker and writer from Belfast. He is author of *Screencraft: Editing and Post-Production* (2001) and coauthor, with Felim MacDermott, of *Screencraft: Screenwriting* (2003). He has taught film at Queens University Belfast and University College Dublin. His most recent film is the BBC and RTE documentary *Mary McAleese and the Man Who Saved Europe* (2015).

PART III

FILM PRESERVATION IN THE DIGITAL AGE

CHAPTER 10

Film Preservation in the Digital Age
A CRITICAL SYMPOSIUM

In 2010, *Cineaste* organized a critical symposium on repertory film programming, calling attention to the cinemas, museums, and film societies around
the country that are devoted to the theatrical exhibition of movies from
throughout the history of cinema and from all realms of film production
(including the noncommercial). A central purpose of that symposium was
to celebrate repertory cinemas' indispensable role in preserving a healthy
and diversified film culture and in fostering access to the films of the past.
Cineaste went so far as to suggest that these institutions, many of which
double as film archives, are engaged in preserving the experience of theatrical moviegoing, especially as films are increasingly viewed nontheatrically.
But however older films happen to find their audiences—whether in a cinema or on DVD, computer, or iPhone—they can do so only if they continue
to exist, a condition that, given the precarious nature of celluloid (as well as
of video formats, whether analog or digital), is not to be taken for granted.
Cineaste editors therefore felt that the logical successor to the repertory film
symposium would be a symposium on film preservation itself, a topic of the
utmost importance to film history and culture, but one that is little understood by the public at large.

It's perhaps a testament to the unique, illusory nature of the medium,
to our perception of it as an ephemeral play of light and shadow, that most
people rarely reflect on the status of films as physical objects (a paradox

Originally published in *Cineaste* 36, no. 4 (Fall 2011); copyright © 2011 by Cineaste, Inc.

that's clearly destined to grow as movies—along with almost all media—transition to purely digital form). And yet, even in an age of mechanical (or digital) reproduction, movies most certainly are physical objects, every bit as prone to disintegration and loss as paintings, manuscripts, or monuments. Indeed, despite the medium's relative youth, countless numbers of films from throughout the cinema's first century have been lost, and hundreds of thousands more are teetering on the edge of oblivion.

For this issue's critical symposium, the editors sent out a questionnaire to a host of individuals engaged in various ways in the mission to collect, preserve, and safeguard films. The contributors represent the country's noncommercial archives, the Hollywood film studios, preservation-oriented foundations, and the film labs that perform much of the actual preservation work. Nearly every one of the participants testifies to the gulf between the volume of films demanding preservation and the number that, for reasons practical and financial, can realistically be attended to before celluloid ceases to be a viable option.

The contributors to the symposium are engaged in an uphill battle against the forces of time and decay, as well as against more culturally determined factors, such as funding shortages, lab costs, lack of understanding of proper storage conditions, and so on. The original goal in organizing this symposium was both to call attention to the individuals and institutions whose efforts to save threatened films take place largely behind the scenes, and simply to increase awareness of the fragile nature of the medium, of the mechanics of film preservation, and of the challenges involved in the field.

As the contributors below make clear, the struggle to preserve film history is ongoing, not just because of the volume of films involved, but also because the awareness of what deserves to be saved—of those films deemed worthy of collecting, preserving, and studying—is constantly evolving. Just as Hollywood films were once considered disposable entertainment, one of the most striking developments in the film preservation field (as in film scholarship) is the increasing recognition of the value (and the past neglect) of "orphan" films, works whose creators or copyright holders have either abandoned them or lack the resources to preserve them—home movies and other amateur footage; industrial, medical, and science films; newsreels, experimental films, and so on. These films have only recently emerged from the state of film-preservation purgatory in which Hollywood cinema once found itself, and as a result, they exist—when they exist at all—in a particularly vulnerable state. Many of the institutions represented in the symposium have increasingly focused on these films, since their orphan status leaves them otherwise unprotected.

And the embrace of "orphan" films is far from the end of the story, as *Cineaste* editor and Anthology Film Archives programmer Jared Rapfogel and Andrew Lampert, also of Anthology, point out in their original version of this introduction (here slightly updated and revised). Inevitably, a dominant theme here is the digital revolution and its impact on the film preservation field, an impact that's no less significant than in film production, distribution, and exhibition. While the debate over the positive and negative aspects of the digital revolution is an open one (with a consensus emerging that digital video is at the very least an invaluable tool for providing access to archival material), almost all the contributors to the symposium point out that digital media are far from being stable enough to constitute a means of long-term preservation. For traditional films, this means that digitization is not, at this point, an adequate preservation replacement for celluloid. But it also means that the legions of movies that today are actually created digitally are in almost as precarious a state as the silent films of one hundred years ago. In other words, film preservation should not be mistaken as something relevant only to those interested in past epochs of film history. As the technology of the cinema evolves, the need to understand how to preserve moving-image works becomes a very contemporary challenge—in the words of Margaret Bodde, director of the Film Foundation, "The preservation of born-digital films is going to be the greatest challenge ever to face archivists." The potential for loss that film preservationists labor mightily against applies to twenty-first-century cinema every bit as much as to the musty, fading, bulky film prints that will soon represent an earlier era of moving-image practice.

From any perspective, the transition from celluloid (and analog video) to digital media that is transforming all aspects of film culture makes this a fascinating moment in the history of archiving and preservation, and hence a perfect time to solicit the observations of those in the field. When this symposium was first published in 2011, *Cineaste* expressed the hope that it would raise the curtain on the processes, the challenges, and the financial, ethical, and cultural issues involved in preserving motion pictures, and focus attention on the individuals who devote themselves to the cause of film preservation.

Contributors responded to the following questions. Next to each participant's name is his or her professional affiliation in 2011. Following each response is an expanded, updated biography of the contributor.

Additional symposium responses can be found on the *Cineaste* website (www.cineaste.com) as part of the Fall 2011 edition.

1. How has the landscape of film preservation changed over the past decade or so? Is there a healthy amount of funding available?
2. Can you outline the decisions and choices that go into deciding how certain titles are prioritized for preservation? What are the factors, both theoretical and practical, informing these decisions? How difficult is it to choose certain films over others?
3. Do you feel there are specific films/eras/modes of filmmaking that are falling through the cracks when it comes to preservation? If you are responsible for an archive, how are you trying to diversify and strengthen your collection through acquisitions and preservation of works not already in your care or possession?
4. How has the digital revolution impacted film preservation? Does transferring a film to digital media qualify as preservation? To what extent is it becoming difficult to find labs/technicians with the expertise to do photochemical preservation work? What are the positive dimensions of the digital revolution to the field? What efforts are being taken to archive, transfer, and preserve works that were produced in video?
5. How do you approach the question of preservation versus access? Are these two goals difficult to balance? How would you characterize the relationship between your preservation work and repertory film exhibition, home video releasing, and/or Internet streaming?

SCHAWN BELSTON, TWENTIETH CENTURY– FOX FILM CORPORATION

1. The most significant change in the film preservation and restoration landscape has been the rise of digital technology. Digital tools have eclipsed traditional photochemical techniques as the standard method for restoration, and fewer and fewer new studio productions actually are shot on film, necessitating greater attention to digital preservation and migration. Over the past decade or so, Fox has invested significantly in making the best possible photochemical preservation elements on our feature film library, systematically inspecting and copying the best possible elements. It was very important to us to make sure that the library was safe, and

that we would have elements available for future restoration. The company remains committed to restoring and protecting the library, both digitally and photochemically.

2. Every new film produced by Fox is preserved on an ongoing basis. Prioritizing library titles for restoration is a bit more agonizing—our goal is to restore as many films as possible, but due to the size of the library and the practical limitations of working resources, we have to prioritize. The biggest motivating factors are market need (DVD/Blu-ray, for instance) and physical condition of elements. Additionally, we consider the cultural/artistic significance of the title. As we work through the library beyond the obvious classic touchstones, the choices become increasingly agonizing—I truly believe that there is something redeemable about every film, something to admire that justifies its preservation and presentation in the most authentic way possible.

3. The early years of digital picture and sound postproduction jump to mind—the lack of standard formats and absence of data migration strategy at the time has created a significant backlog of digital assets that need to be properly protected. This is trickier than it may sound. We must confront not only the issue of playing back the physical media, but also the format of the data on the media once we've played it back. Assuming we can find an XYZ deck and that our XYZ media still plays, we are then confronted with how the data on the tapes was originally formatted and how it was wrapped when written to the tape.

4. Simply copying a film to digital media does not generally qualify as preservation; however, films can be preserved digitally. There are many issues to consider. Here are a few: What is the format of the data that is being preserved? Is it in its original resolution and/or format, or has it been transformed somehow? It's interesting to consider that unlike the traditional photochemical paradigm, "original format" may not be the best idea for digital preservation if that format requires a proprietary system or software to be viable. To improve storage capacity, should the data be compressed (mathematically lossless)? What is the long-term plan to perpetuate the data? Migration? Data redundancy at multiple different geographic locations?

As we work toward a robust digital archive of the future, we continue to make photochemical preservation elements as a safeguard, and we will continue to for the foreseeable future. The saddest part of the digital revolution is the slowly disappearing expertise in specialized photochemical techniques, which remain important. It is increasingly rare to meet younger people who are passionate about and dedicated to learning the magic of the traditional film lab.

On the upside, the digital revolution has made restorations possible that could never have been accomplished using traditional tools—allowing us to see movies more closely than ever before to the original presentation.

5. As I mentioned earlier, we are highly motivated by home video and other distribution channels—Blu-ray is particularly great because it allows the best possible home-viewing experience. We also continue to make 35 mm (or 70 mm, if appropriate) prints of all restoration titles, which are available for repertory film exhibition—allowing our films to be seen as often as possible as originally intended, projected on the big screen.

Schawn Belston is executive vice president for media and library services at the Twentieth Century–Fox Film Corporation. A University of Southern California graduate, Belston started at Fox in 1995, working in postproduction. In 2000 he became the director of media and library services. Among the many notable films he has had a hand in restoring are F. W. Murnau's *Sunrise*, Jules Dassin's *Night and the City*, Fred Zinnemann's *Oklahoma!*, and Luchino Visconti's *The Leopard*.

MARGARET BODDE, FILM FOUNDATION

1. In general, there has been less funding for film preservation in recent years due to the economy. That, coupled with the loss of revenue from DVD sales, will have a dramatic impact on preservation starting with the studios and then spreading beyond.

2. The Film Foundation prioritizes projects for preservation starting with the availability or scarcity of the elements and the conditions of those elements. Our board then considers the film's importance from a cultural, historic, and artistic standpoint. Finally, interest from a potential funder in the film or interest in its genre, director, or actors can also factor into the preservation timeline.

3. One area where we did see a potential problem was the avant-garde; these films often exist in only one print, putting them at particular risk. To help address this problem, the Film Foundation and the National Film Preservation Foundation created the Avant-Garde Masters Grants program

to help save these endangered films. Over the past nine years, this grant has funded the preservation of eighty-eight films.

Independent films in general tend to fall through the cracks, and this problem will be exacerbated with films that are born digital, as their original digital formats become obsolete with the rapid change of technology.

4. One of the greatest advantages of film is that it survives—it can be preserved. We can still screen films from the dawn of cinema—will we be able to say that about films born digital? The preservation of born-digital films is going to be the greatest challenge ever to face archivists. Every studio, archive, film organization, including the Film Foundation, is grappling with this issue, researching, and discussing best practices based on what we know at the moment. There are several issues:

a. No digital format has been found to be acceptable for long-term preservation. 4K digital restorations must be recorded out to film, ideally to new separation masters. Digital tape has not stood the test of time, and we don't know how long it will last. We know that film can last for one hundred years or longer if properly stored.

b. Studios and producers must decide which material to keep, as digital data storage is costly, and an enormous amount of material results from a born-digital production. Some filmmakers have begun to erase takes on set while they're shooting as a way to handle this issue.

c. Tape formats and standards change so rapidly that playback becomes a very real concern. Information must be migrated often and consistently. This is not always realistic or reliable, particularly for independent filmmakers without resources and knowledge about maintaining digital data.

d. In this digital era, people may be mistakenly lulled into complacency by the ready availability of films from every era and every country, accessible with a single click of the mouse. In fact, being able to see a postage-stamp-sized clip of a film or newsreel online does not constitute preservation. Film elements still must be preserved once a new digital master is created. Should something happen to that master, you will need to go back to those originals.

e. Not only do the digital formats change from year to year, digital technology allows every element of a film to be radically altered—which can lead to serious artists' rights issues. There are many attributes to digital filmmaking; unfortunately, preservation is not one of them.

5. The issues of preservation and access are closely aligned—preserved films must be shown and exhibited, and in order to program and provide access, the films need to have been preserved and/or restored. As mainstream and even repertory theaters move toward digital presentation exclusively, it will fall to the museums and archives to preserve not only the films themselves but also the experience of seeing film projected in a theater. In terms of Internet streaming, the greatest threat to the future of film preservation is Internet theft.

Already having an alarming impact on the entertainment industry at large, Internet theft will have a direct impact on the preservation of studio library titles if nothing is done to regulate the illegal downloading and file sharing of films, whether they are current features and independents or classic films; all films will be affected.

The Film Foundation's mission encompasses education, artists' rights, and exhibition as essential components of preservation. The foundation has developed several programs to screen preserved and restored films at festivals, museums, and archives all over the world. In addition, the foundation created a groundbreaking educational program, the Story of Movies, to teach young people about film literacy and the importance of preservation. The program is distributed, free of charge, to over thirty-five thousand middle- and high-school educators, reaching over nine million students.

Margaret Bodde is executive director of the Film Foundation, a nonprofit organization established in 1990 by Martin Scorsese and dedicated to protecting and preserving motion-picture history by providing annual support for preservation and restoration projects at leading film archives. Prior to working with Scorsese, Bodde worked in independent film distribution and exhibition, including three years as director of marketing at Miramax Films. She has produced several documentaries, including *The 50 Year Argument* (2014), *No Direction Home: Bob Dylan* (2005), *George Harrison: Living in the Material World* (2011), and *Val Lewton: The Man in the Shadows* (2007).

PAOLO CHERCHI USAI, GEORGE EASTMAN HOUSE

1. The notion that digital technology has changed the rules of the game in film preservation has become such an article of faith as to become a cliché. There is an implication here that archivists rigorously followed these "rules" in the analog domain, when in practice we know this is not true.

We have all been claiming to bring films back to a form as close as possible to what we presume they looked like originally, but we have frequently done so by making questionable decisions, such as altering image contrast or color grading according to modern taste and cleaning up soundtracks to make them suitable to current standards. For all its flashy righteousness, the catchphrase "ethics of film restoration" can be abused in the name of an arrogant and devious claim of archival authority: we, the practitioners, know our stuff; you, the viewers, should trust our word on what's ethical and what isn't.

It is time to expose this ideology of pseudocuratorial expertise—"ideology" in the sense of false consciousness and false representation. In fact, we might as well take a step further and come to terms with the reality that there is no such thing as "film restoration" in the proper sense of the term. Digital has provided yet another rationale to an ancient betrayal of our own principles, proudly claiming that the images of the past should look like new and therefore have no history, a goal we should all be ashamed of. Audiences are asking, if this is a digital restoration, why are there still scratches on the film? In other words, why does it look so old? The very fact that the question is being raised is the best evidence of what went wrong. Nevertheless, it deserves better than the perfunctory answer based on what digital can or cannot achieve. Instead, we should explain what led us to think that scratches are "bad" and that a moving image made one hundred years ago should be spotlessly clean. Technology has nothing to do with it.

In this sense, too much money is being made available to film preservation. Curators are largely to be blamed for this, as they have relinquished their responsibility to the hands of technocrats and publicity agents. Once upon a time there was "film restoration." That time is over. To achieve respectability, a film of the past must now be promoted as a "digital restoration." This seemingly harmless shift in semantics comes with a hidden financial agenda. In the course of a digital "restoration" process, a film originally made by photochemical means can be subjected to a variety of treatments. Scratches may indeed be reduced, or eliminated altogether; the same applies to dirt, flickering, image instability, contrast, color balance, and so on. However, the new tool also generates an irresistible temptation to not just clean up an image but change it altogether, to "improve" it for the sake of a "digital look," essentially making another film. We are all accomplices in its mutation: if it doesn't look different, you—the viewers—don't feel like calling it a restoration, and we—the "experts"—can't justify the mystique attached to our profession.

Money, as always, plays a crucial role in this perverse equation. Curators ask for an appraisal of what a "digital restoration" will entail; the esti-
mate they receive is normally based on the average time needed to clean
up a frame, multiplied by the number of frames of the film. As soon as
the process has actually started, it becomes evident that there is no clear
end in sight. Laboratories send the digital files to India, where dozens of
underpaid workers do much of the legwork. More time, however, may be
required in working with a fine comb over individual frames, so that the
cost of a high-quality digital work will often entail a multifold increase
from its photochemical equivalent.

Hence the chronic stalemate we are witnessing between the archive
and the laboratory contracted to do the job. The former asks for a reliable
budget; the latter proposes a specific figure based on its past experience
of similar projects. Alternatively, the laboratory responds by presenting its
hourly rate, meaning that the curator may go as far as he or she wants with
the digital tweaking, as long as there is someone willing to foot the bill.
At this point, the curator may either balk at the prospect, or bite the bullet
and spend as much as needed to make the analog film look digital enough,
thereby satisfying the need for a visible difference between "before" and
"after" restoration. The outcome of this modus operandi is often devastating, with the archive blackmailed into spending unforeseen sums in the
name of an unattainable and undesirable perfection.

2. Moreover, this is only the first half of the story, as far as "state-of-the-
art" film preservation is concerned. Its counterpart is the opposite faith in
that awful entry of corporate lexicon called "content delivery." The line of
reasoning behind it is a twisted interpretation of the very legitimate "horizontal" approach to film preservation—good is good enough, as long as it
is applied to the largest possible number of films. If one had to go by the
book, priority should be given to the preservation of films on the verge of
decomposition, beginning with the unique and oldest items in the collection. That's the theory. Truth be told, it rarely works that way. Collecting
institutions preserve what the funders (either private or governmental)
want them to with their money. It is the funders' right to do so, but it is
also the archives' right to decline offers for the "restoration" of works in
no urgent need of intervention. Saying "no" every now and then deprives
them of some media exposure, but goes a long way in upholding their
dignity and purpose.

3. The above framework may be valid in an "analog" context, but is
wholly inadequate to address its nonphotochemical sequel. Digital-born

works are now the most endangered species. Moving-image archives—or, to be precise, those which can afford it—are betting their money into the ongoing migration of digital data, a comfortable mirage that eschews the more substantial issue of selection. Two or three decades ago it would have been financially wise to invest as much as possible into the acquisition of new photochemical prints of carefully chosen titles. It is now too late to do so. Suppose you have compiled a list of one thousand "canonical" films made since the beginnings of cinema, and imagine that you are given an unlimited budget to achieve this goal, the only condition being that the money should be spent in ten years. If such a project was established at the present time, it is highly unlikely that the target could be met. The best hope is to acquire significant works on a case-by-case basis, as the opportunity arises. Which amounts to say that circumstances have already started implementing the very selection process curators should have been responsible for. Let's translate this into pixels. How are curators going to deal with the same concept in a "born-digital" landscape? What will they be allowed to select, if anything, and how? Will the very term "selection" make any sense to them, given the pervasive belief that there's no longer any need to choose?

4. While we wait for these curators to dwell upon the possibility that representing an iPod-viewing event one hundred years from now may be a bit of a challenge, their predigital ancestors are now about to enter that stage where the objects they would like to protect are either seen as liabilities (they shrink, they are bound to decay, they burn), or have definitely gone out of fashion but aren't old enough to be revered as archaeological relics. The expertise required for photochemical grading will soon be compared to the craftsmanship involved in making an eighteenth-century musical instrument according to its original design. Specialists in this kind of skill are regarded as survivors of a bygone era, quietly reaching their age of retirement. Little or no succession plan is in place for them. The few who are equally fluent in digital and photochemical grading are beginning to enjoy the status of laboratory superstars.

There are, of course, superstars in postchemical "restoration," and yet—at the institutional level—the prevailing attitude to the preservation of video and born-digital works may best be defined as high-tech bricolage. Governmental archives in wealthy countries are in a position of relative advantage in relation to private nonprofit organizations, but their strategies tend to take for granted the pattern of media obsolescence genetically implanted by the entertainment industry into its own creations. All of them—rich and poor—seem to share a commitment to the perpetuation of their slavery. The possibility of a nonproprietary infrastructure for digital preservation is often raised as an aspirational goal, but no one really believes in it.

5. The reasons for this bizarre mix of amateurism and utopia are well known, albeit ignored when it comes to its logical consequences at the social and economic level. Self-perpetuation and self-destruction are the key terms of reference for the cultural oxymoron known as "digital collections." In this perspective, outlets such as YouTube and the Internet Archive are a blessing for moving-image preservation, as they ought to relieve collecting bodies from what they shouldn't do. These devices thrive on the notion that "everything can be preserved" and that "access is a form of preservation." They should be encouraged to go ahead and keep basking in their illusion. Moving images are like world population—in the absence of a governance scheme, they will eventually find a mechanism to regulate their own environment, regardless of our intentions. There is nothing apocalyptic about it. We should actually take this as good news for the ecology and, yes, for the ethics of vision.

Paolo Cherchi Usai is senior curator of film at the George Eastman Museum (formerly George Eastman House) and a curator emeritus of the National Film and Sound Archive of Australia. Cofounder of the Pordenone Silent Film Festival, he directed the experimental feature films *Passio* (2007) and *Picture* (2015). He has also authored many books, notably *The Death of Cinema: History, Cultural Memory and the Digital Dark Age* (2001) and *Silent Cinema: An Introduction* (2008), and he coauthored *Film Curatorship: Archives, Museums, and the Digital Marketplace* (2008).

GROVER CRISP, COLUMBIA PICTURES AND TRISTAR PICTURES

1. What has changed is the challenge of dealing with all things digital. Ten years ago we had our first digital intermediate production, shot on film and finished digitally, and over the next decade our productions changed from predominantly film capture/film finish to mostly digital/virtually all digital finish. That is a huge change, for not just how the films are produced but also how we approach the preservation of these productions. So, we have had to go with the flow, so to speak, and we still actively preserve

our productions on film, while at the same time preserving the data. It is a linked dual approach, which I think is essential while we are still in this film and digital era of film production.

Funding is always an issue, in both the public and private sectors. And, of course, times are tough right now for everyone. As a commercial entity, we are fortunate to have a funding base that is usually attainable, though still something to fight for—unlike a public archive, where the funding is very difficult now, even though it always has been. Congress not so long ago committed to another multiyear funding for the National Film Preservation Foundation, so that was a good thing and came in just before the economy took a dive. It will likely be more difficult next time. I am a current member of the National Film Preservation Board, and I know we will do what we can to help the situation. Film preservation at public archives is something my studio has helped to fund for the last twenty years. So, as long as that is available, I will be pushing for it.

2. As a commercial entity, we have to keep in mind what titles in our library are active in the marketplace—what we want to release on Blu-ray, for example. So, that is one aspect to selecting titles that we work on. Beyond that, however, at our studio we have had a firm preservation and restoration foundation in place for many years, and the goal is to make sure everything is properly preserved and available. It is, by its nature, a slow and methodical process, constrained only by time and working within budgets. We try to work on a broad cross section of titles at any one time, from different eras and genres, and prioritize titles based on age, physical properties (nitrate, poor quality film elements, etc.), and so forth.

3. Over the years, we have collaborated with many archives around the world—and especially the Library of Congress, UCLA (University of California, Los Angeles), MoMA (Museum of Modern Art, New York), George Eastman House, the BFI (British Film Institute)—on Columbia Pictures titles for preservation and restoration. We also work with the National Film Preservation Board and the National Film Preservation Foundation on repatriation initiatives for Columbia Pictures films that we may not have good materials on or maybe nothing at all. The recent repatriation of films from New Zealand is a good example of where we will work with a US archive to preserve those films, covering all costs, so that both entities benefit from this recovery of what were truly lost films.

4. There is no concrete long-term digital preservation format for film. We still consider film the most stable and reliable medium for film, which

needs to be handled with care and kept in a proper climate-controlled vault. Having said that, however, I think it is more important to have a well-thought-out plan for dealing with both digital and film, in this digital/film hybrid production era, than it is to just obsess over one or the other. They are no longer at odds, and there is no reason to throw out the basic concepts of conservation just because there are new and somewhat scary things happening in the production environment. Keeping the original material (film, digital files, video, etc.), making multiple verifiable protection copies, testing the integrity of the material, activating a bulletproof geographic separation of assets plan, storing everything in a proper environment, and migrating data to newer platforms as is necessary are some of the most basic things to keep in mind. Eventually, it will be all digital, but I think the basic precepts still apply. If there is no universally agreed-to digital preservation methodology, and there really isn't right now, then you do what makes sense and follow what I would call best practices.

Many of the traditional labs no longer exist, but some of the key labs involved in preservation and restoration are still around, and those labs have technicians who know what they are doing. New-people-coming-up-through-the-ranks, though, is basically a thing of the past. When I am talking to students interested in film preservation, they always want to know how to get into digital restoration. I used to suggest they go get a job, or even volunteer, at a traditional lab because that would help provide the background that I personally think is necessary. Those jobs are not so available anymore. But if you don't understand film from a historical perspective and aren't aware of aspects of different stocks, formats, various printing techniques, and so forth, then you are not going to understand fully what to do with it digitally. And, I must say, I see this all the time in the results of a lot of digital restoration work out in the field. There is this overreliance on the tools available to clean images, for example, often to the point where the restored film doesn't much resemble a film anymore. It's the shiny-plastic syndrome. We just need to understand and control these technologies and not let them control us, and I think that is one of the key aspects of the lack of expertise you refer to. A person fully grounded in the technical and historical aspects of film could transition to digital work much more authentically and successfully than someone who just knows how to turn dials on a console, no matter how expert that person may be.

The ability to fix problems with film, whether it is deteriorating nitrate stock, torn or missing frames from a negative, or just film that is really dirty, is one of the great things about this digital revolution. Digital technology applied to restoration allows us to repair and restore things we could never do in the photochemical world. I still support that world and recognize it for the traditional aspects of the work, of course, but we will at some point be moving on to a purely digital workflow. I think it is important to be mindful of the historical as well as aesthetic implications of digital workflows. So, the old reliable approach to this kind of work of "first, do no harm" is, I think, still a good one. I also firmly support the concept of digital projection—the state of traditional print projection has deteriorated over the years, probably as older technicians retire, and it is very troublesome to restore a film and have pristine prints subjected to substandard projection practices. It is also costly. We have all seen this over and over again. But I think one of the great things about digital projection of legacy films is that it is entirely possible to create a digital-cinema version that is relatively authentic to its time and place, and not have it just look like a large-screen video projection. You have to be very careful in the technical approach to creating this version so that the film still looks like film. Otherwise, what would be the point?

5. Preservation and access go hand in hand. It has been repeated many times, by all of us, that there is no real point to a preservation plan if there isn't a viable access component built into it. Just to lock something away in the vaults is not the point—you must have a viable plan for accessibility, whether that is through distribution of prints or any of the electronic or digital formats.

My department has a very close relationship with both the theatrical-repertory department and our home-entertainment division. On the print distribution side, we try to make sure that the best-quality prints we have are available for booking. This relationship goes back many years, and we actively support the booking of the prints, both domestically and internationally, at archives, festivals, theaters—everywhere. It's important that we share the films that we have worked so hard to restore. On the home-entertainment side, we work closely with the marketing department to determine what, when, and how library titles should be released. We internally developed all the concepts for our box sets (for example, the noir sets, the Sam Fuller set, Rita Hayworth, Kim Novak, Michael Powell, etc.), and home entertainment has welcomed the collaboration.

And we developed our partnership with the Film Foundation as an outgrowth of the personal relationship I've had there for many years. So, it is beneficial for all involved, I think, and the real beneficiaries are the film fans who have been waiting many years for these films to become

Figure 10.1a–b. Grover Crisp explains that at Sony Pictures, home entertainment influences the preservation and release of DVD box sets, ranging from the movies of the venerated British filmmaker Michael Powell to those of the Hollywood star icon Rita Hayworth. (a) From Michael Powell and Emeric Pressburger's *A Matter of Life and Death* (a.k.a. *Stairway to Heaven*) (1946) © Sony Pictures; (b) from *Gilda* (1946) © Sony Pictures.

available. All the work for creating our masters for Blu-ray or DVD is a product of my department, including all new releases, not just the library. Maintaining the quality control of this work is very important to us, and it only makes sense that we oversee the films from initial evaluation for restoration all the way through to exhibition, Blu-ray, and DVD.

Grover Crisp is executive vice president of asset management, film restoration, and digital mastering at Sony Pictures Entertainment. He manages all facets of the asset protection, restoration, preservation, and digital mastering program for the Columbia Pictures and TriStar Pictures feature-film and television libraries at Sony. He has worked in the motion-picture and television industry for over thirty years and at the Columbia/Sony Pictures Entertainment studios since 1984. He oversaw the restoration of *Easy Rider* (1969), *Funny Girl* (1968), *On the Waterfront* (1954), and *Taxi Driver* (1976), among many other films.

DENNIS DOROS AND AMY HELLER, MILESTONE FILM & VIDEO

1. Film preservation has improved dramatically over the past decade. Specifically, the quality of digital-restoration technology has created digital masters that are now indecipherable from film. Photochemical restoration has always had the problem that with each generation (original internegative to interpositive to internegative to projection print), there is a reduction in quality, much like a photocopy of a photograph. Now, a digital scan will be equal to if not better than the original material. And with the ability to time individual frames and dust/scratch removal, they are often better than the original. That said, the costs are still dramatically higher, and a great deal of funding is needed. As Milestone has always been self-funded, I wouldn't be able to tell you about public and private funding opportunities, but with the amount of film that is in danger, there is not nearly enough for the archives to restore all their material.

I would also point out that the founding of the Association of Moving Image Archivists (AMIA) twenty years ago was a major turning point in restoration. It was created to foster better relationships among the archives, studios, professors, students, and distributors and has done an amazing job. There are a far greater number of cooperative efforts among archives and with studios than ever before.

2. The question of prioritization is the most difficult one for any organization, and it is usually based on the rarity of the material, its condition, and the perceived cultural value. As a for-profit company (in theory), the commercial return for a film becomes a real consideration. Milestone specializes in films (such as *Araya* or *The Exiles*) that have seemingly no commercial cachet, however, and then sets out to prove that there is a market for them.

3. Yes, I definitely think that the postwar American independent films have been neglected, especially the more experimental titles. Nitrate films are perceived to be in greater danger so there's less attention paid to these "safety" films, even though they are threatened by vinegar syndrome and color deterioration. Also, Third World cinema is definitely in great danger as there are very limited resources for proper storage. There is splendid work being done by AMIA, the Rockefeller Foundation, the Southeast Asia-Pacific Audiovisual Archive Association, and the World Cinema Foundation to support these smaller archives around the world, but a lot more needs to be done.

A big threat right now is to filmmakers who have stored their film elements in labs. First off, these facilities were rarely designed for long-term storage and usually lack optimal temperature and humidity controls. More importantly, as studios and distributors move to digital, many photochemical labs will be threatened. Already, original materials are disappearing at an alarming rate. We've had serious problems getting materials on some of our releases. I think archives will have to be more proactive in working with labs (and not wait for them to close) to properly ensure the preservation of these materials.

4. As previously mentioned, the digital revolution has greatly impacted film preservation, but more specifically on the restoration side of the equation. As long as there is also digital output to film, I believe this is preservation, and a vastly improved version of it—especially when sound restoration is also done. But I have my doubts on long-term digital storage—and digital output to film is still extremely expensive. There should be a movement among AMIA members to support the photochemical film labs, and, luckily, the best have traditionally been small boutique labs that don't require Hollywood's run of two thousand prints to survive.

5. Milestone is one hundred percent about access—obviously—and our expertise is exhibition and distribution. We are amateur archivists who work with the archives for many of our releases. Much of our success has

Figure 10.2. Milestone Film & Video preserves and releases independent films, including *The Exiles* (1961), Kent Mackenzie's chronicle of twelve hours in the lives of young Native Americans living in Los Angeles. © Milestone Film & Video.

been due to the archives' efforts, and we have repaid them both financially and with increased exposure through the media.

Even though it is self-evident that as film distributors, we are champions of access, we actually believe it is an absolutely essential component of the preservation process. Film culture is not static. Every year, every day, the worlds of filmmaking, exhibition, spectatorship, criticism, and restoration are changing and evolving—now more rapidly than ever, thanks to new technology. With digital media, more and more people have access to a wide range of cinemas and have the ability to create their own films. So as older, rare, more experimental films are rediscovered, restored, preserved, and made available, they become part of the current cinema world. So a freshman seeing *Metropolis* may incorporate themes of alienation and crowd control in his thesis, or may go on to explore other silent films, or may become interested in the restoration process itself. Access opens the door to the wider world of cinema and to the archive itself. It is invaluable.

Archives have long been interested in exploiting their collections, but generally, this has been on a case-by-case basis and not as a part of long-term planning. There are some excellent examples of archives working in distribution, such as the British Film Institute and the Edition Film-museum, but on the whole, archives have rarely known how best to market their holdings and to maximize their commercial possibilities. They tend to see distribution as: (a) crass commercialization, unsuitable for a museum/library, or (b) utterly beyond their capabilities with their limited staffing. There is a major movement of digitizing archive collections for public access. Some of this is very good and some of it, I fear, will prove to be a waste of valuable funding and staff time.

When archives have licensed individual titles to distributors, the archives have seen some excellent results—but often their contribution is relegated to the small print. And when archives have licensed a large part of their collection to distributors, they have seen rather poor results, with many unfulfilled promises. The reality is that access is a commercial enterprise, no different from a museum gift shop or café. With dedication to long-term planning, it can bear excellent results. So whether an archive chooses to go it alone or works with an outside distributor, it is important to set long-range goals and planning to make the archive's work widely available and understood.

Dennis Doros, along with Amy Heller, created Milestone Film & Video in 1990 to discover and distribute films of enduring artistry. Doros serves on the board of directors of the Association of Moving Image Archivists. Previously, he worked at the Athens International Film Festival (Ohio) and served as vice president of Kino International. In recent years, Milestone has begun restoring classic films from American postwar independents, including works directed by Lionel Rogosin, Shirley Clarke, and Charles Burnett.

Amy Heller worked at New Yorker Films and First Run Features before cofounding Milestone Film & Video. In 2011 she and Doros began Milliar-ium Zero, a film distribution company that specializes in films with strong social and political content. She holds an MA in American history from Yale University.

JAN-CHRISTOPHER HORAK, UCLA FILM & TELEVISION ARCHIVE

1. Basically, there is never enough funding, but there has been a sea change in film preservation, influencing both preservation priorities in nonprofit and government archives and overall funding levels for film preservation. Most importantly, major corporate entities with significant libraries of classical Hollywood films have taken responsibility for preserving and circulating their libraries, as compared to the 1990s, when major film archives, like the Library of Congress, UCLA Film & Television Archive, George Eastman House, and the Museum of Modern Art, were investing significant portions of their film-preservation budgets towards preserving studio product.

With the establishment of the National Film Preservation Foundation (NFPF) in 1997, preservation priorities have shifted in public archives towards so-called orphan films, whether public-domain mainstream narrative cinema, amateur film, industrials, medical and educational films, newsreels, et cetera. The Library of Congress, for example, has recently acquired the huge Fred MacDonald and Rick Prelinger collections of "ephemeral films," to use a term first coined by Prelinger. Literally hundreds of moving-image archives have been founded, many parts of larger institutions, like historical societies, and are now receiving funding from the NFPF.

2. Decisions to preserve individual titles depend on a complex matrix of questions and answers, including uniqueness and condition of surviving material, access requests, funding sources—some of which set preservation agendas—curatorial programming, earned-income potential, and historical importance as reflected in film histories. Actually getting titles preserved may depend on technical issues, finding good source material, lab capacities, actual funding, and interests of copyright holders, and projects may take several years to complete.

It is always a choice of one over another title. It is important to strike a balance between various strengths in your collections and to make sure you lose as little as possible, knowing that there will be losses.

3. It is no longer a question of whether specific film types are falling through the cracks, but rather how much material in every genre, era, and style is disappearing because capacities are minuscule compared to need.

The medium facing the greatest crisis, however, is video and television, since there is virtually no public funding for the countless hours of open-access television, guerrilla TV, activist documentaries, regional tele-vision news, produced from the late 1960s through the 1990s. Congress abdicated responsibility for all video preservation, recommending that a private rather than public foundation for funding preservation be created. That foundation has funded no more than thirty projects over ten years.

4. As documented in the Academy's white paper "The Digital Dilemma," digital "preservation" is eleven times more expensive than ana-log preservation, due to the lack of a digital-preservation medium. Fur-thermore, while digitizing films for access purposes is standard procedure now, digitizing for preservation requires that film materials be restored in analog first, since digitality cannot improve what is not there—e.g., when surviving prints or negatives are severely damaged or emulsions too thin. The cost of digital cleanup is also still prohibitively expensive.

While the studios have embraced digital restoration, nonprofit archives have been much slower to jump on the bandwagon, especially since the turnover of digital formats every two years makes long-term storage an iffy proposition. Nevertheless, some archives, like the UCLA Film & Television Archive, have now invested in digital-restoration software and hardware and are proceeding with digital-restoration projects.

The digital revolution has positively influenced access to collections. Before the end of 2011, UCLA will put over six hundred hours of newsreel material online for free access. The archive of the future will be online and transparent, allowing users direct access without the mediation of an archivist, making it a performative space, rather than a closed holding tank. This process, however, will take decades. Our archive holds more than one hundred million feet of material to be potentially digitized.

Video works most endangered are those held on three-quarter-inch tape—which now more often than not need to be baked (literally) before transfer—Sony Portapak half-inch reel-to-reel tape, and other early tape formats. Some archives have already set up automated transfer-to-digital systems for this material, but the sheer volume of unprotected material is staggering.

5. In contradistinction to only ten years ago, access is a huge priority for moving-image archives today, and no preservation project is now under-taken without discussing access issues. Whenever possible, new preser-vation elements are now routinely scanned for the production of a digital master for access purposes.

At the UCLA Film & Television Archive, access occurs through a variety of channels. At the Billy Wilder Theater in Los Angeles, the archive conducts weekly screenings in 35 mm, 16 mm, and video. Every two years, the archive's UCLA Festival of Preservation tours major North American cities, while other screening spaces borrow films from the archive. Through the archive study center, students and other researchers can access collections. Increasingly, the archive is making material accessible as streamed content through its own website, producing its own DVD sets, as well as signing distribution agreements with DVD and Blu-ray producers.

Jan-Christopher Horak is director of the University of California, Los Angeles Film & Television Archive and was named an Academy Scholar by the Academy of Motion Picture Arts and Sciences in 2006. Before his tenure at UCLA, he worked at the George Eastman House (1984–1994), the Munich Filmmuseum (1994–1998), Universal Studios (1998–2000), and the Hollywood Entertainment Museum. Horak is founding editor of *The Moving Image* and has taught at many universities around the world. He is author of numerous books, including *L.A. Rebellion: Creating a New Black Cinema* (2015), *Saul Bass: Anatomy of Film Design* (2014), and *Lovers of Cinema: The First American Film Avant-Garde, 1919–1945* (1995).

ANNETTE MELVILLE, NATIONAL FILM PRESERVATION FOUNDATION

1. The preservation landscape was long dominated by Hollywood sound features, the most celebrated—and visible—side of American filmmaking. The major projects were managed by the studios and the largest nonprofit and public archives—the Academy Film Archive, George Eastman House, the Library of Congress, the Museum of Modern Art, and the UCLA Film & Television Archive, which house most of the nation's surviving nitrate film.

Over the past decade, new institutions have come into the field and brought forward a far more diverse range of films for public viewing and study—the avant-garde, newsreels, home movies, industrial films, town portraits, travelogues, scientific documentation, concert and dance footage, works sponsored by business and advocacy groups, political ads, and animation . . . you name it. Collections not generally associated with film can yield up fascinating works. A good example is *The Blood of Jesus* (1941), a salvation drama made by Spencer Williams for African American audiences. This feature turned up at Southern Methodist University among an impressive collection of nitrate release prints taken in by the university in the 1980s from a warehouse in rural Texas.

The second question concerning adequate funding cannot be entirely serious. Nonprofit archives work on a shoestring, and none but the largest have a budget line for film preservation work. Thus, virtually all film-preservation projects are grant and donor funded. Fortunately, the National Film Preservation Foundation (NFPF) receives federal funds through the Library of Congress to distribute as grants. The funding has remained at the same level since 2006. Little as this is, the support plus the validation brought by the Library of Congress's 1993 preservation study and the Orphan Film Symposiums, begun in 1999, have been major factors in the democratization of the film-preservation community.

2. For the National Film Preservation Foundation, the overriding concerns are the film's historical value, condition, and need for preservation; the uniqueness of the source material; and plans for public access to the preserved film. Because public funding is so limited, we are especially careful to cull out projects that come from commercial entities. Our mandate is to help the public and nonprofit organizations save films that are not likely to survive without public support.

Our recent collaboration with the New Zealand Film Archive brought up an entirely new set of issues. Through this project we are returning more than 160 American silent-era films to the United States. Most survive nowhere else and have been unseen for decades. It was impossible to figure out which titles to repatriate and preserve without doing a careful assessment of their condition and cultural importance. Just figuring out which ones to examine required a judgment call. We invited a group of scholars and archivists to make recommendations. Although everyone had their preferences, there was a surprising consensus once the arguments for each title were clearly articulated.

3. Yes, nonfiction films, especially from the early years of motion pictures. In the press to preserve nitrate features, their less glamorous cousins often fell through the cracks. Many weren't even collected, let alone preserved. Today actuality films can seem like windows into history. Even fragments have important stories to tell. The NFPF worked with the Library of Congress to return from Australia and preserve an eleven-minute

fragment showcasing the US Navy in 1915. Since we started streaming the film on our website last year, it has been viewed more than 150,000 times; it was even used in a presentation by Admiral John C. Harvey at the 2011 Submarine Technology Symposium.

There are hundreds of actuality films like this. Reading the motion-picture trade magazines, you stumble across tantalizing titles that take on new meaning today. Who wouldn't want to see *Modern Architecture*, a 1934 film from Richard Neutra's Studio; or *Farming with Dynamite*, a 1922 film from Dupont? Or *De-Indianizing the Red Man* (1917) or *Life at Hull House* (1911)? If these films survive, let's get them into archives and preserve them!

4. Digitization has already revolutionized the ways archives share films with audiences and researchers, and, as prices drop, it is changing the preservation process as well. For our New Zealand project, for example, the preservation facility scans the less fragile films and posts the copies on a file server for inspection. Archivists on two continents are able to review the copy and return detailed instructions to the technical team. Along the way, archivists provide intertitles, credits, and can even clean up the scan. The corrected version is output to film. As technologies change, the fundamental principle remains the same—use copies to provide access to the film content, and protect the original on film. Film has been around for more than a century and is still the most stable and reliable medium for its long-term archiving.

5. Why preserve a film if no one can see it? It is easy to forget that our notions of film history are determined by film availability. Audiences and scholars cannot appreciate works that are lost or too fragile to view. Such films are forgotten unless they can be made available in some form.

Preservation keeps film alive. The NFPF requires that every institution receiving support share the newly preserved film with the public in some way. We also produce the Treasures DVD series, bringing together films preserved by the American archival community, which, for one reason or another, have slipped from public memory but deserve to be seen. Some Treasures films, such as Christopher Maclaine's *The End* (1953), in *Treasures IV: American Avant-Garde Film, 1947–1986*, have triggered a reassessment of the filmmaker's work (reviewed by *Cineaste*, Winter 2010, www .cineaste.com).

What I am trying to say is this: access is the reason for film preservation, and film preservation makes access possible. The two are flip sides of the same coin.

Annette Melville is director emerita of the National Film Preservation Foundation (NFPF). She was director of the NFPF since it began operations in 1997 until 2014. Under her direction, the NFPF preserved more than 1,800 American films from institutions in all fifty states, the District of Columbia, and Puerto Rico and produced the Treasures from American Film Archives DVD sets. In addition, Melville has worked with the Library of Congress to create a national plan for the preservation of American film.

MICHAEL POGORZELSKI, ACADEMY FILM ARCHIVE

1. The digital transition that the entire industry is going through has had many effects on film preservation. Two of those effects have had an economic impact: (a) The costs of restoring a film digitally are much higher than traditional photochemical preservation or restoration. As a result, archives can achieve superior results with digital but at a much higher cost. Inevitably, the number of projects that can be contemplated must be lower. (b) The cost of restoring a film photochemically will most likely be rising as well. As more mainstream cinema screens transition to digital projection, there will be less need for 35 mm release prints. Thirty-five-millimeter release printing has been the foundation for the business models of the raw-film-stock manufacturers like Kodak and Fuji. With demand evaporating for their biggest-selling film stock, the prices on all stocks will need to go up. These higher costs will mean even fewer projects will be able to be completed in future years, until traditional film printing will no longer be an option at all.

2. The condition of the original elements is, of course, a prime factor. If an original film element is deteriorating and will soon become unprintable, then it moves up in the queue. Films in the Academy Film Archive's collection that are orphans (they have no corporation or government agency that has the resources to preserve them) are given priority over titles that do have such owners. We also try to approach preservation by tackling a filmmaker's entire output. Rather than making judgments of which films are "great" and preserving those judged worthy, we strive to preserve them all. The Satyajit Ray Preservation Project is an example of this approach. Since 1993, the Academy Film Archive has been working to preserve every one of Ray's twenty-eight feature films and eight short films. After eighteen years, we are over halfway through Ray's filmography.

Figure 10.3. Since 1993, the Academy Film Archive has been working to preserve every one of Satyajit Ray's twenty-eight feature films and eight short films, including the landmark Apu trilogy, of which *Pather Panchali* is the first film. © Government of West Bengal, 1955.

3. Along with collecting and preserving films which have won or been nominated for Academy Awards, the Academy Film Archive has been collecting avant-garde and experimental films for many years. These films are often owned and held by filmmakers who do not have resources to properly store their films or actively preserve them. Many avant-garde films pose unique challenges and can be the most technically complicated and time-consuming projects, so we're moving ahead at a painfully slow rate. We are approaching independent filmmakers of all types—animators, documentarians, as well as avant-garde—and offering the archive as a home for their collections or, at the very least, educating them about the importance of preservation and helping them to figure out how to care for their collection.

4. Digital tools are among the most powerful ever available to the preservation field. Things which were "unfixable," such as color fading, emulsion damage, even missing images (as when half of the film frame is simply not there), can now be addressed . . . if you have the budget.

Transferring to digital is not preservation. We've figured out how to make film last for one hundred years or more. We know about proper storage environments and how to safely handle film to prolong its life. But no one knows how to store a digital file for that same period. Solutions are being developed, and not just in the entertainment industry—there are many industries which generate enormous amounts of data they wish to access for hundreds of years into the future. But right now the only way to guarantee a digital file's survival is to actively monitor and migrate it onto a newer, fresher storage (whether that's onto a new hard drive or data tape).

I believe that all video will be preserved as digital files. They will have to be. Maintaining decks and video playback heads for the one hundred plus formats that have been used in the last sixty years will be impossible, and the tapes themselves can begin to experience difficulties in playback within only ten years. But because the files can be much smaller, they will be more manageable.

5. I am very fortunate that I work in an organization (the Academy of Motion Picture Arts and Sciences) that values access just as much as preservation. Prints in the archive's collection are loaned at no cost to the borrowers, and access to items in the collection on-site (in the Pickford Center for Motion Picture Study in Hollywood, where the archive is located) is also free. I think that film-on-film projection will ultimately become the sole purview of archives and museums. Major distributors are already reporting that no 35 mm prints exist on titles in their libraries and they will not be creating any more new prints. The concept of "preservation" will have to expand to curation of individual prints as unique objects, which will need to be handled very carefully and under very specific conditions by highly trained projectionists. The days of, "Well, that print just got scratched so let's just make a new one," are over. That model is not sustainable now and will certainly not be in the future (for archives or distributors like the studios). Only exhibitors who can demonstrate their vigilance and care in safely handling prints will be able to access them from archives in the future.

Michael Pogorzelski received a BA and an MFA in communication arts from the University of Wisconsin–Madison. He was named director of the Academy Film Archive at the Academy of Motion Picture Arts and Sciences in 2000, and has supervised the restoration and preservation of documentaries, experimental films, and animated films, as well as five Academy Award Best Picture winners. Most recently, he helped supervise the digital restoration of *The Life and Death of Colonel Blimp* (1943), *Portrait of Jason* (1967), *Hoop Dreams* (1994), *Rashomon* (1950), and *Peyton Place* (1957).

KATIE TRAINOR, MUSEUM OF MODERN ART (MOMA)

1. I think the film-preservation landscape has changed a great deal over the last ten years. I graduated from the L. Jeffrey Selznick School of Film Preservation in 2001, and since then several other moving-image preservation study programs have emerged. The awareness and state of preservation has entered more into the forefront.

Sadly, I believe there will never be a "healthy" amount of funding available to preserve all of our moving images. That is just practical thought, not pessimistic observation. There are a handful of organizations that dedicate themselves to this cause (e.g., the National Film Preservation Foundation and the Film Foundation), but that is not enough.

2. So many good questions, so little space. In my observation, looking at MoMA's history of preservation, deciding what to preserve has been dictated by several factors. In the early years it was preserving nitrate onto safety stock because of condition and deterioration. I then see a trend of preservation decisions being made by the taste of the current curator's film-history interests as well as funding availability.

Currently, since my time here, we have established a preservation pipeline that meets once a month. This group consists of our chief curator, the curator of access and loans, the film conservator, the circulating film library, and myself and is always open to our exhibition curators to sit in and present their ideas.

This has become a group decision in which factors such as condition, future exhibition needs, collaborative possibilities, and, to be frank, working with filmmakers who are getting older and whose input we would like, all play into how preservation decisions are made.

I do foresee much more collaboration between institutions when embarking on future preservation projects. With the discontinuing of film stocks and costs of digital preservation, sharing the expense is a practicality that I see necessary in the future.

3. I think all films are falling through the cracks to a certain extent, some genres more than others, given the number of films out there that still need to be preserved.

That said, there are many different institutions—including national, regional, university, and historical societies—that are preserving a vast variety of moving images. So my impression is that there is a little bit of everything being preserved. I think no one genre is being neglected.

There is a formal acquisition process at MoMA over which a board presides. The Film Acquisitions Trustee Committee meets four times a year and votes on acquisitions presented to them by the staff of curators. Each curator has his/her "specialties" and areas of interest, so, between them, they cover an amazing expanse of moving-image material, both current and past.

The collection consists of all areas of motion-picture history, and the titles reflect the interest of all the curators that have worked here since 1935. Any film that comes into the collection is considered a work of art and/or the art of the moving image. The collection is diverse. It has its strengths (for example, the Biograph/D. W. Griffith collection, early silent comedy, animation) but also has a wish list of titles to be acquired. There is also the ongoing desire to complete the filmographies of artists in the collection.

It is also important to note that even as an institution continues to acquire, it must also remember to maintain what it already has. Prints can show wear, certain films stocks sadly fade, and the need to preserve from acetate stock to polyester-based stocks is an ongoing process. Therefore, budgeting must consider maintenance as well as acquisition.

4. The question of digital technology's impact on preservation and other issues related to it are million-dollar questions with many different answers, depending on whom you ask. Some folks in this field think the phrase "digital preservation" is an oxymoron. Given the frequent obsolescence of different digital mediums, as well as a multitude of standards being developed that change, it is very easy to fall prey to the school of thought that digital could mean the death of that content. But the digital revolution will be ongoing, and we need to embrace it, understand it, and let those who develop it keep doing what they are doing by supporting their efforts, while also remembering to challenge their outcomes.

This has changed preservation a great deal. We are seeing motion-picture processing labs closing and/or transitioning solely into the digital arena. MoMA has not fully engaged in the digital-preservation arena, as we are still firm believers in the photochemical process. But we are getting our feet wet with the understanding that the preservation process can now include a collaboration of photochemical and digital processes. The positive outcome of the digital revolution is that it allows for more access on several different platforms.

The Department of Film and the Department of Media and Performance Art are actively engaged in migrating all video formats to current media by creating DigiBeta masters and uncompressed files on hard drives. And with that digitization comes the need for a migration plan, more aptly referred to as a Digital Asset Management Program.

5. I think preservation and access work with each other not against. Although, I can see how they can be misconstrued as one force "bullying" the other, so to speak. Balance is definitely difficult to achieve when there are more people who want to see things than there are those who want to contribute to their preservation.

The Film Department has been approached by several different entities that want to help facilitate getting the collection online. But the practicality of the process can be slightly daunting. The cost of digitization and the clearance of rights are serious concerns. Fortunately, the museum has three theaters that provide a constant platform for exhibition. That's not to stay that there is not a hope someday to be able to highlight the collection by having certain films online. I foresee, as these costs start to decline, the greater likelihood of online access.

There is an ongoing debate about putting content on DVDs for sale to the home-video market. The museum already has a successful source for distribution in the retail department. But then we ask ourselves, what is the future of the DVD? Nonetheless it is an area that has not been fully explored.

There is an extremely respectful relationship between preservation and exhibition efforts in the history of MoMA, as one does not exist without the other.

Katie Trainor is film collections manager at New York City's Museum of Modern Art. A graduate of the L. Jeffrey Selznick School of Film Preservation at the George Eastman Museum (formerly the George Eastman House), she was archive manager for the Harvard Film Archive from 1993 to 2000 and is a cofounder of Home Movie Day and the Center for Home Movies. Since 2001, she has managed the Telluride Film Festival's Galaxy Theatre venue.

DANIEL WAGNER, GEORGE EASTMAN HOUSE

1. Excluding the digital revolution for now, I think audiences have become more engaged in what they are looking at on screen. There is a widening disconnect, however, between what they are looking at and how it got there. This is a failing of archivists, and we need to clearly define what exactly we are doing. Where digital does play a part here is when someone asks me, "So, you must do everything digitally now?" No one is interested, including me, in my tiresome reply that digital is fraught with difficulties. A more terse reply of "No" can only be interpreted as archivists being a bunch of Luddites.

The question of funding this is a difficult one. It is easy to say we need more; however, given how the Eastman House is structured, I think there is a healthy amount of funding. I supervise the preservation of six to eight films per year. My two colleagues do the same. I don't know if we could effectively manage any more than that. If this is purely a staffing question, then, yes, we need more funding. It gets tricky. Funding the preservation of a film is romantic. Funding the salary or health insurance of a real person is less so.

2. The driving force behind most preservation projects is money. The vast majority of preservation at Eastman House is reliant on federal and private grant money. The films preserved are proactive responses to those funding agencies. We pair films with agencies that have proven over time to support a certain genre, period, or aspect of film. We also depend heavily on condition and scarcity of material. Historical and regional importance plays a role, but not as big as one might think. Often we use more well-known titles to entice an agency to support a project, but then package it with a short or avant-garde piece that is just as worthy but unknown for any number of reasons. It is easy to understand why *Casablanca* needs to be preserved. It is more difficult to make the case for an early Technicolor test film from the 1920s.

3. Easily the most underrepresented in preservation are the first and second generations of video artists, whose work exists on media that is now nearly impossible to find playback equipment to even begin to consider migrating to a more current format. It is scary how much of this will be lost.

Overall I think the field has a lot to be proud of in expanding its understanding of what is in need of preservation beyond the historically accepted works. Even the Eastman House of just a few years ago was primarily considered an archive entirely dedicated to American silent cinema. In the last few years our program has expanded to a much wider variety. We have preserved sound films like *Born to Be Bad* and *Pandora and the Flying Dutchman*. We have worked on films from independent producers like Danny Lyon, Ross McElwee, Paul Morrissey, Mark Rappaport, and Philip Kaufman. We have preserved home movies from the famous and not so famous.

The larger issue is that the need is so much bigger than what a handful of archives can provide. Home movies, itinerant filmmakers, educational films, industrials, avant-garde, shorts, silents. The need in each of these areas is immense.

4. In no way does any digital media equal preservation. The shelf life of even the best digital media is still being measured in years, not decades, or, in the case of properly stored film, centuries. On the scrap heap of the digital revolution are dozens of formats and carriers that are already unplayable. Perhaps the biggest positive of the digital revolution is the ability to put long-forgotten content in the hands of audiences. BitTorrent, and its brethren, may drive rights holders crazy, but it ensures the survival of so many films that rights holders have forgotten or ignored.

The expertise is still in the photochemical lab, but how long will the lab be there? The era is virtually over when studios had the money to preserve dozens of films a year across multiple labs. If labs were able to make the sacrifice a few years ago, they got a digital scanner to prepare for this moment, but the financial burden is significant. There are so many labs that work with fifty-year-old optical printers. They were built to last, and they still produce a great product. Does anyone think a digital scanner purchased now will still be chugging along in 2060? Who can afford to replace a million-dollar piece of equipment, let alone all of the equipment associated with a digital scanner, every ten years or sooner?

5. We loan to other FIAF (International Federation of Film Archives) archives and approved not-for-profit screening venues. We also screen the collection on-site in the Dryden Theatre. Researchers can travel to Rochester to view collection materials in depth. These are all avenues that have a long-established history. I was not dogmatic about it, but ten years ago I would have said that film should be viewed on film. Now? What archive can afford to be this shortsighted? On one hand, it is a shame that cinema has gone in this direction. I have seen photos of the *Mona Lisa*, but I would

never claim that I have actually seen it in the Louvre. And I think a good many people would hold the same opinion.

Film has never been this way. The cinematic experience has been under-valued since the 1950s, when movies started showing up on TV. Grand movie palaces, multiplexes, neighborhood theaters, drive-ins, church basements, et cetera—any one of these places is a part of the cinematic experience. For decades archives had to battle only TV, and it was easy to exert superiority over those twenty-inch black boxes. But once bad projection and obnoxious audiences became the rule, the moviegoing experience became a chore. Then the only thing that mattered was content. Archives have fought this battle for a while, but they are the only ones fighting it. That battle was lost ten or fifteen years ago and archives have just denied the reality. It's fine to have standards, but the teachable moment is no longer how we see movies, but in fact what kind of movies we "could" see. Maybe, with this approach in mind, archives can transition into the digital world with less hand-wringing and nervousness.

Daniel Wagner has been with the George Eastman Museum (formerly George Eastman House) since 2000, when he graduated from the L. Jeffrey Selznick School of Film Preservation. Since 2005, he has been the preservation officer in charge of digital initiatives. He wrote a description of the special challenges associated with the restoration of the early sound film *Lonesome* (1928) for Criterion's Blu-ray release of the film.

CHAPTER 11

MOD Man
AN INTERVIEW WITH GEORGE FELTENSTEIN

Robert Cashill

Manufacturing-on-demand (MOD) programs continue to be the last best hope for collectors of Hollywood's past, according to *Cineaste* editor Robert Cashill in his article "Life Gone MOD," which appeared in the same issue of the magazine as the interview below. Cashill points out that any discussion about MOD needs to start with the Warner Bros. Archive, which laid the foundation for the Universal Vault Series, Sony Screen Classics by Request (handling Columbia titles), and the MGM Limited Edition Collection (run by Fox but in 2011 offering only MGM and other non-Fox titles). Given the many movies and TV shows underneath the Warner Bros. umbrella, as well as its superior marketing and rare responsiveness to consumer concerns, the Warner Archive would continue to set the pace in MOD, as Cashill saw it in 2011, when he spoke with the Warner Bros. senior vice president of theatrical catalog marketing, George Feltenstein.

An Emmy Award–winner (for the PBS program *American Masters* in 2004), a movie historian, and the executive producer of numerous film-related documentaries aired on Turner Classic Movies or produced as DVD supplements, Feltenstein has held his position at Warner Bros. for nearly a decade. As such, he is the primary spokesperson for the Warner Archive, its MOD discs, and the future of catalog releases on DVD and Blu-ray.

Originally published in *Cineaste* 37, no. 1 (Winter 2011); copyright © 2011 by Cineaste, Inc.

CINEASTE: The Warner Archive will be three years old next March. Has it evolved differently than you thought it might have when it began?

GEORGE FELTENSTEIN: Absolutely. The idea for this began ten years ago. I was involved in a niche CD soundtrack operation with some of our soundtracks as part of a joint venture we have with Rhino Records, where we made a limited number of soundtracks and sold them on the Internet for higher-than-normal prices.

One of my colleagues, Jim Wuthrich, who is now president of international at Warner Home Video and Warner Bros. digital distribution, was working in online marketing then and said, "That's fascinating, I wish I could figure out a way to get a business model like that to work for DVD, but I can't get my brain around it." Every couple of months I'd see him in the hall and he'd say, "I'm still working on it." Around 2006, he said, "I think I've figured out how we could do this—we can manufacture them on demand. Let's see if I can get corporate approval." By then our digital distribution division had grown significantly, and Kevin Tsujihara, who headed the home entertainment group at that time and is now one of our company presidents, blessed it and green-lit it.

What it was when we began was an opportunity for us to take the deepest titles from our library, films that we thought would never have any chance of getting a retail release, and make them available to consumers. That was when Tower, Virgin, and Suncoast were still in business, before the video retail landscape had been so changed and so radically reoriented. We began with a cross section of 150 titles that we felt would nicely supplement our retail activities, and thought we were ready to launch in April 2008—but there were so many problems involved in doing this, not least of which was launching 150 titles all in one go. It took us eleven months longer. Now we're past one thousand releases and have broadened into dual-layer discs, TV series and TV movies, collections, remastering of films—all different components that we never thought of originally. We conceived this as a long-tail business; now I refer to it as a medium-to-long-tail business, as we've upped the ante, partially in response to changes in the marketplace, and our ability to get product out to the consumers that want it, and also to reinvest in the business based on our initial success to continually improve the quality and diversity of the product.

CINEASTE: What's been the biggest obstacle to overcome in launching this business?

FELTENSTEIN: Die-hard consumers who believe themselves to be knowledgeable about how these things work think these are DVD-R discs like they make on their computers at home. They think that one costs us ten cents to make. It actually costs us ten times more per disc to make a DVD-R versus a pressed disc. With the Warner Archive, we're making more of an investment in making the discs, and that's one of the reasons it's been such a challenge to get the price lower. The cost savings comes from us not having to hold inventory and not having to run the risk of returns. In traditional retail, the amount of catalog product returned from retailers had a calamitous effect on all the studios. A lot of product that was pushed out there, the studios did not do well with, and that diminished the possibilities of the channel.

We started with just sales on our shop, and have expanded to the point where most of our video distributors are now carrying Warner Archive product. Business is thriving with our partners, whether it be wholesale or retailers like Movies Unlimited, Critics' Choice, and Oldies.com—bringing them on board has been a godsend, because we want to make sure that people know these films are available. We never anticipated that the sales would be beyond our shop, or that we would be able to make such a huge effort in remastering. It's all very different from where we started, and I'm extraordinarily grateful for that. The changes will continue.

CINEASTE: Special-feature content beyond trailers, like commentaries and vintage featurettes, is now part of some of the titles. Is that part of the evolution?

FELTENSTEIN: Absolutely. We want to increase the value proposition of owning the disc versus watching it on television or streaming it. Part of that was by improving the packaging by using the original artwork. What held us back from doing more was that up until a few months ago we could only use DVD-5s (single-sided, single-layer discs that store 4.7 gigabytes [GB] of data), and adding content to those affected the bit rate. I'd love to do "Warner Night at the Movies" on every release by adding shorts, which doesn't cost us a lot. But if it's going to compromise the feature's bit rate, it's pointless.

DVD-9s (single-sided, dual-layer discs that store 7.95 GB of data) were hard to get to work within the spec of this process until about a year ago, when we finally got it right. And they're a lot more expensive, as the consumer who goes shopping for dual-layer discs knows. Perfecting that process is what's enabled us to add some special features. Or if a film runs over one hundred minutes and it'll look more beautiful with the expanded bit rate, we'll put it on a 9. More commentaries and other special features are coming, and you'll be seeing a lot more collections built around themes and genres and series, like *The Falcon* and *The Saint*.

CINEASTE: They seem like they're turning into pressed discs, without the pressed disc. Is this where the market is for catalog titles?

FELTENSTEIN: The release schedule I would have had for retail, had the market not changed, titles that we hoped to be putting out—now we can release those titles, due to the Warner Archive and the infrastructure. Other companies have now joined in. It's extraordinarily labor intensive (and our staff is smaller than anyone would imagine), but the reward is in bringing so much of the catalog off our shelves and into homes. We've monetized fourteen percent of the company's feature library since we started, and that's really important. We've been able to go back to some of our earlier releases, whose quality I wasn't happy with to begin with, and provide consumers with a better version, giving them a price break as well. It's unusual that a manufacturer will give a prior buyer a break, but as a consumer myself, and a fan and an enthusiast, that's very important to me.

CINEASTE: Unlike the other companies that have started MODs, you use Facebook and Twitter to get the word out.

FELTENSTEIN: Facebook gives us a place to let people make their requests known and for us to answer questions. Someone asked why there's missing imagery in *The Women* and *Hollywood Party* when the films change from black and white to color, and I had to explain the role of the key image layer in early Technicolor. That kind of contact usually isn't possible. And we want to know how we're doing, and what issues are out there. This is the best way possible to have that dialogue on an immediate level.

CINEASTE: Two issues that come up on online forums like the Home Theater Forum regard closed captioning and international distribution.

FELTENSTEIN: There is currently full attention on closed captioning, and including it in the near future is being given heavy consideration. And in the near future as well, the program will start expanding regionally.

CINEASTE: You also provide Archive titles as digital downloads. How is that side of the business doing?

FELTENSTEIN: It's ninety-nine percent disc and virtually zero on the download side. Contrary to the media spin, there are still people who want to own discs, thank God. There are still people who want to have collections, and who know that a file can get corrupted or go away.

The discs have proven themselves, and we stand behind them, and we go out of our way to make that known. Change is never easy to accept. But the positive response we've gotten has been rewarding.

CINEASTE: How did the Archive wind up marketing and distributing the Sony Screen Classics by Request line of MODs?

FELTENSTEIN: A colleague was having lunch with them and they said, "Why don't you guys carry our stuff?" and we said, "Sure." With our newsletters and Facebook page, we can market them in clever, creative ways and draw attention to other things that we have that are like-minded. It's not an exclusive arrangement; several other companies also sell them.

I feel that as an industry we all have to work together to keep disc media alive and to defeat piracy. I can't underscore the impact and devastation of that enough.

CINEASTE: On a related note, is Blu-ray doing its share to keep the market alive for catalog releases?

FELTENSTEIN: It's thriving, growing, and roaring, and for us as a corporation *Citizen Kane* and *Ben-Hur*, released this fall, are generating a strong response. For less well-known classics the market is still a challenge, as you're fighting for shelf and promotional space. And a lot of reviewers working for major newspapers have lost their gigs.

Personally I'm still frustrated that consumers don't understand how incredible Blu-ray is, and how revolutionary the experience of watching a Blu-ray is. So, while very committed to it, we have to be very selective about what catalog titles we release on the market. (All of the remastering that we're doing is in high definition and 2K, a digital scan that produces images with 2,048 pixels or lines of horizontal resolution. It's certainly possible, then, that some of the Archive titles might go to Blu-ray, involving 4K digital scans that produce far superior images with 4,096 lines of horizontal resolution. Of course with Blu-ray you can have a master that looks fine in standard definition but that requires a big investment in dirt cleaning.)

Retail releases of standard DVDs of catalog titles are very much a challenge. A Charlie Chan collection we did last year did really well, so that ensures that there'll be another one at retailers. The stores are gone—I miss Tower Video as much as anybody—and the stores that remain, like Best Buy, Walmart, and Target, will get behind *Citizen Kane* and *Ben-Hur* or even Charlie Chan. But the one-off smaller film, the deep, deep library title, isn't going to get the shelf space from them. It never did.

Five years ago we could have made a movie like *The Prize*, with Paul Newman, available at retail and made a good go of it, but at that time I didn't have a new master and I couldn't put it out in 4:3 letterbox. One of the great things about the Warner Archive is that we reinvest in the business and remaster titles in our library that desperately need a new coat of paint. We have a certain standard for quality that we need to maintain—otherwise we could just release everything right now.

CINEASTE: The Archive has started to release, or rerelease, out of print titles that had been released as pressed discs. Why do that when some of those original discs can still be obtained via, say, Amazon Marketplace?

FELTENSTEIN: We've looked for titles that were extraordinarily rare or hard to find—sometimes they had gone out of print because they were in that old, awful snapper packaging that I despise—and if they were on Amazon Marketplace, were going for high amounts of money. The bottom line is that a lot of people will look for a specific title where they always look to find specific titles, and if they can't find it they won't get it. Now titles won't have to go out of print anymore, and we can bring them back in better shape.

The Warner Archive is becoming the classics division of the company, the niche side, where more attention is put into greater detail, while the big-ticket items continue to get the ultra-deluxe treatment for broad release. That we could remaster *The Woman on the Beach* (reviewed by *Cineaste*, Fall 2011, www.cineaste.com) from a new fine grain made from the camera negative and give proper treatment to Jean Renoir is a beautiful thing, as that would be a very hard title to monetize otherwise. A lot of movies might have gotten lost without the Archive, and given the size of our library, we figure we can keep going at the present rate for another decade.

See biographical note on Robert Cashill in chapter 3, p. 153.

Notes on the Editors

Cynthia Lucia is a professor of English and director of the Film and Media Studies Program at Rider University. She authored *Framing Female Lawyers: Women on Trial in Film* (2005) and coedited *The Wiley-Blackwell History of American Film* (2012) and *American Film History: Selected Readings* (2016). Her essays appear in *Fifty Hollywood Directors* (2015), *Star Bodies and the Erotics of Suffering* (2015), *Modern British Drama on Screen* (2013), *Law, Culture, and Visual Studies* (2013), *Companion to Woody Allen* (2013), and *Oxford's Cinema and Media Studies Online Bibliography*, among other publications. She has served on *Cineaste*'s editorial board for more than two decades.

Rahul Hamid is director of student affairs at New York University's Gallatin School of Individualized Study, where he teaches film and politics, global cinema, and film criticism. He has been an editor at *Cineaste* for more than ten years and is a frequent contributor to *Senses of Cinema* and other film publications. He has appeared on CUNY-TV's *City Cinematheque* and has presented at screenings at many venues around New York City.

Index